Ecology and Land Management in Amazonia

To Martin

Ecology and Land Management in Amazonia

Michael J. Eden

Belhaven Press
A Division of Pinter Publishers
London and New York

© Michael J. Eden, 1990

First published in Great Britain in 1990 by
Belhaven Press (a division of Pinter Publishers),
25 Floral Street, London WC2E 9DS

British Library Cataloguing in Publication Data
A CIP catalogue record for this book is available from the
British Library

ISBN 1 85293 118 3

Library of Congress Cataloging-in-Publication Data
Eden, M.J. (Michael John)
  Ecology and land management in Amazonia

  1. Man – Influence on nature – Amazon River Region.
2. Rain forest ecology – Amazon River Region.
3. Conservation of natural resources – Amazon River Region.
4. Environmental policy – Amazon River Region. I. Title.
GF532.A4E34   1990   333.75'16'09811   90–6927
ISBN 1-85293-118-3

Filmset by Mayhew Typesetting, Bristol
Printed and bound in Great Britain by Biddles Ltd.

Contents

List of photographs   vii
List of figures   ix
Acknowledgements   xi

1. Introduction   1

2. The Amazonian Lowlands   16

3. Amazonian Ecosystems   39

4. Indigenous Resource Exploitation   62

5. Modern Colonisation and Exploitation of the Rain Forest   86

6. Modern Colonisation and Exploitation in Wetlands and
    Savannas   121

7. Alternative Land Development   142

8. Regional Environmental Impact and Conservation Planning   171

9. Integrated Land Management at the Regional Level   186

10. Present and Future   197

Bibliography   218
Index   258

List of photographs

1. Tertiary sedimentary lowland of western Amazonia—the middle Caquetá basin, south-east Colombia 18
2. Upfaulted sandstone block near Araracuara, Caquetá valley, south-east Colombia 18
3. *Várzea* zone of Río Napo, near Iquitos, eastern Peru 27
4. Junction of black water Río Yari and white water Río Caquetá, south-east Colombia 31
5. Rain forest along access trail in lower Tapajós basin, Pará, Brazil 43
6. Surface litter layer with enmeshed fine roots from rain forest in Caquetá basin, south-east Colombia 44
7. Recently burnt *Trachypogon* savanna in the northern Rupununi region, Guyana, with defoliated *Curatella americana* 51
8. *Campo de várzea* along the lower Rio Curuá-Una, near Santarém in the lower Amazon valley 54
9. Forest clearance for indigenous shifting cultivation, Sipapo basin, southern Venezuela 57
10. Sparse regrowth on cleared forest land on white sands of the Berbice Formation, Soesdyke-Linden project, Guyana 59
11. Captive anteater in Andoke village, south-east Colombia 64
12. Andoke woman grating manioc tubers, near Araracuara, Caquetá valley, south-east Colombia 66
13. Manioc-dominated Piaroa field near Uña on the Río Sipapo, southern Venezuela 71
14. Communal Piaroa hut and surrounding yard garden with bananas and fruit trees, Río Cuao, southern Venezuela 74
15. Graft of blight-resistant *Hevea pauciflora* crown onto *H. brasiliensis* stem at Anandineua rubber plantation in Bragantina zone, Pará, Brazil 92
16. Logs at roadside awaiting transport to local sawmill, near Tomé Açu, Pará, Brazil 95
17. Processing of malva fibre near Capitão Poço, Pará, Brazil 102
18. Incipient weed invasion in recently-derived pasture near La Tagua, upper Caquetá basin, south-east Colombia 108

19. Cleared forest land on Suiá Missú ranch, northern Mato
    Grosso, Brazil   116
20. Settlement of Puerto Santander, middle Caquetá valley, south-
    east Colombia   124
21. Santarém on the *terra firme* margin, overlooking the mouthbay
    of the Tapajós river and the turbid Amazon mainstream   126
22. Sugar cane along drainage canal at Uyfluyt estate, Demerara,
    coastal Guyana   133
23. *Criollo* cattle in corral at Lumidpau, southern Rupununi
    savanna, Guyana   137
24. Black pepper cultivation at agricultural experimental station,
    Capitão Poço, Pará, Brazil   147
25. Black pepper plant with root fungal disease, Tomé Açu, Pará,
    Brazil   148
26. Experimental enrichment planting of group of *Bagassa
    guianensis* on previously logged land at Curuá-Una, Pará, Brazil 155
27. Guarico irrigation project in central *llanos* of Venezuela,
    showing the Calabozo reservoir and adjacent cultivated land   164
28. Cultivable floodplain land in the Caquetá valley, south-east
    Colombia, currently in use for impermanent cropping of maize
    and manioc   165
29. Land colonisation along the Tingo María-Pucallpa highway
    near Pucallpa in central Peruvian *oriente*   204

List of figures

1. The Amazonian forest and some associated savannas: 1. Gran Sabana, 2. Rio Branco–Rupununi, 3. Trombetas–Paru, 4. Puciari–Humaitá, 5. Mojos   3
2. Location map of Amazonia   6
3. *Amazônia Legal* of Brazil   8
4. Annual rainfall (mm) in Amazonia   20
5. Mean monthly rainfall (mm) at selected stations in Amazonia   21
6. Geology of Amazonia   23
7. Gauge height above sea level of the Negro/Amazon rivers near Manaus for 1903–1952   29
8. Soils of the *terra firme* and *várzea* zones, central Amazonia   34
9. Savanna 'islands' in the Puciari–Humaitá area, Brazil   50
10. Location map of the lower Amazon region, Brazil   90
11. Location map of the Bragantina zone, Pará state, Brazil   99
12. Location map of the upper Caquetá basin, Colombia, showing *Proyecto Caquetá*   105
13. Location map of northern Mato Grosso, showing forest area and selected development projects   114
14. Location map of the Caquetá valley, south-east Colombia   123
15. Coastal Guyana in the vicinity of Georgetown, showing soils and empoldered land   131
16. Rio Branco–Rupununi savanna   136
17. A compartment model for land management   188
18. A land management model   191
19. The Guianas   199
20. Location map of southern Venezuela, showing national parks, forest reserves and the protected zone of the upper Caroní   202
21. Brazilian Amazonia, showing development poles, POLONOROESTE, and *Programa Grande Carajás*   207
22. *De facto* compartments in Rondônia, Brazil   208

23. National parks in Amazonia, including 1. Canaima National Park, 2. La Neblina National Park, 3. Pico da Neblina National Park, 4. Cabo Orange National Park, 5. Jaú National Park, 6. Amazonas National Park, 7. Pacaya Samiria Nature Reserve, 8. Manu National Park, 9. Manuripi Heath Nature Reserve, 10. Beni Biosphere Reserve/Chimane Reserve, 11. Isiboro-Sécure National Park, 12. Guaporé Biological Reserve, 13. Pacaás Novos National Park   213

Acknowledgements

Over the years, many colleagues have contributed to my studies in South America, not least of all Theo Hills who introduced me to the area in the early 1960s. Other colleagues whose support has been critical during periods of fieldwork relating to the book include Angela Andrade, Carlos Caceres, Antonio Carpanezzi, Walter Coppens, Jean Dubois, Ian Hutchinson, Abraham Lion, César Carneiro Lopes and Duncan McGregor. In preparing the book, I have received cartographic support from Ron Halfhide, Claire Wastie and Justin Jacyno, photographic assistance from Roy Davies, and bibliographic help from Val Allport. All their help is gratefully acknowledged.

1

Introduction

In recent years, increasing concern has been expressed about the scale and rapidity of forest clearance in tropical South America, and particularly Amazonia. The clearance is most widespread in Brazil where vast livestock holdings have been established and where substantial extractive logging and peasant colonisation are occurring. Comparable processes are evident in the eastern lowlands of Peru, Colombia and Ecuador and, to a lesser extent, other parts of the region. Early concern was expressed by Budowski (1972, p. 384), who criticised 'the elimination of an extremely useful type of vegetation cover and its replacement by often terribly degraded lands'. Fosberg (1972, p. 388) suggested that 'there are far better land-uses for at least some of these tropical forests than chopping them down and converting them into submarginal agricultural land'. Restraint has been urged. Denevan (1973, p. 133), warning of the 'imminent demise' of the rain forest, suggested that 'road building and colonization in Amazonia probably should be restricted for now'. Similarly, Sternberg (1973), while recognising the difficulty of any 'hands-off' policy, urged that at least some extensive tracts of non-agricultural land be saved from degradation. Latterly, the requirement for sustainable exploitation as well as protection, of Amazonian forest land has been emphasised and the need for increased ecological and agronomic research stressed (Goodland, 1985; Jordan, 1987; Nogueira-Neto, 1989).

As well as the direct land use implications of forest clearance, concern has also arisen over various broader issues. Attention has focused on the likely effects of clearance on atmospheric carbon dioxide (CO_2) levels and the global heat balance (Fearnside, 1985a; Dobson *et al.*, 1989), on atmospheric nitrous oxide (N_2O) and ozone (O_3) levels (Fearnside, 1985b; Joyce, 1985; Seiler & Conrad, 1987), and on hydrologic cycling and regional rainfall patterns (Salati *et al.*, 1986). While the precise impact of forest clearance in these respects is by no means clear, caution is urged. As Fearnside (1985b, p. 88) emphasises, 'climatic concerns are especially dangerous since delays inherent in the natural systems mean that many of the effects may not be detectable before irreversible processes have been set in motion'. In addition, there is concern over the massive species extinction that is likely to accompany large-scale forest clearance (Myers, 1979a, 1986).

Behind these issues is the assumption that, in spite of the extensive, unexploited land remaining in Amazonia, current development is ecologically and, in the longer term, socially and economically inappropriate. Locally, it will diminish natural resources and create land conditions that are difficult and costly to exploit. At the regional level, climatic and hydrologic regimes may be seriously perturbed and unique genetic resources lost. Even so, the governments controlling Amazonia are mostly proceeding apace with, or readily allowing, forest development. They may acknowledge the ecological implications of their behaviour and formulate comprehensive conservation policies, but the latter are commonly seen as inadequate and are labelled as merely 'symbolic action' (Fearnside, 1986a). As Sternberg (1973, p. 262) remarks, 'the rules of the game are that environmental concern should never impede development'. This attitude is comprehensible. Brazil and the Andean states experience persisting socio-economic problems which may be alleviated by suitable forest development programmes. In particular, migration from settled regions into new forest lands is seen as a way of easing conditions in the former areas, while, in the latter, perceived opportunities for large-scale cash cropping of cacao, oil palm or beef or for commercial extraction of timber or minerals provide further motivation for development (Skillings, 1984). Also, there are cogent geopolitical reasons for occupying Amazonian land (Rosenbaum & Tyler, 1971; Becker, 1974).

In the short term, it is unlikely that the governments in question will terminate or seriously curtail development activities in the face of conservationist pressures. Official expressions of good intent are commonly made, but rarely translated into adequate and lasting conservation programmes. Consequently, it is desirable to ensure that forest development in the future eschews the more damaging forms it has lately pursued, and instead focuses on exploitation that is sufficiently realistic in ecological, as well as economic, terms to accommodate both developmental and conservationist interests. Prerequisite to this is a knowledge of the forest ecosystem and its likely response to specific modes of exploitation. Equally, the status of adjacent ecosystems, notably dry savannas and wetlands, needs to be evaluated in order to determine their potential as alternative or complementary areas for development. Latterly, there has been a significant increase in the scale of environmental investigation in Amazonia, at both local and regional levels, but an inadequate scientific and technical basis for land development exists and repeated failures have occurred where mal-adaptive and unstable agrosystems have been promoted.

The present study focuses on the Amazonian forest region and the exploitation of its renewable resources. Since the forest ecosystem extends somewhat beyond the margins of the Amazon river basin, notably in Venezuela and the Guianas, the forests of the latter are included within

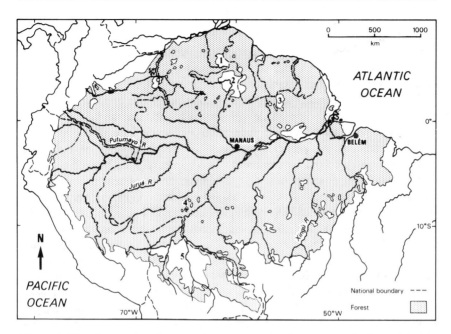

Figure 1 The Amazonian forest and some associated savannas: 1. Gran Sabana, 2. Rio Branco-Rupununi, 3. Trombetas-Paru, 4. Puciari-Humaitá, 5. Mojos

the study area, which corresponds broadly to the phytogeographic unit known as the *hylaea* (Ducke & Black, 1953). In addition, attention is paid to the dry savannas and wetlands which lie within the Amazonian forest. These occupy a fraction of the total area, but are ecosystems which possess distinctive characteristics and resources and provide an interesting and often instructive contrast to the forest. The total forest area involved covers an estimated 613 million ha; this includes the more or less continuous block of forest that extends across the tropical lowlands, with its Andean margin here defined at 1,000 m above sea level. Within the forest area, there are an estimated 15–20 million ha of dry savanna and 28 million ha of herbaceous wetland (see Figure 1).

The study itself will initially review the physical and biological conditions in Amazonia, and then examine traditional and modern modes of land exploitation within the region. Subsequent consideration is given to alternative strategies for land exploitation and management that may more realistically satisfy the requirements of contemporary developmental and conservationist interests. In particular, the desirability of achieving sustainable exploitation and of creating and maintaining national parks and other forms of reserved land is emphasised.

The approach adopted is ecological in the sense that it is concerned with the interactions of humans, other organisms and the physical environment, particularly in relation to the exploitation of renewable resources. The study derives significant conceptual components from ecology *sensu strictu* and also from ecological anthropology. Attention is paid to the temporal behaviour of ecosystems and agrosystems, particularly in relation to the manner in which their stability or otherwise affects patterns of land exploitation. The concept of cultural adaptation is also applied in respect of agrosystems and other modes of land exploitation, and is in places extended to patterns of human population and settlement. The concept is useful because of its explicit emphasis on the dynamic relationship of human behaviour to the environment. This approach goes beyond the one-sided relationship implicit in the traditional concept of limiting factors or the idea of environmental risks or hazards (Odum, 1975; Vickers, 1979). While contemporary land development elsewhere in the world has at times achieved success by overcoming such environmental constraints, it is increasingly evident that ecological systems, whether natural or anthropic, have complex and far-reaching linkages, and require more sensitive and adaptive management than is commonly provided. The latter certainly applies in contemporary Amazonia where a poor understanding of ecological dynamics persists, but where potent technology is increasingly available for land development. Careful attention is thus required to the adaptation of contemporary agrosystems, and caution is needed in the control or correction of perceived environmental constraints, whether involving soil fertility, water supply or crop pests and diseases.

As well as concern with the nature and impact of local development, attention is required to regional land management. Some ecologists have stressed the need to generalise more local data as a basis for a broader science of landscape ecology or resource management (Dasmann *et al.*, 1973; Holling & Clark, 1975), but, as Moran (1981) clearly indicates in Brazilian Amazonia, significant difficulties exist in articulating the local and regional levels of investigation. Furtado (1980) is equally aware of such problems, which he sees as limiting the effectiveness of landscape ecology in the tropics: 'As an emerging area of academic focus, [landscape ecology] has been marked by the survey of adverse economic development impacts on the environment . . . and by the formulation of oversimplified ecological guidelines for economic development . . . There are few general ecological rules and many specific ones for economic development' (Furtado, 1980, p. iv). At the regional level, specialists from other disciplines have contributions to make, including geographers whose concern with regional synthesis is of long standing. To the present author, a geographer by training, this level of study is of particular interest, although clearly not the exclusive preserve of his or any other discipline. From a geographical viewpoint, however, a distinctive contribution can be made by focusing on the regional unit within which numerous, more specialised investigations are also being pursued.

While the present study attempts to achieve some breadth of temporal and spatial investigation, it remains partial in viewpoint and approach and will do little, for example, to overcome the concern expressed by Nugent (1981) and others in regard to the functionalist nature of an ecological approach and of its problematic relationship to sociological explanation. The study focuses explicitly on the exploitation and management of renewable resources. It not only ignores the important mineral resources in the region and their associated industrial potential, but also pays limited attention to the broader socio-economic and political factors which are acknowledged as critical to development. The latter have been the subject of earlier studies by Nelson (1973), Mahar (1979), Bunker (1985) and others, and the present approach is adopted in order to emphasise the significance of ecological factors in land exploitation and to stress the need for their effective consideration in the local and regional management of Amazonia. On this basis, the possibility exists of longer-term exploitation in the region that is adaptive and sustainable in ecological terms and acceptable in socio-economic and political ones.

Colonial contact

The European impact on the Amazon basin commenced in the mid-sixteenth century when Francisco de Orellana (1541–2) and Lope de Aguirre (1560–1) penetrated the region from the Andes and crossed by river to the Atlantic. Subsequently, small settlements were established along the lower Amazon valley and, in 1616, initial occupance of the site of Belém occurred (Soares, 1963). In 1969, a fort was established at the site of Manaus on the lower Rio Negro, and exploration continued along various tributaries, including the Casiquiare which provided a link to the Orinoco basin. By 1750, a few dozen forts and about a hundred missions had been established in Brazilian Amazonia (Soares, 1963). Parallel penetration occurred in Spanish territories. Catholic missionaries from Peru were established in the Iquitos area by the early eighteenth century (Eidt, 1962; Hemming, 1978), and, later in that century, secular expeditions from the north were sent up the Orinoco to counter southerly infiltration by the Portuguese (Ramos Peréz, 1946; Eden, 1971a). Coastal settlement in the Guianas, initiated in the early seventeenth century by Dutch, British and French colonists, was likewise consolidated during the eighteenth century (Lowenthal, 1960) (see Figure 2).

Colonial penetration was disastrous for indigenous society. Introduced diseases, warfare and enslavement reduced the Amerindian population from an estimated 4 million or so at the time of contact to a fraction of that total by late-Colonial times (Denevan, 1976; Ross, 1978a; McNeill, 1979). Early European settlement was concentrated along the larger rivers,

Figure 2 Location map of Amazonia

and few tribal groups survived in these areas. The indigenous population gained some protection in Catholic mission settlements, or *aldeias*, but still succumbed to introduced diseases and was exploited as a ready source of labour (Ross, 1978a). Although indigenous society was effectively destroyed along the main rivers, the colonists assimilated elements of the indigenous population and adopted its cultural practices. This was most evident in Brazilian Amazonia where miscegenation was officially encouraged and indigenous culture was readily absorbed by the emerging peasant, or *caboclo*, society. As Wagley (1964, p. 72) remarks, 'it was the Indian who taught the European newcomer to live in the strange Amazon environment'. Such is apparent from the persistence among *caboclos* of folk beliefs relating to indigenous medicines and supernatural beings. Inherited beliefs and behaviour still influence *caboclo* hunting and fishing, and many indigenous techniques continue to be employed in these pursuits (Wagley, 1964; Moran, 1981; Smith, 1983). *Caboclo* agriculture also replicates indigenous methods in its continuance of small-scale shifting cultivation, based on manioc and other traditional crops.

As well as subsistence activities, the extraction of forest products occupied the Brazilian *caboclo* and his counterpart in other territories. Extractive products included such items as cacao, sarsaparilla, Brazil nuts, oils, resins, timber and animal skins, and these provided the *caboclo* with marginal access to the cash economy. There were also early attempts to establish more permanent land exploitation. In the early eighteenth century, the Jesuits operated estates in Pará that produced sugar cane and cacao, and large numbers of cattle were reared on Marajó island with the aid of Amerindian labour (Hemming, 1978). There were other attempts to establish sugar, cacao and coffee estates in the lower Amazon, but progress was often hindered by labour shortages and competing extractive pursuits (Ross, 1978a; Moran, 1981). Early commercial agriculture was also established in the coastal Guianas, where plantations were developed by the Dutch and British through use of imported rather than indigenous labour (Panday, 1959; Mandle, 1973).

The developmental approach

Although widespread European contact with Amazonia occurred during the late sixteenth and seventeenth centuries, the overall scale of exploitation and settlement was limited. Indeed, most of the region persisted through the eighteenth and into the nineteenth century as an isolated and poorly-known wilderness. Early scientific explorers, however, were at times impressed by the resource potential of the region. They included Alfred Wallace, who travelled widely in Amazonia in the mid-nineteenth century:

> When I consider the excessively small amount of labour required in this country, to convert the virgin forest into green meadows and fertile plantations, I almost long to come over with half-a-dozen friends, disposed to work, and enjoy the country . . . It is a vulgar error, copied and repeated from one book to another, that in the tropics the luxuriance of the vegetation overpowers the efforts of man.
>
> [Wallace 1890, p. 230]

To Wallace and other writers of the time, the Amazonian lowlands remained undeveloped mainly through the lack of energetic exploitation. In Brazil, the problem was perceived as the indolence of the Indo–Portuguese population (Myers & Myers, 1871) and their distaste for 'agricultural and mechanical labour' (Wallace, 1890). Even so, a favourable perception of land resources persisted. The Acre region of south-west Amazonia, for example, was reported by Church (1904, p. 596) to be 'an area of South America which probably has no superior in fertility and varied natural resources', while Marbut & Manifold (1926), although more cautious about the quality of soils, still recognised a large aggregate potential for crop production (see Figure 3).

In the late nineteenth century, the potential of Amazonia seemed to be confirmed by the rubber boom, which occupied Amerindians and new migrants to the area alike and brought great wealth to a few trading companies. But the prosperity was short-lived, ending with the collapse of

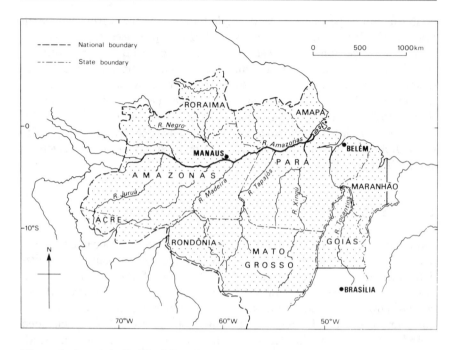

Figure 3 *Amazônia Legal* of Brazil

the local rubber market in 1911–12, as Asian plantation rubber undercut
the wild Amazonian product (Melby, 1942; Burns, 1966). A parallel
setback to development occurred in the Bragantina zone of eastern
Amazonia, where planned agricultural colonisation in the period 1875–
1916 failed to achieve its anticipated success (Camargo, 1948). Some
agricultural activity continued in the region, but, with the demise of
rubber, most of Amazonia experienced a period of 'social regression' and
economic stagnancy (Hanson, 1933; Wagley, 1964; Ross, 1978a). Scattered
efforts were made to revive development. These included attempts in the
1930s to establish plantation rubber in the Tapajós basin and, during the
Second World War, to revive the collection of wild rubber, but success
was limited (Russell, 1942; Wagley, 1964). In the 1930s and 1940s,
marginal colonisation of the eastern Andean lowlands also took place, but
little permanent settlement resulted (Eidt, 1962; Bonilla, 1966; Hegen,
1966). It was only with the 1950s that any broader revival of developmental interest occurred.

In Brazil, the renewed interest was heralded by the creation, in 1953,
of the Superintendência do Plano de Valorização Económica da Amazônia
(SPVEA). The agency itself has long been superseded, but over the years
there has been substantial government-sponsored road construction in
Amazonia and associated promotion of land colonisation. Migrants have

arrived from peripheral areas of eastern and southern Brazil, settling mainly in the states of Pará and Mato Grosso and, latterly, Rondônia and Acre (Valverde, 1979; World Bank, 1981; Goodland, 1986; Almeida, 1987). Since the 1950s, increasing colonisation of the eastern Andean lowlands, or *oriente*, has also occurred and, particularly in Peru, Colombia and Ecuador, there has been a substantial influx of migrants to the forested lowlands (Hiraoka & Yamamoto, 1980; Aramburú, 1984; Ortiz, 1984). As in Brazil, the construction of penetration roads has often provided the immediate stimulus to land colonisation (Nelson, 1973; Schuurman, 1980; Fearnside, 1986a). In general, the colonisation process has focused on the forested interfluves or *terra firme*, with only limited settlement of Amazonian wetlands and dry savannas. A variety of exploitation has occurred, but most has been associated with either small-scale peasant colonisation or larger-scale commercial enterprises. Few examples of medium-scale farming have appeared.

There are several reasons for this renewal of interest in Amazonian development. An important factor in both Brazil and the Andean states has been the assumption that peasant or small-farmer migration to Amazonia would relieve agrarian pressures in the settled periphery of the continent (Katzman, 1977; Mahar, 1979; Schuurman, 1980). An additional, geopolitical factor was the wish of individual states to consolidate their sovereignty over vacant or sparsely-populated territory (Mahar, 1979; Bromley, 1980). Also there was the desire to safeguard and exploit the natural resources of the region (Skillings, 1984), even if knowledge of those resources was at times sketchy. Some resources, like timber and minerals, were evidently present in abundance and capable of providing a high return to those who exploited them. The agricultural and ranching potential of the land also continued to be proclaimed in many quarters, in spite of recurrent difficulties in establishing sustainable agrosystems and consequent emergence of unstable pioneer exploitation.

Nowadays official acknowledgement is made of the difficulties inherent in Amazonian development, but land colonisation continues apace. During the 1970s, many outside observers became increasingly sceptical of the development process, but optimistic appraisals continued to appear. Although cautious about the likely speed of development, Nelson (1973, p. 34) was of the opinion that 'a vast agricultural and forestry potential awaits exploitation' in Amazonia and its adjoining regions. In more specific terms, Alvim (1977, 1980) asserted that favourable prospects existed for tree crops like cacao, oil palm and rubber, which were at the time being widely promoted in Brazilian Amazonia. Similarly, on the basis of field experiments in Peruvian Amazonia, Sanchez *et al.* (1982) emphasised the feasibility of continuous cultivation of annual crops like maize, rice and soyabeans, based on substantial fertiliser inputs. Likewise, in respect of cattle raising, Falesi (1976) claimed that, with good management, cultivated pastures could be developed and maintained for many years on cleared forest land. While the general applicability of such production systems for Amazonia has yet to be confirmed, optimistic appraisals of this kind provided a rationale for continuing land colonisation, particularly on the forested *terra firme*. Such colonisation continues unabated to the present and, as satellite imagery shows, is commonly associated with large-scale forest clearance.

The conservationist approach

Land development in Amazonia has been paralleled in recent years by a growing concern among ecologists, geographers and others with the environmental impact of such development. Associated damage to surviving Amerindian populations has likewise provoked vigorous reactions from anthropologists and others. Many of these issues have been elaborated by foreign media and environmental groups and to a lesser extent by their South American counterparts. The critical reaction to Amazonian development policies has mainly arisen during the last 10–15 years, and is part of the broader environmental movement that has matured during that period. However, some earlier recognition existed of the harsh impact of land development. Camargo (1948) drew attention to the environmental damage inflicted on the Bragantina zone in eastern Amazonia, where early land colonisation had resulted in extensive forest clearance and consequent soil degradation. Eidt (1962, p. 263) also reported damage from colonisation of the vulnerable Andean piedmont in Peru, where 'long years of uncontrolled deforestation on sloping land have resulted in accelerated erosion which has left much of the countryside scarred and useless'.

The emergence of more general concern with ecological aspects of Amazonian development occurred in the 1970s. Seminal publications by Denevan (1973) and Goodland & Irwin (1975) provoked attention to the potential impact of highway development and associated land colonisation, and numerous other studies have subsequently explored these and related issues (Jahoda & O'Hearn, 1975; Kleinpenning, 1975; Eden, 1978; Tricart, 1978; Sioli, 1980; Bunker, 1981; Fearnside, 1985b; Buschbacher, 1986a). The range of ecological concern has been considerable, extending from the local impact of land development on soils and on plant and animal communities to the regional impact of deforestation on climatic and hydrologic systems and on genetic resources. General preservation of the forest has been sought by some writers, notably Lovejoy & Schubart (1980) and Sioli (1980), who envisaged a matrix of forest with only patches or 'islands' of developed land existing within it. Minimal development was also recommended by Goodland & Irwin (1977, p. 214), who advocated the deflection of agricultural colonisation into the adjacent *cerrado*, thus 'alleviating pressure on Amazonia and buying time to determine less destructive courses of action'. Other writers have focused on the need to establish more sustainable modes of agriculture in the region and to create adequate national parks and other reserved land (Pandolfo, 1974; Wetterberg *et al.*, 1976; Jordan, 1987). According to Fearnside (1985a), better understanding of the environmental consequences of deforestation is urgently needed, in order to persuade decision makers to regulate the development of forest areas.

Equally, concern has been expressed about the continuing damage to indigenous populations in the region as a by-product of development (Goodland & Irwin, 1975; Davis, 1977; Branford & Glock, 1985). The concern is essentially humanitarian in character, but also impinges on contemporary development. Indigenous land exploitation, founded on intimate knowledge of local environmental conditions, is widely considered to be adaptive in character and conservative of resources, and as such it provides an instructive model for contemporary development (Eden, 1987). More specifically, anthropologists and others have argued that a familiarity with the strategies and techniques of traditional cultures can play an important role in planning agricultural development, particularly for the small farmer (Smith, 1978; Brush, 1979; Posey, 1983). Indeed Meggers (1971, p. 156) has gone so far as to claim that 'as long as the impetus for Amazonian exploitation comes from alien cultural roots, the possibility of a rational program of development is nil'.

Inevitably, much of the literature on the ecological impact of Amazonian development has been speculative and at times conflicting in character. This is particularly so in respect of macro-regional feedbacks, which involve highly complex climatic and hydrologic variables (Farnworth & Golley, 1974; Fearnside, 1985b; Salati, 1985). Even so, Amazonian governments and their development agencies increasingly acknowledge the need for conservation policies, although immense problems exist in implementing them (Mares, 1986). Not least of the problems is the difficulty of achieving an effective compromise between the cogent political pressures for commercial or socially-orientated land development on the one hand and the less immediate and tangible benefits of conservation on the other. The problem is aggravated by the imprecision of existing conservation models, illustrated for example by the fundamental uncertainty that exists regarding the optimal size of and location for forest reserves (Myers, 1979b). Such uncertainty is inevitable as long as the ecological conditions of the region remain poorly known, and it exposes the vulnerability of the conservationist position in relation to that of the agronomist or economist, whose methods and accounting procedures commonly display greater apparent precision (Nelson, 1973; Alvim, 1977; Myers, 1979a).

Although there is little immediate prospect of a general restraint on

Amazonian development, some practical moves have been made towards conserving the environment. National parks have existed in a few places for several decades, while since 1970 the extent of such land has risen considerably and now covers an estimated 24.2 million ha. Even so, this represents only a fraction (less than 4 per cent) of Amazonian land. Maintaining reserved land also presents immense problems in view of the continuous pressures that exist from developmental interests to trespass thereon. Conditions vary from country to country, but, even in Brazil where appropriate protective legislation exists, invasion of reserved land is commonplace (Brooks *et al.*, 1973; Fearnside & Ferreira, 1984; Fearnside, 1986a).

Attempts to establish sustainable agrosystems in Amazonia are also important components of a conservation strategy. This applies not only in the sense that sustained yield systems are inherently conservative in character, but also that by stabilising the overall pattern of land development such systems facilitate the protection of reserved or unexploited areas. As yet, limited success has been achieved in establishing sustained yield systems in Amazonia, whether through the intensive cultivation of annual or perennial crops or through less intensive systems like mixed-forest silviculture or agrosilviculture. Against a background of continuing land colonisation, however, the pursuit of sustainable exploitation is as critical a component of general conservation strategy as the creation of national parks and other reserved areas.

Integrating conservation and development

In spite of growing recognition of the need for conservation in Amazonia, insufficient progress is being made to counteract the damaging effects of contemporary land colonisation. Negative attitudes commonly exist towards the establishment of sustainable agrosystems and the maintenance of reserved or unexploited land. This attitude is perfectly illustrated by Muthoo & Leader (1978), who, in assessing forestry development in Brazil, referred to the problem of the 'high idleness of forest resources'. Their attitude is comprehensible, but represents a negative perception of the protective and service functions of natural vegetation. Similarly, when reconnaissance land surveys have been undertaken in Amazonia (FAO, 1966; PRORADAM, 1979; Cochrane *et al.*, 1985), the tendency has been to focus on the suitability of land for agricultural or other development, with little or no attention paid to questions of conservation. Latterly, some attempts have been made to adopt a more balanced approach, as in the land surveys of Projeto Radambrasil (Furley, 1986), but effective spatial integration of development and conservation functions is not easily achieved. Similarly, in land development projects, a negative attitude commonly exists towards the long-term diseconomies that derive from the depletion of soil, forest, wildlife or scenic resources; conventional cost–benefit appraisals particularly encourage this attitude (Nelson, 1973; Dubé, 1980; Thompson, 1980). The situation is well-illustrated by contemporary pioneer cattle ranching in eastern Amazonia, but prevails widely across the region (Fearnside, 1980a; Hecht, 1981).

In spite of accelerating land colonisation over recent decades, the environmental impact of development on Amazonia as a whole is still moderate, and time and space exist to create management strategies that incorporate both developmental and conservationist objectives. Such strategies will not emerge spontaneously and official commitment to integrated land management at the regional level is essential. Even with formal commitment, however, effective management is difficult to achieve and progress has as yet been limited. In particular, the broader socio-political environment is critical. This is evident in parts of the Andean *oriente* where, in spite of long-standing official involvement in land management, government functions are periodically obstructed or deflected by the activities of guerrilla groups or *narcotraficantes*. Even in Brazil, where government authority is more secure, land management policies that emerge from the 'unfettered capitalist system' (Kleinpenning, 1979) are by no means always adequate or appropriate. Relevant government agencies, of which there are many, are frequently over-centralised and unresponsive to local conditions and their performance is often disappointing at the individual project level. This is illustrated, for example, by the common practice of allocating geometric land holdings to small farmers in colonisation areas, irrespective of local variations in soil, slope and drainage conditions (Moran, 1981; Leite & Furley, 1985). The selection and support of settlers on planned projects is also poor and levels of success often inferior to those in areas of spontaneous or private colonisation (Nelson, 1973; Schuurman, 1980).

In spite of the problems, continuing government involvement in land management is essential for Amazonia at both local and regional levels. How comprehensive such involvement should be at the local level is clearly debatable, but an approach is required that encourages productive, yet sustainable, agrosystems rather than the existing extractive and pioneer modes of exploitation. Many options exist in respect of crop type and assemblage and of scale and intensity of production, and additional research is required to identify an array of agrosystems that are adapted to local habitats and are appropriate in socio-economic terms.

At the regional level, government involvement is equally essential to co-ordinate broad developmental and conservationist objectives, and thereby to achieve an appropriate mix and distribution of productive and protective land uses. While the data base for such integrated land management has been improved of late, particularly through the use of remote sensing for land survey and monitoring, the conceptual basis for such planning is poorly developed. Goodland (1980) and Fearnside (1983) have undertaken systematic 'environmental' and 'ecological' rankings of forest utilisation as an aid to Amazonian land development. Pandolfo (1974) and Dubé (1980) have proposed optimal land use allocations for Brazilian Amazonia on the basis of a zoning model, and Eden (1978), following work by Odum (1969), has outlined a related spatial model for land management, based on the recognition of 'productive', 'compromise' and 'protective' compartments in the landscape. Latterly, Nogueira-Neto (1989) has called for legislation that formally establishes the concept of 'ecological and economic zoning' in Brazilian Amazonia. Additional investigation of these approaches is urgently required. Meanwhile, the need persists to counter the assumption that undeveloped land is 'idle' or without current value, and to stress that national parks and other reserved areas are, like sustainable agrosystems, desirable and positive modes of land exploitation.

The prospects for establishing a more balanced pattern of land utilisation in Amazonia remain in the balance. Richards (1973, 1977) suggested that most of the existing tropical forests in Amazonia and elsewhere would be destroyed or replaced by seral communities by the end of the century. Many others have foreseen a similar, if less immediate demise (Denevan, 1973; Myers, 1984). On the other hand, formal acknowledgement has been made by South American governments of the need to develop the region without destroying it (Anon., 1976; DAINCO, 1977), and this intention is implicit in the international Treaty for Amazonian Co-operation. The treaty, signed in 1978, specifies that 'economic development and the preservation of the environment are objectives of equal weight, which should be accommodated to one another in such a way that one is not sacrificed for the sake of the other' (Medina, 1980b, p. 66). Whether such objectives represent a realistic target for the governments concerned or will survive only as lip-service to an impractical ideal remains to be seen, but the issue will clearly be resolved within a decade or two. Even if the political will exists, however, there is little chance of the desired objectives being achieved, unless a significant increase occurs in basic and applied research, so that ecologically-sound strategies can be developed for land management at both local and regional levels.

Against this background, the present study aims to explore relevant ecological issues. In Chapter 2, background information is provided on the physical environment of Amazonia, particularly in relation to climate, morphology, hydrology and soils. Chapter 3 examines the major ecosystems in the region, notably the forests of the *terra firme*, the savannas of the *terra firme*, and wetlands and associated aquatic systems. Attention is paid to the dynamics and stability of these ecosystems, both under natural conditions and in the light of human disturbance. Chapter 4 considers the conditions of Amerindian exploitation and settlement in

Amazonia. The adaptive status of traditional exploitation is elaborated and broader aspects of indigenous man–land relationships reviewed. In Chapters 5 and 6, the performance of modern land colonisation and development in the region is examined in a series of case studies. Extractive activities and a range of agricultural and livestock systems are considered, and attention is drawn to the mal-adaptive and unstable nature of much of the exploitation. In Chapter 7, alternative modes of land exploitation are reviewed. These include intensive food and industrial cropping systems, together with compromise systems like agrosilviculture, silvopastoralism and mixed-forest silviculture, which are less productive but more effectively protect the land. In Chapters 8 and 9, the regional impact of modern land colonisation is assessed, particularly in respect of climatic, hydrologic and biotic feedbacks. The need for national parks and other reserved land is discussed, and consideration is given to integrated land management that seeks to balance production and protection in the landscape; the merits of a 'compartment' model are examined. Finally, Chapter 10 summarises the current status of land management in the region, and considers future prospects.

2

The Amazonian lowlands

When one changes the scale from the Amazon as a whole to specific
sub-regions, the homogeneity evident at the regional level yields to
increased variability.

[Moran, 1981, p. 219]

Much of the Amazon basin is Brazilian territory, but parts lie within the
Andean states of Colombia, Ecuador, Peru and Bolivia and also extend
marginally into southern Venezuela and western Guyana. The Amazon
basin is largely covered by tropical forest, but encompasses areas of
wetland, dry savanna and montane vegetation. Since the main focus of the
study is the tropical forest, which itself extends beyond the margins of the
river basin, the larger forest area is here taken to comprise the Amazonian
lowlands (see Figure 1). This region, from which Andean headwater zones
above 1,000 m are excluded, covers approximately 757 million ha, of
which an estimated 613 million ha are under forest (see Table 1).

It is important to recognise the scale of Amazonia. The main river,
rising in the Andean cordillera, flows more than 3,300 km across South
America before reaching the Atlantic ocean, and even tributary basins like
the Madeira and Negro exceed 1,500 km in length. So vast is the Amazon
basin and so abundant its rainfall that the mean discharge of the main
river totals more than 10 per cent of annual world run-off (Morisawa,
1968). This is some twelve times the discharge of the Mississippi river and
several hundred times that of the Thames.

In view of the scale of the region, considerable caution is required in
generalising about its physical status, which is understandably characterised by considerable spatial diversity. On a regional scale, Amazonia can
certainly be regarded as a lowland landscape, and the air traveller is
readily impressed by its continuity and extent. Most of the basin is less
than 300 m above sea level, and the town of Iquitos, located in the main
valley some 2,600 km upstream, lies a mere 100 m above sea level.
Locally, however, the continuity of the landscape is interrupted. Upstand-
ing mountain blocks and large domed inselbergs occur in places, while the
main lowland itself is found, on closer inspection, to consist of a series of
erosional and depositional surfaces of varying elevation and, in places,
considerable dissection (see Photographs 1 and 2).

In spite of its spatial diversity, the Amazonian landscape is commonly

Table 1 The Amazonian lowlands

	Area of lowland Amazonia (million ha)	Percentage of national territory (%)
Bolivia	52.74	48
Brazil	497.82	58
Colombia	45.72	40
Ecuador	9.31	33
French Guiana	9.74	100
Guyana	21.41	100
Peru	65.07	51
Surinam	16.33	100
Venezuela	38.64	42
Total	756.78	

Note: The Amazonian lowlands, as defined, broadly comprise the more or less continuous zone of forest that is centred on the Amazon river basin but extends marginally beyond it. The Andean boundary is defined at 1,000 m above sea level. In the case of Brazil, the area specified comprises the administrative unit *Amazônia Legal*, which includes 70 million ha of savanna outside the continuous forest zone. Detailed breakdown of land cover for the region is given in Table 20.

differentiated on a very broad basis. This is apparent in the familiar sub-division that is made between the *terra firme*, or dryland zone, and the *várzea*, or wetland zone, but this represents an oversimplified view of the region, which increasingly constrains rather than clarifies the appraisal of environmental resources. The traditional distinction between 'white water', 'clear water' and 'black water' rivers in Amazonia is a similar oversimplification which obscures considerable fluvial diversity. While these generalisations are still widely in use, there is need for more refined levels of environmental analysis. The reconnaissance land surveys, based on remote sensing, that have latterly become available for most of the region are a useful starting point for such analysis, but more detailed studies are now required in order to elaborate local landscape variability, allow more specific appraisal of land potential, and generally facilitate resource management.

Photograph 1 Tertiary sedimentary lowland of western Amazonia—the middle Caquetá basin, south-east Colombia

Photograph 2 Upfaulted sandstone block near Araracuara, Caquetá valley, south-east Colombia

Climatic conditions

Amazonia lies within the humid tropical zone. Its climatic regime is strongly influenced by the seasonally-migrating trough of low pressure, known as the Inter-Tropical Convergence Zone. During the months April to July, the convergence zone moves northwards across Amazonia. The movement is associated with south-east trade winds, which enter the continent from a sub-tropical high pressure cell located over the southern Atlantic ocean. The air masses associated with these winds are initially stable, but as they pass across Amazonia they take up large amounts of water vapour and the heating from below destroys their original inversion layer (Nieuwolt, 1977). The passage of the Inter-Tropical Convergence Zone thus brings heavy rainfall, especially in northern Amazonia. At San Carlos de Rio Negro in southern Venezuela, with an annual rainfall of 3,521 mm, mean monthly totals exceed 350 mm from April to June.

With the northward passage of the convergence zone in June and July, drier conditions develop in the central equatorial zone, which continues under the influence of sub-tropical air from the south. At this time, heavier rainfall persists along the Andean foothills and on the eastern coastal zone, where orographic lifting occurs. During July, the convergence zone reaches its northern limit over the Venezuelan *llanos* at about 7–9° N of the equator (Nieuwolt, 1977).

From August the circulation pattern reverses. The trough of low pressure, whose northward movement was generally progressive and well-defined, tends to disintegrate at its northern limit and reform near the equator where convergence is re-established (Pédalaborde, 1963). Within Venezuela, there is a rapid penetration of stable northern air into the continent, with winds coming predominantly from the east and north-east. Rainfall is low in the northern continental interior at this time, but, as the penetrating winds absorb water vapour and veer to the south, humid and unstable air masses develop over the equatorial zone. At Manaus (3°S), heavy rains occur between December and February, associated with easterly waves or eddies in the wind flow within the convergence zone, while along the Andean foothills additional precipitation again results from orographic uplift. The humid north-westerly air current then extends over the southern tropical zone bringing rainfall until March, when the annual cycle is re-initiated.

Variations in solar radiation are relatively low within Amazonia, and this is reflected in temperature regimes. Mean annual temperatures range from 23 to 27°C across the region. The annual range at individual stations is generally low, showing only minor increases with latitude and with distance from the coast, although the latter feature may be obscured by the influence of seasonality (Nieuwolt, 1977). At Belém, in eastern

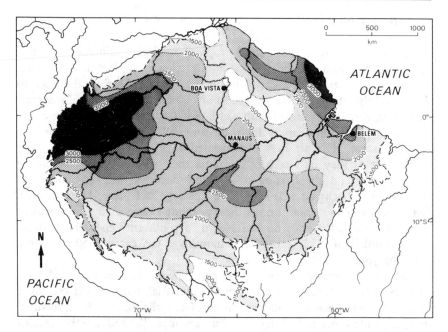

Figure 4 Annual rainfall (mm) in Amazonia (after Reinke, 1962; Haffer, 1974)

Amazonia, the mean monthly temperature ranges from 25.1°C in February to 26.5°C in November. The corresponding figures for Manaus, in the central basin, are 26.9°C for the period February to May and 28.3°C in October.

Diurnal temperature ranges generally show some increase with distance from the coast, but the mean daily range is generally less than 10°C throughout the region (Nieuwolt, 1977). Occasional low temperatures (less than 15°C) are experienced in southern Amazonia as a result of penetrations of polar air from the south, but the region as a whole is generally characterised by high temperatures and, in spite of widespread cloudiness, has rather high values for potential net photosynthesis (Nieuwolt, 1977; Valverde, 1979).

Rainfall regimes show marked variability. The wettest parts of the basin, with annual totals in excess of 3,000 mm, are in west central Amazonia and along the Atlantic coast northward of the Amazon estuary. A zone with annual rainfall in excess of 2,500 mm is located in south central Amazonia across the Madeira–Tapajós basins. Most of the remaining area has 1,500–2,500 mm per annum, including a relatively dry zone that extends transversely across the lower Amazon valley in the vicinity of Santarém and Obidos (see Figure 4). In general, drier parts of the basin have more pronounced seasonality. Boa Vista in northern Brazil has

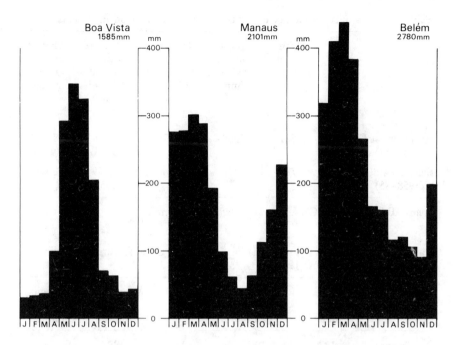

Figure 5 Mean monthly rainfall (mm) at selected stations in Amazonia

annual rainfall of 1,585 mm and experiences five dry months (less than 60 mm) in the year; in contrast, most stations in the region have three dry months or less (see Figure 5).

Inter-annual variability of rainfall is characteristic of Amazonia. It is most marked in drier areas, but is evident throughout the region. At Belém in the lower Amazon valley, with a mean annual rainfall of 2,780 mm, the mean deviation for the period 1958–85 is 14 per cent. The equivalent figure for St Ignatius in south-west Guyana, with a mean annual rainfall of 1,621 mm, is 17 per cent over the period 1930–63 (see Table 2). In seasonal zones, inter-annual variability is commonly linked with the onset and cessation of rainy seasons. Even in wetter zones, unpredictable phases of moisture deficiency may occur in rainy periods, with limiting effects on plant growth (Davis & Richards, 1933; Valverde & Bandy, 1982). Such effects are compounded by high rates of evapotranspiration, which even under cloudy conditions can attain 3–4 mm/day (Eden, 1964; Fränzle, 1979).

Also characteristic of Amazonia is a high intensity of rainfall. Under the forest cover, considerable protection is given to the land surface, but on cleared land intense rainfall induces accelerated run-off and soil erosion. Detailed information on rainfall intensity is not widely available for Amazonia, but daily maxima in excess of 100 mm have been recorded at

Table 2 Inter-annual variability of rainfall for selected Amazonian stations

	Mean annual rainfall (mm)	Mean annual deviation (mm)	Deviation as percentage of mean (%)	Absolute maximum annual rainfall (mm)	Absolute minimum annual rainfall (mm)
St Ignatius, south-west Guyana (1930–63)	1,621	269	17	2,139 (1943)	1,070 (1939)
Belém, Pará, Brazil (1958–85)	2,780	376	14	3,459 (1959)	2,055 (1963)

Source: Eden, 1964; IBGE, *Anuários Estatísticos do Brasil.*

Table 3 Rainfall intensity at St Ignatius, south-west Guyana, during the rainy season, 4 May–21 August 1963

Falls	Total rainfall (mm)	Percentage of total rainfall (%)	No. of falls	Mean rain per fall (mm)	Mean intensity (mm/hour)
> 100 mm	132	10	1	132	16
10–100 mm	642	48	41	16	21
0.5–10 mm	542	40	130	4	n/a
< 0.5 mm	34	2	44	< 1	n/a
Total	1,350				

Source: Eden, 1964.

many stations (Fränzle, 1979). At St Ignatius in south-west Guyana, where intensity data were recorded for one rainy season, heavy falls (more than 10 mm) had a mean intensity of 20 mm/hour (see Table 3).

In general, the combination of high temperatures and high rainfall in Amazonia encourages vigorous and sustained plant growth. Short-term deficiencies in moisture supply occasionally affect crop performance, but are not a major constraint on productivity. The prevailing temperature and rainfall conditions also encourage the proliferation of insects and other micro-organisms, many of which constitute pests and diseases (Nieuwolt, 1977). The absence of marked temperature variability in the region removes a potential control on such organisms, and it is only in areas of significant moisture seasonality, notably savannas and wetlands, that some natural control is exerted.

Past climatic conditions in Amazonia have differed from those of the present. Drier phases appear to have occurred during the Pleistocene and Holocene periods. The precise nature of the fluctuations is unclear, but

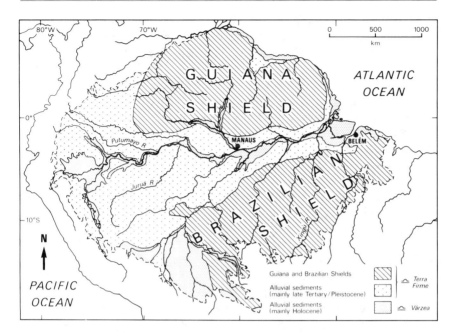

Figure 6 Geology of Amazonia (after Geological Study of America 1964)

they seem to have modified past vegetation distributions and left marks on the contemporary physical and biological landscape (Haffer, 1969; Tricart, 1985). Although the vegetation cover is essentially a dependent variable in these circumstances, it does exert feedback effects on climate. On this basis, current concern exists regarding contemporary large-scale forest clearance. In particular, it is argued that such clearance modifies critical variables like surface albedo, evapotranspiration and run-off, and may lead to significant reductions in regional rainfall and perhaps changed temperature regimes (Potter *et al.*, 1975; Molion, 1976; Sioli, 1980; Salati *et al.*, 1986). Increased carbon dioxide and aerosol inputs to the atmosphere also occur as a result of forest clearance and burning, and will likewise contribute to modified climatic conditions (Fearnside, 1985a; Dobson *et al.*, 1989). While these and related variables, which may be cumulative or counteractive, are unlikely to convert Amazonia into a 'red desert' (Goodland & Irwin, 1975), they may induce positive feedbacks that have significant implications for the human population.

Landscape morphology

The axial belt of the Amazonian lowlands consists of a variably dissected alluvial plain, narrow in the east and widening greatly to the west. The plain rarely exceeds 300 m in elevation and is abruptly defined in the west by the high arc of the Andes. To the east, the alluvial plain is flanked by residual surfaces of the Guiana and Brazilian Shields (see Figure 6).

The Guiana and Brazilian Shields consist of ancient crystalline rocks which are continuous at depth beneath the Amazon valley. The rocks are mainly granites, gneisses and mica-schists of Pre-Cambrian age, although on both Shields early sedimentary rocks locally overlie the basement (Sombroek, 1966; McConnell, 1968). On the Guiana Shield, these include Proterozoic sandstones of the Roraima Formation which extend across the Venezuela–Guyana frontier zone, attaining a summit level of 2,810 m at Mount Roraima; elsewhere, Mesozoic sandstones occur (Gansser, 1974; Maguire, 1979; PRORADAM, 1979). Comparable sediments overlie parts of the Brazilian Shield, including the Mesozoic sandstones that cap water-shed areas like Serra do Cachimbo and Serra do Roncador (Sombroek, 1966).

The Shield landscapes of Amazonia have undergone polycyclic development. Planation surfaces of gently undulating to hilly character, often separated by pronounced scarps, have developed as a result of recurrent landscape rejuvenation. In places, widespread altitudinal accordance exists, although in eastern parts of the Brazilian Shield distortion of individual surfaces has resulted from differential uplift during the Plio-Pleistocene period (FAO–UNESCO, 1971). The planation surfaces are described by L. C. King (1967) in eastern Brazil, where a sequence of five pediplanation levels is identified (see Table 4). These surfaces extend into southern Amazonia. One is evident as an erosion level at 400–600 m across the sandstones of Serra do Cachimbo and Serra do Roncador, and has been provisionally correlated with King's (1967) late Cretaceous Post-Gondwana level (Sombroek, 1966). Farther north on the Brazilian Shield, younger surfaces occur at elevations of 250–400 m and at 100–150 m, equating with King's Sul-Americana and Velhas surfaces (Sombroek, 1966; Camargo & Falesi, 1975).

On the Guiana Shield, McConnell (1968) has identified similar pediplanation surfaces. Designated in Guyana, these include the late Cretaceous/early Tertiary Kopinang surface, developed over the Roraima sandstone, and the Kaieteur and Rupununi surfaces, of later Tertiary age, which are widespread at lower levels over crystalline rocks (see Table 4). Confirmation of these levels exists in French Guiana (Choubert, 1957), Surinam (Zonneveld, 1969), Venezuela (Short & Steenken, 1962) and northern Brazil (Journaux, 1975; Bigarella & Ferreira, 1985), and, although questions arise regarding the age of the surfaces (Berrangé, 1977), their existence is generally acknowledged. The surfaces have been less distorted by tectonic activity than those of the Brazilian Shield and display significant altitudinal accordance. This is most evident with McConnell's (1968) end-Tertiary Rupununi surface. The type area is located in south-west

Table 4 Planation surfaces of the Brazilian and Guiana Shields

Eastern Brazil (after King, 1967)

Gondwana surface	Jurassic
Post-Gondwana surface	Late Cretaceous
Sul-Americana surface	Early Cainozoic (Tertiary)
Velhas surface	Late Cainozoic (Tertiary)
Paraguaçú surface	Pleistocene

Guyana (after McConnell, 1968)

Not named	Not dated	920 m
Kopinang surface	Late Cretaceous to early Tertiary	650–700 m
Kaieteur surface	Late Tertiary	400–600 m & 215–310 m
Rupununi surface	End-Tertiary	100–180 m
Mazaruni surface	Quaternary	75 m

Guyana, but the surface itself is more or less continuously developed around the Guiana Shield at an elevation of 100–200 m (Eden, 1971b; Bigarella & Ferreira, 1985).

Although the surfaces are attributed by King (1967) and McConnell (1968) to pediplanation processes, involving backwearing across a rock surface, Eden (1971b) has suggested from studies in Guyana that etch-planation, involving stripping of a pre-weathered landscape, is a preferable explanation for the characteristic weathering products and inselberg features encountered on the surfaces. A similar view is expressed by Kroonenberg & Melitz (1983) in Surinam.

The axial belt of the Amazonian lowlands contains sedimentary materials of varying age (see Figure 6). The main accumulation of sediments lies within the sub-Andean geosyncline, where early west-flowing rivers deposited materials until the late-Tertiary period. At that time, multiple uplifts of the Andean cordillera took place, which first obstructed and then reversed the original westward drainage. By the mid-Miocene period, the transport of sediments was to the east and a newly-formed Amazon river was draining to the Atlantic (Loczy, 1966; FAO–UNESCO, 1971).

Most of the lowland sedimentary landscape consists of late Tertiary and Quaternary deposits, but peripheral outcrops of older sediments exist. In eastern Amazonia, these include limestones and sandstones of Silurian to Carboniferous age, which are exposed along the Shield margins in the lower Amazon valley. Outcrops of Cretaceous and early Tertiary rocks also occur along the Andean margin, particularly in Peru and Ecuador. Younger Amazonian sediments consist mainly of the Plio-Pleistocene

Belterra clay and localised white sands, Pleistocene terrace deposits and Holocene floodplain alluvium.

The Belterra clay forms a flat terrace-like surface across a large area of the Amazonian lowland (Sombroek, 1966). In the Brazilian Amazon, the surface lies mainly at 100–200 m above sea level. The Belterra clay is 10–20 m in thickness and overlies Tertiary sediments of the Barreiras and Pebas beds. Little information exists on the extent of the Belterra clay in western Amazonia, although Eden *et al.* (1982) have reported comparable materials forming a dissected surface in the Caquetá basin of Colombia. According to Sombroek (1966), the Belterra clay is the product of sedimentation within a shallow lake or inland sea, associated with a high Calabrian (Plio-Pleistocene) sea level, although this interpretation has latterly been questioned (Klammer, 1971; Schubart & Salati, 1982).

Of similar age appear to be the white sand deposits that overlie the margin of the Guiana Shield in the upper Rio Negro basin. Their origin is also in doubt (PRORADAM, 1979; Khobzi *et al.*, 1980) but they probably represent outwash material derived from the adjacent Roraima Formation (Klinge *et al.*, 1977) and could have been deposited as fluvio-deltaic sediments on the margin of an inland Calabrian sea. Similar white sands, designated the Berbice Formation, overlie the eastern margin of the Guiana Shield and appear to be of equivalent age and provenance (Bleackley, 1956; FAO–UNESCO, 1971). Local white sand deposits occur elsewhere in Amazonia, but their age and origin vary (Ducke & Black, 1953; Ab'Sáber, 1982).

Within the sedimentary zone, a complex sequence of Pleistocene terrace levels is developed. They occur widely, especially in central Amazonia, but the associated terrace deposits are often relatively thin, consisting mainly of re-worked Tertiary and older sediments (FAO–UNESCO, 1971). The deposits are of variable texture, but are often more or less sandy and, in places, include gravels (Sombroek, 1966; Eden *et al.*, 1982).

The area of Holocene sedimentation in Amazonia comprises the *várzea* or wetland zone and is conventionally distinguished from the older sedimentary and residual landscapes that form the *terra firme*. Holocene sediments cover only a small part of the Amazonian lowlands, but are separated because of their distinctive characteristics and resource potential. In a strict sense, the term *várzea* is applied to the floodplains of 'white water' or turbid rivers, but in a broader context may be used to describe almost any seasonally-inundated area (Barrow, 1985). The *várzea* zone is well-developed along the mainstream of the Amazon and many of its larger tributaries (Photograph 3). During the late Pleistocene period, the Amazon was graded to a lower sea level than at present, and the existing *várzea* has built up within valleys that, in eastern Amazonia at least, were drowned by rising sea level in the post-glacial period (Sioli, 1975a). Floodplain sediments are mainly fine-textured, with some sandy materials,

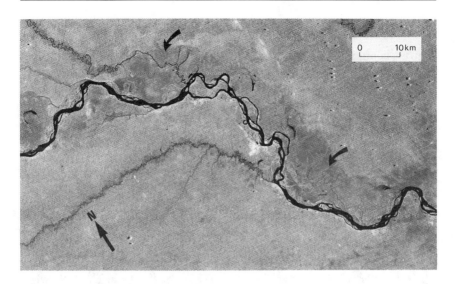

Photograph 3 *Várzea* zone (arrowed) of Río Napo, near Iquitos, eastern Peru. Landsat MSS band 7 image subscene, December 1973, ID no. 1502–14314 (reproduced by courtesy of NOAA)

and their accumulation continues as a result of seasonal overspill of sediment-bearing waters. The *várzea* zone is also subject to recurrent channel migration, achieved by lateral erosional and depositional processes (Salo *et al.*, 1986). Floodplains exist along the lower courses of non-turbid rivers, but they are nowhere near as well-developed as along the turbid rivers; the persisting 'mouthbays' of the non-turbid Xingú and Tapajós indicate the low rate of Holocene sedimentation associated with these rivers (Sioli, 1975a; Barrow, 1985).

Continuous with the mainstream *várzea* are the Amazon estuarine zone and the marginal wetlands extending along the Atlantic coast. Other wetlands in the region include the interior overflow plain of the Mojos savanna in Bolivia, established in a sub-Andean depression, and also parts of the low watershed zones of the Casiquiare and Rupununi on the southern flank of the Guiana Shield. The hydrologic regimes of these wetlands are variable, but all experience periodic flooding and are zones of sediment accumulation. The main contrast that exists is between coastal and estuarine zones, which experience moderate tidal regimes, and interior riparian zones, which, particularly in the central basin, experience marked seasonal hydrologic variability.

Fluvial conditions

Fluvial conditions in Amazonia have been investigated by Gibbs (1967),
Sioli (1967a, 1968a, 1975a & b, 1984), Baker (1978) and others. In these
studies attention is drawn to the coupling of land and water systems and
to associated fluvial regimes. The mean annual discharge of the Amazon
mainstream is estimated at $\geqslant$ 200,000 m^3/sec (Sioli, 1975a; Rich, 1984),
but pronounced seasonal variation occurs in the flow, mainly in response
to rainfall. Hydrographic data for the region are rather scarce, but at
Iquitos and Manaus, where gauging stations exist, annual fluctuations in
river level of 6–7 m and 8–12 m respectively are reported. Further
downstream, the annual range drops to about 6 m at Santarém, with lesser
tidal regimes prevalent in the estuarine zone. The timing of peak floods
varies across the basin. Major right-bank tributaries, like the Madeira and
Purus, achieve their peak in February or March towards the end of the
southern rainy season, while in the north both rainfall and discharge reach
their peak later in the year (Bradley, 1980). In the main channel, where
these flows are integrated, the peak flood is usually in June and low water
in October or November (see Figure 7). Inter-annual flood variability is
characteristic, with very high flood levels occurring from time to time
(Camargo, 1968). It has been suggested that recent deforestation in the
upper Amazon basin has already begun to increase general levels of peak
flooding (Gentry & Lopez-Parodi, 1980; Smith, 1981a). Flood variability
increases risk for human populations in the *várzea* zone, and has long been
a constraint on land exploitation.

Some information is available on the sediment status of Amazonian
rivers, which are broadly categorised as turbid or non-turbid. The Amazon
mainstream is a turbid or 'white water' river, estimated to discharge 731
$\times$ 10^6 t/year of solid and dissolved sediment (Gibbs, 1967). Suspended
sediment concentration in the lower Amazon is in the range 50–200 ppm,
with maximum values attained during the flood season (Sioli, 1966a).
Turbid water is also characteristic of the main western tributaries of the
Amazon, notably the Madeira, Purus, Juruá, Ucayali, Marañon, Napo and
Caquetá-Japurá, as well as the Rio Branco which flows off the southern
flank of the Guiana Shield. The upper Orinoco, draining north across the
Guiana Shield, is similarly turbid. It has commonly been assumed that
white water rivers derive their sediment load from mountain headwaters,
where most erosion occurs, but sediments are also acquired from piedmont
and lowland areas (Sioli, 1975a; Baker, 1978). This is evident in western
Amazonia where both the Purus and Juruá, whose catchments are
confined to the lowlands, have turbid waters. These rivers transport less
sediment than adjacent Andean rivers, like the Ucayali, but still acquire
a significant sediment load by lateral erosion along their sinuous, lowland
channels. White water rivers, which generally have pH 6.2–7.2 (Sioli,

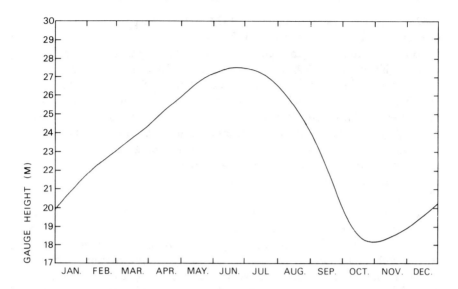

Figure 7 Gauge height above sea level of the Negro/Amazon rivers near Manaus for 1903–1952 (after Oltman *et al.*, 1964; Leopoldo *et al.*, 1985)

Table 5 Erosion rates for selected rivers in the Amazon basin

	Suspended solids (10^6 g/km^2/year)	Dissolved salts (10^6 g/km^2/year)
White water rivers		
Amazon (at mouth)	79	37
Ucayali	307	152
Marañon	251	93
Napo	184	29
Madeira	157	42
Caquetá–Japurá	120	109
Juruá	49	33
Purus	43	30
Clear water rivers		
Tapajós	1	4
Xingú	1	3
Black water river		
Negro	10	10

Source: Gibbs, 1967.

1967b; Thornes, 1969; Chapman, 1977), also transport relatively large quantities of dissolved salts (see Table 5).

Non-turbid rivers in Amazonia are divided into 'clear water' and 'black water'. The principal clear water rivers are the Tapajós and Xingú, which drain areas of low relief on the Brazilian Shield. Similar streams occur elsewhere, in both residual and sedimentary lowlands, where low erosion rates prevail. Although clear water rivers contain little suspended sediment, they are chemically rather heterogeneous. The Tapajós and Xingú have pure waters, but clear water streams in the Bragantina zone of Pará carry dissolved salts derived from limestones of the Pirabas Formation (Sioli, 1968a). Clear water rivers have pH values in the range 4.5–7.8 (Sioli, 1967a).

The principal black water river in Amazonia is the Rio Negro. Its waters, which are non-turbid, derive from an area of low relief on the south-west margin of the Guiana Shield. The white sandy sediments that cover much of its headwater zone are subject to podzolisation, and it is associated soil organic matter, transferred in dissolved or colloidal form to run-off, that gives the Negro its dark appearance and name (Klinge, 1967; Sioli, 1967a). Other black water rivers, similarly associated with sandy soils and areas of low relief, include the Urubú in central Amazonia and the Yari in Colombian Amazonia (see Photograph 4). Black water rivers are relatively uniform in their chemical composition, containing few inorganic ions and being extremely acid (pH 3.8–4.9). Their chemical status and dark colour result in very low biological productivity in relation to most Amazonian waters (Sioli, 1967a, 1975b).

Although preliminary data are available on the sediment status of Amazonian rivers, the level of information on other fluvial attributes is poor. During the 1970s, acquisition of radar and Landsat imagery provided new detail on river patterns, and drew particular attention to the sinuosity of many white water river channels and the contrasts that exist with the more direct courses of clear water and black water rivers. Preliminary analyses of these patterns have been undertaken, but detailed empirical studies have yet to be achieved (Baker, 1978; Holz et al., 1978; Bradley, 1980). A similar situation prevails in respect of Amazonian lacustrine habitats. They often possess high biological productivity and resource potential, but limited data exist on their physico-chemical properties (Fittkau et al.., 1975; Junk, 1984).

Soil resources

Reconnaissance soil surveys have been undertaken for most parts of Amazonia and efforts made to produce comprehensive soil maps. An early attempt of this kind was that of Papadakis (1969), who produced

Photograph 4 Junction of black water Río Yari and white water Río Caquetá, south-east Colombia

individual maps for Amazonian territories using a common soil classification. Subsequently, the South American sheets of the FAO Soil Map of the World became available (FAO–UNESCO, 1971); these were based on studies by FAO staff and others and used a legend formulated by Dudal (1968, 1969, 1970). The FAO map still provides the most useful overview of Amazonian soils, although subsequent local surveys have exposed some imperfections of the original synthesis. Refinement of the FAO map, however, has been constrained by subsequent preference for other classification systems. In Colombia, soil maps produced by the Proyecto Radargramétrico del Amazonas (PRORADAM, 1979), were based on the American Soil Taxonomy (USDA, 1975), while those emanating from the Projeto Radambrasil employed the related Brazilian classification (Brasil, 1973, *et seq.*; EMBRAPA, 1975). Also using the American Soil Taxonomy, Cochrane & Sanchez (1982) produced a generalised soil map covering Amazonia as a whole, although in a later publication (Cochrane *et al.*, 1985) the material was elaborated and attempts made to relate it to the FAO soil map.

In the present account, Amazonian soils are discussed in terms of the FAO soil units (FAO–UNESCO, 1971). According to this classification, the majority of the region is covered by Ferralsols, particularly Orthic and Xanthic Ferralsols. The main subsidiary soils, in free-draining areas, are Acrisols, Nitosols, Arenosols and Lithosols, while, in wetland areas,

Table 6 Approximate correlation of the FAO soil legend and the American Soil Taxonomy, with reference to Amazonia

FAO classification	American classification
Ferralsols	Oxisols
Acrisols	Ultisols
Nitosols	Ultisols/Alfisols
Arenosols	Entisols (Psamments)
Lithosols	Lithic subgroups
Gleysols	Inceptisols (Tropaquepts, Humaquepts, Plinthaquepts)
Fluvisols	Entisols (Fluvents)
Histosols	Histosols
Solonchaks	Aridisols (Salorthids)

Sources: FAO–UNESCO, 1974; USDA, 1975; Sanchez, 1976; Cochrane *et al.*, 1985.

Gleysols are widespread, with subsidiary Fluvisols, Histosols and Solonchaks. The approximate correlates of these units in the American classification are given in Table 6.

Amazonian soils have been significantly influenced by climatic conditions as well as by geology, relief and other variables. Persistent high temperatures and abundant rainfall encourage the weathering and leaching of parent materials, which, particularly on the residual and sedimentary landscapes of the *terra firme*, retain few weatherable minerals and are mainly characterised by quartz sand, kaolinitic clay, and iron and aluminium oxides. Plinthite is present in many profiles and, in places, hardened lateritic outcrops occur. The soil clays generally have a low cation exchange capacity and retain minimal amounts of essential nutrients like calcium, magnesium and potassium (Wambeke, 1978). The exchange complex is frequently occupied by aluminium ions, which create acid soil conditions and may induce toxicity in plants. Phosphorus deficiency is also widespread, with the element in places prone to fixation as aluminium or iron phosphate; highest fixation capacities are associated with acid clayey soils whose improvement can be particularly problematic (Cochrane & Sanchez, 1982; Cochrane *et al.*, 1985). Locally, soils of higher natural fertility occur on the *terra firme*, as for example over basalt parent materials in parts of southern Pará, but chemical infertility is widespread and a major constraint on land exploitation.

Soil physical conditions on the *terra firme* are rather variable. Heavy textured soils are associated with the Belterra clay in eastern Amazonia and with similar sediments in Colombia. Elsewhere, across older Shield landscapes and on Pleistocene terraces, coarser-textured materials commonly occur, giving rise to sandy loam to sandy clay soils. Because of the weathered status of parent materials, the silt content of *terra firme* soils is usually low (Sombroek, 1966). Soil structure is generally well-developed, especially in more clayey soils, and creates favourable conditions for root penetration (Wambeke, 1978). Most soils also drain effectively and are relatively erosion-resistant. However, even under a forest canopy, some erosion occurs, while on land that is cleared and inclined the erosion hazard is greatly increased (McGregor, 1980; Alvarado, 1982).

The existence of a forest cover affects both the physical and chemical status of the soil. As indicated, a forest canopy gives some protection against erosion, while high rates of litter fall and direct nutrient cycling help to offset inherent soil infertility (Burnham, 1975). The accumulation of organic matter in the soil is also important, since it improves cation exchange capacity and is a major source of nitrogen and other nutrients. It also contributes to soil aggregation and improves available moisture retention (Sombroek, 1966; Wambeke, 1978; Swift & Sanchez, 1984). When the forest cover is absent or removed, lower levels of soil organic matter prevail, and associated physical and chemical properties change.

The soils of the *várzea* or wetland zone are notably influenced by parent materials and by local relief and drainage conditions. Floodplain sediments associated with Andean white water rivers usually contain weatherable minerals and give rise to relatively fertile soils, but where the regional landscape is already highly weathered, as on the Guiana and Brazilian Shields, derived floodplain sediments are correspondingly infertile. Floodplain soils display characteristic gleying and mottling and often contain accumulations of plinthite. Soil textures are variable; silty and clayey materials predominate, but some sandy deposits occur. In wetter floodplain sites, organic soils also develop. Similar hydromorphic soils occur in the Amazon estuarine zone and along the Atlantic coastal wetlands; in places, saline soils are also encountered.

Soil types

According to FAO–UNESCO (1971), the most widespread soil type in Amazonia is the Ferralsol, which is present on both residual and sedimentary landscapes (see Figure 8). It corresponds to the Oxisol of the American classification (USDA, 1975) and the Latosol of the Brazilian classification (EMBRAPA, 1975). The Ferralsol is a free-draining soil of low natural fertility, red to yellow in colour, and with a high content of sequioxides. It is defined by the presence of an oxic B horizon containing no more than traces of weatherable primary minerals, like feldspar and mica, and having a cation exchange capacity of < 16 meq/100 g clay (FAO–UNESCO, 1974). Orthic Ferralsols are generally present on Shield landscapes, although in areas of savanna they may be replaced by Acric Ferralsols. On sedimentary landscapes, Xanthic Ferralsols are widely

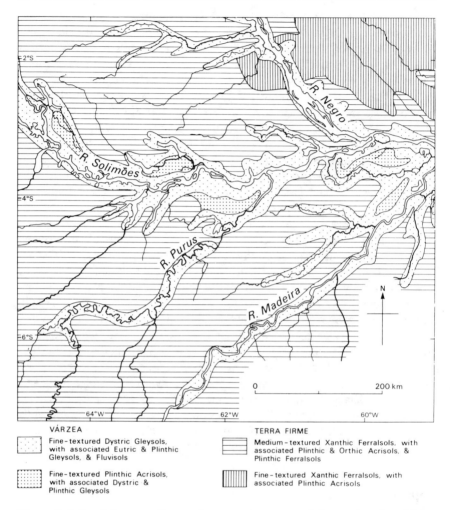

VÁRZEA

| | Fine-textured Dystric Gleysols, with associated Eutric & Plinthic Gleysols, & Fluvisols |

| | Fine-textured Plinthic Acrisols, with associated Dystric & Plinthic Gleysols |

TERRA FIRME

| | Medium-textured Xanthic Ferralsols, with associated Plinthic & Orthic Acrisols, & Plinthic Ferralsols |

| | Fine-textured Xanthic Ferralsols, with associated Plinthic Acrisols |

Figure 8 Soils of the *terra firme* and *várzea* zones, central Amazonia (after FAO–UNESCO, 1971)

reported (FAO–UNESCO, 1971), although later studies indicate that, in western Amazonia at least, the soil type is less extensive than originally assumed (Zamora, 1975; PRORADAM, 1979).

Ferralsols are of low natural fertility and generally unsuited to permanent cultivation, unless nutrient supplements are provided. Deficiencies in trace elements, like zinc and boron, are evident as well as in major nutrients. Under modern management, such deficiencies can be made good by use of fertilisers, but, especially on sandier Ferralsols, fertilisers are prone to rapid leaching (FAO–UNESCO, 1971). Ferralsols are of variable texture, but mostly display favourable structural properties which

Table 7 Analytical data for representative Amazonian soil types

Depth (cm)	Texture	pH (H_2O)	O.C. %	Exchangeable cations (meq/100 g) Ca	Mg	K	Al	H	CEC	P (ppm)
Ferralsol (*Latossolo distrófico*), Rio Uraricuera, Roraima, Brazil										
0–10	Sandy clay loam	4.0	1.8	0.1	0.1	0.1	2.6	7.6	10.5	7
10–20	Sandy clay	3.5	0.9	tr	tr	0.1	2.4	4.9	7.4	2
20–60	Sandy clay	4.0	0.6	tr	tr	tr	1.6	3.0	4.8	2
60–90	Clay	4.3	0.4	tr	tr	tr	1.2	2.1	3.4	3
Eutric Nitosol (*Terra roxa estruturada*), Altamira, Pará, Brazil										
0–8	Clay/clay loam	7.0	2.5	25.2	2.3	0.3	tr	1.4	29.2	8
8–26	Clay	7.3	0.8	6.0	0.7	0.3	0.1	1.8	8.9	2
26–60	Clay	6.9	0.5	3.2	0.6	0.1	tr	1.6	5.5	2
60–100	Clay	6.4	0.3	2.5	0.4	0.1	0.1	2.2	5.3	3
Dystric Gleysol, Santana-Serra do Navio, Amapá, Brazil										
0–20	Clay	4.8	1.1	0.7	0.9	0.2	1.5	2.3	5.9	n/a
20–70	Clay loam	4.9	0.5	0.6	0.7	0.1	0.9	2.1	4.5	n/a
70–130	Clay	5.1	0.5	1.0	1.4	0.3	0.2	2.0	6.7	n/a

Source: FAO–UNESCO, 1971; Brasil, 1975; Cochrane, 1984.

facilitate soil drainage and improve erosion resistance. However, the soils do have rather unfavourable moisture retention characteristics and are susceptible to serious erosion on cleared, sloping land (see Table 7).

Acrisols, which correlate with Ultisols in the American classification (USDA, 1975), displace Ferralsols in many parts of Amazonia. They are acid soils with rather low base saturation. They have red to yellow coloration, and are distinguished from Ferralsols by the presence of an argillic B horizon. Acrisols occur across a range of parent materials, both residual and sedimentary, but more commonly develop on the latter. Acrisols are most widespread in western Amazonia, where they occupy an area significantly greater than that indicated by the FAO soil map (Zamora, 1975; Sanchez, 1976). In Peru and Bolivia, Orthic Acrisols are developed on Tertiary and older sedimentary materials along the Andean margin, as well as on some Quaternary sediments. Plinthic Acrisols also occur over Quaternary sediments in poorly drained areas, such as the Mojos region of Bolivia. In Brazil, both Orthic and Plinthic Acrisols are developed on sediments overlying Shield rocks and, in the Guianas, Orthic Acrisols occur directly on Shield parent materials (FAO–UNESCO, 1971; Zamora, 1975).

Acrisols have rather low natural fertility, although nutrient deficiencies can be made good by fertiliser inputs. In physical terms, Acrisols are less favourable than Ferralsols. They often drain less well and are more susceptible to erosion as a result of strong horizonation. In western Amazonia, Acrisols commonly occupy steeper slopes within dissected landscapes, which increases their susceptibility to erosion (FAO–UNESCO, 1971; Sanchez, 1979a).

Within the broad matrix of Ferralsols and Acrisols, which cover approximately three-quarters of Amazonia (Cochrane & Sanchez, 1982), other soil types are locally encountered. On the *terra firme*, the most important of these are Nitosols, which cover several million hectares. Known as *terra roxa estruturada* in Brazil, they are usually reddish-brown in colour and characterised by a deeply-developed argillic B horizon (FAO–UNESCO, 1974). Nitosols most commonly occur over basic igneous and metamorphic rocks and over some Tertiary and older sediments. Both Dystric and Eutric Nitosols exist widely in the Guianas, associated with gabbro, dolerite and basalt, and Eutric Nitosols occur over similar rocks in Rondônia and Pará, Brazil (Table 7). Eutric Nitosols also occur in the Andean piedmont over parent materials ranging from basic crystalline rocks in Colombia to Tertiary and other sediments in Ecuador and Peru (FAO–UNESCO, 1971). Nitosols are of variable chemical status, but often have relatively high base saturation and are noted, as along parts of the Transamazon highway, for their enhanced fertility (Camargo & Falesi, 1975; Smith, 1982).

Other soil types present on the *terra firme* include Lithosols and Arenosols. Lithosols are shallow, stony soils, usually associated with sloping land. They are most widespread in the dissected central area of the Guiana Shield and, to a lesser extent, the Brazilian Shield. Lithosols are generally unsuited for agriculture. Arenosols are developed over coarse-textured parent materials, notably sandstones of the Roraima Formation in Venezuela and Guyana, and similar rocks in Brazil and eastern Colombia. The alluvial white sands of the Berbice Formation in the Guiana lowlands carry Arenosols (FAO–UNESCO, 1971), as do equivalent sandy deposits in the upper Negro basin. Arenosols, which are commonly associated with black water streams, have extremely low cation exchange capacity and are very acid and infertile. The soils have negligible agricultural value, even using traditional techniques. In the Andean piedmont, where various rock types outcrop, other soils include Dystric Cambisols in southern Colombia and Chromic Vertisols in parts of the Huallaga and Ucayali basins of Peru (FAO–UNESCO, 1971).

Finally, there are the hydromorphic soils of wetland areas. According to FAO–UNESCO (1971), most of these are Gleysols with some Fluvisols, Histosols and Solonchaks in coastal areas (see Figure 8). Gleysols are developed over unconsolidated parent materials, usually floodplain sediments. They are mostly silty to clayey in texture, and give rise to

Dystric Gleysols with relatively low base saturation. Although acid in character, such Gleysols, when developed along white water rivers of Andean origin, usually contain weatherable minerals and are quite fertile. Where the floodplain materials are of Shield origin, the reverse is usually the case (see Table 7). In coastal wetlands, Eutric Gleysols occasionally occur, but along the Brazilian coast and in the Amazon estuarine zone Gleyic Solonchaks commonly develop over marine and brackish-water sediments. Similar areas along the Guiana coast carry Eutric Fluvisols and peaty Histosols (FAO–UNESCO, 1971).

The status of wetland soils in Amazonia mainly reflects parent materials and drainage conditions. Camargo (1958) and others have long considered these soils to possess a high agricultural potential, and there is certainly some direct evidence of this, both past and present (FAO, 1966; Meggers, 1971; Barrow, 1985). Not all wetland soils, however, are of high potential. As indicated, their chemical status varies with the provenance of parent materials, which in places are deficient in nutrients and in coastal areas may give rise to toxic acid sulphate soils (FAO, 1966). Most wetlands also experience periodic inundations, which increase cultivation risk and require highly-adapted agrosystems.

Conclusion

Although reconnaissance soil and terrain surveys have now been undertaken for most parts of Amazonia, there is still very limited information on local environmental conditions. As Moran (1981) indicates, this has at times encouraged planners involved in land colonisation to treat Amazonian landscapes as homogeneous and to neglect critical local soil variations within them. Equally, the need exists to acquire detailed information on temporal environmental variations; this is especially so in areas of high natural variability, notably flood-prone wetlands where increased agricultural exploitation may be desirable.

There are many environmental constraints on land development in Amazonia. In broad terms, they may be summarised as resource deficiencies, resource variabilities, and biotic stressors. Resource deficiencies are mainly evident in respect of soil nutrients, which are frequently in short supply and certainly prone to rapid depletion in forests and savannas of the *terra firme*. Resource variability involves mainly water supply, and is particularly apparent in wetland habitats characterised by seasonal or tidal variations; it is also characteristic of savanna habitats with marked rainfall seasonality. Wetlands and savannas also experience marked inter-annual variability in their water supply. Biotic stressors, notably weeds, pests and diseases, affect land exploitation throughout Amazonia, but are most active, and thus most limiting, under the perennially hot and wet conditions of the forested *terra firme*. Their incidence is reduced, but by no means eliminated, under the more variable water regimes of wetlands and savannas.

Various human responses are possible to the environmental constraints prevalent in Amazonia. Exploitation strategies may be adapted to existing local conditions and make effective use of such natural resources as are available in a particular habitat. This strategy has been broadly characteristic of many pre-Columbian and early Colonial populations in Amazonia, both in *terra firme* and wetland habitats. Alternatively, greater reliance may be placed on controlling environmental conditions through use of technical inputs like fertilisers or pesticides or by engineering works associated with drainage or flood regulation. Both these broad strategies have advantages and disadvantages, but, in either case, successful exploitation still demands an understanding of local environmental conditions and the adoption of specific and appropriate exploitation techniques.

3
Amazonian ecosystems

... the picture of the Amazon ecosystem that is emerging from recent studies is that it is heterogeneous, complex and dynamic.

[Sponsel, 1986, p. 73]

The Amazonian lowlands are largely covered by tropical forest, known as the *hylaea* (Ducke & Black, 1953). Evergreen rain forest is present over large areas, with lesser extents of semi-deciduous to deciduous forest, savanna and wetland vegetation. Immense biological diversity characterises the region, with the greatest floral richness reported to exist in the Caquetá and Guaviare basins in north-west Amazonia (Spruce, 1908). At least one million species of plants and animals, or 10–20 per cent of global species, are estimated to exist in Amazonia, although, on the basis of recent insect studies, it is possible that the true species total for the region is very much greater (Erwin, 1982, 1988; Myers, 1984). The total includes some 30,000 higher plants, of which several thousands are tree species (Myers, 1984). Rodrigues (1967) has recorded 470 tree species in the Manaus region of Brazil, while a survey of Colombian Amazonia resulted in the identification of 550 tree species (PRORADAM, 1979). Savanna vegetation is less diverse than that of the forest, but numerous species still occur. In the Rupununi savanna of Guyana, 494 higher plants have been recorded, of which thirty-eight are tree species (Anon., 1966).

Although field collection in some animal groups in Amazonia is far from complete, similar species richness commonly prevails. This is particularly the case with insects, birds and fishes, which are diverse even by comparison with the Old World tropics (Fittkau, 1969). There are estimated to be 1,800 bird species and 2,000–3,000 fish species in Amazonia (Myers, 1979a; Goulding, 1980). Insects are exceedingly numerous, with thousands of beetle species and hundreds of ant species on record (Fittkau, 1969; Erwin, 1988); micro-organisms are similarly abundant. There is also a considerable number of mammals and reptiles, with bat and rodent faunas particularly well-represented (Hershkovitz, 1969; Bourlière, 1973; Laurent, 1973).

Although widespread plant and animal collecting has been undertaken in Amazonia, general biological information is limited and patchy. In places, the description and classification of vegetation types have been undertaken (Schulz, 1960; Aubréville, 1961; Rodrigues, 1961; Pires, 1973; Prance,

1979b; Pires & Prance, 1985), and in recent years the use of remote sensing, particularly side-looking airborne radar, has greatly advanced the task of vegetation mapping, even though little comparative work has yet been done across national frontiers (Brasil, 1973, *et seq.*; PRORADAM, 1979). A few broader accounts of the Amazonian flora exist, notably that of Ducke & Black (1953), who have identified major phytogeographic zones in the region, and detailed studies of plant distributions have been initiated (Prance, 1973, 1979a, 1982; Prance *et al.*, 1984; Kahn *et al.*, 1988). Similar work has started on many animal groups, including fishes, birds, butterflies, lizards and mammals (Hershkovitz, 1969; Vanzolini & Williams, 1970; Brown *et al.*, 1974; Haffer, 1974; Brown, 1982, 1985; Goulding *et al.*, 1988). Ecological studies of plants and animals are at an early stage, although the scale of investigation is now expanding quite rapidly. Hitherto, investigations have tended to focus on a limited number of study areas, which, for the moment, necessarily provide the basis of preliminary regional generalisations.

In reviewing the nature of the Amazonian *hylaea* and associated vegetation formations, a useful distinction is still made between the *terra firme* or dryland zone and the *várzea* or wetland zone. Both contain tree and herb-dominated communities, but the contrasting physical character of the zones has led to distinctive biotas and resource potentials.

The *terra firme* is mainly covered by evergreen rain forest which represents the climax vegetation for most of Amazonia. In drier areas, the formation grades to semi-deciduous and deciduous forest. Other distinctive forest types of the *terra firme* include the evergreen *caatinga* forest of the upper Negro basin and the *cipoal* or liana forest in Brazilian Pará. Lower forest and shrub vegetation types occur on sandstone uplands. Within the forest itself, there also exist areas of savanna, known as *campos de terra firme* (Pires, 1973). These range from scattered savanna 'islands' like those of southern Venezuela and of the Puciari–Humaitá area of Brazil to more extensive tracts like the Rio Branco–Rupununi and Trombetas–Paru (see Figure 1). The boundary between forest and savanna is usually abrupt, but some transitional categories are identified, notably the *cerradão* and *caatinga baixa* (Rodrigues, 1961; Askew *et al.*, 1970a). The *várzea* or wetland zone contains both woody and herbaceous vegetation. Swamp and marsh forests occur widely on river floodplains, but give way to herbaceous wetlands, or *campos de várzea* (Pires, 1973), along parts of the lower Amazon valley and elsewhere.

Although vegetation maps exist for Amazonia as a whole (Wiebecke, 1965; Hueck & Seibert, 1972; UNESCO, 1981), they contain rather limited detail on the distribution and extent of vegetation types. Supplementary information can be obtained from national or local surveys, but considerable difficulties arise in matching classification units across the region. Consequently, only approximate data are available on the overall extent of individual vegetation types in Amazonia. Estimates by the present author indicate that, in the late 1970s, the forest area of the *terra firme* covered 547.3 million ha, with an additional 15–20 million ha of savanna occurring within that zone. Wetland forest occupied a further 65.5 million ha, and there were 27.7 million ha of herbaceous wetland. In addition, there existed an estimated 28.1 million ha of cleared forest land. By the late 1980s, the area of cleared land had probably increased to 60–65 million ha. These data are elaborated in Chapter 8; for the present, attention is focused on the history, current status and dynamics of Amazonian ecosystems.

Quaternary vegetation history

Although the *hylaea* is an ancient and complex ecosystem that today extends widely across Amazonia, environmental fluctuations appear previously to have caused significant changes in its area and distribution. Such changes provide a perspective on contemporary anthropic deforestation and have been considered of importance to conservation planning. Indications of past changes in the vegetation distribution were reported by Wilhelmy (1952), Hueck (1957), Eden (1964) and others, and early palynological data were provided by van der Hammen (1963, 1972) and Wijmstra & van der Hammen (1966). Subsequently, Haffer (1969, 1974, 1977) developed his seminal refugia hypothesis, based on the study of Amazonian bird distributions, and provided a general model for vegetation changes in the region.

Haffer proposed that during drier phases in the Pleistocene the forest cover was periodically reduced to small isolated tracts, or refugia, which, with the return of wetter conditions, expanded and re-united with each other. Corresponding fluctuations occurred in the extent of adjacent, non-forest formations. The individual forest refugia, which seemingly coincided with areas of persisting wetness, retained bird populations that were differentiated as a result of their genetic isolation. When the refugia expanded and were re-united with each other, complex patterns of hybridisation and sympatry were developed. During successive phases of forest contraction and expansion, extinctions of animal forms also occurred, but the recurrent speciation significantly increased the overall diversity of the forest fauna (Haffer, 1969). The findings from bird populations have been confirmed by studies of lizards (Vanzolini & Williams, 1970), butterflies (Turner, 1971; Brown *et al.*, 1974) and plants (Prance, 1973, 1979a, 1982). Periodic fluctuations in the vegetation cover are also evidenced by the nature and distribution of the savanna islands that are currently scattered through the forest zone. These contain disjunct species and are seen as relics of an earlier, more widespread savanna distribution,

associated with drier conditions (Ducke & Black, 1953; Hueck, 1957;
Eden, 1974a; Prance, 1978; Gottsberger & Morawetz, 1986).

Understandably, some uncertainty and dispute surround the proposed
refugia model (Endler, 1982; Beven et al., 1984; Colinvaux, 1987, 1989;
Colinvaux & Liu, 1987), and precise data on the proposed sequence of
Quaternary climatic and associated vegetational changes are in short
supply. However, it is still widely assumed that drier climatic conditions
and a contraction of the forest to isolated refugia occurred in the late
Pleistocene period (21,000–13,000 BP) (van der Hammen, 1974; Prance,
1978) and were coincident with drier conditions elsewhere in parts of the
tropics (Kershaw, 1978; Sarnthein, 1978; Bonnefille & Riollet, 1988).
Similar conditions and localised forest retreat also appear to have
characterised the mid- to late-Holocene period (van der Hammen, 1974;
Absy, 1985). Earlier patterns of vegetation fluctuation are less clear, but
comparable changes presumably occurred through much of the Pleistocene
period (Vanzolini, 1973; Prance, 1985).

Pleistocene climatic fluctuations and the development of refugia are one
of a number of factors that have contributed to the contemporary species
diversity of Amazonia (Prance, 1978, 1979a). The nature and location of
the refugia are also of some practical importance, since they are areas of
high endemism that contain unique genetic resources, both plant and
animal. On this basis, the refugia have been considered to warrant priority
in the selection of conservation areas (Prance, 1977; Muthoo & Leader,
1978; Brown & Ab'Sáber, 1979). This is a reasonable approach, although
there exist other centres of species diversity in the region that deserve to
be considered for conservation (Salo et al., 1986).

Ecosystems

Forests of the Terra firme

Free-draining soils of the *terra firme* commonly carry evergreen rain forest
in areas where the annual rainfall exceeds 1,800–2,000 mm. The forest is
tall and dense, with a large phytomass and heterogeneous composition (see
Photograph 5). Most of the trees are evergreen, although a few deciduous
species may occur. The forest canopy is continuous and commonly reaches
25–35 m in height, with emergent trees rising to 45 m or more (Schulz,
1960; Klinge & Rodrigues, 1986; Dubois, 1971); species like *Swietenia
macrophylla*, *Mora paraensis* and *Bertholletia excelsa* are reported occasionally to reach 50–60 m (Ducke & Black, 1953). The forest is dense,
frequently containing 100–135 trees/ha (> 25 cm DBH) (Schulz, 1960;
Sombroek, 1966; PRORADAM, 1979). Epiphytes may be present in
abundance.

Photograph 5 Rain forest along access trail in lower Tapajós basin, Pará, Brazil

Photograph 6 Surface litter layer with enmeshed fine roots (shown on sheet of paper) from rain forest in Caquetá basin, south-east Colombia

Although the forest margin, like the canopy above, has a luxuriant and impenetrable aspect, the interior of a mature forest stand is relatively open. Straight trunks ascend, often festooned in lianas, but there is limited growth in the shaded conditions at ground level and human movement through the forest is not greatly obstructed. The ground surface itself is mantled by a layer of leaf litter and other debris, and rooting systems are mainly superficial, with many finer roots extending through the litter layer (see Photograph 6). In the past, it was widely assumed that specific layers, or strata, existed within the forest, but their presence is doubtful. According to Pires & Prance (1977), such stratification is probably lacking in Amazonia, with trees being present at all heights.

Floristically, the evergreen rain forest is heterogeneous. In survey plots near Manaus, large trees (> 25 cm DBH) averaged 65 species per ha (Klinge & Rodrigues, 1968); the total plant population was reported to exceed 600 species/ha, most of which were in the lower part of the stand (Klinge et al., 1975). Other large-tree counts have recorded 79 species/ha (> 20 cm DBH) at Tefé in central Amazonia and 62 species/ha (> 20 cm DBH) at Belém in eastern Amazonia (Black et al., 1950). Such diversity appears to be characteristic of mature rain forest throughout the region. The corollary of high species diversity is that most individual species are present at very low density. In places, a few species may make up a significant proportion of the tree population, but individual species dominance is not characteristic (Boom, 1986). In a survey plot at Mapane in Surinam, the four species *Vouacapoua americana*, *Eschweilera amara*, *E. odora* and *Chaetocarpus schomburgkianus* comprised 35 per cent of the tree population (> 25 cm DBH) (Schulz, 1960). Elsewhere, near Manaus, the four species *E. odora*, *Scleronema micranthum*, *Oenocarpus bacaba* and *Eperua bijuga* comprised 14 per cent of the tree population (> 15 cm DBH) (Prance et al., 1976). The majority of tree species in these stands, however, are distributed very sparsely. According to Ducke & Black (1953), the best represented family among Amazonian forest trees is the Leguminosae. The Moraceae, Lecythidaceae and Sapotaceae also provide many individuals, while the Rosaceae, Meliaceae and Vochysiaceae are well represented. In places palms (Palmae) are common.

Few data are available on the phytomass of the rain forest, but high values generally prevail. On the *terra firme* near Manaus, Klinge et al. (1975) described an evergreen rain forest having a total phytomass of 450–500 t/ha (dry weight). Much of the phytomass consisted of stems (47 per cent), with lesser amounts of roots (26 per cent), branches and twigs (20 per cent), other plants (5 per cent), and leaf matter (2 per cent). Similar forests at Kabo in northern Surinam and San Carlos de Rio Negro in southern Venezuela gave values of 480 t/ha and 390 t/ha respectively (Jordan & Uhl, 1978; Jordan, 1982; Jonkers & Schmidt, 1984; Klinge, 1986). Although few phytomass data are available for Amazonia, supplementary information is

Table 8 Standing timber volume for selected forests in lowland Amazonia

	Tree DBH (cm)	Timber volume (m³/ha)
Evergreen rain forest		
Brazil		
Curuá-Una, Pará (clayey soils)	> 25	233
Curuá-Una, Pará (sandy soils)	> 25	148
Santarém, Pará	> 25	227
Acará, lower Tocantins	> 25	217
Canhumá, lower Madeira	> 25	164
Rio Juami, upper Japurá	> 30	131
Manaus, Amazonas	> 25	102
Benjamin Constant, Amazonas	> 25	100
Rio Puruê, upper Japurá	> 30	82
Colombia		
Caño Tigre, Caquetá river	> 25	140
Maria Christina, Caquetá river	> 25	118
Peru		
Pucallpa, Loreto	> 30	127
Jenaro Herrera, Loreto	> 25	96
Caatinga forest		
Rio Içana, upper Negro, Brazil	> 30	99
Rio Cubate, upper Negro, Brazil	> 30	51
Liana forest (*cipoal*)		
Pará, Brazil	> 25	60–120
Semi-deciduous/deciduous forest		
San José del Guaviare, Colombia	> 25	87
San José del Guaviare, Colombia	> 25	64
Imataca, Venezuela	n/a	69
Açailândia, Pará, Brazil	> 25	62
Wetland forest		
Río Inírida, Colombia	> 25	69–100
Territorio Federal Amazonas, Venezuela	n/a	41–85

Sources: Brazil: Sombroek, 1966; Klinge & Rodrigues, 1968; Brasil, 1977; Colombia: PRORADAM, 1979; Peru: Masson, 1979; Martínez, 1982; *Caatinga* forest: Brasil, 1976; Liana forest (*cipoal*): Dubois, 1971; Semi-deciduous/ deciduous forest: Sombroek, 1966; Wood *et al.*, 1977; PRORADAM, 1979; Wetland forest: Somberg *et al.*, 1973; PRORADAM, 1979.

available in the form of commercial estimates of standing timber volume (see Table 8). As Klinge (1986) points out, estimation techniques are not always consistent between surveys, but the present data do suggest that significant variations exist both within and between forest types in the region. Variations in the timber volume, and presumably phytomass, of the evergreen rain forest do not directly correlate with rainfall levels; according to Sombroek (1966), soil moisture retention may be a more significant factor, but the overall pattern has yet to be explained.

No precise data are available on rain forest productivity in Amazonia, although, under prevailing temperature and moisture conditions, values of at least 20–25 t/ha/year (dry weight) are to be expected (Farnworth & Golley, 1974). At Manaus, estimates have been made of total litter fall at approximately 11 t/ha/year, of which 5.6 t/ha/year comprised leaf litter (Fittkau & Klinge, 1973). Leaf litter fall in a similar rain forest near Belém was reported to be 8 t/ha/year (Klinge, 1977). Such data accord with values from other tropical forests (UNESCO, 1978), but a notable feature of Amazonian forests, which reflects their soil conditions, is the low concentration of nutrients (except nitrogen) in the leaf litter (Klinge, 1977). The supply of litter is matched by high rates of litter decomposition which is mainly achieved by micro-organisms, especially soil fungi (Fittkau & Klinge, 1973).

Other forest types occurring on the *terra firme* include evergreen *caatinga* forest, liana forest or *cipoal*, and, in drier areas, semi-deciduous to deciduous forest. The *caatinga* forest is an evergreen sclerophyllous formation developed over alluvial white sands (Arenosols). The type area for the formation is the upper Rio Negro basin of Brazil, where annual rainfall exceeds 3,000 mm. The main forest, which covers some 3 million ha, is known as *caatinga alta*. A similar area is occupied by *caatinga baixa*, or *campina*, which is a more open, low tree and shrub variant (Pires, 1973; Klinge & Medina, 1979; Anderson, 1981). The *caatinga* extends into adjacent areas of Venezuela and Colombia. The formation as a whole is relatively rich in species, containing many endemics, but individual stands are less diverse than those of the evergreen rain forest (Ducke & Black, 1953; Pires, 1973; Anderson & Benson, 1980).

In the upper Rio Negro, *caatinga alta* forms a relatively open forest, with enhanced light penetration. The canopy trees are of medium stature (20–30 m) and reduced girth, and woody lianas are relatively scarce. Individual communities are commonly dominated by a few tree species, notably *Micrandra spruceana* and *Eperua leucantha*. The *caatinga baixa* is a more open tree and shrub community, reaching approximately 10 m in height and dominated by one or a few species. A notable feature of the *caatinga* forest is its very high root mass, which is seen as a response to the oligotrophic status of Arenosols (Rodrigues, 1961; Klinge *et al.*, 1977; Klinge & Herrera, 1978).

Caatinga forest has also been described from white sands near São Paulo de Olivença in western Brazil (Ducke & Black, 1953), and similar shrub communities are reported in the Manaus area (Rodrigues, 1961) and around Monte Alegre in the lower Amazon (Ducke & Black, 1953). Related communities also occur over white sand deposits in the lowland Guianas and on elevated sandstone terrain elsewhere in the region (Fanshawe, 1952; Egler, 1960; Aubréville, 1961; Sioli, 1967b; King, 1968a; Domínguez, 1975; Ratter *et al.*, 1973; Cooper, 1979). *Caatinga*-type vegetation has traditionally been seen as xeromorphic, but Ferri (1960) expressed doubts that water supplies were generally limiting, attributing its sclerophyllous features to nutrient deficiency. Klinge *et al.* (1977) claimed that in places *caatinga* may suffer periodic water stress, but recognised the general constraint of the infertility of white sand soils.

Liana forest, or *cipoal*, is another distinctive formation within the rain forest zone, covering an estimated 10 million ha between the Tocantins and Tapajós rivers in eastern Amazonia. It forms a relatively low and open stand, with abundant lianas and scattered tall trees (Pires, 1973; Pires & Prance, 1985). Its composition is distinctive and exemplified by the *Orbignya–Bertholletia* association of the Itacaiunas basin (Pires, 1978). The forest experiences a typical Amazonian rainfall regime, and is present over soils of variable fertility. In eastern Pará, Sombroek (1966) associates the liana forest with heavy-textured soils, which are considered to restrict root development and moisture supply. However, the forest is also present on more sandy soils, and Smith (1982) suggests it may be a disclimax attributable to indigenous felling and burning.

Semi-deciduous to deciduous forests occur in more seasonal areas where annual rainfall is below 1,800–2,000 mm. There is usually a gradation from evergreen rain forest to the more seasonal forest types, which are most extensively developed along the southern margins of Amazonia (FAO–UNESCO, 1971). Such forests are of lower stature than the evergreen forest, and their timber volume and presumably phytomass are also reduced (see Table 8).

A 'dry forest' of this type, containing mixed evergreen and deciduous species, has been described from the northern Mato Grosso of Brazil, where it occupies a transitional zone between the main evergreen rain forest and the *cerrados* of central Brazil (Askew *et al.*, 1970b, Ratter *et al.*, 1973). Rainfall data for the area are scanty, but there is an extended drier period in mid-year. The forest has a canopy height of 15–18 m, with scattered emergents rising to 25 m or more. According to Askew *et al.* (1970b, p. 213), the forest consists of 'crowded, often slender trees of many different species of which no single one is dominant. These form an almost closed canopy so that ground vegetation is limited mainly to scattered tree seedlings'. The boundary between the dry forest and adjacent formations is relatively precise, coinciding with a transition from finer to coarser textured soils (Askew *et al.*, 1970a). Similar semi-deciduous forest is reported from drier areas in the vicinity of Boa Vista in northern Roraima (Brasil, 1975); in the adjacent southern Pacaraima mountains of Guyana, areas of 'monsoon-like forest' of deciduous character have also been described (Myers, 1936).

The faunal diversity of Amazonian forests is generally high. Data on spatial patterns of faunal abundance are limited, although Fittkau (1969) has drawn a preliminary distinction between central Amazonia, where sparser animal populations exist, and the more densely populated peripheral areas, particularly the Andean foreland. One general study exists of the heterotrophic structure of rain forest near Manaus (Fittkau & Klinge, 1973). The study reports a total animal biomass of 210 kg/ha, which is extremely low in relation to phytomass. Approximately 75 per cent of the recorded animal biomass consists of soil fauna, including ants and termites, with the balance made up of other insects and larger animals. Beckerman (1979) has suggested that contemporary hunting has depleted the number of larger animals in the study area, but it is questionable whether a substantially increased vertebrate biomass is to be expected in such forests, given the poor-quality foliage and irregular fruit supply of many trees (Sponsel, 1986; Terborgh, 1986). The soil fauna, however, is substantial and confirms the importance of detrital feeding in the system once initial litter decomposition by fungi has occurred. Under prevailing oligotrophic conditions, the detrital pathway appears to be more efficient for nutrient recycling than the faunal consumption of living plant material (Fittkau & Klinge, 1973).

Among the larger forest animals, both terrestrial and arboreal, there is considerable diversity of species, but individual species density is highly variable. Some animals like peccaries (*Tayassu pecari, T. tajacu*) and monkeys (*Alouatta* spp., *Cebus* spp.) occur in groups, but many terrestrial mammals are 'solitary' in habit and present at very low densities (Bourlière, 1973). Large areas of forest are required to maintain effective breeding populations for such species. This is the case, for example, with jaguars (*Panthera onca*) and giant anteaters (*Myrmecophaga tridactyla*), which reportedly occupy individual territories of 10 km^2 or more (Smith, 1976; Robinson & Redford 1986).

Savannas of the Terra firme

Dry savannas, or *campos de terra firme*, cover an estimated 15–20 million ha within the Amazonian forest zone. Such savannas are largely, but not exclusively, confined to drier and more seasonal areas where annual rainfall is less than 2,000 mm. The savanna soils are mostly free-draining, and display similar infertility to forest soils. Individual savannas are usually

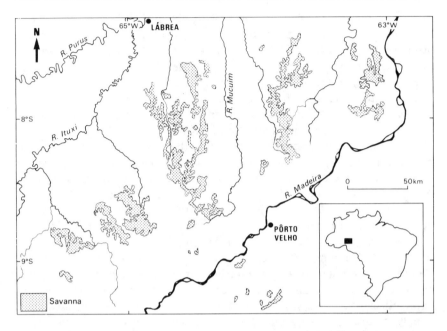

Figure 9 Savanna 'islands' in the Puciari–Humaitá area, Brasil, (1978)

interpenetrated by riparian forest, and their extent is highly variable. They include the relatively large and continuous savannas of the Rio Branco–Rupununi (5.5 million ha) and the Trombetas–Paru (4.5 million ha), but smaller islands of savanna are also dispersed within the forest, as in the Puciari–Humaitá area (see Figure 9).

Savannas are herb-dominated communities that may contain scattered trees and shrubs (Beard, 1953). The herbaceous layer usually consists of deep-rooting, perennial bunch grasses, like *Trachypogon* and *Andropogon*, which grow to a metre or more in height. Tree height and density are variable, and provide the basis for classifying savanna types. The Brazilian *campo cerrado* has a dense but discontinuous tree cover 3–6 m in height, *campo coberto* a moderately dense tree cover 2–4 m in height, and *campo sujo* a sparse cover of low trees and shrubs; treeless savanna is referred to as *campo limpo* (Eden, 1964). Where present, savanna trees are frequently gnarled and contorted, with large brittle leaves. They are usually evergreen, although many trees experience periodic defoliation as a result of herbaceous fires occurring in the dry season (see Photograph 7).

Floristically, the Amazonian savannas are quite diverse. In the Rupununi savanna of Guyana, 494 higher plant species have been recorded (Anon., 1966), while 314 species are reported from the Sipaliwini savanna in southern Surinam (van Donselaar, 1969). Most savannas are floristically distinct from the surrounding forest, but commonly show affinity to each

Photograph 7 Recently burnt *Trachypogon* savanna in the northern Rupununi region, Guyana, with defoliated *Curatella americana*

other and to the flanking *cerrados* of central Brazil or the *llanos* of Colombia and Venezuela. This pattern is taken to reflect a previous continuity of savanna across the Amazon basin in drier Pleistocene times (Hueck, 1957; Eden, 1974a; Haffer, 1977; Gottsberger & Morawetz, 1986). Individual savanna communities are commonly dominated by a few species. In the Rupununi savanna, the bunch grass *Trachypogon plumosus* is widespread and associated with an open tree cover of *Curatella americana*, *Byrsonima crassifolia* and *Plumeria inodora* (Eden, 1964). In southern

Venezuela, similar communities exist which are dominated by *Trachypogon* spp., associated with *C. americana*, *B. crassifolia* and *Platycarpum orinocense*, although on adjacent white sands distinctive savannas with many endemic species occur (Eden, 1974a; Huber, 1982).

The faunal resources of Amazonian savannas are sparse and less diverse than those of the rain forest. Larger mammals include deer (*Odocoileus gymnotis*, *Mazama americana*) and anteater (*Myrmecophaga tridactyla*), with armadillo (*Dasypus novemcinctus*) and various rodents also present (Hershkovitz, 1969; Hills, 1973). Cats (*Felis onca*, *F. pardalis*) and tapir (*Tapirus terrestris*), which are primarily forest animals, occasionally venture into the savanna. Various writers have commented on the general poverty of the savanna fauna. According to Fittkau (1969), true savanna forms are scarce, with many species having been derived from forms with their centre of evolution in the forest. At times, faunal poverty has been taken to indicate a relatively recent origin for the savanna, but this view does not accord with available botanical evidence and overlooks the existence of large herbivorous mammals, now extinct, that occupied the habitat in Pleistocene times (Fittkau, 1969; Hershkovitz, 1969; Medina, 1980a). Of late, cattle and horses have been introduced into most Amazonian savannas, where they co-exist with depleted populations of surviving native herbivores, particularly deer.

Little information exists on heterotrophic relations in Amazonian savannas, although herbivory is clearly of major importance. Some organic decomposition by soil micro-organisms takes place, but the process is limited by the persistence of standing dead leaf material and the slow formation of surface litter (Bulla & Lourido, 1980). Ultimately, a significant proportion of plant material is destroyed by burning rather than biological processes.

Wetlands

Wetlands represent the transition from terrestrial to aquatic habitats, and cover an estimated 93.2 million ha of lowland Amazonia. They comprise 65.5 million ha of swamp and marsh forest and 27.7 million ha' of herbaceous wetland. They are characterised by hydromorphic soils, mainly Gleysols, but a variety of water regimes are encountered. Most of the wetland area experiences seasonal or tidal inundation, but free-draining levees and permanently wet swamps also occur. Soil fertility is variable, depending on local sediment characteristics. Although complex vegetation patterns often exist within wetlands, individual wetland formations frequently display physiognomic and compositional similarity over large areas. Seasonally-flooded marsh forest is the most widespread formation, although it is often juxtaposed with permanently-waterlogged swamp forest. In the lower Amazon valley, between the Negro and Xingú rivers, herbaceous wetlands occur, but they are replaced by tidal marsh forest over much of the estuarine zone. Along the Atlantic coast, marsh and swamp forests again co-exist with herbaceous wetlands, with mangrove forest developed on areas affected by salt water (Sombroek, 1966; Pires, 1973).

Wetland forests are less complex than the evergreen rain forest of the *terra firme*, but they often grow to substantial height. In Guyana and Surinam, riverine swamp forest dominated by *Mora excelsa* achieves a canopy height of 30–40 m (Davis & Richards, 1934), and similar forest dominated by *Qualea* spp. in the Brazilian Mato Grosso reaches 25–40 m (Ratter *et al.*, 1973). Riverine marsh forest in southern Venezuela attains a canopy height of 25–30 m (Williams, 1940), but stands are usually lower in marsh forests along black water rivers and in coastal mangrove forests (Dubois, 1971; Williams *et al.*, 1972; Prance, 1978).

Floristically, wetland forests are less diverse than the evergreen rain forest (Ducke & Black, 1953; Anderson, 1981). Some species are common to both habitats, but clear floristic contrasts are usually apparent (Williams, 1940; Sioli, 1968b; Prance 1978). Floristic distinctions also exist between wetland forests along white water and black water rivers (Williams *et al.*, 1972; Prance, 1978), although many of the characteristic species have water-dispersed seeds and are widely distributed along their respective floodplains (Gottsberger, 1978). Among the trees that recur along the Amazon mainstream, from Peru to the lower valley, are *Ceiba pentandra* and *Olmediophaena maxima* (Ducke & Black, 1953). Near Belém, a stand diversity of forty-one large-tree species/ha (> 20 cm DBH) has been recorded in swamp forest, with four species providing 37 per cent of the tree population (Black *et al.*, 1950).

Herbaceous wetlands mainly occur along the lower Amazon *várzea* and on the Atlantic coastal plain. Both herbaceous marsh and swamp communities are encountered. Along the lower Amazon, the *campos de várzea* occupy wetter floodplain sites, with the forest largely confined to free-draining levees. Characteristic herbaceous species are *Leersia hexandra* in areas of shallower flooding, and *Echinochloa polystachya*, *Paspalum repens* and *Oryza* spp. in areas of deeper flooding. Many of these species develop with the annual rise of flood water, forming 'floating meadows' across the floodplain (Nieuwenhuijs, 1960; Howard-Williams & Junk, 1976; Junk, 1980). In coastal wetlands, flood regimes are less extreme, but *Leersia hexandra*, *Echinochloa polystachya* and *Oryza* spp. recur, together with species like *Typha angustifolia* and *Cyperus giganteus* (Fanshawe, 1954; Dirven, 1965; Pires, 1966). There are also herbaceous wetlands in parts of interior Amazonia, notably on the alluvial overflow plains of the northern Rupununi in Guyana (Eden, 1964) and the Llanos de Mojos of north-east Bolivia (Denevan, 1966a) (see Photograph 8).

Photograph 8 *Campo de várzea* along the lower Rio Curuá-Una, near Santarém in the lower Amazon valley

The faunal resources of wetlands and associated aquatic habitats are commonly abundant, but vary with water quality. The primary productivity of rivers themselves is rather low, with the food chain mainly dependent on supplies from terrestrial sources and from floating vegetation (Roberts, 1973). In white water rivers, primary productivity is limited by poor light penetration in the turbid water (Sioli, 1967a). Productivity improves at the 'mouthbays' of rivers like the Xingú and Tapajós where clear and white waters mix, but along the Rio Negro and other black water rivers, light penetration and nutrient supplies are both extremely limiting. In black water rivers, toxic phenolic substances derived from terrestrial vegetation may also adversely affect aquatic fauna (Janzen, 1974). The Rio Negro has low fish stocks and has been described as a 'hunger river', although by the same token the starving traveller is at least spared the unpleasant attentions of black fly (*Simulium* sp.) and other insect pests (Sioli, 1967a).

In general, fish are most plentiful along river banks and in small streams, where allochthonous plant debris and insects provide a supply of food (Roberts, 1973; Fittkau *et al.*, 1975). This even applies in black water rivers where such inputs can at times sustain a significant food chain (Chernela, 1985; Henderson & Walker, 1986). Favourable conditions for fish also exist in and around floodplain lakes, where in-flowing white waters decant their sediment and mix with run-off from the adjacent *terra firme* (Fittkau *et al.*, 1975; Lowe-McConnell, 1975). Plankton, macrophytes and organic detritus support a complex food chain in these fertile habitats, which sustain many fish species. Herbivores and piscivores abound, including the large pirarucú or paiche (*Arapaima gigas*) and voracious piranha (*Serraselmus* spp.). Aquatic mammals include manatee (*Trichechus inunguis*), dolphin (*Sotalia fluviatilis*) and otter (*Pteronura brasiliensis*). Turtles (*Podocnemis* spp.) and caiman (*Caiman crocodilus, Melanosuchus niger*) also flourish, at least in areas spared intense predation by humans (Smith, 1979, 1981a). Terrestrial animals, like the capibara (*Hydrochoerus hydrochaeris*), tapir (*Tapirus terrestris*) and iguana (*Iguana* spp.) also frequent floodplains, together with abundant bird populations of duck, heron and other species (Goodland & Irwin, 1975). The favourable conditions of the white water *várzea* also extend to the estuarine zone. According to Roberts (1973), regular tidal flooding and the resultant provision of terrestrial food supplies probably render this one of the most productive areas for fish. In addition, large numbers of cattle and water buffalo have latterly been introduced to wetland areas of the lower Amazon (Sutmoller *et al.*, 1966; Nascimento & Lourenço Júnior, 1979).

Ecosystem dynamics

Environmental factors

The luxuriance of the evergreen rain forest creates an impression of favourable growth conditions, which is at least partly justified. There is a high level of solar radiation arriving at the earth's surface in Amazonia, averaging 300–400 langleys/day (Landsberg, 1961). Some seasonal variation in the energy input occurs, but perennial plant growth is possible and potential net primary productivity averages approximately 60 t/ha/year (dry weight) (De Wit, 1967; Sanchez, 1976). Rainfall supply to the evergreen rain forest is also high. Occasional periods of moisture stress occur, but the supply of water is not a general constraint on plant growth.

Nutrient supply is more limiting. In places, eutrophic soils exist, but the vast majority of soils in the region are acid and nutrient-deficient. The forest system has adapted itself to this nutrient-poor environment and is able to achieve relatively high levels of productivity. The adaptation takes various forms, but mainly involves mechanisms that effectively conserve and promptly cycle the limited nutrient supply that is available. According to Richards (1952), 'very nearly closed' cycling of nutrients occurs. In this respect, considerable attention is paid to root conditions. As elsewhere in tropical forests, the Amazonian forest has a well-developed root system which is concentrated at or near the soil surface (Stark, 1971; Jordan,

1985). This results in efficient and rapid uptake of nutrients from the litter layer and mineral topsoil. Most of the available nutrients are held in the litter itself, whence they are transferred to living roots as organic decomposition proceeds. A notable feature of this process is the association that exists between plant roots and mycorrhizal fungi, which encourages a 'direct' transfer of nutrients, particularly phosphorus, from the decomposing litter to living roots (Went & Stark, 1968; Stark, 1971; Jordan, 1985). Such fungi are widespread in Amazonian forests, although Janzen (1975) suggests they are best developed over white sand soils where nutrients supplies are least favourable.

In general, nutrient recovery directly by roots and in association with mycorrhizal fungi limits the downward leaching of nutrients through the soil profile (Herrera et al., 1978b; Stark & Jordan, 1978; Janos, 1983). Slight nutrient leakage occurs in run-off from the system, but studies in southern Venezuela and elsewhere suggest that losses of calcium, potassium, magnesium and phosphorus are generally balanced by atmospheric inputs, both dry and wet. In spite of the limited overall supply of these nutrients, the atmospheric inputs are able to sustain the system (Jordan, 1982; Brinkmann, 1985).

Nitrogen supply in the Amazonian forest is relatively abundant and less limiting to plant growth than other nutrients, particularly phosphorus. Nitrogen is continually being lost naturally from the ecosystem, but biological fixation maintains supply. Symbiotic fixation by forest trees provides some input, while free-living soil bacteria and epiphyllous lichens, algae and bacteria make important contributions (Herrera et al., 1978a; Jordan, 1985).

Soil infertility is also a constraint on plant growth in semi-deciduous and deciduous forests and in savannas, although these systems are more explicitly limited by rainfall seasonality. Their plant productivity reaches a high level during wet seasons, but declines rapidly with the onset of drought when there is leaf-shedding by deciduous forest species and a general die-back of savanna grasses. Evergreen savanna trees apparently survive the seasonal drought by having roots that tap deeper soil moisture supplies. The scleromorphic characteristics of savanna trees have traditionally been viewed as adaptive to seasonal moisture shortage, but, as with caatinga species, are probably more of a response to soil nutrient deficiency (Ferri, 1960; Arens, 1963; Lopes & Cox, 1977).

Little information is available on nutrient cycling in Amazonian savannas, although herbaceous fires, which are a major cause of organic decomposition and hence nutrient recycling, are clearly influential. In general, the savanna ecosystem has a much lower nutrient capital than adjacent forest systems, but its rates of nutrient turnover are higher.

Wetland habitats experience a range of water conditions, which influence their vegetation types. In sites experiencing a pronounced

Photograph 9 Forest clearance for indigenous shifting cultivation, Sipapo basin, southern Venezuela

alternation of waterlogging and drought, tree species other than palms are rarely present, and herb-dominated communities prevail (Eden, 1964; Walter, 1973). Seasonal plant productivity in such areas remains high, especially in white water habitats where regular nutrient inputs occur (Junk, 1980). Where wet conditions prevail for most or all of the year, marsh or swamp forests exist. Within these forests, subsidiary nutrient-related contrasts are evident between white water and black water habitats. In the vicinity of Manaus, white water marsh forest is reported to have a richer flora, taller trees and a greater biomass than adjacent black water marsh forest (Williams *et al.*, 1972).

Anthropic disturbance of forest

Anthropic disturbance of forest has long occurred in Amazonia in the form of indigenous shifting cultivation. Latterly, the scale of disturbance has greatly increased as a result of the activities of modern colonists, and concern exists about the effects of such disturbance on forest regeneration and thus the forest system as a whole.

Indigenous cultivation traditionally involves the clearance of small tracts of forest, usually 0.5–1.0 ha in extent, and their cultivation for periods of two to four years (see Photograph 9). On abandonment, such plots naturally regenerate and in time a mature forest cover is restored. In many respects, this process replicates that which occurs when a natural gap of comparable size is created in the forest (Gómez-Pompa et al., 1972; Uhl, 1982; Whitmore, 1982). In the latter case, heliophytic pioneer trees, like *Cecropia*, *Vismia* and *Trema*, rapidly colonise the ground. The initial growth of such species is rapid, with closed stands of *Cecropia* reaching 10 m or more in height over a period of two to three years (Schulz, 1960; Boerboom, 1974). Similar species occur in abandoned indigenous fields, although in such sites herbaceous weeds may initially be quite prominent and the woody growth slower to re-establish itself (Uhl, 1982; Uhl et al., 1982). In abandoned fields in southern Venezuela, Harris (1971) reports secondary woody growth reaching 4.5–7.5 m in height over two to five years, with *Cecropia* spp. and scattered palms like *Maximiliana regia* and *Jessenia bataua* present.

The appearance of heliophytic pioneer species in a forest gap reflects the ready availability of their seeds, which tend to be small, numerous and easily dispersed, have extended viability, and germinate in response to changing radiation at ground level (Schulz, 1960; Gómez-Pompa & Vázquez-Yanes, 1974; Holthuijzen & Boerboom, 1982). As time passes, however, the pioneer species are less able to compete and gradually give way to late-secondary trees, like *Cedrela*, *Swietenia* and *Cordia*. The latter usually persist for many years, but are also unable to reproduce themselves *in situ*, and are eventually succeeded by primary forest species (Whitmore, 1982). The timescale of such succession is unclear, but extends over many decades. Initial biomass and nutrient re-accumulation is relatively rapid and may justify fresh clearance for cultivation after 15–25 years, but a much longer period is required to restore the primary forest cover.

When forest disturbance occurs on a larger scale, as in areas of cattle ranching or peasant colonisation where blocks of thousands of hectares may be cleared, the regenerative capacity of the forest is impaired (Gómez-Pompa et al., 1972). This would be less worrying if the land in question were destined for permanent exploitation, but in many cases the chances of this are slight and the land is often abandoned after a few years. Weedy shrubs and woody pioneer species readily re-establish themselves, but restoration of a primary forest cover is less assured. This reflects the reproductive characteristics of the primary forest trees, whose seeds tend to be large, rather short-lived, and dependent on animal dispersal (Gómez-Pompa et al., 1972; Kubitzki, 1985). Such species can colonise small gaps, but their re-establishment across extensive tracts of cleared land, where seed sources are lacking and forest animals scarce, is greatly impeded. Gómez-Pompa et al. (1972, p. 764) suggest that primary forest species 'are incapable of recolonizing large areas opened to intensive and extensive agriculture'. This perhaps overstates the case in the light of the apparent

Photograph 10 Sparse regrowth (foreground) on cleared forest land on white sands of the Berbice Formation, Soesdyke-Linden project, Guyana

ability of Pleistocene forests to recover from periodic refugial contractions (Haffer, 1969), but it rightly emphasises the difficulty, on a human timescale at least, of achieving large-scale regeneration of primary forest.

Forest regeneration varies somewhat in relation to local habitat conditions. Periodically-flooded *várzea* forest, for example, generally regenerates more effectively than other forests, because of water-borne seed supplies and higher soil fertility (Ducke & Black, 1953). Conversely, forest regeneration on infertile Arenosols tends to be very slow, as is apparent in parts of lowland Guyana where such soils have locally been cleared for cultivation and later abandoned (Downer, 1979) (see Photograph 10). In areas of seasonal rainfall, forest regeneration is also slower, and there is always the possibility of deflecting the succession to grassland or savanna as a result of burning (Eden, 1974a). In most sites, however, Amazonian forest regenerates after local disturbance, and is only vulnerable when larger-scale clearance occurs. In the latter case, secondary forest may still re-establish itself, but it is likely to remain impoverished in comparison to the original climax forest.

Ecosystem stability

In the past, it has commonly been assumed that, following local disturbance of forest, secondary vegetation develops towards a state of dynamic
equilibrium, which can be described as a forest climax. Some empirical
evidence exists in support of this view. In mature forest on the *terra firme*
near Belém, the total basal area of trees (> 30 cm girth) in a 100 m ×
200 m plot remained nearly constant over a fifteen-year period, in spite
of the growth and death of individual trees (Pires & Prance, 1977). In
similar forest near San Carlos de Rio Negro, the growth of living trees has
also been reported to be approximately balanced by tree-fall (Jordan,
1982). On a larger scale, it is likely that comparable equilibria exist, at
least in the medium term, over tracts of forest containing 'gap' and
'building', as well as mature, phases of growth. However, the fundamental
status of such equilibria is less clear, particularly in relation to larger-scale
disturbance.

Tropical forests were long considered inherently stable in character.
Some writers stressed the constancy of their distribution over time
(Fosberg, 1970), while others emphasised their population stability in the
face of disturbances, attributing it to biotic diversity and complex patterns
of energy flow (MacArthur, 1955; Elton, 1958; Odum, 1971). While the
ability of secondary forest generally to establish itself after disturbance is
not in question (Whitmore, 1982), doubts have arisen about the inherent
stability of the system as a whole. Thus, although adaptation in forest
species appears to be directed towards competitive ability and population
maintenance, it is less obviously directed to reproductive performance.
Primary forest trees, for example, are adapted in their seed and dispersal
characteristics to maintaining existing numbers, but as indicated, are much
less effective in re-establishing themselves after large-scale disturbance
(Gómez-Pompa *et al.*, 1972; Uhl, 1988). Similarly, forest animals,
including many birds and mammals, have relatively low reproductive
rates, which maintain their numbers but do not readily restore population
levels after severe disturbances (May, 1975; Southwood, 1976). At the
systemic level, adaptive nutrient cycling and complex species interactions
involving plants and animals regulate the existing forest system but, if
substantially disturbed, the latter is slow or unable to re-establish itself
(DeAngelis, 1980; Jordan, 1985). In such circumstances, the risk of
extinction of forest species is correspondingly high. According to May
(1975), the tropical forest is thus a dynamically fragile system, which is
adapted to persist in the relatively 'predictable' environment in which it
evolved, but is much less resistant in the face of major human disturbances. Environmental predictability in this context reflects the relatively
equable climatic conditions that assumedly characterise the tropical zone
(Pianka, 1970; Southwood *et al.*, 1974). While this premise needs

clarification in the light of current ideas on Quaternary climatic fluctuations in Amazonia, there is certainly evidence of the inherent vulnerability of the forest system to large-scale disturbance.

If the tropical forest is dynamically fragile, its higher-latitude counterparts may be seen as resilient. In the temperate and boreal zones, biological adaptation appears to be towards reproductive rather than competitive performance, reflecting the seasonal and more unpredictable nature of the environment (Dobzhansky, 1950; Pianka, 1970; Southwood et al., 1974; May, 1975). By analogy, it is arguable that where more 'seasonal' habitats locally exist in Amazonia, as in the case of savannas and wetlands, more resilient systems are also to be expected. Temperature variability in these areas is limited, but they experience seasonal variability in water supply and, in the case of savannas, seasonal burning. On this basis, both savannas and wetlands have been described as 'pulse-stabilised', being adapted to more or less regular disturbance (Odum, 1975), and appear to be correspondingly resilient (Lowe-McConnell, 1977; Walker & Noy Meir, 1982; Sanford & Wangari, 1985).

While various aspects of ecosystem stability are considered in the literature, the precise bio-physical factors involved are by no means clear and certainly more complex than originally assumed (Pimm, 1984). This applies, for example, to the preliminary attempts to relate environmental predictability to systemic stability (Connell, 1978; Wolda, 1978; May, 1979). However, the immediate concern is how far these issues may be relevant to contemporary land management in Amazonia. In this respect, it is arguable that the assumed fragility of the rain forest renders it particularly vulnerable to land colonisation, and demands highly adaptive forms of exploitation. Conversely, the assumed resilience of savannas and wetlands arguably makes them less vulnerable to human disturbance and thus preferable areas for modern exploitation (Goodland & Irwin, 1977; Eden, 1978). Even so, there are limits to the resilience of savannas and wetlands, and careful exploitation of their resources is still required; also, for any such exploitation to succeed, it must be adapted to the prevailing unpredictability of the habitats, most notably in respect of water supply.

It is thus implied that the natural attributes of Amazonian ecosystems are relevant to land management in terms of both conservation and resource development. In the former case, the designation and management of national parks and other reserves can benefit from a clearer understanding of vegetation history and associated ecosystem characteristics. In the latter case, the development of agrosystems can benefit from improved understanding of the nature and likely response of selected habitats and their biological components. In general, examining the stability of natural systems also leads logically to considering the sustainability of managed systems.

4
Indigenous resource exploitation

... the wider society can benefit from tribal people by learning from
them how to adapt to, and utilize, fragile, marginal environments.
[Goodland, 1986, p. 19]

While concern exists regarding the environmental impact of contemporary
colonisation in Amazonia, it is clear that the indigenous population in the
past pursued land exploitation that was broadly adaptive and sustainable
and did not inflict general and irreversible damage on the environment.
Such adaptation was no doubt achieved by trial and error over an
extended period of time. In contrast, contemporary land colonisation is
occurring rapidly and destructively and in a manner that derives little
benefit from past experience, recent or otherwise. Since such colonisation
is harming the long-term prospects of the region and its inhabitants, it is
desirable and potentially valuable to investigate the nature and adaptation
of indigenous resource use systems.

The antiquity of humans in South America is unknown, but Amerindians certainly entered the continent by end-Pleistocene times, and, from
recent findings in north-east Brazil, seem to have been present as early as
32,000 BP (Bray, 1986; Guidon & Delibrias, 1986). Original penetration
was probably within the Andean zone, but there is minimal information
on how the continental lowlands were settled. It is possible that Paleo-
Indian hunters and gatherers first moved into lowland savannas, which in
late Pleistocene times were probably extended at the expense of Amazonian forest (Haffer, 1969; Eden, 1974a). Even before the megafaunal extinctions of the late Pleistocene to early Holocene periods, however, the
dystrophic conditions of most of the tropical lowlands are likely to have
limited food supplies, and human occupance was probably slight except in
the more favourable wetland habitats. In the forest itself, initial penetration is likely to have been along major rivers, with later movements on to
less productive interfluves. Such colonisation has usually been attributed
to groups practising fishing and agriculture (Lathrap, 1968, 1970; Cohen,
1977), but some early hunters and gatherers may also have entered the
forest zone.

The earliest archaeological sites in Amazonia itself are at Abrigo do Sol on its southern margin where evidence exists of human occupance from about 12,500 BP, and in the middle Madeira basin where dates between 7400 and 5200 BP have been obtained at the base of human refuse (Meggers, 1985). In eastern Ecuador, there is microfossil evidence of maize cultivation at about 6,000 years ago (Bush et al., 1989), and, in eastern Peru, a likelihood of fishing and root crop cultivation in riparian settlements some 3,500 to 4,000 years ago (Lathrap, 1970). Later sites have been found elsewhere in the region (Meggers & Evans, 1957; Evans & Meggers, 1968), and it seems likely that forest cultivators have been widespread over at least recent millennia (Cohen, 1977).

At the time of European conquest, the population of Amazonia was low and, on Denevan's (1976) estimates, probably did not exceed 4 million for the present study area. Densities in the *várzea* zone were substantially higher than elsewhere, but over most of the *terra firme* the population was exceedingly sparse. Following European contact, there were major reductions in population as a result of introduced diseases like smallpox, influenza and measles and from warfare and enslavement (Hemming, 1978; Ross, 1978a). The contemporary indigenous population of the region is somewhat less than 500,000 (Denevan, 1976).

Wide-ranging anthropological studies have been undertaken in Amazonia. Those with an ecological emphasis have mainly focused on the relationships between environmental resources and food procurement, and on patterns of population and settlement. It is widely apparent that aspects of tribal culture have become adapted to environmental conditions, although the nature and extent of that adaptation has been the focus of uncertainty and dispute. This applies in the case of both crop production under shifting cultivation (Meggers, 1957; Carneiro, 1961; Harris, 1971; Beckerman, 1983; Eden & Andrade, 1987) and protein acquisition from wild food sources (Lathrap, 1968; Gross, 1975; Lizot, 1977; Beckerman, 1979; Chagnon & Hames, 1979; Chagnon, 1983; Harris, 1984). Irrespective of the precise nature of the cultural adaptation, however, it is evident that indigenous Amazonian populations have subsisted for millennia by the effective use of diverse resources and without grossly degrading the environment. Whether this justifies Meggers' (1973) assumption that traditional culture achieved an equilibrium with the forest environment is open to doubt, but few observers would question the broad adaptation of indigenous land exploitation. In contrast, contemporary land development is often unstable in character, and the question that arises is whether its performance could be improved in the light of indigenous experience and knowledge. A positive view is expressed by Brush, for example: 'The search for intermediate or appropriate technology for use by small farmers has become an important element of agricultural development planning. Scientists who are familiar with the technologies of traditional cultures can play an important role in this search.' (Brush, 1979, p. 114).

Photograph 11 Captive anteater in Andoke village, south-east Colombia

Plant and animal resources

Wild plants and animals continue to provide essential foods and other products for tribal groups in Amazonia, although agriculture has generally been adopted. Game supplies vary from place to place, but are widely sought, as also are wild plant foods. Both provide essential dietary protein. Within the forest, larger terrestrial and arboreal mammals provide highly attractive food sources. Animals like tapir (*Tapirus terrestris*), deer (*Mazama* spp.), peccary (*Tayassu* spp.), monkey (*Alouatta* spp., *Cebus* spp.), paca (*Cuniculus paca*) and agouti (*Dasyprocta aguti*) are commonly sought, as are many other species (see Photograph 11). Birds are also widely hunted. In addition, ants, termites, grubs, beetles and other insects provide acceptable food, while the fruit, seeds and nuts of innumerable wild plants are widely collected and consumed (Boza & Baumgartner, 1962; Denevan, 1976; Beckerman, 1979; Posey, 1983; Dufour, 1987). The protein content of animal products is high (10–30 per cent), as is that of many wild plant foods like Brazil nut (13–14 per cent by dry weight) or palm fruit (5–11 per cent by dry weight) (Gross, 1975; Beckerman, 1979).

In spite of the acknowledged diversity of game resources, the quantity of game in forest areas appears to be rather low. Where estimates of animal biomass have been made, it is not always clear how far the results are affected by modern hunting activities. As previously indicated, however, it is questionable whether a substantial game biomass is to be expected in most *terra firme* forests, in view of the poor quality of foliage and irregular fruit supply of many trees (Sponsel, 1986; Terborgh, 1986).

The animal biomass of the Amazonian dry savannas is also very low. A few game species exist in these areas, notably deer (*Mazama americana, Odocoileus gymnotis*), anteater (*Myrmecophaga tridactyla*) and other smaller mammals, but even prior to the arrival of Europeans and their cattle and related reductions in stocks of native animals, overall game supplies are likely to have been limited.

Fish and other aquatic animals are locally available within the *terra firme*, but are mainly concentrated on larger floodplains, especially along white water rivers. As previously indicated, many wetland habitats contain a great variety and abundance of animals, including fish, mammals, reptiles and birds, and these have long provided valuable sources of protein for indigenous populations. Among favoured food sources are large fish like pirarucú or paiche (*Arapaima gigas*), together with manatee (*Trichechus inunguis*), capibara (*Hydrochoerus hydrochaeris*) and various species of turtle (*Podocnemis expansa, P. unifilis, P. dumeriliana*). Terrestrial animals like capibara are available to hunters throughout most of the year, but many species are only seasonally available. Fishing, for example, is notably unproductive in the flood season, and wildfowl and turtles are less readily available at that time (Smith, 1974a, 1981a; Roosevelt, 1980).

Cultivated plants broadly complement the wild food products. The traditional crop repertoire is diverse at both the species and varietal level. The range of crop plants has been extended during the post-Columbian period, but indigenous cultivation systems are still dominated by New World species. Starch-rich root crops are most commonly grown, in association with fruit and other vegetables. Sugar cane and maize also occur, together with sundry condiments, medicinals and other useful non-food plants. Among the Wai Wai of southern Guyana, twenty-seven species of cultivated food plants are reported (Yde, 1957, 1965; Dagon, 1967), while as many as fifty-four species are used by the Siona-Secoya in eastern Ecuador (Vickers, 1979). Other Amazonian groups cultivate a similar diversity of food crops (Denevan, 1971; Hames, 1983).

Manioc (*Manihot esculenta*) is the staple crop of most indigenous groups in Amazonia. Many varieties of the tuber are grown, with ten to twenty often in use by individual groups (Basso, 1973; Wagley, 1977; Boster, 1983; Hames, 1983). The varieties are broadly classed as bitter or sweet, although no clear separation exists between the two (Coursey & Booth, 1977). Sweet manioc appears to be the earlier cultivar, and its tubers are usually baked or boiled. Bitter manioc contains prussic acid, which must be removed prior to human consumption. Its tubers are valued for their derived, coarse flour and bread which can be stored for extended periods. Both sweet and bitter varieties are used to make beer (see Photograph 12).

Photograph 12 Andoke woman grating manioc tubers, near Araracuara, Caquetá valley, south-east Colombia

Manioc is a drought-resistant plant that prefers free-draining soils. It appears to have originated in a seasonal New World habitat, although the precise focus of domestication is uncertain (Harris, 1972; Pickersgill & Heiser, 1978). The plant itself is of shrubby habit and grows 2 m or more in height. It can be grown on seasonally-draining land in the *várzea*, but is notably tolerant of acid *terra firme* soils. Manioc is a starch-rich crop that gives a high calorie yield, but its tubers provide very little protein (< 1 per cent). Its leaves contain 4–10 per cent protein by fresh weight (Tindall, 1977), but are rarely consumed in Amazonia. Roosevelt (1980) attributes this to their high fibre content, although manioc leaves are eaten elsewhere in the tropics (Terra, 1964; Coursey & Booth, 1977; May, 1984).

Other root crops cultivated by the indigenous population include sweet potato (*Ipomoea batatas*), mafafa (*Xanthosoma sagittifolium*), arrowroot (*Maranta arundinacea, Calathea allouia*) and mapuey yam (*Dioscorea trifida*), as well as Old World introductions like taro (*Colocasia esculenta*) and greater yam (*D. alata*). Many of these plants are widely cultivated, but are of secondary importance to the ubiquitous manioc. Their tubers all contain less than 2 per cent protein. Other cultivated vegetables include legumes like kidney bean (*Phaseolus vulgaris*), lima bean (*P. limensis*) and ground nut (*Arachis hypogaea*), together with pumpkin (*Cucurbita moschata*), chilli pepper (*Capsicum* spp.) and tomato (*Lycopersicon esculentum*). Maize (*Zea mays*), which was introduced prehistorically to Amazonia (Harris, 1972), is widely cultivated. It is better suited to the more fertile *várzea* soils, but occurs on the *terra firme*. Maize has a protein content of 9–10 per cent by dry weight (Roosevelt, 1980). Old World introductions during the Colonial period include pigeon pea (*Cajanus cajan*), castor (*Ricinus communis*), watermelon (*Citrullus lanatus*) and onion (*Allium cepa*).

Among cultivated fruit crops, pineapple is most widely encountered, growing well on acid *terra firme* soils. Numerous fruit trees also occur in indigenous fields and yard gardens, including guamo (*Inga edulis*), cashew (*Anacardium occidentale*), papaya (*Carica papaya*), anón (*Annona squamosa*), avocado (*Persea americana*), guava (*Psidium guajava*), guanábana (*A. muricata*), uvo (*Pourouma* sp.), cacao (*Theobroma cacao*), passion fruit (*Passiflora* spp.), and peach palm (*Bactris gasipaes*). Among Old World introductions are banana and plantain (*Musa* sp.), mango (*Mangifera indica*), and citrus (*Citrus* spp.).

Sugar cane (*Saccharum officinarum*) is also widely cultivated in Amazonia, together with non-food plants like cotton (*Gossypium barbadense*), tobacco (*Nicotiana tabacum*), coca (*Erythroxylum coca*), calabash (*Crescentia cujete*), gourd (*Lagenaria siceraria*), onoto dye (*Bixa orellana*) and sundry fish poisons (*Lonchocarpus utilis, Centrosema carajaense*).

Resource use

At the time of European contact, striking contrasts existed within Amazonia in the pattern of Amerindian resource use and settlement. The main distinction lay between the more intensive exploitation and denser populations of many wetland areas and the extensive exploitation and dispersed population of the *terra firme*. Within the latter, significant variations in resource use also existed, particularly in the relative importance of shifting cultivation, fishing and hunting. This overall pattern reflected the local availability of resources and, in Lathrap's (1962) view, gave rise to an 'ecological zonation of cultures'. European contact had a profound impact on these cultures. Many tribes were extinguished or assimilated, particularly in more accessible riparian zones. Subsequently, many surviving groups have been confined to smaller territories and frequently obliged or encouraged to modify their settlement and subsistence patterns. The introduction of guns, machetes, steel axes and other artefacts has affected methods of resource exploitation. While such impacts clearly complicate any attempts to evaluate traditional cultures, tribal resource use has generally shown more resistance to change than social organisation, and, especially in more isolated areas, many features of traditional exploitation patterns persist. On this basis, the nature and variety of indigenous resource use in forest, dry savanna and wetland zones can usefully be investigated.

Resource use in the forest

A few groups of hunter-gatherers have been encountered in Amazonian forests (Steward & Faron, 1959; Kloos, 1977), but the vast majority of tribal Amerindians practise shifting cultivation as well as extractive activities. The relative importance of starch-rich cultivated crops and the wild foods that supply most dietary protein varies from group to group, as does the degree of dependence on particular wild foods. In interfluvial zones, exploitation tends to focus on hunting and gathering with some shifting cultivation, while groups with access to riverine resources undertake more fishing and devote more time to cultivation (Denevan, 1966b). Throughout the forest area, tribal population densities have always been low, and at the time of contact were an estimated 0.2 persons/km^2 (Denevan, 1976). Individual settlements are usually small, containing 50–250 inhabitants, and are mostly impermanent. Larger settlements are only occasionally encountered (Meggers, 1971).

The extraction of wild food products is variously pursued by indigenous groups, but generally provides their dietary protein. A range of equipment and techniques is used in hunting and fishing, depending on the animals being sought and on local conditions. Nowadays hunting often involves firearms, but has traditionally been undertaken with bows and arrows or blowguns. Arrows and darts, poisoned with curare derived from *Strychnos toxifera* and other vines, are used to great effect (Steward & Faron, 1959; Yde, 1965). Clubs and spears have been employed in some areas, and many groups make use of hunting dogs (Barandiaran, 1962; Yde, 1965; Wagley, 1977).

Among the Sirionó of north-east Bolivia, hunting and gathering have traditionally been the main subsistence activities, with only secondary attention being given to fishing and agriculture (Meggers, 1971). Individual groups settle in one area for several months of the year, but at other times move around in small bands seeking game. Hunting is a male activity and usually undertaken by one or two people. The bow and arrow is the principal weapon, and dogs are not used. According to Holmberg (1963), no animal is considered inedible by the Sirionó, except snakes, and more than forty species of game are sought, including tapir, peccary, anteater, deer, monkey and wildfowl. Gathering is usually done by nuclear or extended family groups, with women and children as well as men being involved. Seasonal fruits from the forest are an important resource (Meggers, 1971).

Among the Makiritare of southern Venezuela, hunting and shifting cultivation are the main subsistence activities. Bows and arrows are traditionally used for hunting larger animals like tapir, deer and peccary, while the blowgun is used for smaller game, especially birds. There is some individual hunting, but communal drives occur where dogs are used to bring animals to the river for killing. Extended hunting expeditions lasting weeks or even months are sometimes mounted, involving the establishment of separate camps away from the main settlement. Fishing and collecting also occur during such trips (Barandiaran, 1962; Wilbert, 1972). Among the neighbouring Piaroa, similar expeditions are made to distant hunting grounds. Both these groups place taboos on hunting particular animals, which are actions that may help to conserve the resource (Ross, 1978b). Among the Makiritare, taboos apply mainly to peccary and anteater (Barandiaran, 1962) and, among the Piaroa, to tapir and opossum (Boza & Baumgartner, 1962).

While periodic excursions increase the availability of game to particular groups, game resources around individual settlements still tend to diminish over time and are a factor that encourages relocation of settlement (Vickers, 1979). Such relocation occurs every few years with most forest groups, although more permanent settlements are not unknown. According to Carneiro (1961, 1968), the Kuikuru of the Xingú basin occupied one location for at least ninety years, although significantly this resulted in hunting activities declining 'to the vanishing point' and protein supply becoming dependent on fishing.

Gathering is generally practised by indigenous groups, who acquire food and other useful products from the forest. Among consumable items, tree fruits, honey and various insects are highly valued. The range of available products is immense. For the Wai Wai of southern Guyana, Yde (1965) lists more than 130 forest plants that provide food and other items. Similarly, among the Kayapó of central Brazil, Posey (1983) reports that some 250 forest plants are sought for their fruits, as well as others for their nuts, tubers and drupes. Many such products are consumed on the spot (Moran, 1982) and few data exist on their precise dietary contribution. Among the Yanomamo of the upper Orinoco, Lizot (1977) estimates that gathered products provide approximately 7 per cent of calorie intake and 9 per cent of protein. Tree fruits and nuts make an important contribution together with wild tubers, fungi, honey, caterpillars, grubs, worms, termites and spiders (Barandiaran, 1967; Chagnon, 1983; Lizot, 1977; Prance, 1985).

Fishing is undertaken by many indigenous groups, although patterns of exploitation are influenced by fish availability in time and space. Headwater or interfluvial groups like the Mekranoti of the Xingú basin and the Yanomamo of the upper Orinoco depend little on fish resources (Lizot, 1977; Werner et al., 1979). In such areas, only small streams and rivers exist, and fish are relatively few in number and small in size (Carneiro, 1968). Conversely, where groups live near larger rivers, fishing acquires more importance, although supplies commonly vary from season to season. Where fishing is relatively productive, populations are generally less mobile and less reliant on hunting, especially of larger forest animals (Ross, 1978b). The techniques and equipment of fishing are diverse and finely adapted to specific habitats. Bows and arrows are frequently used, together with fish traps and plant-derived poisons. In places, the use of spears, fibre nets and bone fish hooks are reported, although introduced items like nylon lines and steel hooks have readily been adopted (Steward & Faron, 1959; Boza & Baumgartner, 1962; Yde, 1965; Lizot, 1977; Wagley, 1977).

Fishing is a major subsistence activity for the Uanano of north-west Brazil (Chernela, 1985). Fish supplies in the area vary in time and space, with specific habitats like floodplain forests and cataract zones being the most favourable. Fishing activities are also adjusted to the pronounced seasonality of the river system, which in this area is most productive at times of high water when significant organic inputs are derived from adjoining forests. Aware of this relationship, the Uanano have long prohibited deforestation along river margins to protect fish supplies, which are their primary source of protein (Chernela, 1985).

Among the Piaroa of southern Venezuela, fishing activities are also seasonally variable, with most fishing taking place in the dry period (Boza & Baumgartner, 1962). Fish poisons, traps, harpoons, and bows and arrows are commonly employed. The relative importance of fishing varies across the tribal territory. Piaroa groups living near larger rivers like the Sipapo and Guayapo acquire most of their protein from fishing, but fishing is much less important than hunting among groups living in head-water areas (Boza & Baumgartner, 1962; Overing & Kaplan, 1988).

Shifting cultivation is practised by almost all indigenous groups in the Amazonian forest, and has long been a focus of ecological interest (Meggers, 1957; Carneiro, 1961). Cultivated fields or swiddens, commonly 0.5–1.0 ha in extent, are cut in mature forest prior to or during drier periods in the year and the resultant plant debris is subsequently burned. Fire destroys much of the debris, but larger trunks and branches mostly survive in a charred state. Burning temporarily eliminates insect pests and weed plants from the field and releases nutrients from the biomass (Eden, 1974b; Gross et al., 1979). Further nutrients become available as the remaining timber debris gradually decomposes (Harris, 1971; Eden & Andrade, 1987). In earlier times, land clearance was undertaken with stone axes and wooden implements, but these have been replaced by steel axes and machetes (Carneiro, 1968; Colchester, 1984). The latter have significantly increased the labour-efficiency of shifting cultivation, but farming technology remains simple and work continues to be undertaken

Photograph 13 Manioc-dominated Piaroa field near Uña on the Río Sipapo, southern Venezuela

by hand (Gross *et al.*, 1979). When crops are planted, they are dispersed amid the timber debris in the field, and a crop canopy develops that increasingly protects the soil from the direct effects of insolation and raindrop impact.

Mixed cropping or polyculture is characteristic of most Amerindian fields, although manioc (*Manihot esculenta*) is usually the dominant crop. Many varieties of sweet and bitter manioc are present in individual fields, where they co-exist with a range of subsidiary fruit and vegetable crops. In places, monocultural production of manioc is also reported (Eden, 1974b; Hames, 1983; Vickers, 1983). The widespread reliance on manioc is in accord with the plant's tolerance of acid Ferralsols and Acrisols on which it produces high and reliable yields (see Photograph 13).

The dominance of manioc is exemplified by Andoke and Witoto cultivation in south-east Colombia (Eden, 1980; Eden & Andrade, 1987). Individual fields commonly contain 10–15 crop species, but in eleven sampled fields 81.7 per cent of all crop plants were manioc, with a range of values from 66 per cent to 91 per cent. Many bitter and sweet varieties were present. Eight other root crops were encountered, including yam (*Dioscorea* sp.), mafafa (*Xanthosoma mafafa*) and taro (*Colocasia esculenta*), but these amounted to only 1.3 per cent of the crop. Fruit plants accounted for a further 10.4 per cent, with minor occurrences of coca (*Erythroxylum coca*) and maize (*Zea mays*) (see Table 9). Similar maniocdominated cultivation is reported from the Jívaro in north-east Peru (Boster, 1983), the Wayãpi in French Guiana (Grenand & Haxaire, 1977), and the Piaroa and Makiritare in southern Venezuela (Fuchs, 1964; Eden, 1974b). Occasionally, distinctive variations in the crop repertoire occur. Among the Wai Wai of southern Guyana, bitter manioc is grown with subsidiary crops like yam (*Dioscorea* sp.), sweet potato (*Ipomoea batatas*) and banana (*Musa* sp.), but neither sweet manioc nor maize are cultivated (Yde, 1957; Dagon, 1967). Among the Yanomamo of southern Venezuela, the principal crop is banana (*Musa* sp.), of which many varieties are grown; subsidiary crops include sweet manioc, ocumo (*Xanthosoma sagittifolium*), and peach palm (*Bactris gasipaes*), but bitter manioc has not traditionally been cultivated (Hames, 1983; Colchester, 1984).

While field areas are relatively specialised in composition, greater diversity commonly exists in yard gardens around dwellings (see Photograph 14). Many food plants are present, especially fruit trees. In addition, the gardens commonly contain condiments like chilli pepper (*Capsicum* sp.), medicinals like hortiga (*Urera caracasana*), and other essential plants like cotton (*Gossypium barbadense*), onoto dye (*Bixa orellana*) and fish poison (*Lonchocarpus* sp.) (Lathrap, 1970; Eden, 1974b; Eden & Andrade, 1987).

In the main fields, harvesting and replanting of crops is progressive. If present, an initial maize crop will be harvested after three months or so, along with various green vegetables. Manioc will be available after six to

Table 9 Aggregate crop composition of eleven Andoke
and Witoto fields in south-east Colombia

Root crops
    Manioc (*Manihot esculenta*) (11)*   81.7%
    Others   1.3%
      Yam (*Dioscorea* sp.) (7)
      Dorodoro (*Calathea* sp.) (4)
      Mafafa (*Xanthosoma mafafa*) (4)
      Yota (*Colocasia* sp.) (3)
      Painhora (*Heliconia acuminata*) (2)
      Sweet potato (*Ipomoea batatas*) (2)
      Bore (*Xanthosoma sagittifolium*) (1)
      Bedungo (unidentified) (1)

Fruit
    Pineapple (*Ananas comosus*) (10)   5.5%
    Bananas (*Musa* sp.) (11)   1.9%
    Fruit trees   3.0%
      Guamo (*Inga edulis*) (8)
      Cucui (*Ficus* sp.) (6)
      Papaya (*Carica papaya*) (5)
      Uvo (*Pourouma ? sapida*) (5)
      Cashew (*Anacardium occidentale*) (4)
      Guacure (unidentified) (4)
      Caimo (*Pouteria* sp.) (3)
      Maraca (*Couroupita* sp.) (3)
      Peach palm (*Bactris gasipaes*) (3)
      Mango (*Mangifera indica*) (1)
      Cacao (*Theobroma cacao*) (1)

Others
    Coca (*Erythroxylum coca*) (5)   2.9%
    Maize (*Zea mays*) (2)   1.8%
    Sugar cane (*Saccharum officinarum*) (7) 1.2%
    Tomato (*Lycopersicon* sp.) (2)   0.2%
    Chilli pepper (*Capsicum* sp.) (5)   0.1%
    Lulo (*Solanum* sp.) (1)   0.1%
    Cowpea (*Vigna unguiculata*) (1)   present
    Auyama (*Cucurbita moschata*) (1) present
    Patilla (*Citrullus vulgaris*) (2)   present
    Job's tears (*Coix lachryma-coix*) (1) present
    Onion (*Allium* sp.) (1)   present
    Cilantro (*Coriandrum sativum*) (1) present
    Tobacco (*Nicotiana tabacum*) (2) present
    Barbasco (*Lonchocarpus* sp.) (1) present
    Calabazo (*Cucurbita ficifolia*) (1) present

Source: Eden & Andrade, 1987.
*The number of field occurrences for each crop is shown
in parentheses.

Photograph 14 Communal Piaroa hut (*churuata*) and surrounding yard garden with bananas and fruit trees, Río Cuao, southern Venezuela

nine months, but its tubers may be left in the ground for eighteen months or more. When part of a field is cleared, manioc and other crops (except maize) will promptly be replanted, which minimises the period of exposure of the soil (Fuchs, 1964; Eden, 1974b; Wagley, 1977). In general, field productivity is high as a result of the emphasis on root crops. Manioc commonly produces 10–15 t/ha/year on *terra firme* soils, providing abundant calories (Carneiro, 1961; Goldman, 1963). Among the Siona-Secoya in eastern Ecuador, Vickers (1979) reports a total crop yield under manioc-dominated mixed cropping of 24.6 t/ha over a two-year period. The total edible calorie yield was 17.6 million calories, of which 10.5 million were provided by manioc; overall protein yield was low (Vickers, 1979).

The cultivation period for individual fields varies, but most are abandoned after two to four years, as crop productivity declines. This partly reflects deteriorating soil conditions. As cultivation proceeds, nutrients are leached, particularly in more sandy soils, and some sheetwash erosion occurs in spite of the protection given by the crop canopy (Dagon, 1967; McGregor, 1980). However, weed invasion is usually a more immediate cause of field abandonment (Kloos, 1971; Eden, 1974b; Denevan, 1976; Moran, 1983). Weeding is commonly undertaken, but becomes an arduous and time-consuming task as more and more weeds invade. Insect pests, particularly ants, also build up in older fields, and after a few years it is generally easier to cut and burn a new field than to persist with an old one (Weber, 1947; Butt, 1970; Eden, 1974b).

Although reference is often made to field abandonment, qualification of the phrase is required. After a few years, it is true that field cultivation usually ceases and the land is invaded by woody plants that herald the regeneration of forest. From a cropping point of view, however, the transformation from a productive field to a forest fallow is often rather gradual. In southern Venezuela, Harris (1971) stresses that fields are not abandoned at one time, but are harvested with decreasing frequency and thoroughness over a longer period. This is evident with longer-cycle crops like banana, whose yield only falls in the fifth or sixth year, when forest regeneration may already be well under way (Harris, 1971). Similar conditions are evident in south-east Colombia, where fruit trees are established in many Andoke and Witoto fields (see Table 9). Planted amid the initial manioc crop, the trees are most productive from about their fifth year by which time manioc cultivation has been abandoned (Eden, 1980; Eden & Andrade, 1987). Indigenous agrosilviculture (Eden, 1980) of this kind, involving ongoing exploitation of long-cycle crops in 'abandoned' fields, has similarly been described from Surinam (Kloos, 1971), central Brazil (Posey, 1983) and eastern Peru (Denevan et al., 1984). According to Posey (1983), the presence of crop plants in old fields also attracts wild game, creating opportunities for hunting as well as collecting.

In spite of persisting exploitation of 'abandoned' fields, forest regeneration generally proceeds apace. Fast-growing pioneers like *Cecropia* spp., *Vismia* spp., and *Trema micrantha* rapidly colonise old fields and a dense woody cover develops amid the residual crop community and associated weeds (Harris, 1971; Uhl, 1982, 1987). The weed plants in effect represent the first stage of succession and facilitate the subsequent forest regeneration (Lambert & Arnason, 1986; Eden, 1987). The regeneration process is beneficial because it leads to nutrient build-up in the accumulating biomass and shades out weeds of cultivation. Premature recultivation, before such processes have advanced, results in lowered crop yields. This is usually avoided in traditional cultivation, where extended fallows of fifteen to twenty years are characteristic. In some areas, cultivation of virgin or primary forest reportedly occurs (Chagnon, 1968a; Wagley, 1977; Gross et al., 1979).

In general, dependence on both cultivated and wild foods is characteristic of Amazonian forest groups, but the relative importance of particular foods varies. In headwaters and on interfluves, a few groups have survived that depend largely on hunting and gathering, but agriculture is usually practised. Among the Yanomamo of the Orinoco headwaters, Lizot (1977) estimates that 76 per cent of caloric intake is derived from cultivation and 69 per cent of protein from hunting (see Table 10). In parts of the

Table 10 Relative dietary contribution of food procurement activities among headwater groups of the *terra firme* forest

	Yanomamo		Achuarä	
	Calorie supply (%)	Protein supply (%)	Calorie supply (%)	Protein supply (%)
Agriculture	75.8	14.2	74.9	20.2
Hunting	14.8	68.8	17.4	51.7
Fishing	1.9	7.6	4.9	26.4
Gathering	7.5	9.4	2.8	1.7
	100.0	100.0	100.0	100.0
	Based on an intake of 1,845 Kcal/person/day and 73.8 g protein/person/day		Based on an intake of 3,257 Kcal/person/day and 107.7 g protein/person/day	

Sources: Lizot, 1977; Ross, 1978b.

Yanomamo territory, fishing has acquired some importance, but still does not approach that of hunting (Chagnon & Hames, 1979). A similar pattern is evident among the Achuarä of eastern Ecuador and Peru, who obtain 75 per cent of their calories from shifting cultivation, and 52 per cent of their protein from hunting (Ross, 1978b). Comparable conditions are reported among the Amahuaca in eastern Peru (Carneiro, 1968) and the Jívaro in eastern Ecuador (Harner, 1972). Forest groups living along rivers similarly depend on shifting cultivation, but fishing is of greater importance. In the case of the Uanano in the Uaupes basin, Chernela (1985) estimates that the bulk of calories are derived from agriculture, while fishing provides some 85 per cent of dietary protein. Similar conditions prevail among the Cubeo in south-east Colombia (Goldman, 1963), the Kuikuru in central Brazil (Carneiro, 1961, 1968), and the Waiyana in Surinam and French Guiana (Butt, 1970).

In response to food procurement activities, many indigenous groups are semi-nomadic and periodically relocate their settlements. This is most evident among groups that are strongly dependent on hunting and gathering. Where fishing is more important, settlements may be larger and more permanent (Siskind, 1973), but in most cases periodic relocations still occur. The precise linkage between settlement pattern and environmental resources has been a matter of dispute. Originally, it was claimed that the characteristic mobility and small size of forest settlements were a response to the low production of shifting cultivation (Meggers, 1957). This view was challenged by Carneiro (1961), who showed convincingly that, even on poor soils, sufficient manioc could be produced around a settlement to sustain a permanent population of 2,000 people or so. That this was not generally achieved in the forest was attributed to internal social stresses that induced fissioning as settlements increased in size (Carneiro, 1961). In contrast, Gross (1975) argued that protein supply, especially animal protein, was only sufficient to sustain small and relatively impermanent settlements. Since protein-deficiency disease was not generally evident, Gross reasonably concluded that indigenous groups stabilised their numbers at levels below the capacity of local habitats to provide the requisite protein.

Other writers have challenged the idea of protein shortage and its assumed constraint on population and settlement (Lizot, 1977;Chagnon & Hames, 1979; Beckerman, 1979; Chagnon, 1983). In respect of the Yanomamo, Lizot (1977) stresses the relative abundance of both plant and animal protein, and asserts that the 'limits of population growth have never been reached'. In his view, the settlement pattern is mainly a result of fission and migration. Chagnon (1983) similarly suggests that the Yanomamo have not yet attained the carrying capacity of their environment, and that raiding and internal feuding, leading to fission, are the primary causes of village relocation. In general terms, Beckerman (1979) also questions the assumption of protein shortage in the forest, concluding that larger populations could have been supported in pre-contact times.

In spite of conflicting views on the precise relationship between resources and socio-demographic conditions in the forest zone, patterns of population and settlement broadly accord with the dynamics of traditional subsistence economies based on shifting cultivation and the exploitation of wild food resources. The more deterministic explanations have understandably been questioned, but, valid or otherwise, they are not critical to the belief that indigenous resource use is adaptive. Even Lizot (1977, p. 515) is prepared to allow that the indigenous economy 'is in harmony with the possibilities of the natural environment'.

Resource use in the savanna

Indigenous groups currently inhabit a few areas of Amazonian dry savanna, including parts of the Rio Branco–Rupununi and the Gran Sabana. Environmental resources, however, are relatively unfavourable in these areas. Savanna soils are mostly infertile Ferralsols, Acrisols and Arenosols and the savanna phytomass lacks the nutrient capital available to shifting cultivators in the forest. Wildlife resources are also sparse (Meggers, 1975; Denevan, 1976; Hammond, 1980). According to Denevan (1976), pre-contact human population densities in the savanna, estimated at $0.5/km^2$, were greater than those of the forest, although this seems unlikely for the present areas. Even so, the proposed density is low and confirms the limited resources of the habitat. A few extra-Amazonian groups, like the Guahibo of the Colombian *llanos*, still effectively exploit savanna as nomadic hunters and gatherers (Morey, 1970), but groups within Amazonia, such as the Wapisiana and Macusi in the Rio Branco–Rupununi and the Akawaio and Pemon in the Gran Sabana, have strong agricultural traditions; they reside in the savanna, but cultivate adjacent forest land.

The Wapisiana and Macusi are most numerous in the Rupununi region of south-west Guyana, where they live in savanna villages along the forest edge (Eden, 1966, 1986a). Their shifting cultivation is located in the forest, where they grow bitter manioc with sweet potatoes, bananas and other crops. In recent decades, they have adopted cattle grazing, and still practise some hunting and fishing in the forest and savanna. Deer (*Odocoileus gymnotis*) are still available in isolated parts of the savanna, and seasonal fishing is possible. Savanna-dwelling Wapisiana and Macusi are also present in parts of the Rio Branco basin, where they again rely on local forest cultivation.

Comparable exploitation of savanna and forest occurs in the Gran Sabana of Venezuela and in adjacent areas of Guyana. According to Butt (1970), the Akawaio of the upper Mazaruni consider the savanna an agreeable place to live, although it is barren and unsuitable for agriculture. Their livelihood is mainly derived from the nearby forest, where shifting cultivation occurs and hunting and gathering are pursued (Butt, 1970). A similar pattern prevails among the Pemon of the upper Caroní, who again prefer to live in the open savanna, albeit close to the edge of the forest and near a river. Shifting cultivation, with bitter manioc as the main crop, is undertaken in the forest, while hunting, fishing and collecting are pursued as resources permit (Matallana, 1937; Layrisse & Wilbert, 1966).

The scale of contemporary indigenous exploitation in Amazonian dry savannas is limited, although such areas are attractive for settlement because of their open aspect and relative freedom from insects and snakes (Butt, 1970). Scattered evidence exists of previous settlement in other Amazonian savannas (van Donselaar, 1969; Prance & Schubart, 1978), and more general early occupance by hunter-gatherers, similar to the Colombian Guahibo, cannot be ruled out. Even so, the paucity of savanna resources is unlikely to have sustained other than sparse human populations, even by forest standards.

Resource use in wetlands

Early European accounts of Amazonia indicate the existence of dense indigenous populations along the main *várzea* zone, particularly in its central and eastern parts (Carvajal, 1934; Acuña, 1942; Ashburn, 1947), and similar conditions apparently prevailed in some coastal areas. Denevan

(1976) estimates the pre-contact population density of the *várzea* at 14.6/km^2 and of coastal areas at or less than 9.5/km^2, compared with 0.2–0.5/km^2 on the *terra firme*. By the early eighteenth century, however, wetland populations were severely depleted, and only limited archaeological and historical data are available on their resource use systems.

Along the mainstream of the Amazon, below the Japurá confluence and in the vicinity of the Tapajós, relatively continuous settlement existed on the higher ground flanking or lying within the floodplain (Meggers, 1971). Confirmation of this settlement, and of its relative permanence, is provided by the existence of *terra preta* soils along the river. These soils are anthropogenic (Eden *et al.*, 1984) and represent 'a cultural layer accumulated at former Indian villages' (Smith, 1980, p. 555). The soils also occur on interfluves, but are most extensive along the *terra firme* margin, overlooking the floodplain of the Amazon and other large rivers. There are extensive *terra preta* soils in the vicinity of Santarém and Manaus, and similar materials have been reported from the Caquetá valley in Colombia and along adjacent rivers in Ecuador and Peru (Sombroek, 1966; Smith, 1980; Eden *et al.*, 1984).

Várzea populations were primarily dependent on the agricultural and wild food products of the floodplain itself. Wetland soils were cultivated following the seasonal retreat of floodwaters, and perennial cropping was undertaken on elevated levees. Adjacent tracts of the *terra firme* were also used for cultivation, providing some insurance against the flood risk of the *várzea*. It has at times been assumed that manioc was the staple crop of the *várzea* as well as of the *terra firme* (Denevan, 1966b; Lathrap, 1970), but maize in fact seems to have acquired considerable importance in the former zone (Carvajal, 1934; Acuña, 1942). Both bitter manioc and maize were cultivated by the Omagua along the middle Amazon, while maize was the principal crop of the Tapajós Indians (Meggers, 1971).

Comparable conditions prevail among the contemporary Shipibo, who are one of the few *várzea* groups that have survived and have retained their cultural autonomy in the face of lengthy outside contact (Hoffmann, 1964). Living along the Ucayali river in Peru, the Shipibo cultivate mainly bananas and maize, together with manioc, beans and other vegetable and fruit crops (Hoffmann, 1964, Bergman, 1974; Denevan, 1984). On *várzea* soils, their banana fields are reported to thrive for fifteen to twenty-five years and their maize crops grow well (Lathrap, 1970; Bergman, 1974). As elsewhere, the main constraint on *várzea* cultivation is seasonal flooding which increases crop risk. In eastern Peru, the timing and magnitude of annual floods vary from year to year, making it difficult to synchronise the agricultural cycle with the state of the land (Hoffmann, 1964). Among the Shipibo, cultivating a range of *várzea* micro-habitats or 'ecological zones' (Denevan, 1984) serves to reduce this flood risk, while allowing advantage to be taken of the favourable soil fertility.

Aquatic faunal resources also provide abundant food for *várzea* populations. The supply varies in time and space. Lacustrine habitats along large white water rivers are the most productive, but fish populations seasonally migrate between lacustrine and riverine habitats and are variously exploited (Lowe-McConnell, 1975; Chapman, 1977). Maximum availability occurs during periods of low water, but the overall catch is increased by using a range of fishing equipment and techniques. In the mid-seventeenth century, Acuña (1942) emphasised the diversity of fishing along the Amazon, which he related to the rise and fall of the river. He contrasted the use of fish poisons in isolated lakes with that of arrows and spears for river fishing. More recently, Chapman (1977) has described the range of fishing equipment utilised by the Conibo in eastern Peru. It includes spears, bows and arrows, and fish poisons which are variously used for different species and habitats. The dry season is the most productive period, but perennial fishing is characteristic, with rivers and lakes being exploited at opposite periods of the flood cycle. *Pimelodus* sp., which is common in the Ucayali river, recurs in dry season catches, while *Erythrinus erythrinus* and *Mylossoma* sp. are acquired from lakes, especially during flood periods (Chapman, 1977). The large paiche (*Arapaima gigas*) is also caught in lakes (Hoffmann, 1964).

Other aquatic animals like manatee (*Trichechus inunguis*) and turtles (*Podocnemis* spp.) have previously been important food sources in the *várzea*, although their numbers, like those of paiche, have declined of late (Bergman, 1974; Smith, 1979, 1981b; Timm *et al.*, 1986). Turtles and their eggs are normally available during periods of low water. According to Acuña (1942), the turtles were placed in corrals, where they were fed with branches and leaves to keep them alive until their meat was needed. In addition, there are many birds and terrestrial animals in the *várzea*, and some game was also available from the adjacent *terra firme* (Meggers, 1971).

While the main Amazon *várzea* is prone to major flood variability and consequent uncertainty in food supply, less extreme hydrologic conditions prevail in coastal wetlands. Within the latter, few indigenous groups survived the initial European impact (Butt, 1965; Kloos, 1971), but there is some evidence of early land exploitation in the coastal Guianas in the form of elevated ridged fields. The fields, now abandoned, date from pre-Columbian times. They are mainly located in herbaceous wetlands in north-east and north-west Surinam, where they co-exist with artificial settlement mounds (Laeyendecker-Roosenburg, 1966; Boomert, 1976, 1980). Similar mounds have been reported in coastal Guyana, and ridged fields may have also occurred there (Goodland, 1964; Boomert, 1978). In general, such structures would be of little utility on the main *várzea* where the annual flood range and variability are high, but they are adapted to the less extreme regimes of the coastal zone. Elevated ridged fields have also been reported from a few interior wetlands of lower flood variability,

Table 11 Relative dietary contribution
of food procurement activities among
the Shipibo of the Ucayali river
floodplain, eastern Peru*

	Calorie supply (%)	Protein supply (%)
Agriculture	84	27
Hunting	3	14
Fishing	13	59
	100	100

Source: Bergman, 1974.
*Based on an intake of 2,288 Kcal/
adult/day and 89 g protein/adult/day.

notably the Mojos savannas and parts of the Venezuelan *bajo llano*
(Parsons & Denevan, 1967; Denevan, 1966a, 1970; Zucchi, 1973;
Denevan & Zucchi, 1978).

No data are available on the cropping systems associated with ridged
fields in the Guianas or elsewhere, although relatively intensive land use
is implied. Crops like manioc and maize were presumably cultivated,
complementing the available faunal resources, and substantial pre-contact
populations probably existed (Kloos, 1971; Boomert, 1980). Further
south, on Marajó island, artificial burial and settlement mounds from
earlier pre-Columbian times have also been reported, although the populations in question were displaced prior to European contact (Meggers &
Evans, 1957, 1973).

Both floodplain and coastal wetlands in Amazonia have traditionally
been exploited for a wide range of plant and animal products, with the
principal emphasis on agriculture and fishing. Even in this nutrient-rich
environment, however, food supplies are seasonally variable, particularly
along the main *várzea* where there is abundant food during periods of low
water but relative scarcity in the flood season. Specific strategies were
adopted to counter this variability, and large sedentary populations built
up along white water rivers, particularly the Amazon mainstream, and also
in some coastal areas. Protein supplies were particularly abundant.
Whether cultivated plants or faunal resources were the main source of
protein is not entirely clear (Lathrap, 1970; Meggers, 1971; Roosevelt,
1980), but both were obviously exploited. There are few detailed accounts
of indigenous wetland resource use, but Bergman's (1974) analysis of
contemporary Shipibo subsistence clearly identifies animal products as the
main protein source (see Table 11).

Indigenous adaptation and modern development

The present account of indigenous resource use adopts the premise that subsistence activities are broadly in harmony with or adapted to the Amazonian environment (Meggers, 1971; Lizot, 1977). Some concern has reasonably been expressed regarding the tendency to view all indigenous behaviour as adaptive and working to protect the environment (Brush, 1979; Moran, 1983), but, in comparison to the behaviour of contemporary colonists, the premise has its attractions. In the case of hunting and gathering, adaptation is apparent in the immense diversity of products sought from the forest and the dispersed and conservative nature of their exploitation. Such activities have long contributed to indigenous diets, but there are still limits to the availability of wild resources. In areas where external contact has created larger and more permanent indigenous settlements, associated for example with the introduction of schools, health posts or missions, more intensive hunting frequently leads to persisting shortages of game (Eden, 1974b; Lizot, 1976). This applies particularly to larger animals, which have low reproduction rates and are more vulnerable to over-predation (Ross, 1978b).

In its traditional form, shifting cultivation is similarly viewed as adaptive, and, while the basis of that view has lately been revised (Beckerman, 1983; Eden & Andrade, 1987), the system itself is still seen as inherently sustainable and productive. Even so, shifting cultivation can be destabilised, if local population pressure leads to abbreviated forest fallowing and a consequent reduction in nutrient capital. This mostly occurs in areas of *colono* settlement, but affects indigenous groups where external contact encourages inappropriate attempts to intensify traditional shifting cultivation (Eden, 1974b).

Wetlands are less prone to resource depletion than the forested *terra firme*. Nutrient inputs from flood sediments help to sustain the fertility of cultivable wetlands and support large populations of fish and other game. Some aquatic species, like manatee (*Trichechus inunguis*) and paiche (*Arapaima gigas*), have been depleted of late, but most fish populations, being adapted to the variable natural conditions, are inherently resilient and less vulnerable to over-exploitation. Relatively large indigenous populations could thus be supported in many wetlands, even though the attendant resource variability, particularly on larger floodplains, created a degree of insecurity in the lives of those dependent upon them (Meggers, 1971).

In order to minimise such insecurity, a diverse pattern of indigenous exploitation was pursued. A range of micro-habitats was habitually cultivated within the *várzea* (Denevan, 1984), different fish were caught using a range of equipment in rivers and lakes (Bergman, 1974; Chapman, 1977), and supplementary foods were obtained from the adjacent *terra*

Table 12 Taboo animals among the Piaroa of
southern Venezuela and the Tapirapé of
central Brazil

Piaroa
    Tapir (*Tapirus terrestris*)
    Amazonian skunk (*Conepatus semistriatus*)
    Common opossum (*Didelphis marsupialis*)
    Water opossum (*Chironectes minimus*)
    Anaconda (*Eunectes murinus*)
    Inia (*Inia geoffrensis*)

Tapirapé
    Deer (*Mazama americana*)
    Tapir (*Tapirus terrestris*)
    Jaguar (*Felis onca*)
    Armadillo (*Euphractus sexcinctus*)
    Alligator (*Caiman* sp.)
    Pirarucú (*Arapaima gigas*)

Sources: Boza & Baumgartner, 1962; Wagley,
1977; Overing & Kaplan, 1988.

firme (Meggers, 1971). In addition, the preservation of dried foods and the
live storage of animals, especially turtles, were traditionally used to reduce
the impact of seasonal scarcity (Meggers, 1971; Roosevelt, 1980).
Although such adaptations only partially countered resource variability,
particularly on the main *várzea*, they served to increase human carrying
capacity. In coastal wetlands, where flood variability is less extreme, a
contrasting strategy was adopted, namely the construction of elevated
ridged fields, which assumedly maximised local crop production and again
increased carrying capacity.

Although the adaptation of subsistence activities can be examined in
isolation, it is possible to apply the approach more broadly. This is evident
in the view that the small size and relative impermanence of forest
settlements are a response to limited wild food resources and the need to
spread acquisition of those resources across time and space (Meggers,
1971; Gross, 1975). Similar attitudes have been adopted towards taboos
and rituals that influence the acquisition and consumption of wild
products. There are many taboos relating to forest animals, and also to
forest plants and some aquatic species (Boza & Baumgartner, 1962;
Harner, 1972; Reichel-Dolmatoff, 1976; Wagley, 1977) (see Table 12).
The functional nature of taboos is stressed by Ross (1978b), who explains
them in terms of the variable productivity of particular habitats. Similarly,
Reichel-Dolmatoff (1976) interprets ritual behaviour relating to the
activities of hunters and fishermen as an adaptive mechanism for the
control and management of game resources.

While such behaviour may well serve beneficially to regulate wild food resources, its efficacy also depends on the density of human population. Some writers have assumed that, prior to European contact, population pressure on resources already existed in Amazonia, and that additional behavioural adaptations arose that directly regulated population density. These included restrictions on the incidence of sexual relations as well as practices like selective female infanticide and senilicide (Meggers, 1971; Gross, 1975; Ross, 1978b). Recurrent inter-group warfare was widespread in pre-contact times and has similarly been interpreted as a response to population pressures on territory or food supplies (Gross, 1975; Meggers, 1971; Harris, 1978; Morey & Marwhitt, 1978).

Such ecological explanations of cultural phenomena are not without their detractors. Some authors have doubted the existence of general population pressure at the time of European contact (Carneiro, 1961; Lizot, 1977) and many prefer socio-cultural explanations for the small size and mobility of forest settlements (Goldman, 1963; Chagnon, 1983), for the existence of taboos (Basso, 1973; Harner, 1972; Smole, 1976), for selective female infanticide (Chagnon, 1968b), and for the occurrence of tribal warfare (Goldman, 1963; Harner, 1972; Lizot, 1977; Chagnon, 1983, 1988). Warfare in particular has been the subject of vigorous debate between proponents of ecological and socio-cultural explanation. In contrast to the ecological view, Goldman (1963) sees warfare among the Cubeo of southeast Colombia as a means 'to seize women' or as motivated by 'revenge'. According to Lizot (1977, p. 515), who is notably wary of ecological explanation, the Yanomamo 'make war to punish insults, avenge deaths, and fulfil kinship obligations'.

The extent to which indigenous culture is an autonomous variable is part of an older and broader philosophical debate that cannot be resolved at present (Sahlins, 1977). However, the idea of adaptive resource use itself is generally acceptable, even if related issues continue to provoke significant disagreement. On this basis, it is concluded that existing models of indigenous resource use, provisional as they are, have some relevance for modern development. The modern colonist may not immediately see indigenous subsistence activities as attractive or instructive, but they deserve attention in view of their persistence over millennia and of the dismal and inferior performance of their modern equivalents. In places, modern exploitation has achieved some success, but frequently it is mal-adaptive, damages the environment and offers little prospect of sustained yield. If modern development is to succeed, it needs to match the adaptability of its indigenous counterpart. This is not to say that indigenous resource use systems should simply be adopted by modern colonists, but it does imply that the indigenous strategy of conservative and sustainable exploitation is an essential principle for modern development. Implicit in this view is acknowledgement of the complex and sophisticated nature of indigenous exploitation and of the fact that indigenous knowledge itself constitutes a valuable resource.

As well as offering a general principle for modern exploitation, indigenous resource use has specific attributes that are of contemporary relevance. Firstly, there is the wide range of habitats that are identified and exploited by indigenous groups. The site-specific knowledge of such groups, both in respect of agricultural and extractive activities is immense and contributes significantly to effective resource use (Chapman, 1977; Posey, 1983; Denevan, 1984). This contrasts with the crude nature of much modern development, which is commonly based on poor knowledge of local land conditions and untested assumptions about land capability. Secondly, the diversity of plants and animals that are exploited by indigenous groups across the range of habitats deserves attention. The species-specific knowledge that groups possess is again immense (Moran, 1983), contributing significantly to the effectiveness of exploitation. This contrasts with the specialised character of much modern land development, which frequently relies on a limited number of familiar, if at times ill-adapted, species. Familiar species have a place in Amazonian development, but their use should be paralleled by greater awareness of the diversity of the indigenous plant and animal repertoire. Thirdly, there is benefit to be gained from adopting specific indigenous cultivation practices that protect soils and crops and maximise the use of available moisture and nutrients. Mixed cropping, frequently promoted in this context, is less apparent in traditional Amazonian agriculture than in some parts of the tropics (Eden, 1988), but experience in the productive use of forest fallow, exemplified by indigenous agrosilviculture (Eden, 1980; Denevan et al., 1984; Denevan & Padoch, 1988), offers significant opportunities for modern Amazonian farmers. Traditional wetland cultivation, albeit largely in abeyance since European contact, is similarly instructive in its ability to exploit nutrient-rich habitats while minimising flood risk (Denevan, 1984). Benefit may also be gained from indigenous experience of controlling agricultural weeds and pests. This emerging research area recognises the profound indigenous knowledge of interactions between crop and non-crop organisms and the related potential for improving weed and pest management in contemporary farming (Gliessman et al., 1981; Chacón & Gliessman, 1982; Lambert & Arnason, 1986; Eden, 1987). Against this background, the investigation of indigenous exploitation systems, which are a product of long selection extending over many generations (Egger, 1981), should be seen as an essential parallel, if not priority, to introducing advanced resource use technology.

5

Modern colonisation and exploitation of the rain forest

Many of these efforts at rain forest development have short-lived results.

[Jordan, 1987, p. 4]

Early European exploitation of the *terra firme* forest was mainly directed towards extractive and subsistence activities, with localised attempts at commercial cropping. Modern exploitation still includes extractive activities, but commercial crop production is of growing importance. A few examples of productive and sustainable cropping exist in the region, but pioneer land exploitation of an unstable and damaging kind is more common. Such exploitation largely reflects the use of agrosystems that are ill-adapted to the *terra firme*, although external factors, particularly relating to the provision of infrastructure and services, also constrain the achievement of more permanent use of the land. In this chapter, selected developments on the forested *terra firme* are examined, while comparable activities in wetlands and dry savannas are considered in the next chapter. These case studies, selected on the basis of the author's interest and experience, cover the range rather than totality of contemporary land development. In the present chapter, they include the exploitation of rubber and of timber, examples of planned and spontaneous peasant colonisation, and large-scale cattle ranching.

Extractive activities have always been an important part of Amazonian land exploitation. Indigenous populations traditionally acquired essential food products in this way, and the Brazilian *caboclo* and his counterpart in other territories readily continued such practices. Extractive products from the forest also provided the *caboclo* with marginal access to the cash economy. Traditional commercial products included sarsaparilla, Brazil nuts, oils, resins, timber and animal skins, but it was during the nineteenth century that one extractive product, namely wild rubber, acquired, for a while at least, a dominant position in the regional economy. Rubber had previously attracted minor attention in the region, but, particularly after 1870, there was rapid growth in its extraction and export. Rubber prices rose, reaching a peak in 1910, but thereafter the local market collapsed in the face of competition from Asian plantation rubber (Hanson, 1933; Wagley, 1964; Ross, 1978a).

Wild rubber is still collected in Amazonia, but other extractive activities now greatly exceed it in importance, notably mining and logging. Mining is rather localised in character while logging is widely dispersed, but both are of growing importance on the *terra firme*. Their environmental impact, both direct and indirect, is often substantial and certainly greater than that of wild rubber collecting which, for all its social problems, is environmentally benign.

Peasant land colonisation in Amazonia has latterly been encouraged by the development of roads. This is well illustrated by the Transamazon highway, which in the early 1970s opened up large tracts of the Brazilian *terra firme* to colonists. Many other penetration roads have been constructed in Brazilian Amazonia and parts of the Andean *oriente*, providing similar access for migrant colonists. Road developments of this kind are sponsored by governments, but the extent to which further official support is given to the colonist varies. In many areas, land colonisation is spontaneous in character, with minimal assistance provided for individual settlers and their families. Elsewhere, planned or directed colonisation occurs, with wide-ranging technical and socio-economic support supposedly available through a variety of government agencies (Nelson, 1973; Schuurman, 1980).

The explicit aim of most peasant colonisation is permanent settlement and cultivation of the land by subsistence and cash cropping. In reality, such colonisation is frequently associated with unstable land exploitation, characterised by soil deterioration, pest and weed problems, and declining crop yields. As a result, colonists are frequently obliged to resort to shifting cultivation after a few years on the land. As local population densities are often quite high in colonisation zones, land pressure develops and fallow periods become abbreviated, causing further land degradation. Exploitation may continue until a new basal equilibrium is attained, involving a low nutrient turnover and biological yield. This constitutes a 'low-biomass steady-state' (Noy-Meir, 1975), which is usually associated with subsistence rather than cash cropping. Alternatively, declining productivity may lead to land abandonment and a regeneration of secondary forest. In either case, substantial ecological resources arc lost and any natural recovery that occurs is slow and managed improvement costly. Degradation of this kind, although by no means inevitable, prejudices the long-term potential of the land, and is as unsatisfactory in socio-economic terms as it is damaging in ecological ones (Eden, 1978).

The development of large-scale commercial agrosystems has occurred alongside peasant colonisation. Some capital-intensive plantations have been established, mainly for the production of rubber and timber, but most attention has focused on establishing cattle ranches on cleared forest land. Many large-scale enterprises were originally intended for sustained production, but this has frequently been impractical or uneconomic and systemic instability has developed. This is most evident on cattle ranches, where nutrient loss, degrading pasture and declining beef productivity frequently occur over time. Under such conditions, fresh clearance of forest land is generally preferable to maintaining existing pastures, which are sold or abandoned to secondary growth. Plantation systems also encounter difficulties. Problems of long-term nutrient supply are again evident and crop pests and diseases can become troublesome, especially with monocultural systems. In these respects, both large-scale and small-scale modes of colonisation suffer similar constraints and instabilities, and questions arise regarding the appropriateness of the agrosystems involved.

Rubber exploitation in Amazonia

In spite of long commercial interest in the exploitation of Amazonian rubber, only limited success has been achieved in establishing it as a cultivated crop in the region and current production is still largely extractive. Rubber (*Hevea* spp.) is a native of Amazonia, occurring throughout the *hylaea*. *Hevea brasiliensis*, distributed across central and southern Amazonia, is the most valued of the latex-producing species (Ducke & Black, 1953). It is present at low density in the forest, with larger trees occurring on the *terra firme*. The latex contains a suspension of rubber particles in an aqueous serum, and has a hydrocarbon content of about 30 per cent (Huffnagel, 1964; Purseglove, 1979). Other species include *H. guianensis*, which is present throughout the region, and *H. benthamiana*, which is confined to northern Amazonia. The latter have an inferior yield and quality of latex, but have been exploited in the wild as well as used for grafting and hybridisation purposes (Russell, 1942; Huffnagel, 1964; Purseglove, 1979). Other forest species exploited for their latex include caucho (*Castilloa elastica*), mangabeira (*Hancornia speciosa*), and balata (*Manilkara bidentata*) (Le Cointe, 1922; Higbee, 1951).

In Europe, occasional use was made of Amazonian rubber in the eighteenth century, but significant demand for the product only developed after 1839, following the discovery of vulcanisation, which improved the elasticity and strength of rubber by heating it with sulphur. From the mid-nineteenth century, rubber was of increasing economic importance in Amazonia and, particularly after 1870, its extraction and export rapidly expanded. Further impetus was provided by the development of the motor car and increasing demand for rubber tyres (Purseglove, 1979).

The collection of latex by regular tapping of wild rubber trees spread widely through Amazonia. The demand for labour was high and many migrants were attracted from drought-prone areas of north-east Brazil. Between 1877 and 1900, an estimated 158,000 people left the latter region for Amazonia to take up rubber collecting (Soares, 1963; Ross, 1978a). Some of the migrants stayed in the lower Amazon, but the majority travelled up-river to western Brazil and the Andean *oriente*. The rubber collectors, or *seringueiros*, settled along Amazon tributaries and worked in adjacent forests. Individual trails, or *estradas*, were established, running 4–6 km through the forest and providing access to 120–180 rubber trees (Le Cointe, 1922; Wagley, 1964). Thence, the *seringueiros*, who were tied by indebtedness to their hazardous jobs, collected and dispatched the crude rubber, via middlemen, to the trading centres of Iquitos and Manaus. Eventually, much of the rubber passed downstream to Belém for export (Burns, 1966). The major collecting areas were located in the upper Juruá, Purus and Madeira basins in the south-west and the Putumayo and Caquetá basins in the north-west; collecting also occurred in the Casiquiare zone and in parts of Pará state (Higbee, 1951; Burns, 1966).

The production of raw rubber in Amazonia increased from 2,700 t in 1860 to 16,400 t in 1890. Peak production of 43,000 t was attained in 1912, by which time immense profits had been accumulated by the local entrepreneurs (Le Cointe, 1922; Huffnagel, 1964). Very little in the way of profit, however, was passed on to the *seringueiros* in the forest, for whom working conditions were appalling and hardship and death commonplace. In areas such as the Putumayo, Amerindians were also involved in rubber collecting, as a result of which many of them perished (Collier, 1968).

While the rubber industry prospered, its fate was in fact sealed as early as 1876. In that year, a consignment of *Hevea* seeds from the Tapajós valley was discreetly removed to Kew Gardens in England, and tree seedlings were thereafter dispatched to the Far East (Wickham, 1908). Rubber plantations were established in Ceylon and Malaya, and by the turn of the century cheaper cultivated rubber was beginning to appear on the world market, undercutting the wild Amazonian product (Burns, 1966; Purseglove, 1979). In the late 1890s, plans had in fact been made to start plantations in the Brazilian Amazon and a few small units were established, but no real progress was made (Le Cointe, 1922; Melby, 1942). Rubber prices in Amazonia peaked in 1910 and over the following two years, as Oriental supplies increased, the local rubber market collapsed and with it the fortunes of the trading centres of Manaus and Belém (Melby, 1942; Burns, 1966). Many people were forced back to the larger towns or returned to north-east Brazil and, although some rubber was still collected, overall production steadily declined and economic activity stagnated (Hanson, 1933; Wagley, 1964; Ross, 1978a).

An initial attempt to revive the rubber industry in Amazonia was made in 1927, when the Ford Motor Company acquired a concession of

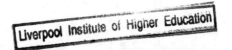

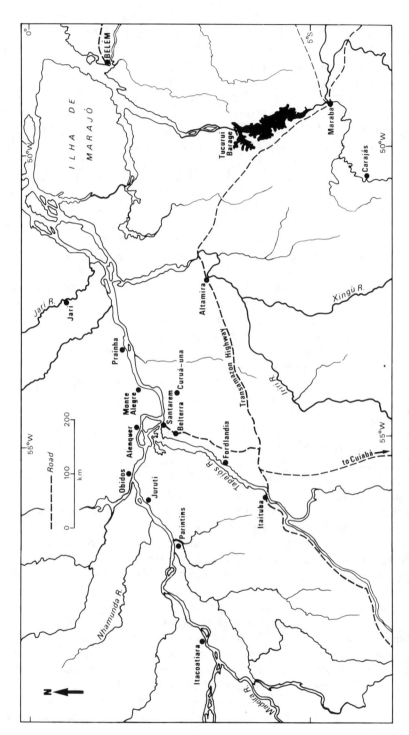

Figure 10 Location map of the lower Amazon region, Brazil

1 million ha on the Tapajós river, intending to start plantation production. At Fordlandia, as it was known, forest clearance and rubber planting began, but problems were soon encountered. The dissected *terra firme* was prone to soil erosion on clearance and poorly-drained bottomlands were found to be unsuitable for planting. On slopes, terracing and cover crops were adopted, but some areas of cleared land had to be abandoned (Russell, 1942). Also fungal diseases and insect pests, which scarcely affect the dispersed *Hevea* in the wild, began seriously to damage the monocultural stands on the plantation. The most serious problem was South American leaf blight (*Microcyclus ulei*), a fungal infection which is most prevalent in perennially-humid areas and kills trees after several defoliations (Tollenaar, 1959; Huffnagel, 1964; Ortolani, 1980). In 1934, with only 3,400 ha of rubber established at Fordlandia, the company exchanged part of the plantation for a new concession, named Belterra, which covered 280,000 ha of flatter land near the mouth of the Tapajós river. Fordlandia was retained as an experimental station (see Figure 10).

At Belterra, soil erosion was less troublesome, but there were persisting disease problems, involving both South American leaf blight (*M. ulei*) and other fungal infections like *Phytophthora palmivora* and *Pellicularia filamentosa* (Langford, 1953; Soares, 1963; Huffnagel, 1964; Alvim, 1982). Eventually, most were controlled through the use of disease-resistant species of *Hevea*, by grafting, and by spraying (Russell, 1942). One approach was to double-graft high-yielding clonal trunks and pest-resistant crowns on to native *Hevea* stock, but this was costly and time-consuming. Progress was also impeded by shortages of labour and, although development activities continued, the company finally sold its interests in Fordlandia and Belterra to the Brazilian government in 1946 (Russell, 1942; Soares, 1963). Plant breeding continued at Belterra under the Instituto Agronômico do Norte, and a small amount of rubber was produced, as it still is today, but the ambitious objectives of the Ford Motor Company were never realised.

During the Second World War, Allied access to Oriental supplies of rubber was lost, and, in the early 1940s, urgent efforts were made to restore the collection of wild rubber in Amazonia. Labour was again brought in from north-east Brazil, but only modest gains in production were made by the end of the war (Wagley, 1964). Other attempts have also been made to establish plantation production in the region (Bonnaire, 1970, Benacchio, 1982). The most successful have been at Igarape-Açú and Anandineua in the Bragantina zone of Pará, where, in the 1950s, small plantations were set up by the Goodyear and Pirelli companies respectively. Production continues to the present on a cultivated area of some 3,700 ha (IBGE, 1984). South American leaf blight (*M. ulei*) exists in the area, but a reasonable level of control has been achieved. At Anandineua, two approaches are adopted. Part of the land is planted with a

Photograph 15 Graft of blight-resistant *Hevea pauciflora* crown onto *H. brasiliensis* stem at Anandineua rubber plantation in Bragantina zone, Pará, Brazil

variety of *Hevea brasiliensis*, which is double-grafted and has a crown of *H. pauciflora*. The latter species has latex of low rubber content, but its leaves are immune to *M. ulei*. Rubber yields are 1,300–1,500 kg/ha/year (see Photograph 15). Elsewhere, the land is planted with FX 25, a blight-resistant clone that was developed at Fordlandia and Belterra. The clone is now susceptible to *M. ulei*, but control is achieved by fungicidal fogging when young foliage is present. Yields are approximately 650 kg/ha/year. At both Anandineua and Igarape-Açú, fertilisers are applied, and leguminous cover crops, mainly *Pueraria* and *Centrosema*, are used to improve soil fertility and for erosion control (Huffnagel, 1964; Penteado, 1967).

Latterly, rubber cultivation in the Brazilian Amazon has been economic under prevailing support prices. However, attempts to raise national production, in the face of increasing imports of natural rubber, have also extended outside Amazonia. Some 25,000 ha of rubber have been established in Bahia (Alvim, 1982), and there have also been plantings in São Paulo, where the crop benefits from the absence of *M. ulei* under drier climatic conditions (Camargo *et al.*, 1977; Benchimol, 1988). Nevertheless, the ready availability of land in Amazonia still makes that region attractive for rubber cultivation, and, in the early 1980s, substantial new plantings were made in the Juruá, Purus and Madeira valleys on the assumption that effective disease control was feasible (Alvim, 1982). However, large areas of this rubber have in fact been lost to *M. ulei* (Benchimol, 1988).

While this recent episode seems to confirm Huffnagel's (1964, p. 39) conclusion that commercial rubber estates 'cannot be recommended' for Amazonia, the search for protection against *M. ulei* continues. Whether it will eventually be feasible to sustain large-scale monocultural production in the region remains to be seen, but some risk seems inevitable with this vulnerable long-cycle crop. Also, rubber yields in Amazonia are still relatively low and production costs high, especially in relation to Old World producers among whose advantages is an absence of *M. ulei*. Nevertheless, import substitution of rubber has obvious attractions for both Brazil and her neighbours, and the pertinent question, in ecological and economic terms, is whether national production should be pursued in Amazonian or extra-Amazonian areas. Meanwhile, the extractive tradition, inefficient as it is, persists to the extent that some 90 per cent of natural rubber produced in Brazil is still obtained by tapping wild rubber trees (IBGE, 1985).

Forestry in Pará

In spite of the massive timber resources in Amazonia, forestry activities have hitherto been mainly concentrated elsewhere in the continent. This is the case in Brazil where total timber production, in 1984, was 210.7 million m³, of which only 33.9 million m³ (16 per cent) were derived from Amazonia, largely through extractive logging. The main Amazonian production area is Pará state, followed by Amazonas and northern Mato Grosso (see Table 13). Less timber is produced in other Amazonian territories, where a higher proportion of logs is destroyed when the forest is cleared for agricultural or other purposes. Improved road access and increasing demand for timber products, however, are encouraging commercial production across the region, and, as the forests of the Old World tropics are depleted, the demand for Amazonian timber is intensifying (Swinbanks & Anderson, 1989).

The lower Amazon region, and particularly Pará state, has been a focus of extractive logging for many decades. In the past, the majority of timber was derived from *várzea* forests, whence it was manually transported to

Table 13 Timber production in Brazilian Amazonia in 1975 and 1984 (million m³)

	1975		1984	
	Timber extraction	Silvicultural production	Timber extraction	Silvicultural production
Brazil	156.33	46.30	175.40	35.32
Amazônia	10.36+	–	32.83	1.04
Acre	0.98	–	1.57	–
Amapá	0.39	–	1.00	–
Amazonas	3.47	–	4.79	–
Mato Grosso (northern)	n/a	–	4.73	–
Pará	5.24	–	19.12	1.04
Rondônia	0.25	–	1.53	–
Roraima	0.03	–	0.08	–

Source: IBGE, *Anuários Estatísticos do Brasil*.

nearby rivers and floated downstream to sawmills (Palmer, 1977; Muthoo & Leader, 1978). Since the mid-1970s, access to *terra firme* forests has greatly improved as a result of road building, and logging has extended into these areas. Mechanised operations have become more common, and there is now much greater reliance on road than river transport (Dubé, 1980). There is also a greater range of available species on the *terra firme*, among which *Swietenia macrophylla*, *Hymenolobium excelsum*, *Dinizia excelsa*, *Bowdichia* spp. and *Ocotea* spp. are commonly sought (Brune & Melchior, 1976). In total, there now exist some 3,000 sawmills in Pará state (Uhl & Vieira, 1989).

Some sawmills in the state have their own land for timber extraction, and a few multi-national companies have acquired large holdings to sustain their milling and other operations. These include subsidiaries of Toyomenka of Japan and Georgia-Pacific of the United States, which are reported to hold areas of 300,000 ha and 400,000 ha respectively (Garrido Filha, 1980). Timber extraction, however, is little regulated and a great deal of logging has hitherto been undertaken at low cost by small, independent operators who supply timber to local sawmills (see Photograph 16). Some sawmill owners have also themselves lately acquired logging vehicles and other equipment, and, after purchasing logging rights from landowners, are undertaking their own logging and transport operations (Uhl & Vieira, 1989). Some 200 tree species are currently in industrial use, although the bulk of production is derived from far fewer. Individual sawmills commonly accept 20–40 species, and the number used is only slowly increasing (Muthoo & Leader, 1978; Dubé, 1980; Rankin, 1985). As forest stands are generally diverse, logging is highly selective and the volume of timber extracted is low, averaging 10–40 m³/ha in

Photograph 16 Logs at roadside awaiting transport to local sawmill, near Tomé Açu, Pará, Brazil

many areas. This compares with an estimated standing timber volume for the Brazilian *terra firme* of 178 m³/ha (Pandolfo, 1979).

Because of the rather low volume of timber extracted, initial clear-cutting is not generally apparent in Pará. Damage inevitably results from the selective cutting and removal of trees, but much of the original canopy survives and the forest is able to regenerate, provided further disturbance is avoided. Even so, selective logging can lead to over-exploitation of individual species. This has been the case with pau rosa (*Aniba roseodora*) which was heavily cut in the past for rosewood oil and eliminated in many areas (Heinsdijk, 1958a). Similar problems have arisen with mahogany (*Swietenia macrophylla*) and maçaranduba (*Manilkara huberi*) (Valverde, 1981). However, the most serious effect of extractive logging is indirect and derives from the establishment of logging trails in the forest. These provide ready access for ranchers and itinerant farmers, who subsequently establish themselves on the land and complete the process of clearance. While the impact of selective logging is still localised in Pará, the industry is growing rapidly and there is an urgent need for more positive forest management. Some official action has been taken, but, as in the case of rubber, there is little incentive at present to abandon traditional extractive methods.

Government involvement in forestry in Brazilian Amazonia has been intermittent in character. Extensive forest inventories were made in the period 1954–62, with assistance from the Food and Agriculture Organization (FAO). An area of 200,000 km^2 was surveyed to the south of the Amazon mainstream, extending from the Atlantic coast of Pará to the Madeira river (Heinsdijk & Miranda Bastos, 1963). Subsequently, interest in the area declined when the Transamazon highway was established further to the south, and little use has been made of the information collected (Palmer, 1977). More recently, in the 1970s, comprehensive land surveys of Pará state were undertaken as part of the Projeto Radambrasil, including assessments of timber reserves and of the feasibility of their exploitation. Such data are clearly relevant to formulating sound forestry policies, but, in spite of sundry proposals from government agencies, progress at the policy level has been slow. In the early 1970s, the Superintendência do Desenvolvimento da Amazônia (SUDAM) stressed the need to modernise timber exploitation, and recommended the creation of 'income forests' (Florestas Regionais de Rendimento) and 'national forests' (Florestas Nacionais) for sustainable, large-scale commercial exploitation (Pandolfo, 1974). As yet, only the Tapajós National Forest (600,000 ha) and the Caxiuaná National Forest (200,000 ha) have been established, both located in Pará. In addition, proposals for various types of logging concession were put forward by the Instituto Brasileiro de Desenvolvimento Florestal (IBDF) (Schmithüsen, 1978), but few such concessions have been granted. The first significant example was for the salvage extraction of natural forest in the reservoir basin of the Tucuruí barrage in southern Pará, but the concession was reportedly a complete failure (Rankin, 1985).

Even if broad policy directions were clarified, a persisting problem would be the slow progress in developing silvicultural techniques for sustainable exploitation of mixed-forest stands (Eden, 1982). When the FAO inventories were undertaken in the 1950s, the agency also initiated silvicultural experiments at Curuá-Una near Santarém (Pitt, 1961, 1969), but interest in this important programme was not sustained and few relevant results emerged (see Figure 10). In the late 1970s, fresh experiments were started at Curuá-Una into mixed-forest management, with particular attention to regeneration techniques (Jankauskis, 1978; SUDAM, 1978), and similar studies were also begun in the Tapajós National Forest south of Santarém (Carvalho, 1980; Costa Filho et al., 1980; Yared et al., 1980). Crucial as these experiments are, the scale of investigation is small and few useful results are likely to emerge in the short term.

At present, the only major silvicultural enterprise in the forest zone is the Jari project, which is based on short-cycle plantation production rather than mixed-forest management. The project covers 1.6 million ha on the Jari river in northern Pará. It was initiated in 1967 by the American entrepreneur D. K. Ludwig, although it subsequently has been transferred to Brazilian ownership (see Figure 10). The project is primarily concerned with wood production, although subsidiary rice cultivation, livestock rearing and mining activities were also developed. Wood production is mainly for pulp and paper, for which a processing plant was established on the site in 1978. A sawmill also exists for handling forest hardwoods (Greaves, 1979; Dubé, 1980).

Approximately 100,000 ha of forest land have been cleared and planted at Jari. *Gmelina arborea*, *Pinus caribaea* var. *hondurensis* and *Eucalyptus* spp. are the main trees in use. *Gmelina arborea* is a native of south-east Asia that has been widely cultivated in the tropics (Lamb, 1968). It is a fast-growing deciduous tree, which at Jari is grown on clayey soils and currently occupies about a fifth of the planted area. *Gmelina* was previously cut for pulping at 5–7 years, but cycles have now been reduced to 3–4 years (Greaves, 1979; Hornick *et al.*, 1984; Fearnside, 1987). *Pinus caribaea*, a later introduction, occupies more than a third of the planted area. It is grown on sandy soils that are unsuitable for *Gmelina*, and rotations are cut at nine years (Hornick *et al.*, 1984; Fearnside, 1987). Latterly, *Eucalyptus* has been planted in large numbers, and now covers a similar area to *Pinus*. *Eucalyptus deglupta* was originally preferred, but has been superseded by *E. urophylla* and some *E. urograndis* (Fearnside, 1987). High wood yields have previously been reported at Jari for both *Gmelina* (38 m³/ha/year) and *Pinus* (27 m³/ha/year) (Alvim, 1977), but average growth on properly managed stands is a relatively low 13 m³/ha/year (Hornick *et al.*, 1984; Jordan, 1985).

Although tree cropping has been effectively established at Jari, questions arise regarding the sustainability of the system. There is, firstly, concern over long-term nutrient supply. Fertilisers are not generally used to sustain tree growth, and net nutrient losses are occurring from the system, mainly through the removal of logs (Jordan & Russell, 1983). Potassium and calcium are being lost, and longer-term reductions in nitrogen supply are evident. The losses are expected to reduce wood production in later rotations (Jordan, 1985). While the use of fertilisers would resolve the immediate problem, the resultant costs would be high and possibly uneconomic (Fearnside & Rankin, 1980; Rankin, 1985). In addition, there is concern over the long-term pest vulnerability of the monocultural stands at Jari. Pest attacks have been reported over the years, including damage to *Pinus* from leaf-cutting ants (*Atta* spp.) and to *Gmelina* from unidentified leaf-eating moth larvae. *Gmelina* is also affected by a canker-producing fungal infection (*Ceratocystis fimbriata*), which is widespread among native and introduced trees in Amazonia and unlikely to be eradicated at Jari (Muchovej *et al.*, 1978; Rankin, 1985). Other fungal and bacterial infections affect *Eucalyptus* spp. (Fearnside, 1987). Although pest damage has not as yet caused major economic losses, a gradual build-up in pest numbers may occur and create long-term risks for the project

(Fearnside & Rankin, 1980; Rankin, 1985).

The Jari project inevitably invites comparison with the earlier plantation ventures at Fordlandia and Belterra. As yet, Jari has not encountered as serious ecological problems as the latter, but such cannot be discounted. Jari has certainly displayed a similar appetite for investment, absorbing an estimated US$850–1,000 million by the early 1980s (Anon., 1981; Knight, 1982). Immediate profits were not anticipated on the project, but, by 1982, the low return on investment became unacceptable to D. K. Ludwig who sold his interest in the venture to a Brazilian consortium (Rocha, 1982; Hornick et al., 1984). The poor economic performance of the project was partly due to lower wood yields than anticipated and to falling prices for cellulose on the world market, while technical and social overheads were very high. How far the specific costs of operating the plantation under Amazonian conditions constrained overall financial performance is difficult to determine, but the production difficulties do not appear to have been resolved under recent Brazilian management (Anon., 1981; Knight, 1982; Fearnside, 1987). As at Fordlandia and Belterra, an ambitious agro-industrial project, based on imported technology and expertise, has been established in the forest, but its long-term sustainability is uncertain.

In spite of the difficulties encountered at Jari, the possibility of intensive wood production on cleared forest land is favourably viewed in some quarters. According to Goodland (1980), forestry plantations are much less damaging than most of the development alternatives for Amazonia, and certainly preferable to converting the forest for annual crops or cattle pasture. Similarly, Hornick et al. (1984) argue that intensive management of relatively small areas, like Jari, will reduce overall land pressure and thereby permit larger areas to remain under natural forest. Whether the Jari project will eventually confirm these views remains to be seen. Doubts exist that it represents the viable, long-term development model that Ludwig envisaged (Fearnside & Rankin, 1980), but it remains an important experiment that deserves careful monitoring, notably in respect of nutrient and pest dynamics. The outcome is of more than local interest, moreover, since similar plantation production is scheduled for the Carajás project in central Pará. The aim in this area is to cultivate Eucalyptus spp. for charcoal for smelting locally-produced iron ore, and an eventual plantation area of 2.5 million ha of forest land is envisaged. Similar ecological problems to those encountered at Jari are likely to arise, although the scale, and hence risks, involved are of much greater magnitude (Rankin, 1985; Fearnside, 1987). Meanwhile, extractive logging remains commercially attractive in Pará, and continues to expand. Its current production far exceeds that of silviculture, whether by mixed-forest management or industrial plantations. However, the environmental impact of extractive logging is less favourable, especially where forest land is opened up to

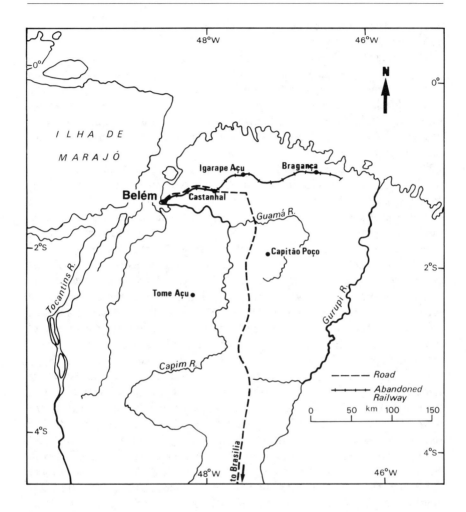

Figure 11 Location map of the Bragantina zone, Pará state, Brazil

ranchers and itinerant farmers, and more sustainable modes of timber exploitation are required.

Peasant colonisation of the Bragantina zone

The Bragantina zone covers approximately 1.2 million ha of *terra firme* east of Belém in Pará state (see Figure 11). More than a century ago, it was the scene of a major attempt at planned colonisation, which aimed to settle small farmers permanently on cleared forest land and produce food and other supplies for the expanding population of Belém. In retrospect, the endeavour is more notable for its environmental impact than its agricultural achievements.

The Bragantina zone lies at less than 100 m above sea level, and comprises a sedimentary landscape of broad valleys and gentle slopes and terraces (Soares, 1963). Annual rainfall is approximately 2,500 mm, and a well-developed rain forest originally covered the area. The presence of forest was taken to indicate favourable soil conditions, but, as land colonisation proceeded, the falsity of this assumption became apparent. Soils in the area, which are classified as Xanthic Ferralsols (FAO–UNESCO, 1971), are mostly acid (pH 4.5–5.5) and of low natural fertility, with deficiencies in both major and trace elements (Soares, 1963; Vieira *et al.*, 1967).

The site of Belém was occupied in early Colonial times and became an important focus in the lower Amazon valley. The settlement gradually increased in size, attaining some 15,000 inhabitants by 1850, but thereafter its growth accelerated in response to the rubber boom. By 1867, its population had reached 30,000, mainly through migration from north-east Brazil, and many thousands more were passing through the settlement on their way up-river (Penteado, 1967). One result of the expansion of Belém and the general preoccupation with rubber was a growing shortage of locally-produced foodstuffs, and it was the need to resolve this problem that led to planned colonisation in the Bragantina zone (Kass, 1976).

In 1875, a first agricultural colony was founded at Santa Isabel de Benevides, some 30 km east of Belém, and between then and 1916 a further nineteen colonies were established over the 200 km distance to the town of Bragança (Biard & Wagenaar, 1960). Between 1883 and 1908, a railway link was also built from Belém to Bragança (Kass, 1976). These developments were coincident with and financed by the revenues of wild rubber collection in Pará state. All went well as long as the rubber industry prospered, but when the rubber boom ended just before the First World War, government investment in land colonisation came to a halt. Agricultural activity in the area continued, but the early momentum was lost.

The original land colonisation was undertaken by foreign migrants, mainly of French and Spanish origin. Few remained on the land, however, and settlement was mostly effected by *nordestinos*, particularly from Ceará state. The arrival of these migrants usually coincided with droughts in north-east Brazil. Severe droughts occurred in 1888–9 and 1899–1900, which sent thousands of migrants to Pará and beyond (Biard & Wagenaar, 1960). By 1902, the established colonies were reported to contain 10,112 settlers, of whom 8,396 were Brazilian and 1,726 foreigners (Penteado, 1967).

In the colonisation areas, land holdings of 25 ha were usually allocated to individual families (Biard & Wagenaar, 1960; Penteado, 1967). Initially

Table 14 Agricultural exports by
railway from the Bragantina zone in
1915 (tons)

Farinha (processed manioc)	11,328
Maize	3,609
Rice	1,032
Alcohol/*cachaça*	788
Fruit	519
Beans	204
Tobacco	145
Others	160

Source: Biard & Wagenaar, 1960.

several hectares of each holding were cleared and burnt, and then interplanted with rice, maize and manioc. Sugar was often cultivated as a cash crop, along with cotton and tobacco. Yields were reasonable on newly-cleared land, but declined after a few years as soil conditions deteriorated and weeds invaded. Individual fields were then abandoned, reverting to secondary forest or *capoeira*. For a family confined to a 25 ha plot, such a regime soon involved re-cultivation of immature *capoeira*, where even first harvests were rather poor. As a result, colonists began to abandon their original holdings, turning to pioneer shifting cultivation in the surrounding forest (Biard & Wagenaar, 1960). Pressure on the *capoeira* and forest was further increased by the demand for timber for domestic and commercial purposes, including fuel for railway engines.

As long as stands of primary forest, with attendant nutrient capital, were available for exploitation, colonists were able to support themselves by impermanent cultivation, but, over the years, the forest cover was gradually replaced by a mosaic of scattered fields and degraded *capoeira*. Crop productivity declined, which in turn impoverished the rural population and encouraged out-migration. Productivity data are unavailable for the early period, but the general pattern of production is evident from the agricultural goods carried on the railway; the importance of manioc, maize and rice cropping is apparent (see Table 14).

Although rural poverty has provoked out-migration from Bragantina, the net population of the area has grown steadily in recent decades by natural increase. In 1939, the Bragantina zone (excluding Belém) had a population of 131,000; by 1985, the number had increased to 423,000, giving an average density of 36.5/km^2 (Kass, 1976; IBGE, 1986). Some local redistribution of population has occurred in the zone, mainly in response to the establishment of the Belém–Brasília highway through its western part, but most of the population is still involved in dispersed agricultural activities. Shifting cultivation is still widespread, even though the available *capoeira*, often no more than 5–10 years old, provides a poor basis for crop

Photograph 17 Processing of malva fibre near Capitão Poço, Pará, Brazil

production. Manioc yields of 9,000–10,000 kg/ha are still obtained, but yields of rice and maize are extremely low, mostly in the range 500–900 kg/ha (Biard & Wagenaar, 1960; IBGE, 1980a). Rainfall variability partly explains the poor crop performance, but the principal constraint is the low nutrient capital of the *capoeira*. Traditional low-yielding crop varieties are still in use, but are at least adapted to local environmental conditions and sustain basal yields (Biard & Wagenaar, 1960; Penteado, 1967; Kass, 1976).

In recent decades, some attempts have been made to improve land exploitation. An early innovation was the cultivation of malva, a local fibre product used for making bags and cord (see Photograph 17). The fibre is obtained from several plants, notably *Urena lobata* and *Pavonia malacophylla*, which exist as weeds of cultivation on degraded land in the area. Since the 1940s, malva has been produced as a cash crop within the shifting cultivation system (Biard & Wagenaar, 1960; Soares, 1963). In the 1950s, black pepper (*Piper nigrum*) was introduced to the area, mainly by Japanese smallholders, who used fertilisers for its cultivation. Attempts have also been made to develop horticultural production, and, as previously indicated, small rubber plantations have been established. Some progress has been made with these cash crops, but various problems arise. Fruit and vegetable crops, which need to compete with low-cost imports from southern Brazil, require the use of costly pesticides and fertilisers (Kass, 1976). Serious fungal diseases also variously constrain the

Table 15 Agricultural
exploitation in the Bragantina
zone in 1979

Manioc	21,079 ha
Maize	11,713 ha
Rice	8,527 ha
Malva	7,057 ha
Black pepper	5,516 ha
Beans	4,449 ha
Melons	913 ha
Cotton	856 ha
Tobacco	836 ha
Papaya	647 ha
Cacao	584 ha
Others	1,275 ha
	63,452 ha

Note: an additional area of
approximately 3,700 ha was
under cultivation for rubber
(1982).
Source: IBGE, 1980a.

production of black pepper and rubber crops. In total, less than a tenth of the land area is reportedly cultivated at any one time, and of this most is still devoted to the traditional staples of manioc, rice and maize (see Table 15).

Against a background of poor agricultural performance and natural population growth, the Bragantina zone has latterly experienced significant out-migration. Even in early times, some colonists returned to north-east Brazil and over the years many others moved to Belém, which, by 1985, had attained a population of 1.1 million. New areas of pioneer colonisation have also developed elsewhere in Pará. The Guamá valley was a favoured area that drew migrants in the 1940s, after malaria was brought under control. Further south, forest land around Capitão Poço and Tomé Açu was likewise colonised in the 1950s, while the development of the Belém–Brasília highway in the 1960s offered further opportunities for local migrants (Valverde & Dias, 1967; Mueller, 1975). The long-term prospects in many of these areas are no greater than in Bragantina, but the opportunity to colonise fresh forest land remains as attractive as a century ago.

Meanwhile, in the Bragantina zone, impoverished and stagnant conditions have persisted, and the area largely remains one of 'degraded vegetation and decadent agriculture' (Valverde & Dias, 1967). In western Bragantina, where the Belém–Brasília highway traverses the original colonisation area, some economic regeneration has occurred, with towns

Table 16 Population data for selected *municípios* in the Bragantina zone, 1950–85

	Castanhal (western zone)		Igarape-Açú (central zone)		Bragança (eastern zone)	
	Population	Density per km²	Population	Density per km²	Population	Density per km²
1950	14,261	14.0	15,370	12.7	57,888	13.9
1960	21,618	21.6	21,315	17.6	69,005	16.6
1970	37,921	37.8	15,973	21.1	62,026	19.0
1980	65,251	65.1	23,007	30.4	85,087	26.1
1985	90,014	89.7	27,730	36.7	97,942	30.1

Note: between 1950 and 1960, the *município* of Castanhal was reduced from 1,018 km² to 1003 km²; between 1960 and 1970, that of Igarape-Açú was reduced from 1,213 km² to 756 km² and of Bragança from 4,163 km² to 3,258 km².
Source: IBGE, *Anuários Estatísticos do Brasil.*

like Castanhal lately increasing in size and prosperity, but further to the east, along the route of the old railway line, there is limited evidence of recovery from the original impact of colonisation. Out-migration from the latter area is higher and traditional agricultural practices more persistent (see Table 16).

Various factors have contributed to the failure of early planned colonisation in the Bragantina zone. Some observers have drawn attention to the limited agricultural experience of many of the original settlers (Kass, 1976), and to the archaic and rudimentary cultivation techniques they employed (Penteado, 1967). These factors need also to be set against the local environmental conditions, which, in the absence of fertilisers and other technical inputs, were bound to preclude permanent cultivation of most short-cycle crops. In these circumstances, the assumptions behind the original colonisation were clearly over-optimistic and the consequent mal-adaptive exploitation scarcely surprising. In the late nineteenth century, it is understandable that the existence of luxuriant forest should have been taken to indicate favourable soil conditions, but unfortunately the assumption was false. Latterly, some attempts have been made to achieve sustainable land exploitation with the aid of fertilisers and pesticides, but efforts have been belated and of limited significance in relation to the overall extent of forest clearance. According to Sioli (1980), some 3.0 million ha of forest land have now been colonised and degraded in and around the Bragantina zone.

Peasant colonisation in the upper Caquetá basin

More recently, pioneer colonisation of forest land has been undertaken by

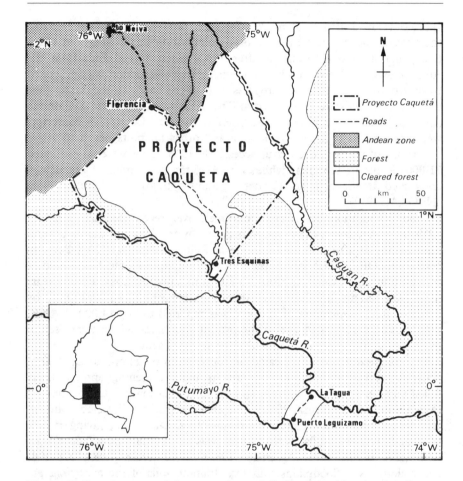

Figure 12 Location map of the upper Caquetá basin, Colombia, showing *Proyecto Caquetá* (after Benilla, 1966; Landsat images)

migrant farmers in parts of Colombian Amazonia. In contrast to Bragantina, the colonisation has mostly been spontaneous in character and involved the development of unintensive cattle rearing. Colonisation first occurred in the upper Putumayo and Caquetá basins, and has latterly extended into the Guaviare basin (Wesche, 1967; Kirby, 1978; Ortiz, 1980). The most extensive of the colonisation zones is that of the upper Caquetá, where an estimated 2.5 million ha of lowland forest have been cleared and settled, mainly since the 1950s (Domínguez, 1987) (see Figure 12).

In the late nineteenth century, extraction of wild rubber, quinine and other forest products was taking place in the upper Caquetá. The small settlement of Florencia, which was established by Catholic missionaries in

1902, developed as a local market for such products. During the 1920s, there was some government-sponsored colonisation in the area, but effective penetration only occurred after 1932, when a road link from the Andean town of Neiva reached Florencia. Its construction was provoked by a frontier war then in progress with Peru, and at the same time military outposts were established at Tres Esquinas and Puerto Leguízamo (Crist & Guhl, 1957; Bonilla, 1966). After the war, Colombian conscripts were encouraged to settle in the area and other migrants began to arrive as a result of the improved road access. By 1938, there were an estimated 21,000 people in the area, while, by 1951, the population of the newly-designated Intendencia del Caquetá amounted to 41,000 (Bonilla, 1966; INCORA, 1973).

Land colonisation has largely continued over recent decades. Between 1959 and 1961, colonisation was supervised by the Caja Agraria and thereafter by the Instituto Colombiano de la Reforma Agraria (INCORA). In 1963, INCORA established the Proyecto Caquetá which covered a colonisation zone extending from Florencia to Tres Esquinas. Recent years have seen serious political and other disturbances in the area, but, by 1985, the total population of Caquetá was reported to be 214,000 (DANE, 1986); most were located within the project area, although scattered settlement extended along the Caquetá river to La Tagua.

The colonisation zone is located on the Andean piedmont at 250–500 m above sea level. Rainfall in the area is high, averaging approximately 4,000 mm per annum at Florencia, with somewhat lower totals to the east (Ministerio de Agricultura, 1985). The area comprises a dissected sedimentary landscape. Parent materials are mostly fine-textured, giving rise to acid and infertile soils with high levels of exchangeable aluminium (Benavides et al., 1975; Alvarado, 1982). More fertile parent materials occur along river floodplains, but free-draining soils of the terra firme are mostly Orthic or Xanthic Ferralsols (FAO–UNESCO, 1971).

Colonisation of the upper Caquetá has been undertaken by migrants from Andean Colombia, who commonly left the highlands as a result of rural violence and inequitable land ownership (Hayter & Watson, 1985). Migration to the lowlands has been encouraged by the government, who viewed it as a means of relieving pressure on overcrowded Andean cities. When the Caja Agraria programme was initiated in 1959, 700,000 ha of forest land around Florencia were formally designated for colonisation. The Caja Agraria, primarily a credit agency, focused its attention on three areas of planned colonisation near Florencia. Holdings of 50–75 ha were allocated as well as some larger units of 267 ha, and over a three-year period several hundred families were settled (Bonilla, 1966). In the same period, several thousand other migrants arrived and settled spontaneously on the land.

In 1961, INCORA assumed responsibility for land colonisation, and soon afterwards established the Proyecto Caquetá which extended the formal colonisation zone to 1.3 million ha. Under INCORA, some support for planned colonisation continued, but assistance was mostly given to spontaneous colonists who were arriving in increasing numbers. On their behalf, INCORA sought to allocate land holdings, provide credit, and build roads, hospitals and schools (Ortiz, 1984). Originally, it was planned to allocate individual holdings of 85–100 ha, of which 75 ha or more were intended for pasture development, but the majority of holdings did not in fact attain this size (Kirby, 1976). During the 1970s, the INCORA programme was supported by major loans from the World Bank which were specifically, if not always effectively, expended on 'integrated rural development' in areas of spontaneous colonisation (Hayter & Watson, 1985).

While land colonisation in the upper Caquetá is broadly concerned with the establishment of pasture on cleared forest land, a transitional agricultural phase usually occurs. After initial cutting and burning of the forest, colonists plant crops like maize and manioc for two or three years on the ash-enriched soil. Thereafter, a few hectares may be devoted to manioc, sugar cane or bananas, but most of the holding is converted to pasture and cattle are introduced (Bonilla, 1966; Ministerio de Agricultura, 1985). Beef production is the priority, with only a few holdings devoted to dairying. Beef herds, mainly of zebu-*criollo* stock, are reared on an unintensive basis. Overall livestock density has been estimated at 0.84 animals/ha (INCORA, 1973), with local variations reflecting pasture quality and management. Various reasons exist for the regional emphasis on cattle rearing, not least of which is the social status attached to the activity. It is also relatively easy for an unskilled colonist to clear an area of forest and create pasture. Capital or credit is required to obtain cattle, but, once established, the animals are a marketable commodity which can be readily walked from isolated holdings and trucked to Andean urban centres (PRORADAM, 1979; Ortiz, 1980).

In spite of the basic attractions, cattle rearing creates problems for colonists. After initial land clearance and cultivation, improved pastures are normally established with grasses like *Hyparrhenia rufa*, *Brachiaria decumbens* or *Axonopus micay*. Initially, these pastures support relatively high cattle densities, but pasture productivity is difficult to sustain and carrying capacities fall (PRORADAM, 1979). At La Tagua, initial densities of 2 animals/ha are reported, but they drop to 0.5–0.8 animals/ha within a few years of clearance (Benavides et al., 1975). The low inherent nutrient status of the soil, particularly in respect of phosphorus, and reduced pasture productivity as ash inputs are depleted are mainly responsible for the declining carrying capacity. Conditions are further aggravated by the overgrazing that commonly occurs as carrying capacity itself declines. Trampling and compaction of the clayey soils tend to result,

Photograph 18 Incipient weed invasion in recently-derived pasture near La Tagua, upper Caquetá basin, south-east Colombia

which in turn lead to drainage and erosion problems. Careful land management can mitigate the worst of these effects, but other problems arise in the form of persistent weed and shrub invasion, particularly on overgrazed land (see Photograph 18). Such invasion can be controlled by burning, but this complicates attempts to maintain improved pastures and fencing. As a result of weed and shrub invasion, pastures are commonly abandoned to woody regrowth after a few years, although they may be cleared again within 5–10 years (Benavides *et al.*, 1975; Alvarado, 1982).

The poor quality of pasture in the upper Caquetá directly affects the condition of livestock. This is particularly apparent in the low reproductive rates of cattle and the incidence of nutritionally-related diseases (Ministerio de Agricultura, 1972; PRORADAM, 1979). Livestock also face other health problems, including brucellosis, foot and mouth disease, and various parasitic infections. Some attempts are made to provide food supplements in the form of salt licks and to supply animal health care, but the general levels of management are poor and rearing mostly remains unintensive. As a result, beef production in the area is low, with an annual extraction of only 80,000–90,000 animals from a beef herd in excess of one million (Ministerio de Agricultura, 1985).

The development of cattle rearing is further constrained by the pattern of land holding. In spite of INCORA's original intention to allocate individual holdings of 85–100 ha, many earlier allocations were less than

50 ha, which, under existing conditions, were frequently insufficient to support a colonist and his family. Some colonists managed to survive on such holdings with 25–35 cattle, but many were unable to produce an adequate saleable surplus of animals and were obliged to sell out. Some remained on the land as sharecroppers or leaseholders, but many moved on to clear fresh forest land (Kirby, 1978). As a result larger holdings emerged through amalgamation, although these were rarely more intensively used and provided employment for only a few people. Landholding patterns have fluctuated somewhat of late, but the general trend towards larger holdings has persisted. By 1984, some 50 per cent of farms in the area were 50–500 ha in extent, covering about 80 per cent of the settled area; the remaining settled area was broadly divided between small (< 50 ha) and large (> 500 ha) holdings (Domínguez, 1987).

Over the years, some attempts have been made to encourage more intensive agricultural activities as an alternative to cattle raising. In the 1960s, areas of oil palm (320 ha) and rubber (400 ha) were planted by INCORA, but recurrent technical and other problems were encountered and no substantial development of the crops has occurred (Bonnaire, 1970; PRORADAM, 1979; Ministerio de Agricultura, 1985). Cacao and coffee have also been established, but production levels remain low, while the prospects for commercial cultivation of short-cycle crops like rice or sugar cane are limited by competition from more favourable Andean areas such as the Cauca valley (Kirby, 1976, 1978). Much of the agriculture in the upper Caquetá thus remains transitional and impermanent in character and is orientated towards subsistence or local markets. An exception to this, of course, is coca (*Erythroxylum coca*), which is produced locally as a cash crop, and also illicitly imported and processed for re-export as cocaine.

In spite of the principal emphasis in the area on cattle rearing, limited progress has been made towards more intensive pasture exploitation. Some experimental work has been initiated with forage grasses and legumes (PRORADAM, 1979, Alvarado, 1982), but the main trend is towards amalgamation of smaller holdings and clearance of fresh forest land as a basis for continuing low-input beef production. Government involvement in the colonisation process has focused on the allocation of land holdings and the provision of services and infrastructure, but levels of support have often been poor and limited efforts have been made to control the spread of extensive exploitation. Unstable pioneer colonisation widely prevails and, although in places private investment has been made in the land and some successful rancher-colonists have emerged, little opportunity exists for the majority of settlers permanently to establish themselves on the land. Meanwhile, the dispersed nature of the population complicates the provision of basic government services, which have in any case latterly been disrupted or deflected by the activities of guerrilla groups and *narcotraficantes* (Bagley, 1986; Domínguez, 1987). Admittedly, there is abundant land in the Caquetá basin to accommodate spontaneous colonists, but, as in the adjoining Putumayo and Guaviare zones, such colonisation offers poor prospects for most settlers and causes widespread forest destruction. A few attempts have been made to establish forest reserves in the colonisation zone, but these have failed, while the area of cleared and degraded forest land continues to expand (Spears, 1980; Hayter & Watson, 1985).

Peasant colonisation of the Altamira zone

Small-scale land colonisation has also been attempted along the Brazilian Transamazon highway. Following an acute drought in north-east Brazil in 1970, construction of the highway was ordered by President Médici who saw it as a means of giving *nordestinos* access to Amazonian forest land. In broader terms, the aim was to integrate the resources of Amazonia into the strategy of national economic development, for which purpose a new Programa de Integração Nacional (PIN) was created (Moran, 1981). By 1972, the Transamazon highway had extended as far as Itaituba on the Tapajós river, passing through the settlements of Marabá and Altamira, and, by 1974, it had reached Humaitá on the Madeira river. From Estreito in the east to Humaitá in the west the Transamazon highway covered a distance of 2,320 km (INCRA, 1972; Kleinpenning, 1979; Smith, 1982).

The forest land along the highway was reserved for small-scale planned colonisation, with initial settlement occurring in the Marabá–Altamira–Itaituba sector (see Figure 10). High rates of malaria around Marabá and poor soils in the vicinity of Itaituba, however, resulted in most attention being focused on a stretch of highway 20–120 km west of Altamira (IPEAN, 1974; Kleinpenning, 1979; Moran, 1981). Altamira itself lies on the Xingú river some 270 km above its junction with the Amazon mainstream. The settlement, which originated in the seventeenth century, had previously developed as a minor centre for the extraction of forest products. It underwent some expansion during the rubber boom but, by 1960, had a population of only 3,500 (Moran, 1981). The construction of the highway provided a major boost for Altamira, which, by 1980, contained approximately 30,000 people (Smith, 1982). A similar number was reported to have settled along the highway west of the town, where planned and some spontaneous colonisation occurred. By mid-1976, the total area brought under cultivation in the Altamira zone was estimated at 22,000–25,000 ha (Kleinpenning, 1979).

The Altamira zone is drier than many parts of Amazonia, with a mean annual rainfall of 1,705 mm. Rainfall varies inter-annually, but there are generally 4–5 dry months in the year (Falesi, 1972; Moran, 1981). Soils in the area are mostly acid Ferralsols, although west of Altamira, where the Transamazon highway skirts the margin of the Brazilian Shield, there are local occurrences of *terra roxa estruturada*, or Eutric Nitosols. These soils are developed over diabase and basalt rocks and are relatively fertile (Falesi, 1972; Camargo & Falesi, 1975; Smith, 1982). Much of the land along this part of the highway, however, is of undulating relief and is very susceptible to soil erosion when the forest is cleared (Fearnside, 1980b; Smith, 1982).

The colonisation programme envisaged planned settlement of peasant farmers on land along the Transamazon highway. The intention was to construct nucleated villages, or *agrovilas*, at intervals of 10 km along the highway and on side-roads into the forest (Smith, 1982). New urban centres, known as *agrópoles* and *rurópoles*, were also to be built. Around the *agrovilas*, individual families were allocated rectangular plots of 100 ha, although it was decreed that at least 50 per cent of each holding should remain under forest (Goodland & Irwin, 1975). The Instituto Nacional de Colonização e Reforma Agraria (INCRA) assumed general responsibility for the settlement process, including the selection of colonists, allocation of land and provision of technical support. Other agencies were responsible for providing credit, education and health facilities. The plan was to settle 100,000 families along the highway by 1974. Originally, it was intended to settle *nordestinos*, but this was soon modified to allow the inclusion of more 'suitable' settlers from other parts of Brazil (Martine, 1980; Moran, 1981). Initially, dry rice cultivation was promoted and there were longer-term plans for the production of high-value cash crops, notably cacao, black pepper and coffee (Smith, 1982).

In reality, the planned colonisation fell far short of its objectives. According to Kleinpenning (1979), only twenty-nine *agrovilas* were completed, and, as early as 1973, INCRA had abandoned their construction as many colonists preferred to live on their dispersed individual holdings. By end-1974, INCRA had settled 5,717 families along the Marabá–Altamira–Itaituba sector of the highway, of whom 3,095 (54 per cent) were located in the Altamira zone. Only a third of the colonists were direct migrants from north-east Brazil (Chaloult, 1980).

In spite of the existence of some *terra roxa* soils along the highway, agricultural productivity was disappointing. The initial emphasis was on dry rice cultivation, but unsuitable varieties were introduced and weed and pest problems were encountered. According to Smith (1978), rice yields in the years 1972–4 averaged only 1,243 kg/ha, and there were problems with local transport and marketing that further impaired crop profitability. Even poorer yields were recorded for maize and beans, which suffered from fungal disease and pest damage (Smith, 1978; Moran, 1981). Some of the problems could have been reduced by use of fertilisers and pesticides, but few colonists used them (Kleinpenning, 1979). The recommended cash crops like cacao and black pepper were similarly in need of

Table 17 Production of principal crops in
the Altamira colonisation zone in 1972/1973
and 1977/1978 (tons)

	1972–3	1977–8
Rice	5,873	24,000
Beans	580	875
Maize	2,131	1,758
Black pepper	–	877
Cacao	–	274
Sugar cane	–	280,000

Source: Chaloult, 1980.

fertilisers, and were also vulnerable to fungal diseases like witches' broom (*Marasmius perniciosus*) and black pod (*Phytophthora palmivora*) in the case of cacao and the root fungus *Fusarium solani* in the case of black pepper (EMBRAPA, 1978; Fearnside, 1978; Allen, 1983). Other crops planted along the highway were manioc and bananas, as well as sugar cane which was intended to supply a newly-built mill and alcohol processing plant west of Altamira. A few settlers also acquired cattle (see Table 17).

Peasant colonisation along the Transamazon highway in the early 1970s did not make an immediate and significant contribution to regional agricultural production, and as a result there was a shift in official policy towards larger-scale commercial development (Kleinpenning, 1979; Martine, 1980). In 1973, INCRA began promoting the sale of larger land holdings in the area, and in the following year this policy was formally incorporated into the new Programa de Pólos Agropecuários e Agro-minerais da Amazônia (POLAMAZONIA). The programme, which moved away from a linear development model associated with highway colonisa-tion, sought to achieve a more concentrated pattern of regional land development; among the areas designated for development was the *polo agropecuário* Altamira (Anon., 1976; Mahar, 1979; Smith, 1982). Therein, INCRA continued its original colonisation activities on a limited scale, increasing the number of families on smallholdings from 3,095 at end-1974 to 3,595 at end-1978 (Kleinpenning, 1979; Smith, 1982). In addition, it devoted attention to opening up new forest areas with larger holdings of 3,000 ha and above. These were located beyond the original smallholdings and were intended for commercial cattle rearing. Some medium-sized units of 500 ha were also allocated. Altogether 2.7 million ha of forest land were designated for larger land holdings (Kleinpenning, 1979; Chaloult, 1980; Smith, 1982). A trend to larger units also developed in the original colonisation zone where amalgamation of some of the 100 ha holdings occurred, again mostly with cattle rearing in view (Moran, 1981).

While these changes constituted a clear shift in emphasis from socially-orientated to more commercial land development, the official view was also expressed that they would 'promote the maintenance of the ecological balance' (Martine, 1980). The prospects for cattle ranching did not justify such optimism. As in the upper Caquetá, severe problems of pasture maintenance arose as a result of progressive nutrient depletion after clearance and of weed and shrub invasion. Much of the pasture that was established along the Transamazon highway became choked with secondary growth within a few years of establishment, and livestock carrying capacities fell to low levels (Fearnside, 1979; Smith, 1982). Speculative profits could still be made from land sales, but the economic return on ranching itself was limited. Any recuperation of the pasture soils for crop cultivation was also viewed as extremely difficult without massive additions of fertiliser and possibly ploughing (Smith, 1982).

While the crop and livestock systems established in the Altamira zone were in many respects mal-adaptive, particularly in the absence of fertilisers and other technical inputs, institutional factors have also constrained development. In particular, it has been pointed out that inadequate preliminary land surveys and economic feasibility studies were undertaken, and that, once colonists were established on the ground, levels of agronomic assistance, road maintenance, and general social provision were poor (Kleinpenning, 1979; Martine, 1980). In more fundamental terms, such problems are seen to reflect the centralised and bureaucratic nature of Brazilian officialdom (Martine, 1980; Moran, 1981).

In spite of the perceived failure of early Transamazon colonisation, some small farmers managed successfully to establish themselves along the highway, and it has been argued that the small-scale colonisation programme was prematurely abandoned (Moran, 1979, 1981; Martine, 1980). In 1973–4, however, the overall results of small-scale colonisation in the Altamira zone, with its low average productivity, its slow progress in cash cropping and its high turnover of colonists, were not overly impressive, and it was easy enough for the Brazilian government, under pressure of commercial interests, to re-direct the colonisation programme (Branford & Glock, 1985). Unfortunately, the resultant encouragement of larger-scale cattle rearing in the area was not the way to achieve more productive use of the land or to reduce rates at which the land was being cleared and degraded.

Cattle ranching in northern Mato Grosso

Comparable lessons were also being learnt elsewhere in Brazilian Amazonia, notably in northern Mato Grosso and eastern Pará where similar, large-scale cattle ranching on cleared forest land was under way. In northern Mato Grosso, forest clearance mostly commenced in the

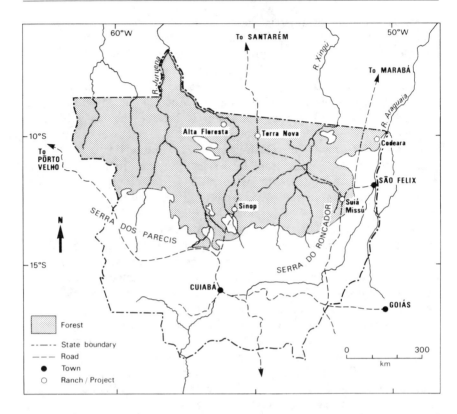

Figure 13 Location map of northern Mato Grosso, showing forest area and selected development projects

1960s. By 1980, there were probably 1–2 million ha of derived pasture in the area (Davis, 1977; Serrão *et al.*, 1978; Hecht, 1981), since when a further several million ha seem likely to have been cleared (Nelson *et al.*, 1987; Margolis, 1988a). The main ranching areas in northern Mato Grosso are Barra do Garças and Luciara, which form part of the *polo agropecuário* Xingú-Araguaia, designated in 1974 (Anon., 1976).

Northern Mato Grosso, lying astride the *hylaea-cerrado* margin, has annual rainfall in the range 1,500–2,500 mm, with a marked dry season in mid-year. The forest zone in the north is drained by rivers originating in the sandstone plateaus of Serra dos Parecis and Serra do Roncador (see Figure 13). Arenosols occur in the latter areas, but recent forest clearance is mostly located on adjacent land with medium to fine-textured Acrisols and Ferralsols (FAO–UNESCO, 1971).

In earlier times, the eastern part of the Mato Grosso forest was largely closed to settlers because of attacks from Xavante Indians (Davis, 1977). The Indians were 'pacified' in the mid-1940s and, following construction of the Belém–Brasília highway, colonisation of the area began in earnest. During the 1960s, many large ranches were established on forest land and, particularly from 1966, rates of forest clearance increased in response to the fiscal incentives provided through the newly-established Super-intendência do Desenvolvimento da Amazônia (SUDAM). The incentives, in the form of tax rebates to companies taking up ranching, were intended to encourage large-scale beef production for export and the national market. By 1979, there were at least thirty such livestock projects approved by SUDAM on forest land in northern Mato Grosso (Pandolfo, 1979). Many of them were set up by business groups from São Paulo. They included the vast Agro-Pecuária Suiá Missú, covering more than 500,000 ha, and the Companhia de Desenvolvimento do Araguaia (CODEARA), occupying 196,000 ha. Over the years, many other holdings of 20,000 ha and above have been established (Davis, 1977; Branford & Glock, 1985).

Forest clearance on these large ranches is necessarily progressive in character. In places, peasant farmers may already occupy part of the land which is then appropriated and turned over to pasture. Elsewhere, farmers are allowed on to as yet uncleared land for a year or two until it is ready to be converted to pasture. Direct conversion also takes place where the forest is cleared by labour gangs or with caterpillar tractors (Kleinpenning, 1975; Denevan, 1981). Clearance itself takes place in the dry season, at the end of which the accumulated forest debris is fired. Further cutting and burning is often required for another year or two to dispose of the residual debris and regrowth, but thereafter the pasture becomes established. The cattle in use are zebu, often Gir and Nellore breeds. At Suiá Missú, where forest clearance began in the early 1960s, Smith (1971) reported that 250 men with axes were able to fell 1,200–1,400 ha during each dry season, after which the debris was fired. Introduced grasses sown on the ash-enriched soil were *Panicum maximum*, *Hyparrhenia rufa* and *Pennisetum purpureum*. Once a grass cover was established, cattle were brought in and a breeding programme started. By the late 1960s, the Suiá Missú ranch had 15,000 cattle on 12,000 ha of cleared land, at a density of 1.25 animals/ha. By 1979, the number had risen to 85,000 cattle on 78,500 ha, although, in subsequent years, degrading pastures enforced a major reduc-tion in the cattle population (Smith, 1971; Branford & Glock, 1985) (see Photograph 19).

Throughout northern Mato Grosso, colonião (*Panicum maximum*) has been the most widely introduced forage grass. Using nutrients from ash residues, the species provides good initial pasture on cleared forest land, and has in fact been claimed to improve soil fertility levels (Falesi, 1976). The claim is questionable, however, since favourable pasture productivity usually only persists for a period of four or five years. Thereafter, there is a marked decline in yield and parallel reduction in livestock carrying

Photograph 19 Cleared forest land on Suiá Missú ranch (arrowed), northern Mato Grosso, Brazil. Landsat MSS band 5 image subscene, July 1978, ID no. 378208–124801 (reproduced by courtesy of CNPq/INPE, Brazil)

capacity (Serrão *et al.*, 1978; Fearnside, 1979; Serrão & Toledo, 1988). On older pastures, carrying capacities rarely exceed 0.3 animals/ha (Sioli, 1980).

As elsewhere in Amazonia, a critical constraint on pasture growth is nutrient supply. Nutrient losses occur as a result of burning of forest debris and of subsequent soil leaching and erosion, while low phosphorus availability is prevalent in areas with more acid soils. The latter problem is most acute in clayey soils, and, although it can be overcome by applications of fertiliser, this is not usually seen as economic (Fearnside, 1980a; Hecht, 1985). With time, soil nitrogen supplies also tend to become limiting. Soil physical changes, particularly topsoil compaction, also adversely affect the growth and maintenance of pasture grasses. As well as *Panicum maximum*, other grasses have been introduced into the area. They include the less demanding and more aggressive *Brachiaria decumbens*, although its use has been curtailed by serious attacks of spittle bug (*Deois incompleta*); latterly, *B. humidicola* has also been widely introduced. In general, these grasses provide good initial forage, but their performance is still limited by declining soil fertility and other problems as pastures age (Serrão *et al.*, 1978; Hecht, 1981; Dias Filho, 1983; Branford & Glock, 1985).

As elsewhere, declining pasture productivity is paralleled by weed invasion. As the vigour of forage grasses diminishes, herbaceous and woody weeds increasingly invade the pasture. Some of the weeds provide useful browse, but readily dominate the introduced forage grasses. Weeding and periodic burning are undertaken and some use is made of biocides, but weed control becomes increasingly difficult and costly as the years pass (Serrão *et al.*, 1978). As well as suppressing forage grasses, invading weeds also include toxic species that can kill livestock (Gonçalves *et al.*, 1974; Dantas & Rodrigues, 1980).

As a result of deteriorating soils and weed invasion, large areas of derived pasture in northern Mato Grosso have become degraded and in places been abandoned. Conditions vary locally. Serrão *et al.* (1978) cite the existence of productive 17-year old pastures of *Panicum maximum* which have never been fertilised, but conditions are rarely as favourable. Surveys made by the Instituto de Pesquisas Espaciais (INPE) in Barro do Garças in the late 1970s showed that about half the pastures in the area were degraded (Hecht, 1981). In these cases, the condition of the pasture is usually related to grazing intensity. In places, ranchers are prepared to overstock newly-cleared land for five years or so and then dispose of it in a degraded state. The land is initially used for fattening steers, which are robust and tolerate weedy pastures better than breeding cows with calves (Hecht, 1971). The overstocking accelerates the rate of weed invasion and general pasture deterioration, but profits accrue from the sale of animals, while the land itself appreciates in value in spite of its condition. The

profits are available to underwrite continuing speculative exploitation at
the expense of land resources (Fearnside, 1980a). While not all ranchers
are as predatory, this pattern has been a common one in northern Mato
Grosso and reflected in a high turnover of land titles (Mahar, 1979; Hecht,
1981).

The problems of sustaining extensive ranching on cleared forest land
have become apparent to ranchers and government alike (Goodland &
Irwin, 1977; Fearnside, 1980a; Buschbacher, 1986a). In theory, the
production system could be sustained with technical inputs and lower
stocking levels, but this strategy is scarcely economic and certainly less
profitable than pioneer ranching based on short-term overstocking and
early land disposal. Damaging as the latter system is, it represents a
rational course of action for the individual rancher, especially when fiscal
incentives are on offer (Fearnside, 1980a) and it continues in many areas.
However, in the late 1970s, reductions were occurring in the tax rebates
available to ranching companies, and this, added to the problems they
were experiencing on the ground, obliged them to review their status and
prospects. As indicated, a common strategy was to sell land after over-
exploiting it for a few years, but, although this accommodates the vendor,
it fails to resolve the problems of what is best for the land itself. In the
cases of both Suiá Missú and CODEARA, the policy has been to try to
sustain livestock production, in spite of recurrent problems with pasture
quality and general profitability. During the 1980s, however, both
companies have sought to diversify their operations by planting cash crops
like rubber, sugar cane, cacao and soya bean (Branford & Glock, 1985).

Elsewhere in northern Mato Grosso, a similar trend is apparent with the
emergence of privately-sponsored land development schemes. In this case,
development companies acquire large tracts of land and sub-divide them
into small or medium-sized holdings. The holdings are then sold, often at
considerable profit, to migrant farmers from southern Brazil and
elsewhere, who are encouraged to develop cash cropping. Several projects
of this kind, notably Sinop, Terra Nova and Alta Floresta, have been
established along the Cuiabá–Santarém highway (see Figure 13). It is
difficult to evaluate the long-term prospects of these ventures, although
their early performance has at times been encouraging (Dubé, 1980; Branford & Glock, 1985). Irrespective of their prospects, however, the
existence of such schemes is a measure of the failure of large-scale cattle
ranching to provide a sustainable basis for forest exploitation in northern
Mato Grosso.

Conclusion

The present studies of land exploitation on the forested *terra firme* cover traditional extractive activities, small-scale land colonisation and larger-scale commercial enterprises. Individual areas vary in the nature of their exploitation, but some commonalities exist. In the case of rubber and timber, traditional extraction persists in the face of ecological and other problems encountered in attempts at cultivation. Such extraction varies in its impact on the forest; rubber collecting is relatively benign, while selective logging is more disruptive. However, both activities are associated with the frontier of settlement and neither is readily maintained in the face of extending agriculture or cattle ranching. In the longer term, extractive activities are only likely to survive, if at all, in dedicated managed reserves (Sternberg, 1987; Gradwohl & Greenberg, 1988).

In the case of pioneer land colonisation, initial production from cleared and burnt forest land is favourable, but difficult to sustain, whether the area is used for crop cultivation or livestock rearing. Progressive land degradation tends to occur and the settler is frequently obliged or chooses to move on to fresh forest land. Such pioneer colonisation is undertaken by both peasant and large-scale producers on the *terra firme* and is, by its very nature, self-perpetuating. The 'degraded vegetation and decadent agriculture' (Valverde & Dias, 1967) of the long-settled Bragantina zone illustrate perfectly the depressing aftermath of this process, which is now widespread on the *terra firme*.

Unstable land colonisation of this kind is comprehensible in ecological terms. Nutrient depletion and other soil changes consequent upon land clearance commonly limit crop or pasture growth and result in lowered yields. Biotic stressors also reduce the productivity of crop plants and livestock. Weeds are a particular nuisance in derived pastures, but compete with crop plants wherever the forest cover is removed. Crop pests and diseases are equally troublesome. As is apparent, their impact on long-cycle trees crops is particularly damaging, but short-cycle crops and pasture grasses are also vulnerable. In the case of rubber, prolonged research has been undertaken into South American leaf blight (*Microcyclus ulei*) and a degree of control achieved, but there are many other susceptible crops and innumerable potential pests and diseases.

Unstable exploitation is often inherent in the agrosystems employed on the *terra firme*, especially when fertilisers and other industrial inputs are lacking or little used by reason of cost or colonists' inexperience. This applies at the crop plant level, when farmers or farm managers seek to cultivate species or varieties that are unsuited to local conditions. This is exemplified by the nutrient-demanding grain crops that were initially promoted along the Transamazon highway. Pest-prone pasture grasses, like *Brachiaria*, have likewise been introduced on ranches in northern Mato Grosso and elsewhere, with limiting effects on productivity. At the crop community level, mal-adaptive systems have also been introduced. This is most evident in the case of monocultural plantings of crops like rubber and cacao, which are highly vulnerable to particular fungal infections. Clearly, more attention is required to selecting crops and designing agrosystems that are adapted to the particular conditions of the *terra firme*.

Agrosystem performance also depends on external factors relating to infrastructure and services. Road building is often the initial spur to land colonisation, but if colonisation is to succeed, roads also need to be properly maintained. Equally, colonisation of new areas is dependent on adequate preliminary land surveys and agronomic experimentation. If such are not undertaken, unsuitable crops and agrosystems will be encouraged and prospects for longer-term development undermined. In addition, the success or otherwise of land colonisation depends on the quality of extension services, credit provision, marketing facilities and the like. While shortcomings in these directions were understandable in the Bragantina zone a century ago, inadequate or mal-orientated support for the contemporary colonist, and consequent encouragement of pioneer exploitation, represent a lamentable failure to learn from earlier experience. Unless proper support is provided at institutional and ultimately political levels, it is unrealistic to expect sustainable land development to occur, irrespective of the nature of the colonisation involved.

Such of course assumes that sustainable production is the aim of land colonisation. This is broadly so, but explicit pursuit of unstable exploitation does occur and can be a rational enough strategy for the individual concerned. This certainly applies in ranching areas like northern Mato Grosso, where forest land is progressively cleared, heavily grazed for a few years, and then disposed of in favour of fresh clearance. This provides continuous access to productive, newly-established pasture as well as the considerable profit of disposing of land that has appreciated in value while deteriorating in quality (Mahar, 1979; Fearnside, 1980a). In ecological terms, the impact of such colonisation is probably no more damaging than where the original land user sought, but failed, to achieve permanent exploitation, but eventual stabilisation of land use may be more difficult.

Although both extractivism and pioneer colonisation are widespread on the *terra firme*, it is obvious that sustainable agrosystems will eventually have to be introduced, as land exploitation progressively removes existing forest. The increased market value of cleared, albeit degraded, forest land is presumably some indication of long-term commercial confidence in this view. However, more immediate pursuit of sustainable exploitation is required not only to increase land productivity, but also to curtail forest clearance and thus minimise positive feedbacks on regional climate and hydrology and on genetic resources. These broader issues will later be discussed, but consideration is first given, in Chapter 6, to contemporary exploitation of Amazonian wetlands and dry savannas.

6

Modern colonisation and exploitation in wetlands and savannas

Not all of Amazonia is covered with tropical moist forest . . .
[Goodland, 1980, p. 6]

The rivers of Amazonia provided the pathways of early European exploration, and many new settlements were established along riparian zones. Although indigenous society was largely destroyed in these areas, the emerging *caboclo* or *colono* society included elements of the indigenous population and adopted many of its cultural practices. A range of resources was exploited by colonists, although the specific emphasis on *várzea* cultivation that characterised pre-Columbian society was not generally reproduced. Colonists made occasional use of the *várzea* for food cropping, but more attention was devoted to shifting cultivation on the margins of the *terra firme* (Ross, 1978a). Attempts were also made to produce cash crops like sugar cane and cacao on the *várzea* and in coastal and estuarine wetlands, but few such developments survived into the present century (Le Cointe, 1922; Panday, 1959). More recently, other cash crops like jute and wet rice have been introduced to the Amazon valley, but it is only in the coastal Guianas that substantial commercial wetland cultivation has persisted from Colonial times to the present (Mandle, 1973). In contrast, the indigenous tradition of fishing has been widely maintained in the *várzea* zone, and cattle have been reared in the lower Amazon valley and estuarine zone since their introduction in early Colonial times (Sutmöller *et al.*, 1966; OEA, 1974).

Although less accessible than many wetlands, Amazonian savannas were often explored and settled in Colonial times. This was the case with the Rio Branco–Rupununi savanna, to which cattle were introduced in the late eighteenth century (Rivière, 1972). The Gran Sabana in Venezuela was similarly penetrated in late Colonial times, coming under the influence of missionaries who likewise brought in cattle (Anon., 1949; Layrisse & Wilbert, 1966). Some isolated savannas remained unvisited, notably the Ariramba savanna of the Trombetas basin and the Puciari–Humaitá savannas which were reputedly unexplored until the late nineteenth century (Braun & Ramos, 1959; Egler, 1960). Cattle-raising apart, Amazonian savannas offered few opportunities for the early colonist and they mostly remained as sparsely settled as in pre-Columbian times. Recent decades have seen only scattered and tentative attempts to upgrade their exploitation.

With a few exceptions, Amazonian wetlands and savannas have been neglected in recent development planning in comparison to the forested *terra firme*, and little attention has been paid to their environmental future. Some local interest exists in the agricultural development of wetlands and their potential for protein production is recognised, but Amazonian savannas have received scant consideration. Nevertheless, the overall extent of wetlands (93.2 million ha) and savannas (15–20 million ha) is substantial and, particularly in the light of their perceived natural resilience and reduced pest incidence (Goodland & Irwin, 1977), they warrant additional attention. On this basis, selected wetlands and savannas are here examined in order to illustrate the nature and range of their contemporary settlement and resource use; consideration is given to riparian exploitation in the middle Caquetá valley and along the mainstream of the lower Amazon, to agricultural exploitation in coastal Guyana, and to cattle ranching in the Rio Branco–Rupununi savanna.

Resource use in the middle Caquetá valley

The Caquetá–Japurá river, a major north-western tributary of the Amazon, illustrates the pattern of settlement and exploitation that characterises many of the more isolated riparian zones in the region. Substantial settlement apparently existed along parts of the river in pre-Columbian times (Eden *et al.*, 1984; Andrade, 1986), but most of the valley is today very sparsely settled. Peasant migrants from Andean Colombia have colonised the upper Caquetá basin in recent times (see Chapter 5), but within the middle Caquetá valley from Tres Esquinas to La Pedrera, a distance of some 700 km, the population totals only 9,000–10,000 people and the adjacent forest hinterland is virtually unoccupied (PRORADAM, 1979). Mid-way along the river lie the twin settlements of Araracuara and Puerto Santander, which are the main foci in the region, but their combined population is only a few hundred and local land development is minimal (see Figure 14).

The Caquetá itself is a white water river that fluctuates several metres in level each year. The river meanders within its floodplain, which is mostly 5–10 km in breadth. Seasonal flooding deposits sediments on the land and the resultant soils, mainly Dystric Gleysols, are more fertile than those of the adjacent *terra firme*. In places, the river channel abuts on the elevated margin of the *terra firme* where most settlement occurs.

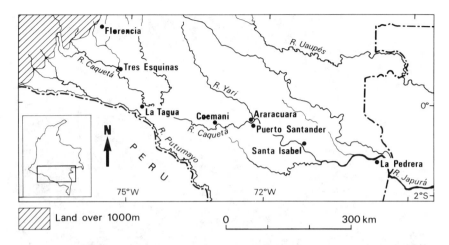

Figure 14 Location map of the Caquetá valley, south-east Colombia

Araracuara itself is located where up-faulted sandstones narrow and obstruct the main channel of the Caquetá, creating severe rapids and impeding river traffic (Eden *et al.*, 1982). Other settlements occupy elevated terrace sites along the river.

In the seventeenth century, Christóbal de Acuña made passing reference to the Caquetá, but there are no early accounts of exploration in the valley (Acuña, 1942; Hegen, 1966). For a long time, the hazardous rapids at Araracuara and other points along the river discouraged outside penetration and served to protect the indigenous population. With growing demand for wild rubber in the nineteenth century, however, these natural obstacles were overcome and first Colombian and then Peruvian rubber traders entered the adjacent Caquetá and Putumayo basins, which were at that time disputed territory (Camacho, 1975; Gómez Latorre, 1978). In subsequent decades, the Amerindian population was cruelly exploited and many thousands were exterminated, mainly at the hands of the infamous Anglo-Peruvian rubber company Casa Arana (Casement, 1912; Collier, 1968). Among the main victims were the Andoke, who once numbered 10,000 people, but today scarcely total 200 (Whiffen, 1915; Guzman, 1971; Corry, 1976).

The Colombian–Peruvian war of the early 1930s finally established the Caquetá basin as Colombian territory, and terminated the activities of Casa Arana (Corry, 1976). The settlement of Araracuara was established in 1939 and, with Puerto Santander, has developed as a regional administrative and service centre, with an air link to Bogotá (see Photograph 20). Elsewhere, scattered settlements occur along the river, often consisting of no more than a hut or two. There are occasional larger villages. Upstream of Araracuara, the first settlement of any size is Coemani, 65 km distant,

Photograph 20 Settlement of Puerto Santander, middle Caquetá valley, south-east Colombia

while downstream the village of Santa Isabel is 150 km away. Much of the population is of Amerindian ancestry, and many of the colonists in the valley have long acquaintance with it.

The middle Caquetá illustrates the traditional pattern of settlement and exploitation that persists in Amazonia beyond the frontier of modern land colonisation. Poorly-connected to the outside world, the valley remains relatively isolated and stagnant, and the present environmental impact is slight. Some local contrasts exist between indigenous and *colono* resource use, but subsistence exploitation is widespread and dependent on a variety of products from the floodplain and flanking *terra firme*. Both *colonos* and Amerindians practice shifting cultivation on the margins of the *terra firme*, growing mainly root crops and fruit trees. The *colonos* also cultivate the floodplain, which can be used for repeated seasonable cropping of maize, manioc and bananas. Higher yields can be obtained from this land, but cultivation is more risky and periodic crop losses occur as a result of untimely or excessive flooding. For *colonos*, the potential yields fully justify their use of this land, but Amerindians are much less inclined to exploit it (Eden & Andrade, 1988).

Hunting and fishing are also widespread. Game is available from the forest hinterland where tapir, deer, paca and other animals are acquired. The river is rich in fish, especially at times of low water when large catfish (*Brachyplatystoma* sp.), gambitana (*Colossoma* sp.) and other species are caught (Ramírez, 1958; PRORADAM, 1979). Local protein needs are mainly met from these sources, although small numbers of beef cattle are also available. In recent years, some commercial fishing has developed at Araracuara, based on small-scale refrigeration plants and air-freighting to Bogota.

In spite of the export of a few high-value products, including fish, small amounts of wild rubber and, in recent years, illicit coca (*Erythroxylum coca*), the economy of the middle Caquetá is still largely a subsistence one, supplemented by local trading. Resource use is highly diverse, but there is minimal pressure on the land, which today carries a much lower population than in earlier times.

While there seems no immediate risk of large-scale land colonisation in the middle Caquetá, any attempts to extend roads to the area from the Andean piedmont would induce substantial settlement and require effective land management. Periodic interest has been expressed in resource developments around Araracuara, both in respect of hydro-electricity generation and permanent agriculture (Panero, 1967; DAINCO, 1977), but colonisation activities are currently focused on more accessible parts of Colombian Amazonia. For the moment, the middle Caquetá valley, like other such zones, is protected by its relative isolation, although there are clearly no guarantees for the future.

Resource use in the lower Amazon valley

The lower Amazon valley was the scene of early European settlement, and many of its present centres of population date from Colonial times. Many settlements were located on the elevated margins of the *terra firme*, overlooking the mal-drained *várzea* and providing access to the resources of both habitats. The lower valley itself, extending from the Madeira to the Xingú river, is approximately 800 km in length and its floodplain, in places 50 km across, covers an estimated 1.8 million ha (Camargo, 1958). The main channel of the Amazon is frequently 5–10 km wide, and its waters seasonally overflow to inundate vast areas of the floodplain (see Photograph 21). At Manaus, above the Madeira confluence, the annual fluctuation in river level is 8–12 m, declining to some 6 m at Santarém and 4 m at the mouth of the Xingú (Camargo, 1958; Smith, 1981a). Flood levels vary from year to year, but the main flood season extends from March to August. At that time, the natural levees mostly remain above water, but large areas of the *várzea* are flooded to a depth of several metres and vast lakes are formed. These contract as the flood season passes, but many permanent water bodies exist (Nieuwenhuijs, 1960; Sutmöller *et al.*, 1966).

As in the middle Caquetá, the seasonal overflow of turbid waters

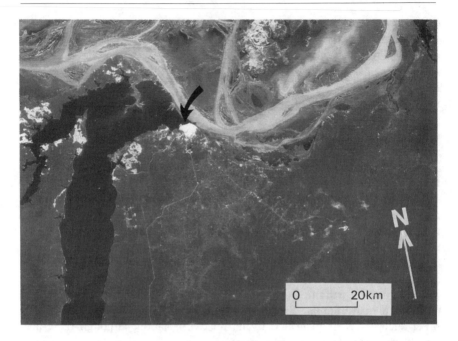

Photograph 21 Santarém (arrowed) on the *terra firme* margin, overlooking the mouthbay of the Tapajós river and the turbid Amazon mainstream. Landsat MSS band 5 image subscene, August 1975, ID no. 275219–130731 (reproduced by courtesy of CNPq/INPE, Brazil)

deposits sediments on the *várzea*, giving soils of higher fertility. Fine-textured Dystric and other Gleysols are mostly encountered, although considerable local variations occur in their physical and chemical properties (Sombroek, 1966; FAO–UNESCO, 1971). West of Parintins, the *várzea* is mostly under forest, but, further east, grassland or *campo de várzea* covers large areas behind the forested levees. Flanking areas of the *terra firme* are mostly under forest, although tracts of dry savanna also exist, as in the vicinity of Monte Alegre.

Permanent occupance of the *várzea* is limited by seasonal flooding, and most larger settlements occur on the elevated margins of the *terra firme*. Santarém at the mouth of the Tapajós river is the largest urban centre, with a population in excess of 100,000. The town originated as a mission settlement in the mid-seventeenth century and has gradually emerged as a regional trading and administrative centre. Only in the 1970s, however, was the town connected to the national road network by construction of the Santarém–Cuiabá highway (see Figure 10). Other towns, like Itacoatiara and Obidos, have developed to the north of the river, and innumerable smaller settlements are distributed along the valley. According to Ross (1978a, p. 193), most of the population lives 'in isolated dwellings or in loose clusters on the river itself or along its many small tributaries and peripheral lakes'. The total population of the lower valley is estimated at 700,000–800,000 (IBGE, 1987). Average density exceeds that of most parts of Amazonia, but there are many sparsely-populated areas between the larger urban centres. The rural population is commonly of Amerindian ancestry, and contemporary peasant or *caboclo* society is still widely dependent on traditional shifting cultivation, fishing and collecting (Soares, 1963; Ross, 1978a). As yet, there is limited modern land development in the zone.

Agriculture has a pre-eminent place amid the variety of exploitation in the lower Amazon valley. There is less dependence on *várzea* cultivation itself than was the case in pre-contact times, and contemporary production derives mainly from the *terra firme* margins, where shifting cultivators grow manioc, dry rice, beans and maize (Soares, 1963; Ross, 1978a; Nugent, 1981). Benefit is often gained from the residual fertility of *terra preta* soils in these areas. In addition, there have been periodic attempts to encourage cash cropping through local agricultural colonisation schemes, notably around Santarém, Monte Alegre and Alenquer (Soares, 1963; Sioli, 1973). Where cultivation does occur on the *várzea*, short-cycle crops like maize and beans are usually planted after recession of the annual flood waters. In spite of the enhanced fertility of *várzea* soils and supposed reductions in weed and pest levels as a consequence of annual flooding, crop cultivation is still vulnerable to flood variability, and there have been few attempts to develop commercial agriculture in the zone. Some 3,000 ha of wet rice were established as part of the Jari project and other experimental rice schemes have been promoted under the PROVARZEA programme, but as yet only preliminary developments of this kind are under way. Close to urban markets, some vegetable cultivation on the *várzea* has also been initiated (Barrow, 1985; Fearnside, 1985c).

One established commercial crop in the lower valley is jute (*Corchorus capsularis*). The crop was introduced by Japanese settlers in the 1930s and is well-adapted to the *várzea* where it is planted on levee sites at times of low water (Pinto, 1966; Pires, 1966). The plant is an herbaceous annual which requires plentiful water during the growing season and can tolerate a degree of flooding when mature (Cobley, 1967; Purseglove, 1979). The crop is mostly grown by small farmers on 3–4 ha plots, without mechanisation or use of fertilisers (Barrow, 1985). The cultivated area varies from year to year, ranging from 11,000 ha to 37,000 ha in the early 1980s (IBGE, 1985, 1986). The main production areas are around Itacoatiara, Juruti and Parintins. Jute fibre has traditionally been used to make sacking, and, although there is increasing competition from plastic products, a market for the fibre persists (Mahar, 1979; Fearnside, 1985c). Smaller quantities of fibrous malva (*Sida rhombifolia*) are also produced in the zone (Junk, 1980; Smith, 1981a).

Extractive activities persist within the lower Amazon valley. Logging has long been practised, involving manual extraction from *várzea* forests and subsequent floating of logs to downstream sawmills. A favoured *várzea* species is *Virola surinamensis*, which is well-established in overseas markets (Palmer, 1977; Muthoo & Leader, 1978). Other commercial species in the zone include *Carapa guianensis*, *Cedrela odorata* and *Ceiba pentandra* (Dubois, 1971; Brune & Melchior, 1976). Although extractive logging is today mostly developing away from the *várzea*, the area is still a useful source of timber.

The extraction of food protein from the *várzea* zone, particularly fish, is of major importance. Fish like pirarucú (*Arapaima gigas*) and other aquatic animals like manatee (*Trichechus inunguis*) and turtles (*Podocnemis* spp.) have been depleted in many areas, but significant fish stocks are still available. *Várzea* lakes and flood forests are productive, and good catches have traditionally been obtained at the mouths of the clear water Tapajós and Xingú rivers (Fittkau *et al.*, 1975; Lowe-McConnell, 1975). Fish supplies in turbid waters of the Amazon mainstream are less abundant, but commercial exploitation has latterly extended there.

As in pre-Columbian times, fishing techniques vary with the species and prevailing water conditions. In places, traditional nets, traps and harpoons are still employed. These are mostly used in *várzea* lakes and smaller channels, where species like tucunare (*Cichla* spp.), carauaçú (*Astronotus ocellatus*) and tambaqui (*Colossoma macropomum*) are sought (Wagley, 1964; Smith, 1981a). Larger-scale exploitation has developed in recent times. Synthetic fibre nets first became available in the 1960s, and have been widely adopted by commercial fishermen, operating powered craft on the Amazon mainstream and in *várzea* lakes. Along the mainstream, migrating shoals of jaraqui (*Semaprochilodus* spp.) and sardinha (*Triportheus* spp.) are caught in this way, as well as catfish (Pimelodidae). Large catfish, weighing 50 kg or more, are also obtained from the river on trotlines at periods of low water (Smith, 1981a). While there are important local markets in the lower valley at places like Itacoatiara and Santarém, fish supplies are also taken to the large and expanding Manaus market as well as exported overland to southern Brazil (Smith, 1981a; Goulding, 1983). Commercial fishing has greatly extended of late, with recent freshwater catches for Pará as a whole attaining 50,000–70,000 t/yr (IBGE, 1985, 1986). The industry, however, is currently 'in a state of virtual non-management' (Lovejoy, 1985a), which bodes ill for the future. Even though most fish populations of the *várzea* are resilient and productive, limits exist to the levels of extraction and effective regulation of commercial fishing is required.

While fishing provides an important and relatively cheap source of protein for residents of the lower Amazon valley, there are other sources of animal protein. Wild game makes some contribution away from the main centres of population, while beef cattle are raised widely on the *campos de várzea*. Earlier estimates have put the cattle population of the lower valley at some 200,000 (Sutmöller *et al.*, 1966). Many smaller ranches exist in the area, each with a few hundred animals which have traditionally been supplied to local markets (Sutmöller *et al.*, 1966; Bunker, 1981). Cattle raising is adapted to the distinctive conditions of the lower valley. At periods of low water, cattle are grazed on the relatively nutritious pastures of the *campos de várzea*, but, as seasonal flooding extends, this pasture largely disappears. Thereafter, some animals are retained in the zone on raised wooden platforms, or *marombas*, where they are fed on floating grasses, like *Echinochloa polystachya* and *Hymenachne amplexicaulis*. Other animals are moved from the *várzea* to adjacent *terra firme* savannas around settlements like Prainha and Monte Alegre, but pasture quality in such areas is usually poor and results in serious loss of condition. According to Sutmöller *et al.* (1966), nutritional deficiencies involving sodium, potassium and other elements occur, which provoke wasting diseases like *mal de cai*. The direst stress of seasonal transhumance is also harmful, causing animal mortality or weight loss (Bunker, 1981). Of late, the traditional pattern of livestock movement has been extended. Nowadays, as the flood season approaches, some *várzea* cattle are sold or transferred to *terra firme* ranches on newly-cleared forest land (Bunker, 1981; Barrow, 1985).

As in pre-Columbian times, diversity of resource use is characteristic of the lower valley and, by Amazonian standards, a relatively high human population continues to be supported. The *várzea* itself is not as extensively cultivated as in the past, but production of animal protein from the zone is still very important. The riparian population also continues to exploit the flanking margins of the *terra firme*, which provide complementary resources to those of the *várzea*.

Agricultural exploitation in coastal Guyana

The coastal Guianas are a comparable wetland habitat to the floodplains of interior Amazonia, although, under tidal influence, they experience less extreme hydrologic variability. Their cultural status also differs as the coastal zone was an enclave of British, Dutch and French colonisation within the broader Iberian sphere of influence. Guyana, which acquired its independence from the United Kingdom in 1966, is the largest and most populous of the three Guianan territories. Its coastal zone covers 1.83 million ha and has a population of approximately 770,000, which represents 95 per cent of the national total. The coastal zone is the mainstay of Guyanese agriculture, which is dominated by sugar cane and wet rice cultivation.

The coastline of Guyana is some 400 km in length and backed by wetlands that extend 15–60 km inland. The zone is flat and low-lying and
mostly below the level of high tides. Inland, the zone is flanked by white
sands of the Berbice Formation. Both forested and herbaceous wetlands
exist, although large parts of the zone have now been empoldered (see
Figure 15). The polders commonly extend several kilometres inland,
beyond which exist un-reclaimed wetlands that remain under water for
much of the year (Ahmad, 1960; Naraine, 1974a). The coastal climate is
wet, with annual rainfall in the range 2,000–3,000 mm. Marked inter-
annual variability in the onset and duration of the double rainy seasons is
reported, and extended periods of drought can occur (King, 1968a; Key,
1974).

The coastal zone consists of marine sediments, transported by currents
from the mouth of the Amazon, and some local fluvial deposits. Saline
soils are present near the sea, but the area mostly carries clayey Eutric
Fluvisols (Gasser, 1961; Ahmad, 1965). The latter require effective
drainage for cultivation, but are inherently fertile and can be renewed
more or less indefinitely by flood-fallowing (Lowenthal, 1960). Eutric
Fluvisols are most widespread in the eastern and central coastal zone, thinning out to the west (FAO, 1966). Further inland, more leached and acid
parent materials occur over which peaty Histosols, or *pegasse*, are
developed. These soils have high levels of exchangeable aluminium and
lose their natural fertility with cultivation (IBRD, 1953; Ahmad, 1960).
Associated with them are Thionic Fluvisols or 'cat clays', which contain
iron and aluminium sulphates and are of minimal agricultural value (FAO,
1966).

The coastal zone of Guyana is intersected by the Essequibo, Demerara
and Berbice rivers, along whose lower courses British and other settlers
established themselves in the late sixteenth and seventeenth centuries
(Lowenthal, 1960). Food crops, tobacco and sugar cane were grown on
early plantations, as well as some cacao and coffee (IBRD, 1953). In the
eighteenth century, the cultivated riverine soils declined in fertility and
plantations were gradually shifted onto the more fertile marine clays, as
land reclamation proceeded (Naraine, 1974a). The reclamation was largely
organised by Dutch companies and implemented by African slave labour.
Once empoldered, the land was very suitable for permanent cultivation
(Lowenthal, 1960).

The polders were gradually extended inland from the sea wall.
Individual polders were narrow, but stretched inland for 5–10 km or
more. They were drained by channels discharging into rivers or the sea
through tidal sluices. When required, fresh irrigation water could be
introduced from the swamps behind the 'backdam' (Mitchell, 1969;
Naraine, 1974a). This system of water management underpinned the
successful development of coastal agriculture, and was gradually extended

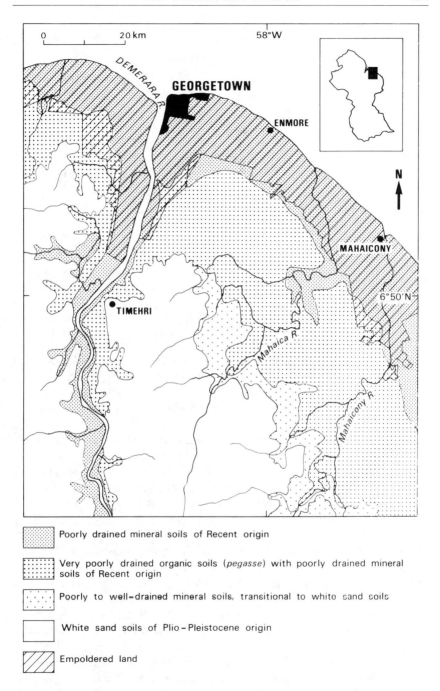

Poorly drained mineral soils of Recent origin

Very poorly drained organic soils (*pegasse*) with poorly drained mineral soils of Recent origin

Poorly to well-drained mineral soils, transitional to white sand soils

White sand soils of Plio-Pleistocene origin

Empoldered land

Figure 15 Coastal Guyana in the vicinity of Georgetown, showing soils and empoldered land (after FAO, 1966)

Table 18 Sugar cane and rice production in Guyana, 1974–86

	Sugar cane		Rice (paddy)	
	Production ('000 t)	Harvested area (ha)	Production ('000 t)	Harvested area (ha)
1974	3,842	56,000	215	116,000
1975	3,632	41,000	292	134,000
1976	4,040	54,000	227	84,000
1977	3,290	51,000	355	136,000
1978	4,160	56,000	305	115,000
1979	3,900	57,000	240	88,000
1980	3,660	52,000	282	95,000
1981	4,190	57,000	276	88,000
1982	3,910	52,000	303	95,000
1983	3,630	51,000	246	76,000
1984	3,210	48,000	312	97,000
1985	3,270	39,000	265	78,000
1986	3,360	42,000	357	92,000

Source: FAO, *Production Yearbooks.*

through the collaboration of plantation owners (Naraine, 1974a). The expertise of Dutch engineers, using techniques familiar in the Netherlands, was critical. Coffee and cotton and then sugar cane became increasingly important, and, when the British formally acquired control of the colony in 1796, these were the crops dominating the agricultural economy (IBRD, 1953; King, 1968a).

During the nineteenth century, sugar cane emerged as the main plantation crop. Its production suffered from periodic labour shortages and later from the competition of European beet sugar, but the industry persisted on a plantation basis (Mandle, 1973). In parallel, the coastal zone saw the gradual emergence of a peasant farming sector, which latterly came to rely on rice cultivation. The development of small-scale farming independent of the plantation began when escaped and, later, freed slaves established themselves on abandoned or vacant land; the process was continued when indentured plantation labour of East Indian origin also became free to settle (Farley, 1953; Adamson, 1972; Key, 1974). Cattle-raising and then rice cultivation were adopted, mainly by East Indian farmers. In 1897, some 2,600 ha of rice were under cultivation and, by 1918, the area had risen to 23,000 ha (IBRD, 1953; Richardson, 1972; Mandle, 1973). Expansion has continued and, by 1986, rice occupied 92,000 ha as against 42,000 ha of sugar cane (FAO, 1987); of late, the area of cane has declined somewhat, as marginal land has been taken out of production (see Table 18). The two crops currently account for about three-quarters of the value of national agricultural production, and are major export crops (IDB, 1982, 1987).

Photograph 22 Sugar cane along drainage canal at Uyfluyt estate, Demerara, coastal Guyana

Sugar cane production is nowadays under government control and derives mainly from eight large estates clustered in Demerara and Berbice (see Photograph 22). Current yields of sugar cane, averaging 80.1 t/ha in 1986, are favourable, but local rainfall conditions generally result in a lower sugar content than elsewhere (IBRD, 1953; FAO, 1987). Cane production benefits from the long-established water management practices in the area and from technical investments that were made in the latter decades of private ownership. Suitable fertiliser regimes are established and integrated with traditional flood-fallowing, which improves the physical and chemical status of the soil (Williams, 1954; Reubens & Reubens, 1962). New cane varieties have been introduced to improve yields and counter crop diseases. The area has been relatively free of serious disease problems, although constant development of disease-resistant varieties is necessary, as elsewhere, to maintain crop productivity. In 1951, the main varieties in use succumbed to leaf scald disease and had to be replaced, while smut and rust diseases have latterly been trouble-some (Williams, 1954; Anlauf, 1980; IDB, 1982).

Sugar yields have always tended to fluctuate from year to year. Some ecological factors are involved, notably rainfall variability and disease incidence; however, in recent times, poor labour relations and shortages of agricultural chemicals, farm equipment and spare parts, have also seriously affected the industry (IDB, 1982, 1984; Graham-Yooll, 1988).

Of late, rice farmers have experienced as many problems as sugar producers. Rice cultivation is mainly undertaken on smallholdings, often less than 1 ha in size, which are unsuited to modern production techniques based on irrigation, fertiliser usage, and pest and disease control (Richardson, 1972; Thomas-Hope, 1987a). Much rice cultivation takes place on old plantation land with established drainage and irrigation facilities, but water management is poor and inadequate for modern high-yielding varieties (Richardson, 1972; Naraine, 1974a). Elsewhere, cultivation relies directly on rainfall and is vulnerable to the natural variability in supply. In spite of favourable soil conditions, rice cultivation is a rather inefficient and uncertain business. Labour-intensive cultivation is scarcely justified, and, even where mechanisation has occurred, increased productivity has not always resulted (Richardson, 1972; Thomas-Hope, 1987a).

Over the years, government-backed attempts have been made to increase rice production. Several major drainage and irrigation schemes were established for small farmers in the 1950s and 1960s, notably the Black Bush polder (12,600 ha) in Berbice and the Tapakuma project (14,800 ha) in Essequibo. In spite of major investment, however, neither of these projects was very successful, and, where higher yields have been achieved, they have mostly come from independent rice farmers (McWatt, 1964; Naraine, 1974b; Vining, 1977). Since the 1960s, there have been attempts to introduce high-yielding varieties, but many farmers continue to use traditional varieties, which are hardier and better able to withstand the periodic droughts and flooding that characterise the area (Richardson, 1972; Rubinstein, 1985). As with sugar cane, rice cultivation has been seriously hindered by input shortages, especially fertilisers, pesticides and farm equipment (IDB, 1982), and, although yields have latterly increased, overall productivity is rather disappointing by modern standards. From average rice yields of about 2,000 kg/ha in the late 1960s, yields had reached 3,200–3,900 kg/ha by the mid-1980s (Richardson, 1972; FAO, 1987).

Sugar cane and rice are the main crops of the coastal zone, but there is some diversification. 'Provision crops', mainly vegetables and fruit, are produced for the domestic market, and coconuts and small amounts of coffee and cacao are grown. Dairy cattle are also raised, mainly near the urban centres of Georgetown and New Amsterdam. In spite of the numerous constraints on Guyanese agriculture, which often reflect fundamental shortcomings in the state-controlled production sector (Latin America Bureau, 1984), the coastal wetlands are an important agricultural zone. Their soil quality is variable and water management presents problems, but parts of the area have been used for sugar cane or rice cultivation for 200 years or more, and agricultural potential is high. Naraine (1974b) reported that coastal cultivation and pasture land covered approximately 400,000 ha, and the present exploited area seems unlikely to exceed 600,000 ha. The extent of cultivable land in the zone has been estimated at 1.1 million ha (Naraine, 1974b), and much of the balance is presumably reclaimable. The current population of the coastal zone is around 770,000, of whom a quarter live in Georgetown, and, although overall population density, at 44/km^2, is high by Amazonian standards, the carrying capacity could be increased, given more effective management of land and water resources.

Cattle ranching in the Rio Branco–Rupununi savanna

The Rio Branco–Rupununi savanna occupies 5.5 million ha astride the Brazil–Guyana frontier (see Figure 16). The area had always been sparsely settled, and when cattle were introduced in the late eighteenth century only a very dispersed ranching community established itself, co-existing with scattered groups of Amerindians. The area long remained isolated and inaccessible, and its cattle-based economy was aptly described by Rivière (1972) as 'subsistence ranching'. By 1943, the savanna had a population of 18,000 people, and, although construction of a road link with Manaus in the late 1970s has increased opportunities in the savanna, it is still very much an economic backwater. By 1985, the population of the savanna was an estimated 100,000, of whom 66,000 were resident in

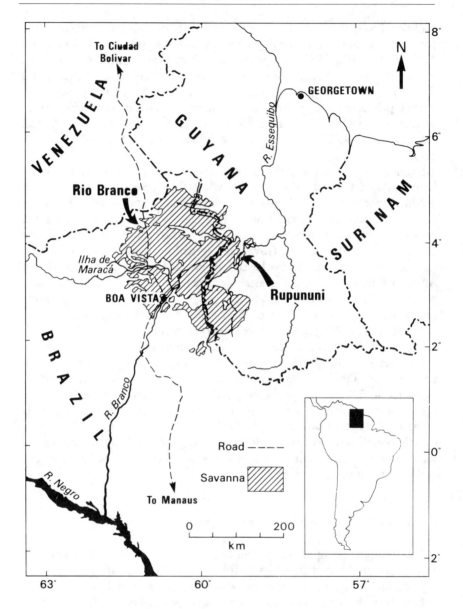

Figure 16 Rio Branco–Rupununi savanna

the regional capital of Boa Vista (Eden, 1966; Migliazza, 1978; IBGE, 1986).

Although located within the broad *hylaea* zone, the Rio Branco–Rupununi savanna is floristically related to the *llanos* as well as other Amazonian savannas (Goodland, 1966; Eden, 1974a). It also experiences

Photograph 23 *Criollo* cattle in corral at Lumidpau, southern Rupununi savanna, Guyana

the characteristic moisture seasonality of the *llanos*. Boa Vista, in the southern savanna, has an annual rainfall of 1,585 mm, with five dry months (< 60 mm) in the year. Inter-annual rainfall variability is high. The savanna itself occupies an undulating land surface at 100–180 m above sea level. The area mostly carries open wooded savanna developed over free-draining soils, but there are also poorly-drained tracts of herbaceous savanna, or *campo de baixada*. Riparian forests locally intersect the savanna. The soils in the area are mainly Orthic Ferralsols and Plinthic Acrisols (FAO–UNESCO, 1971), which are highly weathered, acid (pH 4.0–5.0) and extremely infertile.

The cattle population of the savanna rose steadily during the nineteenth and early twentieth centuries, totalling some 350,000 or more by the 1930s (Brock, 1964; Kelsey, 1972; Rivière, 1972). Numbers subsequently declined, but have now returned to the earlier level. Overall density is currently < 0.1 animals/ha (IBGE, 1987). Most of the land is held in units of 1,000 ha or more, with a few holdings in excess of 10,000 ha. Ranching has traditionally operated on the open range system, with little investment in land or stock. Most of the savanna was unfenced and cattle roamed around in a wild state. Nowadays, the animals, although in places upgraded with zebu, still often show affinity with the ancestral Spanish longhorn or *criollo* stock (see Photograph 23). The latter were hardy

animals and well-adapted to the open range, although growth and reproduction rates were poor (Brock, 1964; Kelsey, 1972). Traditional management consisted of little more than periodic round-ups, which resulted in
annual marketing of 5–10 per cent of the stock. In earlier times, animals
were exported seasonally to Manaus, via the Rio Branco. An overland trail
was opened to the Guyanese coast in 1919, but survived only briefly, and
marketing in that direction has latterly depended on vintage freight
aircraft. In the late 1970s, conditions were eased, at least on the Brazilian
side, by opening of the all-weather road between Manaus and Boa Vista.

Although improved marketing opportunities exist, cattle ranching is still
seriously constrained by environmental conditions, which limit carrying
capacity and stock productivity. The prime constraint is rainfall
seasonality which reduces the availability of grazing in the dry season and
confines animals to scarce moister pastures. In the southern Rupununi,
such pastures cover less than a third of the total grazing area (Turner,
1938). A related problem is the supply of drinking water, which for
several months each dry season tends to be inadequate, over-used and
contaminated. Also characteristic of the dry season are savanna fires, over
which there are differing views (Mott & Popenoe, 1977). Some benefits
accrue under traditional ranching in that fires eliminate old herbage and
encourage more palatable fresh growth. They also help to control shrubby
invasion of pastures and kill ticks, snakes and other pests harmful to
stock. On the other hand, recurrent fires are inimical to the maintenance
of fences and improved pastures, and generally constrain improved stocking and management (Kelsey, 1972). While more progressive ranchers
nowadays seek to control fire, most of the savanna is still burnt at least
once every year.

A further constraint on livestock production is nutrient supply. Few
detailed studies exist, but it is clear that the infertile savanna soils support
grasses of low nutrient content and feed value (Brasil, 1975). This is
particularly true of *Trachypogon plumosus* and similar bunch grasses that
dominate the free-draining savanna, while even the more palatable species
of the *campo de baixada* are usually of modest nutritive value. Extreme
phosphorus deficiency is characteristic of grasses in the Rupununi, and
there are also frequent deficiencies of calcium and potassium; trace
element deficiencies are also reported, notably of cobalt (Duthie, 1939;
Loxton *et al.*, 1958). Consequent nutritional stress reduces animal growth
and lowers calving rates. Nowadays, cattle may be supplied with mineral
supplements, which at least ameliorate the more extreme effects of
malnutrition.

In the past, serious problems of animal health have existed in the
region. As well as nutritionally-related diseases, afflictions like rabies,
brucellosis, and foot and mouth disease have recurrently harmed livestock.
Rabies in particular has been a problem, at times killing tens of thousands

of animals (Kelsey, 1972). In many parts of the savanna, multiple vaccinations are now undertaken and such diseases are broadly under control. Treatment is also given for parasitic infections, while general levels of veterinary care, which in the past were abysmal, have improved. This is particularly so in the more accessible and progressive parts of the savanna where improved stock has been introduced and veterinary investment is readily justified on economic grounds.

Several decades ago, Turner (1938, p. 234) summarised the status of the rancher in the savanna: 'He is caught in a vicious circle, since his poor quality cattle bring low prices, and these allow of no surplus to be expended on the improvement of stock'. In general, this statement is still true for more isolated parts of the Rio Branco–Rupununi savanna, but there have been some recent improvements in the quality of ranching. The most obvious is in the quality of the livestock itself. Some attempts were made in the 1950s to upgrade the local *criollo* stock, but it was only in the 1970s that widespread zebu introductions began, especially of Nellore and Guzerat breeds. These animals tolerate the hot, dry conditions of the savanna and show improved fecundity and productivity (Kelsey, 1972). In addition, attempts have been made to improve the supply and quality of pasture. There have been sporadic efforts over the last fifty years to introduce new grasses, but again it was only from the 1970s that wider use began to be made of species like colonião (*Panicum maximum*), jaraguá (*Hyparrhenia rufa*) and, latterly, kikuyu (*Brachiaria humidicola*). Even so, improved pastures occupy only a very small area, and extensive grazing of natural pastures remains the rule for most of the savanna. Also, there has been an increase in the provision of fencing, and some measure of rotational grazing has developed. However, none of these steps resolves the fundamental regional constraints of moisture seasonality and nutrient deficiency. To some extent, they are being overcome by direct mineral supplementation and by the construction of local earth dams and use of wind pumps. But livestock growth and reproduction rates in most areas are still low, and the overall carrying capacity, traditionally reckoned at < 0.1 animals/ha, has not been significantly increased (Turner, 1938; Brock, 1964; Kelsey, 1972).

Although the carrying capacity of the Rio Branco–Rupununi savanna is low, even by Amazonian standards, it is difficult to identify immediate technical or managerial improvements to the system that would be economic under prevailing market conditions. In parts of the region, notably in the vicinity of Ilha de Maracá, ranching is currently extending to cleared forest land, but, in spite of initial nutrient benefits, increased productivity is unlikely to be sustained. Ranching in the savanna itself remains extensive and low-yielding, and, although adaptive and sustainable at a level commensurate with the prevailing 'low-biomass steady-state' (Noy-Meir, 1975), its profitability is also low. In view of increasing

demand for beef in the region, extensive savanna ranching will no doubt
continue, but there are few local indications of how the system might
intensify.

Conclusion

The range of exploitation in Amazonian wetlands and dry savannas is
considerable, but the contemporary human impact in many areas remains
slight. Denser settlement and more intensive land use occur in a few
wetlands, notably the coastal Guianas and scattered parts of the lower
Amazon valley and estuarine zone. Elsewhere, riparian zones contain
isolated centres of population and exploitation, but settlement along many
rivers is sparse, as in the case of the middle Caquetá. The Amazonian
savannas are thinly populated, even where cattle ranching is established.

Wetland and savanna habitats are distinctive but variable in character.
Wetland areas, whether riparian, estuarine or coastal, often have relatively
fertile alluvial soils, but are subject to intermittent natural flooding. Such
flooding creates serious risks for cultivation, and periodic crop losses can
result. Where the flood variability is less extreme, notably in coastal areas
under tidal influence and along smaller rivers, empoldering, which is
essentially a modern analogue of pre-Columbian ridged fields, permits
permanent agriculture. In central Amazonia, the more extreme flood range
effectively precludes empoldering, but post-flood cultivation of the kind
practised in pre-Columbian times is feasible. The different exploitation
strategies are adapted to contrasting hydrologic regimes, but variously
allow productive land use.

The role of wetlands as a source of animal protein is very important.
Amazonian fisheries have expanded greatly in recent times. However,
there are still significant fish stocks in many areas, and, although current
extraction is often excessive, high levels of sustainable production are
possible, given effective fisheries management. Additional protein supplies
are provided by livestock rearing in herbaceous wetlands, mainly in the
lower Amazon valley and estuarine zone.

Amazonian savannas also experience variable water regimes. Cattle
ranching adapts to this by local stock migration between wet and dry
season pastures, but overall livestock productivity is limited by water
seasonality, as also it is by soil infertility. Conditions can be ameliorated
by technical inputs, but the latter are rarely economic or readily compatible with the prevailing extensive mode of ranching. The ranching system
is sustainable in its present form, but there are no easy options for its
intensification.

In comparison with the forested *terra firme*, Amazonian wetlands and
savannas have been neglected in recent times. Localised development has

occurred, but the areas are generally seen as having lesser potential than the forested *terra firme*, particularly for commercial development. Some authors have argued the case for increased exploitation of wetlands and also savannas (Camargo, 1958; Goodland & Irwin, 1977; Eden, 1978; Goodland, 1980; Smith, 1982), but such areas are not generally perceived as attractive development alternatives to the forested *terra firme*.

7

Alternative land development

The greatest challenge confronting agricultural scientists working in the humid tropics is to find a production system which is ecologically suitable for the area.

[Alvim, 1977, p. 349]

Many attempts at Amazonian land development have led to unstable and unintensive exploitation, especially on the forested *terra firme*. In earlier times, this was often attributed to the shortcomings of the colonists themselves who were seen as failing to exploit a favourable environment (Myers & Myers, 1871; Wallace, 1890). Contemporary colonists as well as the government agencies who seek to assist them are still often held responsible for the poor achievements of land development, but there is now increased recognition of the limiting nature of the Amazonian environment itself and of its negative effects on development (Gómez-Pompa *et al.*, 1972; Goodland & Irwin, 1975). In reality, of course, both cultural and environmental factors are influential and contribute to unstable land exploitation. Precise understanding of the causality involved is not easily achieved, but, in the present context, it is argued that existing land exploitation systems, themselves dynamic expressions of the inter-action between environment and the human population, critically influence the quality of land development. Since many such systems are currently mal-adaptive, the question arises as to what alternative modes of land exploitation might better be employed.

In the present context, the prime requirement of land exploitation systems is that they should be adapted to local resource deficiencies and variabilities, particularly in respect of soil nutrients and water resources, and to prevailing biotic stressors in the form of weeds, pests and diseases. Some technical inputs may be applied, but the ecological and economic implications of such usage require careful evaluation. Broader factors relating to the level of supporting infrastructure and services also affect land exploitation systems, but the systems still need to be environment-ally-adaptive if sustainable development is to occur. Thereafter, the onus is on individual land users to implement the systems and on governments to maintain the institutional framework within which such can occur. Any resultant development will be a function of both the environmental and cultural variables involved.

In this chapter, alternative exploitation to the prevailing extractive and pioneer colonisation systems is considered. Various modes of more permanent and sustainable exploitation are reviewed, most of which already exist locally or experimentally in the region. The main emphasis is on agrosystems for the forested *terra firme*, which occupies most of the study area and is the primary focus of current land colonisation. Firstly, consideration is given to intensive cropping systems. These commonly require higher levels of technical input, are more costly to maintain, and relatively risky in operation, but they can be productive and may have a place in Amazonian development. Secondly, less intensive modes of silviculture and livestock rearing are considered, together with integrated agrosilvicultural and silvopastoral systems. These are broadly characterised by lower productivity, but require limited technical inputs, involve less risk, and more effectively protect the environment. Finally, consideration is given to increased exploitation of Amazonian wetlands and savannas, which have been relatively neglected of late, but are in places seen to have development potential.

Intensive cropping systems

In spite of the persistence of extensive pioneer cultivation on the forested *terra firme*, some observers have been optimistic about the prospects for more permanent and intensive land use. Vicente-Chandler (1968), for example, argued that intensive management and fertiliser use were the key to successful agricultural exploitation of the region. Such views were seemingly confirmed by Sanchez *et al.* (1982), who demonstrated under experimental conditions in eastern Peru the technical viability of permanent, fertiliser-based cropping on the *terra firme*. Admittedly, most attempts at intensive cultivation of this kind, whether involving annual or perennial crops, have done little to justify such optimism, but it is clear that benefits would accrue from the development of sustainable intensive cropping systems and it is desirable to explore the possibilities. The simple introduction of mid-latitude cropping techniques is unlikely to succeed; any intensive systems that emerge will need to be explicitly adapted to local environmental conditions, particularly in respect of soil resources and biotic stressors.

The soil conditions of the *terra firme* create particular problems for permanent and intensive cultivation. In spite of favourable soil structure, marked topsoil compaction and erosion commonly occur when land surfaces are bared. Cleared sloping land is especially vulnerable to erosion. The maintenance of chemical fertility is also a major problem under intensive cropping. Low cation exchange capacity and base saturation frequently prevail, and other problems arise involving aluminium toxicity

Table 19 Fertiliser requirements for continuous cultivation of annual rotations of rice, maize and soyabeans or rice, peanuts and soyabeans on acid soils at Yurimaguas, eastern Peru

Input	Amount per ha	Frequency
Lime	3 tons	Once every 3 years
Nitrogen	80–100 kg N	Maize and rice only
Phosphorus	25 kg P	Every crop
Potassium	80–100 kg K	Every crop, split application
Magnesium	25 kg Mg	Every crop (unless dolomitic lime is used)
Copper	1 kg Cu	Once a year or once every 2 years
Zinc	1 kg Zn	Once a year or once every 2 years
Boron	1 kg B	Once a year
Molybdenum	20 g Mo	Mixed with legume seeds only

Source: Sanchez *et al.*, 1982.

and, in places, phosphorus fixation (Sanchez, 1979a; Cochrane *et al.*, 1985). With traditional shifting cultivation, such constraints are largely circumvented by field rotation, but under continuous cultivation nutrient supplements are soon required. The use of inorganic fertilisers is technically feasible in such circumstances, and appropriate fertiliser regimes have been developed for acid *terra firme* soils. The most notable experimental work has been undertaken at Yurimaguas in Peru, where rotational cropping of rice, maize, peanuts and soyabeans has been sustained on free-draining Ultisols by soil liming and applications of major and trace elements (Sanchez *et al.*, 1982). The inclusion of peanuts and soyabeans in the rotation supplies useful organic nitrogen to the system, but, as Table 19 shows, large quantities of chemical fertilisers are still needed to sustain crop production. Elsewhere, in Brazilian Pará, high yields of black pepper (*Piper nigrum*) have been obtained through regular, heavy applications of inorganic fertilisers, supplemented by organic inputs of bone meal and animal dung (Sombroek, 1966; Homma & Miranda Filho, 1979).

Fertiliser costs in Amazonia are high and affect the viability of intensive cropping. In the case of a crop like black pepper, fertiliser costs are generally covered by the high value of the product. Similarly, under experimental conditions at Yurimaguas, it is claimed that rotational cereal/legume cultivation is profitable over a range of crop and fertiliser prices (Sanchez *et al.*, 1982). However, recurrent doubts are expressed about the provision of regular supplies of fertilisers and other inputs in isolated frontier areas, and also about the longer-term economic viability of such systems, as global stores of inexpensive energy and nutrient supplies are depleted (Fearnside & Rankin, 1982; Nicholaides *et al.*, 1984; Fearnside, 1985c; Goodland, 1986). To some extent, such problems can be circumvented by concentrating on areas of eutrophic soils, such as the Nitosols that exist along the eastern Transamazon highway and in parts of Rondônia. Admittedly, the extent of such soils is limited, but they offer higher potential productivity for given levels of fertiliser input and are the most promising areas for intensive cultivation on the *terra firme* (Alvim, 1980).

Although effective fertiliser regimes can be devised for intensive cropping on the *terra firme*, it is desirable to explore alternatives to this costly, high-input approach. One possibility is to make greater use of organic inputs as supplements to inorganic fertilisers. The nitrogen-fixing capacity of leguminous crops is already exploited in permanent cropping systems at Yurimaguas and elsewhere (Biard & Wagenaar, 1960; Sanchez *et al.*, 1982; Sanchez & Benites, 1987), and there is scope for additional use of organic residues. Manuring with plant refuse is a technique employed by indigenous cultivators in southern Venezuela and elsewhere (Eden, 1974b), while mulching with grass and other plant residues is undertaken by Japanese black pepper cultivators in Brazilian Pará. Experiments with organic inputs, including mulches, green manures and compost, have also been initiated at Yurimaguas, with some encouraging results (Wade, 1978; Nicholaides *et al.*, 1984; Sanchez & Benites, 1987). The value of retaining organic matter in the soil has not always been acknowledged (Vicente-Chandler, 1968), but recycling organic residues as a supplement to inorganic fertilisers will certainly enhance soil nutrition, especially in respect of nitrogen and phosphorus. Organic matter also improves soil aeration and moisture retention capacity, and helps to control soil erosion (Harrison, 1982; Swift & Sanchez, 1984; Ewel, 1986).

Another appropriate strategy is to concentrate on the cultivation of long-cycle tree or shrub crops on the *terra firme* (Camargo, 1948; Watters, 1971; Goodland, 1980). Tree crops provide good protection against leaching and soil erosion, and are less vulnerable than annuals to the occasional dry spells that occur. Tree crops also cycle their own nutrients. Where the crop product is oligotrophic, like rubber latex, the crop will have low overall fertiliser requirements. Other perennials like cacao and coffee require heavy applications of fertilizer under intensive cultivation, but, as with black pepper, their high product value generally facilitates economic production. In the case of wood species like *Gmelina arborea* or *Pinus caribaea*, which require destructive harvesting, the long-term prospects may be less favourable on account of high nutrient loss in removal of the crop and low unit product values (Jordan & Russell, 1983). Clearly, particular crops need to be evaluated on their merits, but there are no doubt many perennial species that can be intensively cultivated on the *terra firme* as far as soil conditions are concerned. Among those currently being investigated or developed are oil palm (*Elaeis guineensis*), guaraná (*Paullinia cupana*), papaya (*Carica papaya*), Brazil nut (*Bertholletia excelsa*) and copaíba (*Copaifera* spp.) (Alvim, 1982; Balick, 1985; Goodland, 1986).

Biotic stressors create more risk for intensive cultivation on the *terra firme* than do soil conditions. The incidence of crop disease is particularly high in forest areas, where environmental conditions encourage the continuous and rapid growth of micro-organisms. Fungal and viral diseases are common, with the pathogens tending particularly to build up in areas of continuous monoculture (Wellman, 1972; Hecht, 1982; Sanchez *et al.*, 1982; Fearnside, 1985c). Crop pests, ranging from shoot borers and leaf-cutting ants to various larger birds and mammals, also damage many crops, both annuals and perennials. According to Wellman (1972), pests and diseases result in average field losses of 24–32 per cent annually for major neotropical crops. Further losses also occur in storage.

Maize, rice and short-cycle leguminous crops like beans (*Phaseolus vulgaris*), cowpea (*Vigna unguiculata*) and peanut (*Arachis hypogaea*) are subject to sundry pests and diseases, especially under monocultural cropping (World Bank, 1981; Smith, 1982; Valverde & Bandy, 1982). Perennial monocultures are similarly at risk. The classic example is plantation rubber, with its recurrent infection by the leaf fungus *Microcyclus ulei*. Cacao (*Theobroma cacao*), which is widely cultivated in areas like Rondônia and parts of the Andean *oriente*, is another native species that suffers debilitating fungal diseases, notably witches' broom (*Crinipellis perniciosa*) and black pod (*Phytophthora palmivora*). Witches' broom was first reported in Surinam as long ago as 1895 and a continuing reservoir of infection exists among wild cacao in the forest (Wellman, 1972; Smith, 1982). Current plantings are mostly 'disease-resistant', but individual trees, with a potential lifespan of eighty years or more, remain vulnerable to the fast-breeding and evolving pathogens (Fearnside, 1978). Commercial plantings of coffee are also vulnerable to sundry pests and diseases. In eastern Peru, coffee borer (*Hypothenemus hampei*) and coffee rust (*Hemileia vastatrix*) are reported to be particular problems, which can be caused by a 'large extension or excessive density' of the crop (OEA, 1987a). Even black pepper (*Piper nigrum*), introduced to Pará state in the 1930s and once proclaimed as 'the first example in Amazonia history of what rational intensive agriculture can do' (Pires, 1978, p. 616), has lately suffered serious damage, mainly from the root fungus *Fusarium solani*. The disease, which shortens the productive lifespan of the plant, has widely affected black pepper cultivation since the 1960s (see Photographs 24 and 25).

Monocultural wood crops are equally vulnerable. In Brazil, experimental plantings of mahogany (*Swietenia macrophylla*) and cedar (*Cedrela odorata*) have suffered serious damage from shoot borers (Horn, 1957; Dubois, 1971). In the Guianas, *Eucalyptus deglupta* seems to tolerate plantation conditions, but other eucalypts (*E. grandis*, *E. saligna*) suffer severe fungal damage and are considered unsuitable for plantation cultivation (Boerboom & Maas, 1970; Vega, 1979). Similar problems are encountered at Jari,

Photograph 24 Black pepper cultivation at agricultural experimental station, Capitão Poço, Pará, Brazil

Photograph 25 Black pepper plant with root fungal disease, Tomé Açu, Pará, Brazil

where *Gmelina arborea* and *Eucalyptus* spp, appear increasingly vulnerable to fungal and other infections (Muchovej *et al.*, 1978; Rankin, 1985; Fearnside, 1987). In new plantations, initial pest and disease damage may be slight, but, particularly in large-scale monocultures, a progressive build-up of pest populations and increasing levels of crop damage are likely to occur over time (Fearnside & Rankin, 1982). While immediate control of crop pests or diseases is often possible by use of biocides, the technical and economic problems associated with recurrent usage are immense, given the huge reservoir of pest and disease organisms in the forest and their genetic plasticity. Effective long-term protection of any intensive cultivation systems, annual or perennial, seems more likely to lie with mixed cropping, rotational cropping and other biological control strategies.

In the face of prevailing bio-physical constraints, it is difficult to identify a clear pathway ahead for intensive cultivation on the forested *terra firme*. Hitherto, most attention has focused on soil constraints, especially relating to chemical fertility. In technical terms, such problems are generally manageable, although cost factors clearly affect the prospects for particular crops. Biotic stressors present more intractable problems and create significant risks that increase with the extent and uniformity of cropping and with the passage of time. Additional risk derives from the dependence of intensive systems on external linkages, which range from the supply of fertilisers and other technical inputs to the operation of extension and marketing services (Buschbacher, 1986a; Sanchez & Benites, 1987). The general provision of infrastructure and services is frequently inadequate in new and isolated production areas, and seriously limits opportunities for intensive cultivation. Small farmers are most vulnerable to such constraints, which are particularly critical in high-input systems (Nicholaides *et al.*, 1984; Fearnside, 1985c; Jordan, 1987).

Whether existing systems of intensive cropping on the *terra firme* can be made more adaptive and sustainable without sacrificing overmuch in the way of productivity is not yet clear. Some important advances have been made both in rotational annual cropping of cereals and legumes (Sanchez *et al.*, 1982; Sanchez & Benites, 1987) and in mixed cropping of shade-tolerant commercial perennials like cacao and black pepper with such species as coconut, peach palm and Brazil nut (Alvim, 1982). However, until both the technical basis and supporting infrastructure and services for such agrosystems are more secure, caution is required in the pursuit of intensive cultivation. Even so, some agrosystems of this kind are desirable on the *terra firme* both as a means of increasing overall production and of reducing the pressure on adjoining forests by providing an alternative to pioneer exploitation. Intensive cultivation inevitably involves relatively high risk, ecologically and economically, but investigation of the possibilities needs to continue, particularly for areas of eutrophic soils.

Agrosilvicultural systems

Less intensive, sustainable cultivation systems have better prospects on the forested *terra firme*, and deserve detailed consideration. Although involving lower productivity, such systems are less dependent on external inputs, have lower crop risk, and are more easily maintained. One option that has latterly received attention in Amazonia is agrosilviculture or agroforestry, which offers small farmers the possibility of permanent land exploitation through long-cycle mixed cropping. Agrosilviculture is a 'multi-strata production system' that aims to integrate short-cycle food crops with timber or other tree crops in order to achieve sustained yields (Combe & Budowski, 1979; Peck, 1982). Both subsistence and cash crops are commonly involved. In practice, the system is likely to be relatively labour-intensive and less reliant on technical inputs than intensive cropping. Its productivity will be lower, but the system appears sustainable and to protect the land. It represents a compromise between production and protection, and is particularly useful as a recovery system for areas of *terra firme* degraded by earlier pioneer colonisation.

Agrosilviculture is usually seen as derivative of the *taungya* cultivation system of Burma, in which shifting cultivators establish young stands of valuable forest trees amid food crops in order to create a subsequent productive fallow (Baur, 1964). In recent decades, similar cropping systems have been established in West Africa (King, 1968b; Olawoye, 1975), central America (Aguirre, 1963; De las Salas, 1979) and other tropical regions. According to King (1968b), agrosilvicultural systems have worked well in many areas, and there is growing recognition of their potential in Amazonia (Watters, 1971; Dubois, 1971, 1979; Brienza Junior, 1982; Hecht, 1982). Occasional doubts have been expressed about the utility of the system on the grounds that it tends to be associated with low standards of living (Baur, 1964), does not encourage farmers to improve their socio-economic status (Budowski, 1983), and is less easy to modify and improve than equivalent monocultures (Spears, 1980). Nevertheless, the system offers various technical and economic benefits to the small farmer, and provides a possible basis for gradual intensification of land use (Spears, 1980; Raintree, 1986).

As previously indicated, a clear model for agrosilviculture already exists among indigenous shifting cultivators in Amazonia. Among the Venezuelan Waika, Harris (1971) reports that fruit crops like banana and papaya continue to be harvested in old field areas that are regenerating to forest after manioc cultivation. Similarly, in eastern Colombia, Witoto and Andoke farmers interplant manioc with fruit trees, like guamo (*Inga edulis*), cucui (*Ficus* sp.) and uvo (*Pourouma* sp.), which are harvested in the early years of subsequent forest fallowing (Eden & Andrade, 1987). Comparable 'swidden-fallow management', involving ongoing exploitation of fruit trees in old field areas, is also reported among the Bora Indians of eastern Peru (Denevan *et al.*, 1984; Denevan & Padoch, 1988).

Although such practices have infrequently been reported among *caboclo* or *colono* cultivators in Amazonia (Anderson *et al.*, 1985; Padoch *et al.*, 1985), sundry experimental programmes involving intercropping of short-cycle food crops with timber and other tree crops have been initiated. At Belterra plantation, there were early attempts to intercrop rice and beans with young rubber trees (Huffnagel, 1964). More recently, an agrosilvicultural demonstration project was established by forestry staff near Pucallpa in Peru, where a local market existed for wood pulp and timber products (Masson, 1978, 1979). The project, targeted at small farmers, involved initial plantings of rice, manioc and bananas in association with pulp and timber species like *Gmelina arborea*, *Jacaranda copaia* and *Simarouba amara*. The food plants were cultivated for up to four years, after which the land was devoted to tree crops. According to Masson (1978), sale of the latter would allow fertilisers to be purchased for application in succeeding crop cycles. Similar experiments were started in the adjacent Tingo María colonisation zone (Reátegui, 1979).

In Brazil, small-scale agrosilvicultural experiments have been initiated by forestry staff along the northern stretch of the Santarém–Cuiabá highway. In this area, colonists were encouraged to plant tree seedlings amidst regular food crops of maize, beans and manioc. The trees included timber species like *Bagassa guianensis*, *Cordia goeldiana*, *Carapa guianensis* and *Swietenia macrophylla*, together with rubber (*Hevea brasiliensis*). In places, mango (*Mangifera indica*), papaya (*Carica papaya*) and cashew (*Anacardium occidentale*) were also planted (Eden, 1982). Similar experiments have been undertaken at Mapane in Surinam, where *Cordia alliodora* was interplanted with rice, manioc and bananas (Vega, 1979). The approach at Mapane differed in that overall control of the system was exercised by the forestry department, who retained ownership of the final tree crop. The department organised initial land clearance and tree planting, after which selected farmers were allowed on the land. They grew their own food crops and were responsible for weeding the tree crop, although, after two years when the latter was established, they were required to move to fresh forest land (Vega, 1979).

Such experiments cover various crop combinations, but all involve the integration of short-cycle and long-cycle crops. In the Surinam example, agrosilviculture is essentially an extension of forestry activities, but the main potential in Amazonia would seem to be for establishing pioneer cultivators more permanently on cleared forest land, and thereby reducing the pressure on adjacent forest. Field evaluation of agrosilviculture will inevitably be slow because of its extended cropping cycle of 10–15 years or more, but the technical feasibility of the agrosystem is already evident from indigenous cultivation (Eden, 1982).

Among the perceived advantages of a mixed cropping system like agro-silviculture are its more efficient use of solar radiation and available soil nutrients (Sanchez, 1976). Individual crop plants also improve micro-climatic and other conditions for the growth of associated plants. The tree components in the system are particularly useful in that they enhance the production of organic matter, help generally to maintain soil fertility, conserve water, and reduce soil erosion (Raintree, 1986). More specific nutrient benefits also accrue if leguminous trees, like *Inga* spp. and *Enterolobium* spp., are incorporated in the system (Hecht, 1982; Peck, 1982). In addition, mixed cropping is claimed to reduce pest and disease problems, thereby lowering the risk of crop failure (Sanchez, 1976). Various mechanisms are suggested, including the reduced apparency of a pest's target in a mixed crop, the low density of potential target species within a matrix of non-susceptible species, and the physical interference with the movement of pests through a dense crop community (Ewel, 1986). The prospects for cultivation of species like rubber, cacao and mahogany (*Swietenia macrophylla*), which are highly vulnerable to pests under monoculture, are greatly improved in agrosilviculture. Trials with other fruit, fuelwood and timber species will no doubt reveal many more that can usefully be incorporated in agrosilvicultural systems.

Given appropriate crop combinations, low-input agrosilviculture is sustainable on the forested *terra firme*, and offers advantages to small farmers. It provides a range of subsistence and cash crops on a relatively secure basis, which is an asset in pioneer colonisation zones where infrastructure and services are frequently poor. Achieving more permanent settlement on the land is also advantageous, since it in turn increases the chances of eventually providing those services. In the longer term, there are also possibilities of upgrading the agrosystem. As Masson (1978) indicates, the harvesting and sale of a final tree crop provide income that can be invested in the land as a possible step towards intensification.

There are still problems to be overcome with agrosilviculture. Additional data are required on appropriate crop combinations and cultivation regimes, as well as further information on the optimal size and organisa-tion of individual holdings. The system also needs to be backed by improved land tenurial arrangements which will allow longer-cycle cultiva-tion to occur without risk of land invasion or appropriation by other land users. In addition, there is need for closer co-operation, at both research and extension levels, between agriculture and forestry agencies both of whom have obvious interests in agrosilviculture (Muthoo & Leader, 1978; Spears, 1980) Given progress in these and related directions, agrosilviculture provides opportunities for sustainable Amazonian land exploitation.

Mixed-forest silviculture

Mixed-forest or natural forest silviculture is another less intensive mode of crop production that has potential in Amazonia. It is based on the management, rather than replacement, of the original forest cover and involves an extended tree-cropping cycle of 25–30 years or more. Although primarily concerned with timber production, possibilities also exist for simultaneous, managed harvesting of non-wood products from the forest, notably rubber latex, Brazil nuts and tree fruits. An important feature of mixed-forest silviculture is that the compositional diversity of the original forest is largely retained, which lowers risk from biotic stressors and permits growth of tree species that are vulnerable under monocultural production. The productivity of the system is lower than that of industrial plantations, but effective land protection is achieved and the genetic resources of the forest are conserved (Wood, 1976). Like agrosilviculture, mixed-forest silviculture is a compromise between production and protection, and it offers an explicit and sustainable alternative to extractive logging.

In Amazonia, mixed-forest silviculture has received limited attention. Most tropical experience of the system has been gained in Far Eastern forests where timber-cropping techniques of this kind were introduced from Europe in the nineteenth century (Whitmore, 1975; Wadsworth, 1987). Various methods have been applied, including monocyclic systems, which involve the initial removal of all commercial timber from a stand, and the managed regeneration of a new tree crop, which usually consists of light-demanding species. The Malayan Uniform System, for example, works well in Far Eastern dipterocarp forests where adequate seedlings are present in a stand to provide a basis for the next tree crop. After initial logging, poison-girdling of the residual canopy is usually undertaken to ensure release of the seedlings (Whitmore, 1975; Schmidt, 1987). Elsewhere in the Far East, polycyclic systems have been applied. These involve a lighter initial logging of the stand, followed by the selective encouragement of surviving trees of commercial value, which then become harvestable after a shorter interval. Such systems are more difficult to operate than monocyclic ones, but can in places be used to rehabilitate exploited dipterocarp forest at moderate cost (Whitmore, 1975; Hutchinson, 1980; Schmidt, 1987).

While logging in Amazonia has greatly increased in recent years, there has been little attempt to develop sustainable exploitation of mixed-forest stands. Large areas of forest are now accessible to extractive loggers, and there is little incentive to develop long-term treatments for improving the growth of native commercial species. Some experimental work started in Surinam in the 1950s, with emphasis on pre-logging refinement of stands. Subsequently, post-logging refinement has been investigated through poison-girdling of less valuable species, and favourable preliminary results have been obtained in both ecological and economic terms (Schulz, 1960; Jonkers & Schmidt, 1984; Boxman *et al.*, 1985).

In the 1950s, silvicultural experiments were also begun in Brazil under the auspices of FAO (Pitt, 1961, 1969; Dubois, 1971). At Curuá-Una, attention was focused on both pre-logging and post-logging refinement treatments, aimed at improving the performance of desirable timber species. Among species responding favourably were *Vochysia maxima*, *Goupia glabra* and *Didymopanax morototoni*, but higher-value species like *Cedrela odorata* performed poorly (Dubois, 1971). Enrichment treatments were also investigated at Curuá-Una as a means of improving the quality of regenerating stands. Line and group plantings of species like *Carapa guianensis* and *Bagassa guianensis* were undertaken on logged land, but the results have been variable, partly because of irregular experimental control (see Photograph 26). In the late 1970s, there was renewed interest in mixed-forest silviculture in Brazil. New experiments, based on natural regeneration, were initiated at Curuá-Una and in the nearby Tapajós National Forest (Jankauskis, 1978; Carvalho, 1980; Eden, 1982). Also during the 1970s, similar silvicultural studies were started in the Imataca Forest Reserve in Venezuelan Guayana and in the Bosque Nacional Alexander von Humboldt in east central Peru (Wood *et al.*, 1977; Masson, 1979). `

Although experimental programmes of this kind are clearly important, fundamental problems arise in that the timber cropping cycles in question extend over 25–30 years or more. In Amazonia, there are very few experimental results available for this length of time, which makes current design of operational programmes difficult. Where such programmes are initiated, problems arise in maintaining the crop over the requisite period in the face of changing institutional and political interests and of competition from other land users, especially migrant farmers and extractive loggers. According to Schmidt (1987), silvicultural management initiated in the Tapajós National Forest in Brazil has already stalled, while the programmes in Venezuela and Peru have either not been implemented or not sustained.

In spite of these problems, it is desirable to establish a sound technical basis for Amazonian mixed-forest silviculture and to identify appropriate options. In this respect, it is noted that current extractive logging mostly involves rather few species and relatively low timber volumes (10–40 m³/ha). This suggests that polycyclic systems, relying on low-cost refining treatments and a cutting cycle of 25–30 years or so, may be appropriate. Liberation thinning, for example, which encourages the emergence of established trees in residual stands, may be a suitable technique (Hutchinson, 1980, 1987). At the same time, the number of commercial species in the forest is gradually increasing, which will lead to more

Photograph 26 Experimental enrichment planting of group of *Bagassa guianensis* on previously logged land at Curuá-Una, Pará, Brazil. One of 13 trees in the group is intended for final crop, but no selection has taken place 17 years after planting

complete harvesting and favour the adoption of longer-term monocyclic systems. Available results from Curuá-Una and elsewhere suggest that natural regeneration of desirable commercial species will not easily occur in these circumstances (Dubois, 1971; Jonkers & Schmidt, 1984). Experimental data from the Tapajós National Park are more optimistic (Carvalho, 1980), but it seems doubtful whether natural regeneration of commercial species in more heavily logged Amazonian forest will generally approach the required levels (Wadsworth, 1987). In this case, enrichment treatments will be needed to regenerate a satisfactory commercial crop. Preliminary experiments in Surinam suggest that species like *Cedrela angustifolia* and *Cordia alliodora* may be suitable for this purpose (Vega, 1979). Additionally, enrichment with species like rubber (*Hevea brasiliensis*) or Brazil nut (*Bertholletia excelsa*) may be appropriate.

The pathway ahead for mixed-forest silviculture is neither clear nor straightforward. Sustainable timber production from the *terra firme* is obviously desirable, and technical options can no doubt be found that will allow exploitation of the forest in a semi-natural state. Such forest would retain much of its compositional diversity, conserving genetic resources and also providing longer-term market flexibility. Even so, it will be difficult to maintain mixed-forest silviculture in a region attuned to extractive logging and impermanent cultivation. Nor are the economic prospects seen as entirely encouraging. According to UNESCO (1978, p. 460), 'it seems probable that the cost per m^3 of such sylviculture will be rather high and that it will have to be justified either by the quality of the products or by the role of the tropical forest biome in the biosphere'. On both counts, however, such justification is surely available in Amazonia, and indeed likely to increase with time as additional forest is cleared and timber potential depleted. If other natural products such as rubber, Brazil nuts and tree fruit are also harvested from the managed stands, the economic return will be further enhanced. While a transition from extractive logging to mixed-forest silviculture will not readily be achieved, unless implemented within designated forest reserves, such silviculture represents an adaptive and sustainable long-term option for the *terra firme*.

Semi-intensive livestock rearing

In seeking a sustainable alternative to extensive pioneer ranching on the forested *terra firme*, attention has mostly focused on the prospects for semi-intensive cattle rearing on mixed grass–legume pastures. The use of legumes in this context is intended to improve pasture quality and productivity and to facilitate maintenance of a permanent pasture cover. In some other neotropical lowlands, attempts have been made to establish intensive cattle rearing, based on confined breeding systems or the use of heavily fertilised pastures (Vicente-Chandler, 1975; Fernández-Baca *et al.*, 1986). In places, the performance of intensive rearing systems has been favourable, but costly inputs are required and there is little scope for immediate developments of this kind on the *terra firme*.

Early investigations of the potential of tropical legumes for livestock rearing were undertaken in Australia during the 1940s (Schultze-Kraft & Giacometti, 1979). The development work included use of plant material from Latin America, which is the richest source of germplasm for tropical forage legumes (Sanchez, 1979b). Subsequently, interest in such legumes developed in Latin America itself. Some Australian cultivars were repatriated to their centre of origin, but the modified material often failed when re-exposed to neotropical conditions. Attention in Latin America thus shifted to indigenous sources of germplasm, with the emphasis having lately been on the collection and testing of such legume genera as *Centrosema*, *Pueraria*, *Stylosanthes* and *Desmodium*. Parallel work is also taking place in respect of grass genera like *Brachiaria*, *Panicum* and *Andropogon*. As yet, very few legumes have been introduced into commercial pastures in Amazonia, but, particularly in Brazil, Colombia and Peru, there is growing technical interest in their potential (Schultze-Kraft & Giacometti, 1979; Sanchez, 1979b; Serrão & Toledo, 1988).

As with extensive cattle rearing on the *terra firme*, semi-intensive systems are subject to soil nutrient constraints that affect both the quantity and quality of pasture. The value of pasture legumes lies in their ability to contribute nitrogen to the grass and to improve the overall nutritional content of the pasture (Sanchez, 1976). Nitrogen fixation will not realise the full growth potential of available grasses (Hutton, 1979), but overall productivity and quality will exceed that of unimproved grasslands and the requirement for costly nitrogenous fertilisers will be avoided. Even so, some fertiliser inputs are needed. According to Santhirasegaram (1975a), phosphate fertiliser is the most critical, although small amounts will generally suffice for pasture establishment and early growth. In places, soil liming has also been undertaken to neutralise exchangeable aluminium and reduce levels of phosphorus fixation, but this approach is costly for beef production and it is preferable to focus on the selection of forage species with enhanced tolerance of acid soils (Sanchez, 1979b; Sanchez & Isbell, 1979; Toledo & Serrão, 1982; Serrão & Toledo, 1988). Applications of sulphur may also be required, as well as small amounts of molybdenum, zinc and other trace elements (Spain, 1975; Hutton, 1979).

A 'utilisation model' for Amazonian forest soils has been formulated by Serrão *et al.* (1978) on the basis of experiments conducted along the Belém–Brasília highway in Pará and Mato Grosso. The model, which elaborates earlier work in Peru (Toledo & Ara, 1977), is designed for upgrading existing pastures of colonião (*Panicum maximum*) and is based on the introduction of adapted legumes, like *Pueraria phaseoloides*, and the application of phosphate fertilisers at rates of 25–50 kg P_2O_5/ha every two to three years. A similar approach has been tested at Marabá in Pará state, where grass–legume pastures containing jaraguá (*Hyparrhenia rufa*), *Pueraria phaseoloides* and *Stylosanthes guianensis* have been established with fertiliser applications of 50 kg P_2O_5/ha. At stock densities of 1–2 animals/ha, significantly higher liveweight gains are achieved than on traditional *H. rufa* pastures (Camarão *et al.*, 1980). At Pucallpa in Peru, increased liveweight gains have also been reported on experimental pastures of *H. rufa* and *S. guianensis* after similar fertiliser treatments; according to Toledo & Morales (1979), highest liveweight gains are achieved at densities of 2.6 animals/ha. The improved economic performance of grass-legume pastures compared with traditional colonião (*Panicum maximum*) pastures has also been demonstrated (Kitamura *et al.*, 1982).

While preliminary experiments in recent years have been encouraging, additional investigation is needed to determine local fertiliser needs and other management requirements. In the latter context, selection of suitable germplasm of grasses and legumes is considered to be of primary importance (Serrão & Toledo, 1988). Many Amazonian plants have evolved a natural tolerance of high levels of soil aluminium and make efficient use of the limited supplies of phosphorus in the soil. Selection of such species and their ecotypes is highly desirable and is expected to contribute to improved pasture productivity (Santhirasegaram, 1975a; Toledo & Serrão, 1982). In addition, pasture performance will depend on the specific grass-legume associations adopted. In many instances, it appears that tropical grasses grow faster than pasture legumes and are capable of shading the latter, causing their elimination from the sward (Santhirasegaram, 1975b). Many of the existing pasture legumes, for example, do not easily co-exist with the recumbent *Brachiaria* spp. that have lately been introduced on much cleared forest land (Rayman, 1979; Hecht, 1982). However, some suitable associations involving *Brachiaria* spp. have been identified (Dias Filho, 1983), and erect grasses like *Hyparrhenia rufa*, *Panicum maximum* and *Paspalum plicatulatum* certainly appear, under proper management, to be compatible with familiar legumes like *Centrosema pubescens*, *Pueraria phaseoloides* and *Stylosanthes guianensis* (Santhirasegaram, 1975a; Sanchez, 1976). Experimental work with other legumes, such as *Desmodium*, *Arachis* and *Calopogonium*, is also under way with a view to identifying further grass-legume associations that are suitable for specific Amazonian habitats (Alarcón *et al.*, 1980; Serrão & Toledo, 1988).

Other factors influence the productivity and stability of semi-intensive pasture systems. Under traditional extensive ranching, weed and shrub invasion is a major constraint on pasture maintenance, and similar problems arise with grass–legume associations. The establishment of a well-developed pasture layer helps suppress weed invasion, but manual and other controls are periodically required. As pastures are improved, it is desirable to avoid burning as the basis for weed control, as the practice tends to undermine longer-term pasture quality. Other biotic problems exist in that current forage cultivars are susceptible to pests and diseases. The vulnerability of *Brachiaria* spp. to spittle bug (*Deois* spp., *Zulia* spp.) has been widely reported, while other insect pests and also fungal infections attack sundry forage grasses and legumes (Hecht, 1981; Dias Filho, 1983; Serrão & Toledo, 1988). Temporary reversion to agricultural cropping is one management strategy recommended for pastures that have been degraded by biotic or edaphic processes (Sanchez, 1979a), but sustaining the original pasture cover is in many respects preferable. Against this background, the development of new forage cultivars that are better-adapted to nutrient-poor soils, more resistant to existing pests and diseases, and sufficiently fast-growing and persistent to reduce weed competition is seen as the critical basis for improved pasture management (Serrão & Toledo, 1988).

Once improved pastures are established, additional attention is required to the livestock itself. Controlled rotational stocking is essential, since any overgrazing will tend to upset the grass–legume balance and aggravate weed problems, leading to reductions in livestock productivity (Roberts, 1979; Camarão *et al.*, 1980; Nicholaides *et al.*, 1983). Zebu stock are suitable for semi-intensive rearing systems, but increased attention to animal health and nutrition is required. Whilst improved pasture quality will itself increase stock productivity and reproduction, additional responses may be expected from direct mineral supplementation (Santhirasegaram, 1975a; Sanchez, 1979a).

Semi-intensive pasture systems offer an alternative to extensive pioneer ranching on the forested *terra firme*. Their aim is to establish sustainable low-input beef production on cleared forest land, with stock densities of 1–4 animals/ha. Some fertiliser inputs and mineral supplements are required, but at levels that are compatible with the financial return of the system. The incorporation of legumes is critical in this respect, since they provide the pasture with significant natural inputs of nitrogen. According to Santhirasegaram (1975a, p. 435), the use of grass–legume pastures will be 'in harmony with the socio-economic conditions and level of technology practicable in the region for quite some time to come'. Even so, it must be emphasised that appropriate experimental work has only been initiated in a few areas and that numerous problems remain to be resolved, not least of which are the provision of well-adapted forage germplasm and of appropriate grass–legume associations as a basis for sustained pasture productivity. Nevertheless, grass–legume systems appear feasible in ecological and economic terms, and, provided modest technical inputs and support are available, offer a more stable basis for Amazonian beef production than extensive pioneer ranching.

Silvopastoral systems

Another possible option for the forested *terra firme* is silvopastoralism, which includes a variety of integrated crop–livestock activities. Like agrosilviculture, silvopastoral systems are designed to achieve sustained production at low levels of technical input. Silvopastoral systems in a strict sense refer to the grazing of livestock on herbaceous cover crops grown within tree plantations (Hecht, 1982), but also included here are small-scale farming systems in which livestock production is integrated with mixed short-cycle and long-cycle cropping, i.e. agrosilvopastoral systems, as described by Combe & Budowski (1979).

Previous experience with silvopastoralism has been acquired in central America and south-east Asia (Holdridge, 1951; Payne, 1976; De las Salas, 1979), but little experimental work has taken place in Amazonia. An important exception is a government-sponsored programme of integrated small-scale farming at Limoncocha in eastern Ecuador (Bishop, 1978). According to Kirby (1976), the programme is based on the principles of European peasant farming, combined with some of the technology of local indigenous groups. From the European tradition derives the idea of recycling nutrients through domestic animals, so that the land benefits from a concentration of manure when arable cultivation is restored after pasture fallowing. Elsewhere in Amazonia, there have also been scattered attempts to establish livestock rearing within commercial tree plantations (Hecht, 1982).

In ecological terms, silvopastoralism derives specific advantages from its mixed-crop status. As with agrosilviculture, more efficient utilisation of solar radiation and available soil nutrients occurs. Nitrogen-fixing species can be incorporated in the system for forage or other purposes, while the involvement of livestock also serves to enhance nutrient cycling. In addition, the risk of crop pests and diseases is diminished in mixed silvopastoral systems, and reductions in the level of weed invasion are to be expected (Bishop, 1979a).

The approach at Limoncocha in eastern Ecuador involves small-scale farming based on the 'rotation of agricultural production with a forest-pastoral "fallow"' (Bishop, 1978, p. 460). One example cited is a swine–forestry–production system. This is based on initial cultivation of maize, manioc and beans over a two-year period during which perennial forage species like *Desmodium ovalifolium*, *Canna edulis* and *Musa* sp. are interplanted. The latter are intended to provide feed for pigs, which are introduced in the third year of the cycle. Tree crops are also planted, including peach palm (*Bactris gasipaes*), whose fruit are a useful feed, and the fast-growing legume *Inga edulis*, which provides firewood. The system is intended to operate as an eight-year rotation on 10 ha units (Bishop, 1978, 1979b). A longer-cycle rotation has also been devised for integrated cattle and timber production on 40 ha units. Experiments are reported with grass–legume pastures of *Brachiaria humidicola* and *Desmodium ovalifolium*, among which the commercial timber *Cordia alliodora* is planted. Grazing commences when *C. alliodora* reaches 3 m in height, and cattle densities of 2 animals/ha are maintained. The tree crop is intended for harvesting after twenty years, and the system is seen as particularly suitable for renovating older pastures on cleared forest land. In practice, a cattle–timber unit can be combined with a swine–forestry unit to produce a 50 ha family farm, which is a common size of holding allocated to colonists in eastern Ecuador (Bishop, 1979c, 1982; Hiraoka & Yamamoto, 1980).

Cattle rearing in commercial tree plantations has also been initiated in parts of Amazonia. The best-known example is on the Jari project, where cattle were established on pastures of *Panicum maximum* and *Brachiaria humidicola*, amid *Pinus caribaea*. Over 20,000 ha of such pasture were planted, with the aim of reducing the cost of weed control in the tree plantation (Fearnside & Rankin, 1982; Hecht, 1982). Cattle raising under *P. caribaea* has also been reported from Surinam (Kirby, 1976) and occurs under plantation rubber at Anandineua in Pará.

Current experience with silvopastoral systems in Amazonia is limited, and few long-term data are available. However, the systems are considered to be sustainable at low levels of technical input and to provide economic returns from the sale of livestock and tree products (Bishop, 1982). Many tree species can usefully be incorporated, especially on small-scale farming units. Commercial timber species that occur naturally in Amazonian pastures, like *Bagassa guianensis* and *Cordia goeldiana*, are suitable for inclusion (Hecht, 1982). Trees like mango (*Mangifera indica*), coconut (*Cocos nucifera*) and cashew (*Anacardium occidentale*) can also be incorporated, and many other lesser-known forest species are likely to have silvopastoral potential. Among these are possible leguminous browse species, like *Leucaena glauca* and native *Cassia* spp. (*C. fastuosa*, *C. grandis*), which can provide livestock feed in the form of green foliage or edible fruit and seeds (Hecht, 1982; Peck, 1982).

Like agrosilviculture, silvopastoral systems offer a sustainable basis for land exploitation on the *terra firme*. They have ecological advantages over monocultural systems, and provide a basis for commercial production at lower levels of input and yield. Various plant–animal combinations are feasible, although further experimental work is required to identify a range of options that are adapted to local conditions. Considerable silvopastoral experience has been acquired elsewhere in the tropics, and provides a relevant source of information and expertise. Admittedly, in Amazonia, there are continuing commercial attractions in pioneer cattle-ranching and extractive logging, but silvopastoralism provides a possible long-term alternative to these profitable, but damaging pursuits.

Savannas and wetlands

While recent Amazonian development has mainly focused on the forested *terra firme*, some observers have argued the desirability of directing more attention to savanna and wetland areas. Camargo (1949, 1958) was an early advocate of exploiting the Amazonian *várzea*, urging the development of intensive cultivation of rice and other annual crops on its relatively favourable soils; such development was seen as a means of avoiding damage of the kind that had occurred in the Bragantina zone. Other authors who have emphasised the cropping potential of the *várzea* include Sioli (1973), Goodland & Irwin (1975), Katzman (1977), Eden (1978) and Smith (1982). In addition, Goodland & Irwin (1977) have argued the case for increased use of the *cerrados* and also Amazonian savannas; this is seen as an explicit alternative to forest exploitation, which, in their view, is not sustainable under existing practices and is leading to 'increasingly severe and possibly irreversible environmental destruction' (Goodland & Irwin, 1977, p. 214). Furley (1980) similarly favours exploitation of the *cerrados* as a means of 'buying time' to allow slower and more controlled development in forest areas.

Underlying these views is the assumption that savanna and wetland systems, which experience particular natural stresses associated with water supply, are inherently resilient and less vulnerable to irreversible damage than tropical forests. On this basis, savannas and wetlands are seen as suitable areas for additional exploitation and settlement and as alternative foci for colonisation. Even so, it must not be assumed that such areas are immune to over-exploitation or environmental damage. As elsewhere, any agrosystems employed need to be adapted to local environmental conditions and any extractive activities commensurate with available natural resources.

The main savanna zones in tropical South America are the *cerrados* and *llanos*, which have traditionally been used for extensive cattle ranching (Cole, 1960; Parsons, 1980). Latterly, they have also been exploited for agricultural purposes and thus offer instructive models for Amazonian savannas. In the Brazilian *cerrados*, a significant extension of agriculture has occurred in recent years, with development mainly concentrating on dry farming of crops like soyabean, wheat, maize and coffee (Cunningham, 1980; CETEC-IBS, 1980; Bertrand, 1988; Furley & Ratter, 1988). Local crop production is at times affected by short-term droughts during the rainy season, but climatic conditions are generally favourable and rainfall seasonality tends to reduce pest populations (Goodland & Irwin, 1977; Sanchez, 1979a). *Cerrado* soils are similarly infertile to those of the Amazonian *terra firme*, but local supplies of limestone and rock phosphate are available and provide relatively cheap means of soil improvement (Soares *et al.*, 1975; Goodland & Irwin, 1977). Agricultural development has also occurred in the *llanos*, mainly in Venezuela, where a range of capital-intensive irrigation schemes has been developed; cereals, fruit and other cash crops are cultivated, as well as improved pastures (Eden, 1974c; Parsons, 1980) (see Photograph 27). In the eastern *llanos*, local dry cropping of sorghum and groundnuts also occurs, and a large plantation of *Pinus caribaea* and *Eucalyptus* spp. has been established (CVG, 1969).

Recent agricultural experience in the *cerrados* and *llanos* indicates that a higher land potential exists than that offered by traditional extensive ranching. This would presumably also apply in Amazonian savannas, like the Rio Branco–Rupununi or Puciari–Humaitá, were the provision of fertilisers and other inputs less costly in these remoter areas. In more accessible Amazonian savannas, occasional commercial crop production has been attempted. This includes soyabean and groundnut cultivation and *Pinus caribaea* plantings in savannas of the coastal hinterland of the Guianas, but the prevailing Arenosols in the area are highly infertile and the results have not been very encouraging (Wagenaar, 1966; Bajracharya, 1980). *Pinus caribaea* has also been established in savannas of southern Amapá, where a plantation of 120,000 ha is being developed (Dubé, 1980; McDonald & Fernandes, 1984); initial progress with the project appears satisfactory, although, as elsewhere, questions exist over longer-term provision of nutrients.

The other option is to try to upgrade cattle ranching in Amazonian savannas. As indicated in the Rio Branco–Rupununi, marginal improvements can be made to existing livestock systems, but ranching in most Amazonian savannas remains extensive and low-yielding, and it is difficult to identify further improvements that would be economic under prevailing market conditions, especially in more isolated areas. As on cleared forest land, the best long-term prospect for improved livestock production seems to be grass–legume pastures. Studies have been undertaken in the Colombian *llanos* (Spain *et al.*, 1986), and local experiments are under way in some Brazilian Amazonian savannas. In Amapá, *Brachiaria humidicola* and *Paspalum plicatulatum* have been grown in association with legumes like *Stylosanthes capitata*, *S. guianensis*, *Desmodium ovalifolium* and *Pueraria phaseoloides*. Results are encouraging when phosphate fertilisers are applied, and, although problems exist in maintaining the grass–legume balance, the approach holds promise (Dutra *et al.*, 1980; Souza Filho *et al.*, 1980). Continuing investigations are clearly required.

Even so, in terms of deflecting colonisation from the forest zone, Amazonian savannas are unlikely to make immediate and significant contributions. Their long-term prospects for development may be favourable, but this has yet to be demonstrated, and, in any case, depends on the provision of improved infrastructure and services. Continuing

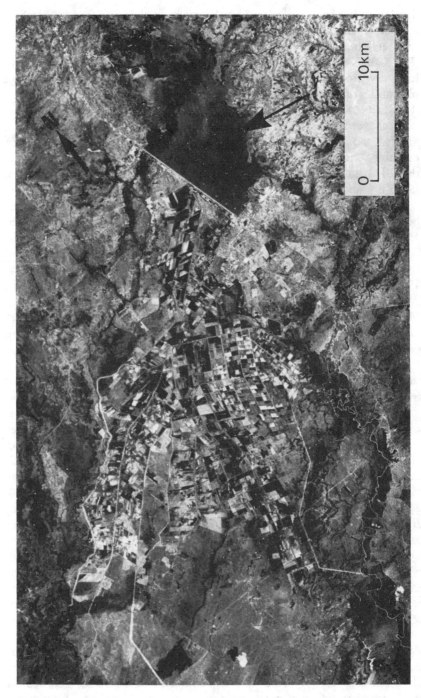

Photograph 27 Guarico irrigation project in central *llanos* of Venezuela, showing the Calabozo reservoir (arrowed) and adjacent cultivated land. Skylab image (red band), February 1974, ID no. G40AOA5386 (reproduced by courtesy of NOAA)

Photograph 28 Cultivable floodplain land in the Caquetá valley, south-east Colombia, currently in use for impermanent cropping of maize and manioc

development of the more accessible *cerrados* and *llanos* will no doubt occur, but, for the moment, most Amazonian savannas provide no great focus of development opportunity.

In general, it seems preferable to direct more attention to the resource potential of Amazonian wetlands and related aquatic habitats. The main advantages of wetlands, as a function of recurrent flooding, are their enhanced soil fertility and reduced incidence of weeds, pests and diseases (Sioli, 1966b; Goodland, 1980; Smith, 1982). Enhanced fertility is not ubiquitous, being confined to white water floodplains and coastal wetlands, but these cover a significant area and, as pre-Columbian experience indicates, are generally cultivable (see Photograph 28). Flood variability makes their exploitation somewhat risky, but does not preclude it (Katzman, 1977; Eden & Andrade, 1988). The areas of lowest flood risk are coastal and estuarine wetlands under tidal influence, and it is there that most permanent wetland cultivation currently occurs. This includes the long-established sugar and rice cultivation in empoldered, coastal Guyana, as well as comparable activities in adjacent coastal Surinam (Thomas-Hope, 1987b) and along the Guamá valley in Pará (Camargo, 1958; Alvim, 1977). Further inland, intensive rice cultivation has been undertaken on the Jari river floodplain (Fearnside & Rankin, 1982) and similar exploitation is clearly feasible along other rivers of lower flood range in both eastern and western Amazonia (PRORADAM, 1979; Norgaard, 1981; Barrow, 1985).

In central Amazonia, where the annual flood range attains 10 m or more, agricultural development is more problematic. Earlier proposals for regulating the Amazon mainstream by means of a dam, 30 m or more in height, at Monte Alegre were imaginative, but quite inappropriate in spite of the vast hydro-electric potential involved (Panero, 1967; Goodland & Irwin, 1975). As Norgaard (1981) indicates, scope may exist for more modest agricultural engineering works, but adaptation to, rather than control of, flood waters is likely to be more appropriate where flood range is high. It should be possible to develop floating rice cultivation in such areas and to upgrade post-flood cultivation with improved varieties of maize, beans and manioc (Biard & Wagenaar, 1960; Barrow, 1985). Overall, a substantial area of cultivable wetland exists along the Amazon valley and in adjacent estuarine and coastal zones. According to Lima (1956), the estuarine zone alone contains more than 1.5 million ha suitable for rice cultivation; extensive undeveloped wetlands also exist in adjacent coastal Amapá.

Although the merits of wetland agriculture have commonly been canvassed, much less actual development has occurred than on the forested *terra firme* and less research has been undertaken. Nor should it be assumed, in spite of pre-Columbian achievements in the zone, that wetland exploitation is easily established. As elsewhere, preliminary land surveys and agronomic experiments are required to identify adaptive modern agrosystems and avoid the kind of problems that have beset colonisation on the *terra firme*. Elsewhere in the tropics, there is much experience of wetland cultivation, especially rice cropping, but limited information exists on Amazonian wetlands and more is required. As experience in the Orinoco delta indicates, modern land drainage and reclamation schemes may initially increase agricultural potential, but can also induce positive feedbacks that complicate longer-term production (Ruddle & Chesterfield, 1976; Eden & Potter, 1979). Even where the technical aspects of wetland cultivation are resolved, infrastructural and institutional constraints on development also need to be overcome (Petrick, 1978).

Amazonian wetlands have considerable potential for producing animal protein. Cattle are already present in many areas, and also water buffalo (*Bubalus bubalis*) which were introduced to the Amazon estuarine zone in the late nineteenth century. The zone currently contains more than 200,000 water buffalo, which exploit perennial supplies of nutritious feed (IBGE, 1980b). The animals are reared for their milk and meat, and are generally more productive than cattle; particular efforts are being made to develop their potential on Marajó island (Nascimento & Lourenço Júnior, 1979; Nascimento et al., 1979; Marques et al., 1980). A few buffalo herds also exist along the Amazon valley and elsewhere, but the animal has not yet been widely adopted beyond the estuarine zone (Soares, 1963; Junk, 1980).

The wild fauna also offers opportunities for managed exploitation. Experimental rearing of capibara (*Hydrochoerus hydrochaeris*) has been successfully undertaken in the Venezuelan *bajo llano* (Ojasti & Medina, 1972; Ojasti, 1980), and the species warrants attention in Amazonia. Turtles, which have long been under intense pressure and are now an endangered resource (Smith, 1979), are also suitable for managed exploitation, which would simultaneously help conserve the species. A pre-Columbian precedent exists for such exploitation, which in the case of *Podocnemis* spp. is reported by Smith (1974a) to be of higher productive potential than cattle rearing. There is already a market in the region for capibara and turtle, while other native species like tapir, deer, peccary and caiman are also seen as candidates for managed exploitation (Sternberg, 1973; Smith, 1981b; Dourojeanni, 1985; Myers, 1988a).

Substantial fish stocks also exist in the wetland zone. Productive habitats include *várzea* lakes and estuarine waters, although stocks are generally lower in the turbid Amazon mainstream and poor in black water rivers (Fittkau *et al.*, 1975; Lowe-McConnell, 1975). Traditional fishing methods are still widely used, and, although local over-exploitation sometimes results, such methods generally allow sustained production. Commercial fishing, however, has greatly expanded in recent years and serious over-exploitation has become apparent. The use of powered boats and nylon nets, particularly by fishermen from larger centres like Belém, Manaus and Iquitos, has greatly increased fish production, which now provides exports to southern Brazil and the United States as well as supplies to local urban markets (Chapman, 1977; Smith, 1981a; Goulding, 1983). Reported fish production in Amazonas state in Brazil, for example, has risen from an average 10,800 t/yr in 1960–5 to 44,780 t/yr in 1980–5.

Fish stocks are also coming under indirect pressure as a result of environmental disturbance. The clearance of *várzea* forest is particularly damaging since it reduces the supply of fruit, seeds and other organic matter to rivers and lakes. Organic matter of this kind is an important food source for fish species like tambaqui (*Colossoma macropomum*) and jatuarana (*Brycon* sp.) which swim into flooded *várzea* forests at times of high water (Goulding, 1980; Lovejoy, 1985b). Also, general forest clearance modifies terrestrial run-off, and, in the longer term, will affect water quality and biological productivity (Marlier, 1973). In addition, fish populations are affected by hydro-electric developments. Major fish kills have been reported after completion of dams at Brokopondo in Surinam and Curuá-Una in Pará (Paiva, 1977a, 1977b). Other major developments have recently taken place, including the massive Tucuruí dam on the Tocantins river, and other hydro-electric projects are under construction or scheduled for the near future. All are liable to cause permanent damage to fish stocks (Smith, 1981a; Lovejoy, 1985b; Goodland, 1986; Barrow, 1988).

Although many Amazonian fish populations are supposedly resilient (Lowe-McConnell, 1979), the overall effects of current commercial extraction and habitat disturbance bode ill for the future. If long-term fish stocks are to be maintained, more positive management of what is currently treated as a free resource is required. In north-east Brazil, fisheries development has involved pond culture of species like *Arapaima gigas* and *Colossoma bidens* (Lowe-McConnell, 1975; FAO, 1978a). Pond culture can be highly productive, especially when fertilisers are used, and some Amazonian research of this kind is desirable in respect of both local and exotic species (FAO, 1978a; Goulding, 1980). More attention, however, needs to be devoted to managing natural habitats and their fish populations than developing artificial ones. Natural habitats that benefit from the inherent fertility of Amazonian white waters can be very productive, and, given effective management, are capable of sustained high fish yields. Where artificial lakes are created as a result of hydro-electric projects, it may be appropriate to develop new fisheries to compensate for lost riverine species (FAO, 1978a; Smith, 1981a), but managing existing fish stocks is the immediate priority.

Fisheries management for sustained yield can take various forms in Amazonian waters. Possible control measures range from the imposition of closed seasons to limits on the number of fishermen or the size of catch. In places, relevant legislation already exists. In Brazil, killing of pirarucú (*Arapaima gigas*) is technically prohibited from October to March each year, and other regulations nominally control the minimum lengths of species that may be kept for sale or consumption (Smith, 1981a). However, the current implementation of such regulations is lax, while basic data on fish productivity, population dynamics and the like, which are essential for formulating efficient long-term management strategies, are in short supply. In these circumstances, the prospects for Amazonian fisheries are extremely uncertain, in spite of the potential for substantial, sustained production.

Conclusion

Sustainable exploitation is feasible in Amazonia. In places, intensive agricultural production of food or industrial crops can be established, although cropping risk may at times be high. Such exploitation is best located in more fertile habitats, particularly wetlands and local areas of eutrophic soils on the *terra firme*. Wetlands and associated aquatic habitats also offer high potential for sustained animal protein production, provided effective resource management occurs. In parallel, it is desirable to explore the prospects for less intensive, but sustainable exploitation on the forested *terra firme* as an alternative to prevailing extractive and pioneer exploitation systems. Sustainable exploitation, whether involving agriculture, silviculture, livestock rearing or some combination of these, is desirable both to safeguard long-term regional production and to minimise the positive feedbacks of forest clearance. In respect of possible 'laterization' (McNeil, 1964) or 'desertification' (Goodland & Irwin, 1975) in the region, localised clearance does not create serious cause for concern. In the Bragantina zone, forest clearance began more than a century ago, and, although much of the area is now seriously degraded, it is by no means a desert, lateritic or otherwise. Nevertheless, more general forest clearance is likely to induce positive feedbacks that will affect climatic and hydrologic regimes and deplete genetic resources. Such feedbacks give genuine cause for concern and reinforce the need for adaptive land exploitation.

Sustainable exploitation of Amazonian land will not easily be achieved. There are multiple environmental constraints, particularly relating to resource deficiencies, resource variabilities and biotic stressors, that variously complicate attempts to establish sustainable agrosystems. A number of options have been discussed, but the present technical basis for their development is often inadequate and further research is required. Also, the development of sustainable exploitation is constrained by inadequate infrastructure and services and by the fact that such exploitation is, at least initially, likely to be less profitable than established extractive or pioneer options. However, given effective land planning and management, none of these factors need be an absolute constraint on the development of sustainable exploitation, for which a basic model has been provided by indigenous resource use. Admittedly, the latter emerged through trial-and-error over a period of millennia, while the current requirement is more urgent. Nevertheless, it is appropriate to emphasise the need for sustainable exploitation and to recognise the possibility of learning from the indigenous experience.

What is required in practice is, firstly, recognition of the need to identify and exploit a range of Amazonian resources. This applies to plant and animal species and to habitats. More diversified resource use is no guarantee of sustainable land development, but should lower the overall level of risk in exploitation and expose promising directions for the future. Secondly, exploitation needs to be adapted to the explicit constraints of the physical environment, particularly nutrient deficiency and hydrologic variability. Technical inputs and capital-intensive agricultural engineering may have some place in this process, but alternative strategies based, for example, on biological management of soil fertility (Swift & Sanchez, 1984) or small-scale drainage and irrigation works (Norgaard, 1981) are likely to be more practical. Thirdly, exploitation needs to be adapted to biotic stressors. Again alternative solutions based, for example, on biological control mechanisms (Gliessman *et al.*, 1981) are preferable to reliance on chemical biocides, which are costly for the farmer and often of dubious efficacy in the humid tropics. It is of course arguable that more, rather than less, advanced technology is the means to overcome environmental constraints. Genetic engineering, for example, with its potential for enhancing pest resistance in vulnerable crop plants (Gould, 1988) or for extending nitrogen-fixing capacity among non-leguminous crop species (Döbereiner, 1977) has obvious attractions, but it would be unwise to assume the early viability or local cost-effectiveness of such treatments. For the moment, the best course is to explore sustained yield systems that are securely adapted to local Amazonian conditions.

Although the emphasis of this chapter is on alternative modes of land development, this must not be taken to imply that general development of the Amazon region is desirable, even on a sustainable basis. The forest itself has intrinsic value, and its conservation is as important as any sustainable development that is established within it. The two functions are related, moreover, in the sense that selected forest areas can only effectively be conserved if sustainable development replaces the extractive and pioneer exploitation systems that are currently damaging the forest on a broad front. For such replacement to occur, improved planning and management are required at both agrosystem and regional levels. Hitherto, the agrosystem level has mainly been discussed, and the regional level now requires attention. In Chapter 8, consideration is given to the regional environmental impact of forest clearance and to general conservation planning. In Chapter 9, the critical issue of integrating land development and conservation at the regional level is examined.

8

Regional environmental impact and conservation planning

. . . over the next few decades, the world will lose the bulk of the rain forest remaining today.

[Mabberley, 1983, p. 124]

Existing agrosystems in Amazonia are variable in performance and quality. Many of them display serious shortcomings, being characterised by low or declining productivity associated with rapid depletion of nutrient supply or a proliferation of weeds and pests. Some alternative agrosystems exist that are better adapted to local conditions and sustainable in character. The adaptive status of agrosystems is a critical consideration in Amazonian land management, but it is only part of the issue. Regional factors also need to be considered. Any agrosystem, sustainable or otherwise, will to some extent modify its physical and biological environment. Locally, this impact may be minor or temporary, but the cumulative effect of multiple impacts over a large area can generate positive feedbacks that affect human populations across and even beyond the region. Such feedbacks relate mainly to climatic and hydrologic conditions and to genetic resources. At the regional level, land management in Amazonia thus needs to concern itself with conservation as well as development, and in particular with the array and patterning of productive and protective units on the ground.

In the present chapter, the overall scale of human impact on the Amazonian forest is reviewed, the broader physical and biological feedbacks of forest clearance and land development are considered, and the ecological basis of general conservation planning is discussed. This provides the background for an examination in Chapter 9 of the regional relationship between conservation and development.

Contemporary environmental impact

Imprecise knowledge exists of the overall environmental impact in Amazonia. Recent surveys of vegetation and land use are available for large parts of the region, allowing some estimate of present land cover, but older baseline data are mostly lacking or of poor quality, and preclude realistic estimation of longer-term rates of land cover change. One approach adopted has been to compare the notional 'climax area' of forest with the existing forest area. On this basis, Sommer (1976) estimated that the extent of South American moist forest, largely but not exclusively Amazonian, had already been reduced by some 37 per cent. Although a useful starting point, this approach does not provide definite information on whether the climax area had in fact been previously forested, nor yield data on actual rates of clearance. Latterly, the advent of Landsat and other environmental satellites has offered the possibility of relatively prompt and precise monitoring of land cover over large areas. In Brazil, where a Landsat receiving station was established in the mid-1970s, a forest monitoring programme was initiated and preliminary information acquired on the extent and rate of forest clearance in the Amazonian region (Tardin et al., 1980). Subsequently, responsibility for such monitoring was transferred between government departments, and information on forest clearance was not made widely available. Only in the late 1980s has such information again become generally accessible, although it is currently the subject of some technical uncertainty and dispute (Neto, 1989a, 1989b).

In Table 20, an estimate is given of land cover in Amazonia for the late 1970s. This estimate, which provides a baseline for the region, is derived from available official data for Brazil (Tardin et al., 1980; Hecht, 1981; Benchimol, 1985) and from examination by the present author of Landsat imagery and other sources for the remainder of the region. The total forest area in the late 1970s was estimated at 613 million ha, and the area of cleared forest land at 28 million ha. The forest cover is mainly evergreen to semi-deciduous in character, but includes some drier deciduous forest in parts of eastern Bolivia and the Brazilian Mato Grosso. Approximately 66 million ha (11 per cent) of the forest area is wetland forest. Included within the forest area is an unknown extent of older regenerating forest, which is not distinguishable from primary forest on Landsat imagery. In addition, herbaceous wetland covers an estimated 27–28 million ha within the main forest zone, while dry savanna covers 88 million ha, of which an estimated 15–20 million ha lie within the forest zone. The remaining savanna, in Mato Grosso, Goiás and Maranhão states of Brazil, lies outside the main forest zone, although it is officially part of Amazônia Legal.

The estimated area of cleared forest land in Amazonia in the late 1970s is 28 million ha (see Table 20). This figure is mainly based on Landsat data, and refers to larger areas of more or less continuous clearance. The Brazilian data are derived from Tardin et al., (1980), extrapolated by Hecht (1981), and from UNESCO (1981). Elsewhere, the data are directly derived from Landsat images, as available, with supplementary information from UNESCO (1981) and other sources. Precise and uncontroversial

Table 20 Estimated area (million ha) of the main land cover types in the Amazonian lowlands

	Amazonia	Total forest area*	Terra firme forest	Wetland forest	Total non-forest area	Dry savanna	Herbaceous wetland	Cleared/cultivated land (end-1970s)
Bolivia	52.7	36.6	30.5	6.1	16.1	0.6	14.5	1.0
Brazil[†]	497.8	388.2	348.3	39.9	109.6	80.1	12.1	17.4
Colombia	45.7	42.0	38.1	3.9	3.7	1.3	–	2.4
Ecuador	9.3	8.4	7.6	0.8	0.9	–	–	0.9
French Guiana	9.7	9.6	9.4	0.2	0.1	tr	0.1	tr
Guyana	21.4	18.6	18.1	0.5	2.8	2.1	–	0.7
Peru	65.1	60.3	51.1	9.2	4.8	–	0.1	4.7
Surinam	16.3	15.0	13.5	1.5	1.3	0.1	0.5	0.7
Venezuela	38.6	34.1	30.7	3.4	4.5	3.8	0.4	0.3
Total	756.6	612.8	547.3	65.5	143.8	88.0	27.7	28.1

Sources: Landsat images; Bajracharya, 1980; Benchimol, 1985; Bromley, 1980; Hecht, 1981; ORSTOM, 1979; PRORADAM, 1979; Tardin *et al.*, 1980; UNESCO, 1981.

* The total forest area comprises the more or less continuous zone of forest that is centred on the Amazon river basin, but extends marginally beyond it. The Andean boundary is defined at 1,000 m above sea level.

[†] Brazilian Amazonia is taken to comprise the administrative unit *Amazônia Legal*, which includes 70 million ha of savanna outside the continuous forest zone.

data on more recent rates of forest clearance are not easily acquired. A realistic estimate for Amazonian clearance during the early 1980s is probably 2.0–3.0 million ha/year (Hecht, 1981; Buschbacher, 1986a; Fearnside, 1986b; Salati et al., 1986). Assuming a cleared area of 28 million ha in the late 1970s (Table 20), it is likely that, by end-1985, total clearance had risen to some 40–45 million ha, or 6–7 per cent of the forest area. Latterly, clearance rates have increased, especially in Brazil, where satellite-derived data indicate that, in 1987, a massive 8.3 million ha of primary forest were cleared; a similar area seems to have been lost in 1988 (Margolis, 1988a, 1988b). On that basis and on the assumption of continuing clearance elsewhere in the region, the total area of forest clearance in Amazonia, by end-1988, was probably 60–65 million ha, or 10–11 per cent of the forest area.

Fearnside (1982, 1986a) has drawn attention to the problems of using Landsat imagery for land cover analysis, particularly in respect of identifying small areas of clearance and also older cleared areas where forest regeneration is occurring. Even allowing for this, however, the present level of clearance is well below Sommer's (1976) estimated 37 per cent reduction on the notional climax forest area and also other estimates of actual clearance, notably the 20–25 per cent proposed by Gentry & Lopez-Parodi (1980) and the 33 per cent suggested by Myers (1979a). The latter estimates may more closely approximate the extent of Amazonian forest that has lately been subject to human disturbance, but they exaggerate actual clearance. Where clearance has occurred, the most common causes appear to be cattle-ranching and peasant colonisation.

In parallel with forest clearance, the regional population of Amazonia has increased. From a total of about 10 million in 1970, the population rose by an average 4 per cent per annum to some 15.5 million in the early 1980s. In a few urban areas like Manaus and Belém and in some older colonisation zones, relatively high concentrations of population have developed, but most parts of the region are very sparsely populated. In the early 1980s, the overall population density was approximately 2.1/km^2 (see Table 21).

Various estimates have been made of the likely, long-term impact of population growth and land colonisation on the forest cover. An oft-cited prediction for the tropics as a whole is that of Richards (1973), who concluded that by the end of the present century very little of the rain forest would remain. A similar view is expressed by Mabberley (1983). In respect of Amazonia itself, Myers (1979a) has suggested, from extrapolation of earlier estimated rates of clearance, that the forest could disappear by the year 2040. Estimating future clearance is obviously very difficult, and both more and less pessimistic predictions continue to appear (Fearnside, 1982, 1986b; Buschbacher, 1986a; Raven, 1988). Whatever the prospect, the present level of forest clearance allows no grounds for

Table 21 Population in the Amazonian lowlands

	Land area (million ha)	Population in early 1980s (million)	Population density (km²)
Bolivia	52.7	0.70 (est.)	1.3
Brazil	497.8	11.19	2.3
Colombia	45.7	0.66 (est.)	1.4
Ecuador	9.3	0.28 (est.)	3.0
French Guiana	9.7	0.06	0.6
Guyana	21.4	0.81	3.8
Peru	65.1	1.25 (est.)	1.9
Surinam	16.3	0.37	2.3
Venezuela	38.6	0.23 (est.)	0.6
Total	756.6	15.55	2.1

Sources: Anon., 1987; Aramburú, 1984; Bajracharya, 1980; DAINCO, 1977; Denevan, 1976; IDB, 1984, 1987; Kleinpenning & Volbeda, 1985; OCEI, 1987; Portais, 1983; Uquillas, 1985.

complacency, especially in areas where extractive logging is reinforcing the effects of cattle ranching and peasant colonisation. Nevertheless, it should be emphasised that the Amazonian forest cover has not as yet suffered gross damage on the regional scale. Such could easily occur in the next decade or so, but, given the appropriate political will and effective regional planning, the possibility still exists of achieving a rational compromise between development and conservation.

Climatic and hydrologic effects of forest clearance

It is widely assumed that large-scale replacement of the forest cover will affect regional climatic and hydrologic conditions, and will induce changes that are significant in human terms. Earlier suggestions that widespread deforestation would upset the global oxygen balance have been discounted (Bryson, 1972; Farnworth & Golley, 1974; Sternberg, 1986), but the impact of deforestation on the heat balance and hydrologic cycle continues to give cause for concern. The processes involved are complex and prediction of effects is very difficult, but regional and even global environmental changes are anticipated. The complexity is well-illustrated by Potter *et al.* (1975) in a computer simulation of the climatic effects of general deforestation in the zone 5 degrees N to 5 degrees S. The initial result of such clearance was predicted to be increased land surface albedo and reduced energy absorption. This would in turn modify local evaporation, convection and rainfall processes, as well as affect extra-tropical energy and moisture flows. Within the tropical zone itself, a slight temperature lowering was envisaged, together with a marked reduction in rainfall at the equator and an increase towards the tropics. Computer simulations of this kind involve many questionable assumptions (Sagan et al., 1979; Dickinson, 1981), but they emphasise the complex interactions involved and indicate the kind of climatic modifications that may occur. Refined simulations continue to appear, which similarly indicate temperature and/or rainfall adjustments as a result of forest clearance (Henderson-Sellers & Gornitz, 1984; Dickinson & Henderson-Sellers, 1988).

Many investigations in Amazonia have concentrated on the relationship between deforestation and rainfall (Portig, 1968; Marques et al., 1977; Salati et al., 1978, 1986; Fränzle, 1979; Lettau et al., 1979; Salati, 1985). According to Molion (1976) and Salati et al. (1979), the supply of water vapour in Amazonia is initially derived by air flow from the Atlantic ocean, but approximately 50 per cent of regional rainfall is attributed to local evapotranspiration and re-precipitation. The existence of a forest cover, which lowers rates of terrestrial run-off, is assumed to facilitate this local recycling and thus enhance rainfall levels. Conversely, if deforestation occurs, terrestrial run-off is likely to increase and evapotranspiration and rainfall be correspondingly reduced. According to Sioli (1980), replacement of a freely-transpiring forest by a 'steppe-like' cover might lower evapotranspiration to one-third of the present level, causing a significant reduction in rainfall total and increased rainfall seasonality. At what scale of clearance such effects would become apparent is less clear. Fränzle (1979, p. 97) considers that localised forest clearance 'limited to the areas adjoining transport routes and settlements' would have little influence on precipitation levels. However, more than localised clearance will occur if current rates of land colonisation continue, and an appreciable hydrologic feedback seems possible.

Consideration has also been given to the effect of rain forest clearance on atmospheric carbon dioxide (CO_2). The latter is currently increasing as a result of net carbon release from fossil fuels as well as from decomposing forest biomass and soil organic matter. Such release is generally expected to induce changes in both global and regional climates. During the last 100 years, atmospheric CO_2 has increased by 20–25 per cent, giving a present concentration of some 350 ppm. The net annual atmospheric increment commensurate with the current rate of increase is 2.9×10^9 t/C/yr, and continuing additions at this rate will probably double the atmospheric concentration at some time during the next century (Hare, 1980; Walsh et al., 1981; Detwiler & Hall, 1988). How significant Amazonian deforestation is to this process is uncertain. The amount of carbon stored in the biomass of Amazonia is estimated at 115×10^9 t (Sioli, 1980, 1985), but the net flux from this pool will depend as much on the nature of the replacement land cover as on the extent of forest clearance itself. The situation is further complicated because the dynamics of the global carbon cycle are imperfectly understood, making it difficult to determine what proportions of released forest carbon pass to the atmospheric and the oceanic pools (Richey et al., 1980). Nevertheless, it has recently been estimated that global forest clearance is currently contributing 20–30 per cent of atmospheric CO_2 build-up, with Amazonian clearance probably responsible for at least a third of that total (Dobson et al., 1989). Resultant modifications to the atmospheric 'greenhouse effect' are expected to cause rises in global temperature and sea level, as well as changes in rainfall. The effects will vary from region to region; temperature increase in the tropical zone may be less marked than in higher latitudes (Hansen et al., 1981, 1988; Fearnside, 1985b; Peters, 1988), but any rise in sea level is likely to have significant implications for coastal, estuarine and lower Amazon valley wetlands.

The overall impact on Amazonian climate is uncertain. Modified surface albedo and evapotranspiration will occur as a result of deforestation, while local, as well as general, increments of CO_2 will continue to be added to the global atmosphere. Also, forest clearance and burning are causing a net flux to the atmosphere of trace gases like nitrous oxide (N_2O) and possibly methane (CH_4) and also raising aerosol levels, all of which, directly or indirectly, impinge on the heat balance and may affect climate (Fearnside, 1985a; Joyce, 1985; Seiler & Conrad, 1987; Margolis, 1988a; Pearman & Fraser, 1988). While the precise prospect is unclear, drier and possibly warmer conditions may develop within Amazonia on a timescale of decades.

Forest clearance and replacement by a less substantial plant cover will cause accelerated surface water run-off, especially on steeper slopes, and will lead to increased fluvial discharge and sediment load. Even if rainfall totals decline, similar tendencies will be apparent. During drier periods of the year, river levels may not be greatly modified, but peak flood levels are likely to increase.

Flood responses of this kind have been widely reported in Asia (Myers, 1984). The clearance of forest from Himalayan mountain slopes has notably increased flood damage in lowland agricultural areas in India, Pakistan and Bangladesh (Polunin, 1980; Myers, 1988a). In China, excessive flooding along the Yangtse river has been attributed to large-scale logging in its upper basin (Bonavia, 1981). Similarly, in Amazonia, increased flooding is to be expected, if extensive clearance takes place in lowland areas or adjacent headwater zones. Indications of this may already be evident in western Amazonia. Using data from Iquitos, Gentry & Lopez-Parodi (1980) have reported an increase of more than 2 m in the annual high-water level of the Amazon river since the early 1960s, which they attribute to increased run-off due to upstream deforestation in Peru and Ecuador. The analysis is complicated by rainfall variability over the study period (Nordin & Meade, 1982), but the preliminary results accord with the assumed link between forest clearance and flood conditions.

Any impact of modified fluvial regimes will be most evident in the *várzea* zone. Increased peak flooding will extend the area of seasonal inundation, putting settlements and cultivated land at risk. In addition, river sediment levels will increase and patterns of channel erosion and deposition vary. In places, the aquatic fauna may be directly affected by sediment change (Marlier, 1973), and indirect damage is likely to result from modified light penetration, which will in turn affect primary aquatic productivity and the food chain (Richards, 1977). Aquatic resources will generally be at risk.

In some areas, specific environmental changes will occur as a result of hydro-electric projects. As yet, only a few major developments of this kind have been undertaken in the region, notably those at Guri in south-east Venezuela, Brokopondo in Surinam, and Tucuruí in Brazilian Pará. However, numerous potential hydro-electric sites have been identified, especially in Brazil, and additional projects are under way or scheduled for the near future (Pandolfo, 1974, 1979; Junk & de Mello, 1987; Barrow, 1988). Attention is currently focused on a series of dams planned along the Xingú river, which are expected to flood 8 million ha of land (Anon., 1988), and on the massive Balbina project, 140 km north of Manaus, where a shallow lake covering 240,000 ha is due to be created. Hydro-electric projects of this kind inevitably involve substantial destruction of forest in and around their reservoir areas, while the aquatic fauna is generally at risk. Also human populations are commonly displaced, and there is a clear need for more balanced appraisal of future projects. Where they do proceed, hydro-electric projects should be integrated into a broader conservation strategy. As is widely recognised, their lakes are vulnerable to sedimentation and infilling, especially when associated with upstream deforestation, and this vulnerability, when set against the high capital costs of projects, provides a cogent reason for forest protection. Even where rivers that are presently less turbid are involved (Junk & de Mello, 1987), forest areas lying upstream of existing or planned hydro-electric projects should be seen as priority conservation areas and attention given to their protection on economic, as well as environmental, grounds.

Biological implications of forest clearance

Widespread clearance of primary forest in Amazonia will have permanent and damaging biological effects. The main effects will be a massive extinction of plants and animals and consequent loss of genetic resources (Myers, 1986; Wilson, 1988). Any biome is prone to damage when disturbed by humans, but tropical forest is particularly vulnerable as a function of its composition and dynamics. Not only is it exceptionally diverse and thus prone to multiple extinctions, but also many of its species are specialised and inter-related and are intolerant of general disturbance. Evolutionary factors, including the creation of Pleistocene forest refugia (Haffer, 1969), have resulted in a localised distribution of many organisms, which are correspondingly vulnerable to localised forest clearance (Prance, 1977; Myers, 1980). No precise estimate is possible of the likely scale of plant and animal extinctions in Amazonia, but Myers (1978) has suggested that, if large-scale clearance continues, some half million species might disappear from all tropical moist forests by the end of the century. In respect of Amazonia, the scale of extinction will depend on the extent and location of clearance, but there is no question that very significant losses could occur.

Loss of Amazonian genetic resources is undesirable for many reasons. Firstly, it will limit the capacity of the forest to reproduce itself. Pioneer plant species capable of initiating regeneration on cleared forest land will generally survive, but primary forest species are biologically more vulnerable and prone to extinction. Such vulnerability is apparent, for example, in the lower availability of their seeds, reflecting basic seed production, dispersal and germination characteristics as well as the sparse distribution of individuals of each species (Gómez-Pompa et al., 1972; Kubitzki, 1985; Uhl, 1988). In view of the increasing area of forest that is subject to exploitation and deflection to secondary growth, it is essential to safeguard primary forest species. Their regenerative capacity is the fundamental insurance against anthropic disturbance.

Secondly, the extinction of Amazonian species represents a loss of particular resources of direct value to humans. Numerous natural plant and animal products have already been identified and commercially exploited in the forest, but many other species of potential value exist there. The latter are vulnerable because their utility is often unrecognised or only locally known. They include many potential cultigens of value for the production of food, fibres and fodder (Tosi & Voertman, 1964). The number of Amazonian forest trees, for example, that produce edible fruit or nuts is immense and, although a few like cacao (*Theobroma cacao*) and Brazil nut (*Bertholletia excelsa*) are already of major commercial importance, many others have unrealised potential as food products (Benchimol, 1988). In Peruvian Amazonia, for example, Pinedo del Aguila (1967) identified more than thirty species of fruit tree of local economic value, few of which are widely known; a further twenty-two species were listed yielding useful fibre products. As far as Amazonian commercial wood production is concerned, a relatively small number of tree species currently provides most of the timber, plywood, veneer and pulp that is obtained from the region. Many more species could be used for such purposes, and diversification of this kind is both feasible and desirable, at least in a silvicultural context.

Also of potential value are phytochemical products, or extractives, which exist in individual plants or taxa and have widespread industrial and other uses (Goldstein, 1979). Such products include latex, oils, waxes, resins, dyes, tannins and other natural compounds. Latex, an emulsion of hydrocarbons and water, is familiar as the raw material for the production of rubber from *Hevea brasiliensis*. Latterly, investigations have been initiated with another Amazonian tree species, *Copaifera langsdorfii*, using its hydrocarbon fluids as a direct source of vehicle fuel. The product appears to perform satisfactorily, and experimental plantations have been established in Brazilian Amazonia (Myers, 1984; Calvin, 1987). Plant oils for human consumption and other uses are also being sought from the region. African oil palm (*Elaeis guineensis*) has been widely introduced, but many indigenous palms, like babaçu (*Orbignya phalerata*), patauá (*Jessenia bataua*), urucuri (*Attalea excelsa*) and caiaui (*E. melanococca*), produce oil-bearing fruit that are of similar value and already locally in use (Mors & Rizzini, 1966; Müller, 1980; Balick & Gershoff, 1981; Balick, 1985; Anderson & Overal, 1988). Many other species of comparable potential exist in the forest and warrant investigation.

Forest plants also contain chemical compounds of medicinal value. Lovejoy & de Padua (1980) point out that the Amazon basin is one of the best places to seek such compounds, because the evolutionary processes that induce their development have been aided by the constant natural competition in the forest between plants, insects and other organisms. Natural products of this kind have been widely used by indigenous populations, and some have been exploited by modern society. The traditional remedy ipecac (*Cephaelis ipecacuanha*), which contains alkaloid substances, has been used in the treatment of amoebic dysentery, bronchitis and bilharzia (Myers, 1984). Curare, derived from a range of alkaloid-bearing plants and used as a hunting poison, contains an active ingredient that has long been employed as a muscle relaxant in surgery (Mors & Rizzini, 1966; Reis Altschul, 1977). Other forest species reported to be of medicinal value include guaraná (*Paullinia cupana*), copaiba (*Copaifera reticulata*), pedra-ume-caá (*Myrcia* spp.) and tunadí (*Alexa canaracunensis*) (Pandolfo, 1979; Lewis & Owen, 1989); tunadí, a leguminous tree species, is of special interest as it contains the alkaloid castanospermine which, under laboratory conditions, exhibits activity against the AIDS virus (Lewis & Owen, 1989). Meanwhile, the screening of many other forest plants continues in a search for natural compounds that will serve either as the direct constituents of medicines or drugs, or provide a starting point for their laboratory synthesis. The present screening of forest species is broadly focused, but has immense possibilities in fields ranging from AIDS and cancer control to fertility regulation (Myers, 1984; Prance, 1985).

Other extractives are of use as biocides. Rotenone, derived from

Lonchocarpus spp. (*L. urucu, L. nicou, L. utilis*), has traditionally been employed as an Amazonian fish poison, but is also the basis of a biodegradable insecticide. The food industry obtains a range of colouring agents and flavouring substances from the forest. Urucu (*Bixa orellana*) bears fruit that contain a tasteless and non-poisonous red dye which has traditionally been used as an Amerindian body paint as well as serving to deter insects; it is today used as a food colorant (Mors & Rizzini, 1966; Gottlieb & Mors, 1978; Posey, 1983). Forest species are of value to the perfume industry. In the past, pau rosa (*Aniba duckei*) was widely used for this purpose, and other species of similar potential include casca preciosa (*Aniba canelila*), cumarú (*Dipteryx odorata*) and puxuri (*Licaria pucheri*) (Pandolfo, 1979; Benchimol, 1988). Many resources of this kind exist in the forest and are at risk if general clearance occurs.

Thirdly, a loss of Amazonian species would not only limit the development of new forest products, but also put established products at risk. Forest species that have been brought into cultivation are still dependent on the genetic resources of their wild relatives and primitive cultivars for breeding purposes. Even when major plant improvements have been made in respect of energy and nutrient conversion or of stress resistance, continuing plant breeding is required and depends on the availability of a large and diverse gene pool. This applies as much to established commercial species, like rubber and cacao, as it does to any new domesticates, plant or animal, that may emerge from the forest. In the case of rubber, the productivity and disease resistance of which have been of major concern to plant breeders for more than fifty years, the long-term viability of the crop is still dependent on wild plants growing in the forest (Allen, 1980). Cultivated cacao similarly relies on the genetic diversity of wild Amazonian cacao to maintain disease-resistant varieties and to improve yield characteristics (Allen, 1983). In the case of staple food crops, much less attention has hitherto been paid to plant breeding, but any future improvements will depend on the availability of traditional cultivars. As contemporary land colonisation extends, this material is as vulnerable to genetic erosion as are wild forest species. Attempts can be made to conserve traditional cultivars outside the forest, as in the case of manioc at the Centro Internacional de Agricultura Tropical (CIAT) in Colombia. The forest itself, however, is the fundamental gene pool, and its wild plants and traditional cultivars, which are increasingly at risk as deforestation proceeds, are optimally conserved in the natural habitat where maximal genetic variability is maintained.

Conservation planning

While damaging environmental feedback is likely to result from extensive deforestation, its precise scale and impact are not easily determined. In these circumstances, it is understandable that speculative and at times exaggerated predictions have been made and received wide publicity. This has not been entirely unproductive, as public attention has been drawn to the issues involved. However, realistic appraisal of the scale and impact of clearance is now required, if politicians and planners are to respond objectively to the need for Amazonian conservation. This echoes Alvim's (1977, p. 349) call for 'scientific *facts* rather than . . . mere prognostications' as the basis for promoting forest protection, but the problem remains that the requisite data on the effects of clearance are not easily acquired and may indeed only emerge as an obituary to lost forest resources.

Reconnaissance surveys and land cover monitoring are providing additional data relevant to conservation planning, and systematic studies of the feedback effects of deforestation are increasing. How rapidly these studies will clarify the situation remains to be seen, particularly in respect of the atmospheric system whose likely response to large-scale clearance is extremely difficult to anticipate (Hare, 1980; Sioli, 1980). The biological effects of clearance are more predictable, and, on such grounds alone, the case for substantial forest conservation can readily be made. However, in spite of increasing awareness of environmental issues in Amazonia, there is still an urgent need to raise levels of 'conservation consciousness' (Steyermark, 1977) at both popular and political levels, and also to resolve outstanding technical questions regarding the integration of conservation objectives with those of land development. The questions concern, firstly, the kind of spatial balance that is required between development and conservation activities in order to sustain productivity and protect resources, and, secondly, how that balance can best be expressed at the regional level.

At present, there are few empirical data on which to base an Amazonian conservation strategy. However, it is evident that several kinds of reserve are required in the region. Firstly, there is the need for 'national parks', which are essentially unaltered areas where the natural flora and fauna can be conserved and genetic resources protected (Dasmann, 1973). While their main function is biological, national parks also provide physical protection for the environment. Secondly, Indian reserves are required where tribal groups can sustain traditional food-procurement and other activities. Such reserves also provide some broader physical and biological protection. Thirdly, 'forest reserves' are required where physical protection of the environment is pre-eminent. Such areas support a general tree cover, but controlled or rational exploitation is permissible; some biological protection is also likely to be achieved.

Preliminary consideration has been given to the required extent and distribution of national parks in Amazonia. On the basis of island biogeography theory (MacArthur & Wilson, 1967; Diamond & May,

1976), it has been suggested by Myers (1979a) that conserving 1 per cent of the Amazonian forest might safeguard 25 per cent of the region's species. If 10 per cent of the forest area were conserved, 50 per cent of its species might be saved, while conserving 20 per cent of the forest area should safeguard most of its species. These data are no more than 'an informed first guess' (Myers, 1979a), and will in any case be affected by how the reserves in question are distributed. In this respect, national parks are likely to be more effective if they include areas within each of the main phytogeographic sub-regions of Amazonia. According to Ducke & Black (1953), seven such units exist, each of which is characterised by distinctive biological assemblages. Within these units, it has generally been accepted that national parks should focus on Pleistocene refugia, since the latter are areas of high natural endemism and are probably best able to provide material for natural re-colonisation of land disturbed by humans (Prance, 1977, 1985; Muthoo & Leader, 1978; Wetterberg et al., 1981). The postulated refugia, however, are not exclusively coincident with centres of species diversity, and some broadening of the basis for selecting forest conservation areas may be necessary (Myers, 1979b; Salo et al., 1986). Also, it is desirable to ensure that examples of subsidiary habitats, particularly wetland and dry savanna, are conserved alongside areas of forest. In general, regional planners need to continue the challenging task of establishing national parks in Amazonia, especially in areas of existing or developing land pressure. No longer is it adequate merely to designate parks in areas of low economic potential or isolated location.

Consideration is also required of the optimal size of individual national parks. On theoretical grounds, it is usually assumed that relatively large and compact units are desirable in order to minimise extinction rates and to maintain adequate gene pools for organisms that are present at low densities (Diamond, 1975; Myers, 1979a). Estimates of the minimum area required for such purposes, particularly in respect of birds and mammals, suggest that individual units of 250,000 ha or more are generally necessary for rain forest areas (Terborgh, 1974; Myers, 1979a; Higgs & Usher, 1980). Smaller reserves in a region are also of some value for protecting unique micro-habitats or localised species distributions (Myers, 1979a). In addition, consideration is required of the optimal shape for individual reserves, which may be circular and compact or of extended linear form (Diamond, 1975; Game, 1980). Further studies are needed to clarify these issues.

While broad guidelines exist as a basis for conservation planning in Amazonia, they often derive from scanty empirical data. However, one important project in Brazil, namely, the Minimum Critical Size of Ecosystems project, is trying to reduce this problem. The project itself was jointly established by the Instituto Nacional de Pesquisas da Amazônia (INPA) and the World Wildlife Fund–US. Within a 60,000 ha area north of Manaus, artificial forest 'islands' of different sizes, namely, 1, 10, 100, 1000 and 10,000 ha, are being created and inventoried before and after isolation (Lovejoy *et al.*, 1983, 1986; Lewin, 1984). Differential rates and levels of species loss are anticipated, and the data acquired are expected to contribute in the future to the design and management of conservation areas. Preliminary experimental results are available from smaller forest islands isolated in the early 1980s (Lovejoy *et al.*, 1986; Powell & Powell, 1987; Schwarzkopf & Rylands, 1989), although many of the more interesting findings will only become apparent on a longer timescale. Meanwhile, as Zimmerman & Bierregaard (1986) indicate, many other data, especially autecological ones, are urgently required to support immediate conservation objectives.

Some estimates have been made of the overall requirement for national parks in Amazonia. Wetterberg *et al.* (1976, 1981) formulated a plan involving the creation of twenty-four larger (500,000 ha) and twenty-four smaller (100,000 ha) parks in the region, which gave a total conserved area of 14.4 million ha or 2.4 per cent of the forest area. These parks were to be distributed across the major phytogeographic sub-regions, with particular concentration on Pleistocene refugia. Other writers have suggested that at least 10 per cent, and possibly as much as 20 per cent, of the forest area should be designated for biological conservation (Pandolfo, 1974; Myers, 1979a, 1984). Whatever the level adopted, however, it must not be assumed that the remaining forest is available for clearance, since far more than a 10–20 per cent forest cover is required to safeguard climatic and hydrologic systems. Even so, not all the additional reserved land need be under natural forest, since forest reserves containing agrosilviculture, mixed-forest silviculture and the like will provide effective physical protection. The total area of national parks, Indian reserves and forest reserves needed to achieve general physical and biological protection is not known, but it seems highly desirable to maintain at least 50 per cent of the land, and perhaps appreciably more, under permanent tree cover of some kind. A 50 per cent cover accords with the general level of environmental protection recommended by Odum & Odum (1972), although the case is arguable for an even higher level of cover as a component of a global strategy to limit further increase in atmospheric CO_2 and minimise likely climatic and other feedback effects (Nisbet, 1988; Dobson *et al.*, 1989).

In spite of the uncertainties, designating national parks, Indian reserves and forest reserves in Amazonia is arguably more straightforward than maintaining them. There are recurrent examples of the invasion of existing reserved land by road builders, ranchers, small farmers, miners and mining companies, and, as long as pioneer colonisation and the like continue, the pressure for more 'productive' use of reserved land will inevitably persist (Spears, 1980; Anon., 1984, 1986; Fearnside & Ferreira,

1984; Schwarz & Rocha, 1989). Nevertheless, the recommendation of 50 per cent tree cover for Amazonia is a minimum requirement. Legislation of this kind — the so-called '50 per cent rule' (Pandolfo, 1974; Goodland & Irwin, 1975) — was established in Brazil in 1965, and what is now needed is a broader acceptance and implementation of this general approach, based on an invigorated strategy of national parks, Indian reserves and forest reserves. Difficult as implementing this order of land protection might seem in the face of current rates of land colonisation, implementation will be much easier if it coincides with a transition from pioneer colonisation to more sustainable land exploitation. The key to conserving the forest ecosystem thus lies in an integrated approach to the management of reserved and developed land. In the next chapter, consideration is given to how integrated management of this kind can be achieved at the regional level.

9
Integrated land management at the regional level

Zoning the landscape would require a whole new order of thinking.
[Odum, 1969, p. 269]

In previous chapters, the case has been argued for establishing a range of sustainable agrosystems in Amazonia and for creating substantial areas of reserved land as national parks, Indian reserves and forest reserves. Two critical questions arise in this context: firstly, how can these functions be effectively integrated at the regional level, and, secondly, what are their prospects for implementation in the face of prevailing extractive and pioneer exploitation? In the latter respect, it is clear that implementation will only occur as a result of revised political and planning attitudes on the part of the national governments involved. In places, there are encouraging signs in this direction in that some experimental work on sustainable agrosystems has been started, significant areas of reserved land have been designated, and an increasing, if belated, awareness of the broader ecological issues involved has begun to emerge. At the same time, the required move away from damaging extractive activities, pioneer exploitation and large-scale forest clearance has yet to occur. On the assumption that it will occur, however, it is important to have available a sound technical basis for integrating productive and protective exploitation. In the present chapter, this question is examined, notably in the light of Odum's (1969) 'compartment model'.

In one respect, the prospects for developing integrated land management at the regional level have improved in recent years in that the geographical data base for Amazonia has been greatly enhanced by reconnaissance land surveys, based on remotely-sensed imagery. Even so, full use has yet to be made of the available data for integrated planning purposes. This is particularly so in respect of the land potential or land capability mapping that commonly forms parts of such surveys. An early example of the procedure was the land capability mapping of Guyana, which was undertaken as part of a general soil survey based on aerial photographs (FAO, 1966). Similar land potential or land aptitude mapping formed part of the radar-based reconnaissance surveys of Brazilian Amazonia (Brasil, 1973, *et seq.*) and of south-east Colombia (PRORADAM, 1979). Land potential assessment likewise underlies the land systems mapping of Amazonia undertaken by the Centro Internacional de Agricultura Tropical (CIAT) and Empresa Brasileira de Pesquisa Agropecuária (EMBRAPA) (Cochrane *et al.*, 1985). While providing a useful aid to regional planning, such surveys tend to adopt a narrow, development-orientated approach that focuses on the quality of land for crop production. Less favourable terrain may be designated as 'non-agricultural land' (FAO, 1966) or 'unsuited for utilisation' (PRORADAM, 1979), and is, by default, available as reserved land. The approach, however, neglects the positive requirements of reserved units in respect of their individual size and location and their overall extent. Some attempt has been made to resolve this problem in the Brazilian radar survey (Projeto Radambrasil) by explicit designation of reserves on land potential maps, but the status of such units remains subordinate to the primary concern of the maps, namely, the 'economic utilisation' of land (Brasil, 1973).

A more useful approach, founded in systematic ecology but having explicit spatial expression, has been formulated by Odum (1969) and outlined in relation to Amazonia by Eden (1978). Recognising the contrasting characteristics of natural successional and climax communities, with their respective emphasis on growth and production and on stability and protection, Odum (1969) has applied the same distinction to land exploitation. Landscape planning, he argued, could be implemented either in terms of a compromise between moderate yield and moderate quality over all the landscape or by 'compartmentalizing' the landscape 'so as to simultaneously maintain highly productive and predominantly protective types as separate units subject to different management strategies' (Odum, 1969, p. 267). His main options, namely, production, protection, and compromise, along with urban-industrial use, were incorporated in a 'compartment model' that offers an integrated framework for regional planning (see Figure 17).

In similar vein, Odum & Odum (1972) formulated a 'management model' which emphasised the need to allow for both 'natural lands' and 'developed lands' within a region. Natural lands, which are sustained by solar or natural energy, range in character from 'little-used wildernesses to moderately used forests, grasslands, rivers, estuaries, and oceans, which produce useful products and recycle wastes on a continuous basis'; they are seen as a necessary 'life support system' for developed lands (Odum & Odum, 1972, pp. 179–80). Natural lands equate with Odum's (1969) protective and compromise compartments, while developed lands, which are fuel-powered or energy-subsidised, equate with Odum's (1969) productive and urban-industrial compartments (Odum & Franz, 1980). In conclusion, Odum & Odum (1972, p. 183) suggested that for the present 'it would be prudent for planners everywhere to strive to preserve 50 per cent of the total environment as natural environment.'

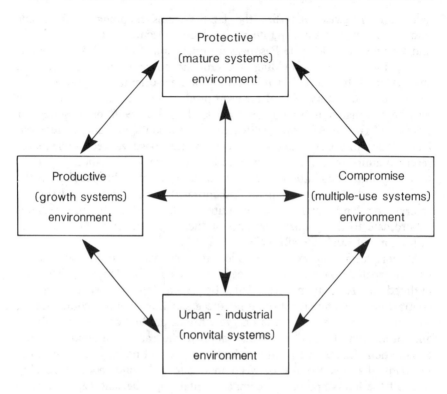

Figure 17 A compartment model for land management (after Odum, 1969)

Although theoretical in character, such models are usefully applied in Amazonia where they offer a balanced and integrative basis for regional planning and management. Eden (1978) explored the importance in Amazonia of the relationship between protective and productive units, and emphasised the particular relevance there of compromise units. In practice, Odum's (1969) protective compartment was seen as analagous to the national parks that are required in Amazonia, while the productive compartment would include any intensive, sustainable agrosystems that were established, whether involving short-cycle food cropping or industrial plantation production. The compromise compartment would contain less intensive, sustainable production systems such as agrosilviculture or mixed-forest silviculture which would simultaneously function as forest reserves (Eden, 1978). Similar ideas have been explored by Pandolfo (1974) and Dubé (1980) in respect of Brazilian Amazonia. In that area, Pandolfo (1974) argued for an '*institucionalização do zoneamento regional*'; her proposal was to undertake simultaneous demarcation of land areas for preservation of flora and fauna, agricultural colonisation, cattle projects and sustainable forestry. In similar vein, Dubé (1980) called for a

Table 22 Proposed regional zoning of Brazilian Amazonia

(a) Amazonian forest area		
Areas cleared for non-forestry purposes		78.8 m ha
Areas cleared for agricultural purposes		40.0 m ha
Natural pastures		15.0 m ha
Floodplains, swamps and mangroves		9.5 m ha
Indian reserves		20.0 m ha
National Parks and Biological Reserves		43.0 m ha
Sustained yield production forests		53.7 m ha
	Total	260.0 m ha
(b) Amazonian area		
Indian lands		70 m ha
Agricultural colonisation		50 m ha
Agro-silviculture and related forest use		50 m ha
National Parks and Ecological Stations		150 m ha
National production forests		60 m ha
	Total	380 m ha

Sources: (a) Pandolfo, 1974; (b) Dubé 1980.

'zoneamento ecológico-econômico da região', and both authors gave pre-liminary areal expression to their thinking (see Table 22). The approach has also recently been re-iterated by Nogueira-Neto (1989), who has called for legislation to formalise the concept of 'ecological and economic zoning' in Amazonia.

Other writers have examined the ecological status of Amazonian land use options in purely systematic terms. Goodland (1980) formulated an 'environmental ranking of utilization of the tropical moist forest' in which he considered twenty-five alternative modes of land use. These ranged from 'intact forest', through tree plantations and agrosilviculture, to agriculture and livestock rearing, being so ranked 'that the environmentally preferred precede the less desirable activities' (Goodland, 1980, p. 20). A similar approach was adopted by Fearnside (1983) who undertook an 'ecological evaluation' of fourteen possible land uses for the Brazilian *terra firme*, roughly ranking them in order of 'environmental perturbation'. His sequence, broadly similar to that of Goodland (1980), ranged from 'untouched forest', through various forms of silviculture and plantation production, to annual cropping and pasture (see Table 23). Fearnside (1983, p. 66) wisely stressed that 'no single option should be considered desirable for the entire Amazon, but rather a patchwork of areas in different uses'. Systematic appraisals of this kind, covering the range of land use options from the protective to the productive, are clearly critical inputs for any compartment-based approach to regional planning.

The compartment approach is valuable because it focuses attention on

Table 23 Development options for the
Brazilian *terra firme*, ranked in descending
order of environmental perturbation

Untouched forest
Extraction of forest products
Shelterwood forestry
Highgrading with replanting
Highgrading without replanting or regulation
Enrichment and/or selective poisoning
Silvicultural plantations
Clearcutting without replanting
Perennial crop plantations
Taungya
Annuals in shifting cultivation
Annuals in continuous cultivation
Pasture with fertiliser
Pasture without fertiliser

Source: Fearnside, 1983.

broad practical issues. In particular, its concern with multiple land uses
raises fundamental questions relating to the appropriate overall mix in
Amazonia of protective, compromise and productive activities, and to their
spatial distribution. In considering these issues, the starting point is
preferably a macro-regional one that takes account of the broad ecological
variables relating to land protection and land productivity. Once a macro-
regional framework has been established, intermediate and local-scale planning can follow on a similar integrated basis. The exercise in question is
essentially one of land classification, based on the subdivision or analysis
of the larger area as opposed to synthesis of smaller ones. The approach
has obvious antecedents in the methodology of early geographers like
Herbertson (1905) and, latterly, of landscape ecologists like Troll (1963).

A compartment strategy for Amazonia

The compartment approach is applicable through the 'management model'
of Odum & Odum (1972) which initially distinguishes between 'natural
lands' and 'developed lands' (see Figure 18). Various criteria are involved
in spatial designation of these land units, but the authors' premise that at
least 50 per cent of the forest area should be held as natural or reserved
land and, by implication, that the remaining 50 per cent may eventually
be developed is here adopted as one model. Also an alternative 'green'
model is formulated, which is primarily a response to growing concern
over increasing levels of atmospheric CO_2 and their likely climatic and
other effects (Dobson *et al.*, 1989); this model designates a higher

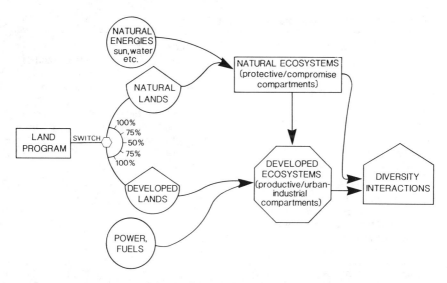

Figure 18 A land management model (adapted from Odum & Odum, 1972)

proportion, namely 75 per cent, of Amazonian forest as natural or reserved land. As Figure 18 indicates, the ratio of land usage can be switched to accommodate such alternatives, but implicit in this is the important assumption that any adjustments will be based on consideration of the relative merits of the 'natural' and 'developed' land options, rather than the apparent desirability or otherwise of one option, usually the latter.

Natural lands: protective and compromise compartments

The specific requirements for reserved or natural land have been discussed in Chapter 8. The primary functions of such land are to maximise the conservation of genetic resources and to minimise the effects of forest clearance on climatic and hydrologic systems. The former function is relatively place-specific in the sense that the location and form of individual reserves, i.e. national parks, need to be adapted to the compositional and distributional features of the regional flora and fauna. The total area of national parks can reasonably be expected to cover at least 15–20 per cent of the forest area (cf. Pandolfo, 1974; Myers, 1979a, 1984). The regulation of climatic and hydrologic systems requires a greater extent of reserved land, but the requirement is less place-specific and is as readily satisfied by tree-based, compromise usage, e.g. forest reserves based on agrosilviculture or mixed-forest silviculture, as by protective usage, i.e. national parks. Indian reserves also fall within the compromise compartment, although, in contrast to forest reserves, they are likely to be

Table 24 Proposed Amazonian compartments

Forest land exploitation	Model 1 (after Odum & Odum, 1972) Forest area		Model 2 ('green' model) Forest area	
	%	million ha (approx.)	%	million ha (approx.)
Natural lands				
Protective compartment (National parks)	15–20	105	25–30	170
Compromise compartment (Forest reserves/mixed forest silviculture/agrosilviculture, Indian reserves, etc.)	30–35	200	45–50	290
Developed lands				
Productive compartment				
Wetlands, and eutrophic *terra firme* soils	5–10	45	5–10	45
Dystrophic *terra firme* soils	40–45	260	15–20	105
Urban–industrial compartment	c.1	c.6	c.1	c.6

Note: Amazonian dry savannas and herbaceous wetlands occupy an additional 15–20 million ha and 27–28 million ha respectively. These areas have productive potential, but substantial areas again need to be designated as 'natural lands'.

relatively place-specific. If the total area of natural lands is set at 50 per cent (Odum & Odum, 1972), the extent of forest reserves and Indian reserves will cover up to 30–35 per cent of the forest area; alternatively, if the total area of natural lands is set at the higher 75 per cent, such reserves might occupy up to 45–50 per cent of the forest area (see Table 24). National parks, Indian reserves and forest reserves will be mainly located on the *terra firme*, but some parallel conservation of wetland habitats is also required.

Developed lands: productive and urban-industrial compartments

Developed lands, as defined herein, include productive agricultural and also urban-industrial compartments. The present concern is mainly with the former, whose specific functions will broadly influence their distribution. The agrosystems in question are intended to be sustainable and relatively intensive in character. They may require industrial inputs in the form of fertilisers, pesticides and the like, but selective exploitation of more favourable habitats should lessen this requirement. In edaphic terms, wetlands and eutrophic areas of the *terra firme* are preferred for productive exploitation, while wetlands and dry savannas are attractive on account of their assumed lower incidence of weeds, pests and diseases. How far the productive compartment can reasonably extend on dystrophic soils of the *terra firme* is open to question. It may be feasible to establish industrial plantations for timber, fuel crops or wood chemicals on such land, and pressure may also increase to develop intensive, annual food cropping there. However, as Chapter 7 indicates, the longer-term implications of intensive exploitation of dystrophic *terra firme* soils are unclear, especially in forest areas, and, although relevant agronomic experiments need to continue, a cautious approach is currently required.

Ecological aspects of the urban-industrial compartment are currently of lesser significance, although conditions need to be monitored, particularly in areas of expanding mining activity. In the case of hydro-electric projects, the most significant impacts will derive from localised flooding of forest land, although, as previously indicated, the long-term efficiency of such projects may well depend on maintaining the forest cover in head-water zones. In view of the capital-intensive nature of hydro-electric projects, the incentive to protect such forests is considerable and provides an opportunity that should be fully exploited for general conservation purposes.

Thus, regional planning in Amazonia requires initial designation of natural lands and developed lands (see Figure 18). The data base for achieving this is by no means complete, but the impact of current extractive and pioneer exploitation is sufficiently acute to warrant prompt implementation of an integrated planning approach of this kind. No extreme problems should emerge in identifying the respective planning units, since intended natural lands will mainly coincide with the forested *terra firme*, while developed lands will, initially at least, be largely located outside that zone. For the moment, some extractive and pioneer exploitation will obviously persist on the forested *terra firme*, but such exploitation is not yet of sufficient overall extent to preclude the requisite designation of natural lands. However, critical to the success of the proposed strategy is an early reduction of damaging extractive and pioneer exploitation and its replacement by more permanent and sustainable agrosystems of suitable intensity on both the *terra firme* and in adjacent wetlands. Such a transition will not easily be achieved, but is an urgent requirement. In this respect, it is assumed that encouragement of productive activities on the *várzea* will help to slow colonisation of the forested *terra firme*, and in turn safeguard the hydrological status, and thus potential, of the *várzea* itself.

Designation of compartments

The broad relationship between natural lands and developed lands, as defined by Odum & Odum (1972), has been elaborated. In respect of natural lands, designation of the protective compartment, i.e. national parks, needs to be undertaken at the macro-regional level, in order to achieve adequate representation across the Amazonian biological spectrum. The designation of other compartments can largely be achieved at a lower planning level. In the latter case, the planning regions need to be sufficiently large to incorporate a range of bio-physical conditions and, at the same time, small enough to avoid subordination of ecological considerations to broad economic and political strategies of the kind that have hitherto dominated Amazonian planning (Eden, 1978). The resultant pattern of compartments will vary from area to area, depending on local environmental conditions and policy concerns.

Following initial designation of the protective compartment, with a target area of at least 15–20 per cent of the forest, the specific location of the productive compartment needs to be considered. Initially, its constituent parts will be mostly located on more favourable soils, notably those of the *várzea* and of eutrophic areas of the *terra firme*. The extent of these soils will obviously vary from one planning region to another, but is unlikely to exceed 5–10 per cent of the forest area. In Brazilian Amazonia, for example, the extent of wetland forest is approximately 40 million ha, or some 10 per cent of the forest (see Table 20); in addition, there are approximately 1 million ha of more fertile *terra roxa* soils or Nitosols (Pandolfo, 1979). Similar proportions of such land exist in other Amazonian territories. Not all this land should be intensively developed, but it represents the preferred location for the productive compartment (see Table 24). Any extension of this compartment on the dystrophic soils of the *terra firme* must be dependent upon the development of sustainable agrosystems for such areas as well as careful assessment of the maximum acceptable level of general forest clearance in relation to likely macro-environmental feedbacks. For the moment, intensive development on dystrophic forest soils should proceed with caution and is best focused on land already degraded by pioneer colonisation.

In general, the dystrophic soils of the *terra firme* are better exploited by compromise systems. Considerable flexibility is possible in this compartment, allowing account to be taken of both local environmental and socio-economic conditions. Forest reserves, for example, may be established for watershed protection in association with hydro-electric projects, or used as buffer zones around national parks; as appropriate, such areas can also be used for agrosilviculture, mixed-forest silviculture and the like. Indian reserves also represent an important element of the compromise compartment (see Table 24).

Mixed-forest silviculture has significant potential as a compromise system for dystrophic soils of the *terra firme*. Additional research and development are required, but, particularly if basic timber production can be supplemented by managed harvesting of natural non-wood forest products, the system is likely to be profitable as well as sustainable (Sternberg, 1987; Gradwohl & Greenberg, 1988). Even if specific pressures arise for the system, once operating, to move towards more intensive, plantation-type timber production, as has happened elsewhere (Lawton, 1978), such can occur within the present strategy provided the new systems are sustainable and do not exceed the designated extent of the productive compartment. Nor should the areal implications of any such development give serious cause for concern. As Pandolfo (1979) indicates, even if ten to twenty projects similar to that of Jari were established in the Brazilian Amazon, they would occupy less than 2 per cent of the forest area. Some risk obviously attaches to opening up forest land for silvicultural purposes, intensive or otherwise, but the alternative is likely to be continuing extractive logging of a more damaging and extensive kind.

Agrosilviculture has similar potential for dystrophic soils of the *terra firme*. Additional research and development are again required, but the system offers significant opportunities, especially for peasant farmers. Land holdings of adequate size are essential, but agrosilviculture should help to stabilise land use and settlement and at the same time provide significant environmental protection. The system can be established in existing forest or employed for recovery of land already degraded by earlier colonisation. If local livestock traditions are strong, silvopastoral or semi-intensive livestock systems can likewise be implemented.

In respect of non-forest lands, a similar integrated strategy should be pursued. Some commercial exploitation already occurs in dry savannas and wetlands, and given the development of adequate infrastructure and services, both food and industrial cropping could surely be extended. Within Amazonia, dry savannas and herbaceous wetlands cover an estimated 15–20 million ha and 27–28 million ha respectively. Not all this land, particularly less accessible areas like the Rio Branco–Rupununi savanna, is currently suitable for more intensive exploitation, but, in general, longer-term development potential exists, particularly within herbaceous wetlands. As elsewhere, national parks also need to be designated to conserve distinctive biotas.

A compartment strategy (Odum, 1969) for Amazonia is intended to provide a balance between conservation and development at the regional level. The approach involves a positive attitude towards conservation of land and resources as well as emphasis on sustainable development. The land allocation outlined in Table 24 is provisional, but offers alternatives for longer-term land exploitation. In ecological terms, the decision whether to adopt a more or less 'natural' or 'developed' model will depend on the prospects for establishing sustainable, intensive production systems on dystrophic *terra firme* soils and on the clarification of maximum acceptable levels of general forest clearance in relation to likely climatic and hydrologic feedback. In broader terms, the decision is clearly contingent upon prevailing political attitudes, both within and beyond Amazonia. Meanwhile, in order to keep critical planning options open, a major political initiative is required to limit damaging extractive and pioneer exploitation on the forested *terra firme*, which is currently the key area in implementing any general, long-term land management strategy. In parallel, continuing acquisition of ecological and other data on compartment structure and functions is required as a basis for reappraisal and refinement of existing compartment models. Admittedly, an integrated compartment strategy, as outlined, is more readily formulated than implemented, but, if effective long-term regional exploitation is to occur, such a strategy is required. As the final chapter will show, some recognition of this view is emerging in Amazonia.

10
Present and future

Government involvement in the colonisation and development of Amazonia has generally increased in recent decades. The level and quality of involvement differs from country to country, and there is varying recognition of the need for integrated land management. Even where the approach is broadly acknowledged, moreover, its implementation is difficult because the requisite ecological and other data are often in short supply, the necessary physical infrastructure and services deficient, and the institutional support inadequate. Even so, signs are emerging of a more effective basis for land management in the region. Numerous land surveys have been undertaken at reconnaissance and other levels, and the scale of environmental and agronomic research is increasing. Institutional advances have also occurred including the establishment of various regional development agencies and of the broader Treaty for Amazonian Co-operation. Such advances are no guarantee of more effective land management, but they are a basis for progress in that direction. In this chapter, the current status of land management in Amazonia is examined, region by region, and the general prospects for developing a more integrated approach to land management are reviewed.

At the national level, notable contrasts exist in the attitude of individual countries to the exploitation of Amazonian land. In the north, Venezuela and the Guianas have periodically displayed interest in developing their forest interiors, but such interest has rarely been sustained. By contrast, in the Andean *oriente*, large-scale forest colonisation has occurred more or less continuously in recent decades, although the process has generally been spontaneous rather than planned in character. In Brazilian Amazonia, there has been similar large-scale colonisation, but more positive efforts have been made by the government and its agencies to manage the process at both local and regional scales. Contrasting levels of conservation activity have also characterised the various territories.

Present land planning and management

The Guianas

The territories of Guyana, Surinam and French Guiana cover about 6 per cent of Amazonia. Their total population is approximately 1.24 million (see Table 21), of whom most are located in the coastal zone as a function of more favourable environmental conditions and of earlier Colonial linkages. The long history of agricultural settlement in coastal Guyana was outlined in Chapter 6, and similar, if less extensive, development has occurred in coastal Surinam. French Guiana, still a colony, is in a retarded state, with minimal agricultural or related activities (ORSTOM, 1979).

Little development has taken place in the interior of the Guianas, which are still largely forested. In both Guyana and Surinam, bauxite has been produced from the coastal hinterland since the First World War, and in Surinam there are associated hydro-electric developments, including the large Brokopondo project (Leentvaar, 1973; Dew, 1978; Potter, 1979). Agricultural and silvicultural projects have also been initiated in the coastal hinterland, but have rarely been successful on the infertile Arenosols (Wagenaar, 1966; Vining, 1977; Downer, 1979; Bajracharya, 1980; Jonkers & Schmidt, 1984).

Deeper penetration of the interior has been limited. Some extractive logging has occurred, and extensive cattle ranching persists in the Rupununi savanna of Guyana (see Figure 19). Many years ago, Buck (1919) proposed the construction of a rail link from the coastal capital of Georgetown to the Rupununi, and periodic efforts have been made to develop the route; latterly, the main interest has been in constructing a road to the Rupununi that would connect with the Brazilian highway system. However, interior development projects of this kind have mostly been conceived in isolation and, despite periodic production of national development plans in both Guyana and Surinam, there has been little attempt over the years to achieve integrated management of the respective territories.

In one important respect, Surinam has progressed in that a series of national parks has been created which cover 582,500 ha or some 3.5 per cent of the territory; in addition, a further 1.77 million ha or 10.8 per cent of the territory have provisionally been designated for such use (see Table 25). However, in both Surinam and Guyana, the majority of settlement and economic activity is still concentrated in the coastal zone, with only localised exploitation of the sparsely-populated interiors (Mittermeier & Milton, 1976; Baal *et al.*, 1988). Nor is this pattern likely to change in the immediate future, given the difficult economic and political conditions that prevail in both countries. Admittedly, the present circumstances help to protect the interior forests, but, in the longer term, a more positive approach to land management is required.

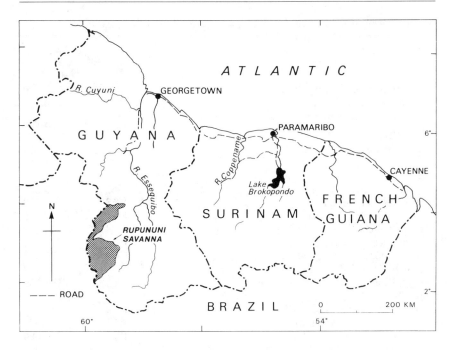

Figure 19 The Guianas

Southern Venezuela

The forested south of Venezuela occupies approximately 5 per cent of Amazonia and, like the interior of the Guianas, has a very low population density (see Table 21). The traditional focus of Venezuelan economic activity has been the coastal and Andean uplands, and, when periodic expansion from this zone has occurred, it has generally been into adjacent areas of the *llanos*, where nowadays old-established cattle ranching co-exists with commercial agriculture. In the early 1960s, however, agricultural and urban-industrial development was also extended to the lower Orinoco zone, where the growth pole of Ciudad Guayana was established by the newly-formed Corporación Venezolana de Guayana (CVG). At the same time, CVG acquired responsibility for parts of southern Venezuela. At that period, there was little colonisation pressure on the south, but, in the late 1960s, a newly-elected national government formulated policies for its occupance and development, primarily for reasons of national security. A *Conquista del Sur* was proclaimed and regional development pursued through the Comisión para el Desarrollo del Sur (CODESUR), whose main aims were to improve transport facilities and organise frontier colonisation. However, this political momentum was not sustained, and, although various agricultural and livestock projects

Table 25 National parks in Amazonia, with date of establishment and area

National park	Date	Area (ha)
Bolivia		
Isiboro-Sécure National Park	1965	1,233,000
Manuripi Heath Nature Reserve	1973	1,844,375
Beni Biosphere Reserve	1982	} 1,633,000
Chimane Reserve	1987	
Total in Bolivia		4,710,375
Brazil*		
Adolfo Ducke Reserve	1963	10,000
Walter Egler Reserve	1968	750
Amazonas National Park	1974	1,000,000
Pico da Neblina National Park	1979	2,200,000
Pacaás Novos National Park	1979	764,800
Rio Trombetas Biological Reserve	1979	385,000
Jaru Biological Reserve	1979	268,150
Lago Piratuba Biological Reserve	1980	395,000
Jaú National Park	1980	2,272,000
Cabo Orange National Park	1980	619,000
Maracá Ecological Station	1981	92,000
Anavilhanas Ecological Station	1981	350,000
Maraca-Tipioca Ecological Station	1981	70,000
Rio Acre Ecological Station	1981	77,500
Iquê Ecological Station	1981	200,000
Abufari Biological Reserve	1982	288,000
Guaporé Biological Reserve	1982	600,000
Gurupi Biological Reserve	1988	11,400
Total in Brazil		9,603,600
Colombia[†]		
Amacayacu National Park	1975	170,000
Cahuinari National Park	1987	575,000
Total in Colombia		745,000
Ecuador		
Yasuni National Park	1979	400,000
Cuyabeno Faunal Reserve	n.a.	30,000
Total in Ecuador		430,000
French Guiana		
None		
Guyana		
Kaieteur National Park	1929	11,655

Table 25 *contd*

National park	Date	Area (ha)
Peru		
Tingo María National Park	1965	18,000
Manu National Park	1973	1,532,800
Pacaya Samiria Nature Reserve	1977	1,387,500
Total in Peru		2,938,300
Surinam[‡]		
Raleighvallen-Voltzberg Nature Reserve	1961	56,000
Wia Wia Nature Reserve	1961	36,000
Brinckheuvel Nature Reserve	1961	6,000
Eilerts de Haan Nature Reserve	1966	220,000
Tafelberg Nature Reserve	1966	140,000
Copenamemouth Nature Reserve	1966	12,000
Brownsberg Nature Park	1969	8,400
Galibi Nature Reserve	1969	4,000
Sipaliwini Nature Reserve	1972	100,000
Herten Rits Nature Reserve	n.a.	100
Total in Surinam		582,500
Venezuela		
Canaima National Park	1962	3,000,000
La Neblina National Park	1978	1,360,000
Duida-Marahuaca National Park	1978	210,000
Jáua-Sarisariñama National Park	1978	330,000
Yapacana National Park	1978	320,000
Total in Venezuela		5,220,000
Total area		24,241,430

[*] Three additional parks have been created in 1989.
[†] Additional parks covering c. 4 million ha have been created in 1988/89.
[‡] Additional parks covering 1.77 million ha have been proposed.
Sources: Baal *et al.*, 1988; Bajracharya, 1980; Herrera-MacBryde, 1988; IBGE, 1987; IUCN, 1982; Margolis, 1989b; Palca, 1987; Pires, 1978.

were initiated, the overall impact was slight. Even today, economic activity in the south continues to be largely based on local subsistence and traditional extractive production (Benacchio, 1982; Buschbacher, 1986b).

Meanwhile, there have been significant conservation initiatives in southern Venezuela (see Figure 20). In 1962, the Canaima National Park was created, and four other parks were designated in 1978; together these cover 5.2 million ha or 14 per cent of the region (see Table 25). The parks, however, are mainly focused on elevated sandstone plateaus, or *tepuis*, rather than areas of lowland forest; the *tepuis* are of undoubted

202 Present and future

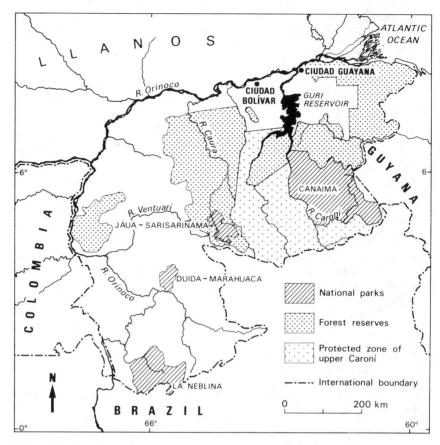

Figure 20 Location map of southern Venezuela, showing national parks, forest reserves and the protected zone of the upper Caroní (after Arvelo-Jiménez, 1980; Gorzula & Medina-Cuervo, 1986)

biological importance (Steyermark, 1977), but additional areas of lowland forest need to be conserved. To some extent, this has been achieved by the designation of four large forest reserves and other related units, which in total cover about 11.2 million ha of land, but these are primarily intended for sustained silvicultural production rather than biological protection. Some further conservation is achieved within a special 'protected zone' that has been designated across the upper Caroní basin in order to safeguard the Guri hydro-electric barrage and reservoir on the lower Caroní river (UNESCO, 1978; Arvelo-Jiménez, 1980; Gorzula & Medina-Cuervo, 1986).

In general, the existence of multiple reserved units in southern Venezuela signifies official recognition of the need for integrated land management. Thus far, the strategy has been relatively easy to implement because of limited colonisation pressures in the region (Gorzula & Medina-Cuervo, 1986). Conditions in this respect may be less favourable in the future, but important preliminary steps have been taken that now result in some 55 per cent of the southern region being designated for protective or compromise exploitation.

The Andean Oriente

The *oriente* zone, covering the eastern lowlands of Colombia, Ecuador, Peru and Bolivia, has been widely settled by migrants from the Andes. Most of the colonisation has been in the piedmont zone, with lesser penetration of the extensive forests further east. The mean population density of the *oriente* is estimated at 1.7/km² (see Table 21). Earlier migrants to the region were mainly concerned with extracting forest products, but, particularly since the 1930s, spontaneous land colonisation has become increasingly important; in places, planned colonisation has also occurred, and commercial oil exploration been initiated. By the 1960s, the *oriente* frontier could justifiably be described as 'a fluctuating pulsating zone of contact, linear penetrations, and even conquest of space' (Hegen, 1963, p. 433).

Although some planned agricultural colonisation has occurred in the region, the scale has been small and the process frequently associated with high turnover rates among colonists and inadequate support from official agencies (Bonilla, 1966; Hiraoka & Yamamoto, 1980; Schuurman, 1980; Uquillas, 1983; OEA, 1987a). Spontaneous colonisation has been more widespread and commonly associated with the construction of penetration roads (see Photograph 29). Early roads of this kind included those built to Florencia in Colombia in the 1930s and to Pucallpa in Peru in the 1940s. Over the years, some technical and social assistance has been provided to spontaneous colonists, but the scale of support has generally been modest. In many areas, land settlement patterns have been unstable, and heavy environmental and social costs have been incurred. Spontaneous colonisation of this kind has been described in the upper Caquetá basin of Colombia (see Chapter 6) and is evident in the adjacent Putumayo and Guaviare basins. Comparable colonisation has taken place in Peru, where extensive forest clearance for crops and livestock has occurred on the eastern Andean slopes and in the piedmont zone, as, for example, in the vicinity of Tingo María; a few isolated colonisation areas exist further east (Eidt, 1962; Masson, 1978; Gazzo, 1982; Myers, 1980). Similar settlement has taken place in parts of eastern Ecuador (Hiraoka & Yamamoto, 1980; Bromley, 1981; Rudel, 1983), and also in eastern Bolivia where forest land has been colonised on the Andean flanks, or *yungas* region, and in scattered parts of the lowlands (Dozier, 1969; Fifer, 1982; Healy, 1986; OEA, 1987b).

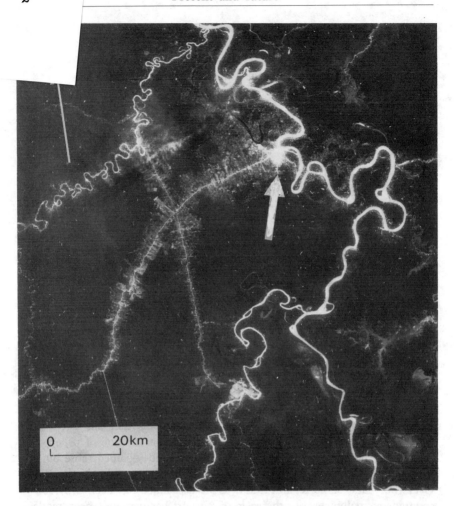

0   20km

Photograph 29 Land colonisation along the Tingo María-Pucallpa highway near Pucallpa (arrowed) in central Peruvian *oriente*. Landsat MSS band 5 image subscene, August 1981, ID no. 281236–142002 (reproduced by courtesy of CNPq/INPE, Brazil).

Some attempts have been made to develop sustainable agrosystems in the *oriente*. At Yurimaguas in Peru, continuous cultivation of annual crops has been rigorously investigated (Sanchez *et al.*, 1982; Sanchez & Benites, 1987), and some of the earliest agrosilvicultural and silvopastoral experiments in Amazonia have been initiated in eastern Ecuador and Peru (Masson, 1978; Bishop, 1982). Efforts have also been made to establish commercial crops in the region. The cultivation of oil palm and rubber has been attempted in eastern Colombia and Ecuador and of coffee and cacao in eastern Peru. Some large cattle projects have also been started.

However, progress has often been slow and some serious failures have
occurred (Watters, 1971; Kirby, 1976; Hiraoka & Yamamoto, 1980;
Aramburú, 1984; OEA, 1987a).

Since the mid-1970s, one traditional crop that has expanded commercially on the eastern Andean slopes and piedmont zone is coca (*Erythroxylum coca*). In Peru and Bolivia, currently the major producers, there are
an estimated 100,000 ha and 50,000 ha respectively of this profitable crop
(Kendall, 1985; Eastwood & Pollard, 1987; Morales, 1988). However,
even if the damaging social effects of exported cocaine are for a moment
disregarded, there are dubious longer-term benefits to be gained from
large-scale, export-orientated cultivation of coca in the *oriente*. In many
cases, coca has displaced established food crops, while the influence in
production areas of *narcotraficantes*, and in places associated guerrilla
groups, undermines government authority and functions (O'Shaughnessy,
1985; Pacini & Franquemont, 1986; Strug, 1986; Eddy *et al.*, 1988). Over
the years, numerous government agencies have been involved in attempt-
ing to develop the *oriente* and, while their plans have often been flawed
and their objectives thwarted by the sheer scale of spontaneous colonisation, some framework for land management has been established. Agencies
with explicit regional functions have been created, such as the Departamento Administrativo de Intendencias y Comisarías (DAINCO) in
Colombia and the Instituto de Colonización de la Región Amazónica
(INCRAE) in Ecuador. Sectoral agencies also operate in the region,
including several concerned with conservation. A few national parks have
been designated, mainly in Peru and Bolivia, and, although these cover
less than 5 per cent of the total *oriente*, important experience of conservation has been gained (see Table 25). At the same time, attempts to
improve land management are commonly hampered by local security problems and uncertain or corrupt government control, and, until greater
political stability is achieved, longer-term land management prospects for
large areas of the *oriente* remain poor.

Brazilian Amazonia

By far the largest part of Amazonia lies in Brazil, where the designated
Amazônia Legal covers 498 million ha. In 1980, the population of this area
was 11.2 million, of whom 1.6 million were located in the cities of Belém
and Manaus. Overall population density was 2.3 persons/km^2 (see Table
21). Brazilian Amazonia is the area where the most pronounced attempts
have been made to implement regional land planning and management. At
institutional levels, there have been recurrent efforts to control and direct
land exploitation, and, although official agencies have been widely
criticised for the technical deficiencies and the damaging environmental

npact of their policies, some basis for integrated land manage-
egun to emerge.

rary exploitation in Brazilian Amazonia has developed from a
active base to that of other parts of the region. Traditional
extractivism reached its peak with the rubber boom of 1870–1910, which
coincided with significant early attempts at planned agricultural colonisation in Bragantina. Subsequent decades, however, were a period of general
economic stagnation and, after some unsuccessful efforts to revive rubber
production in the 1930s and 1940s, it was recognised that a broader
approach to regional development was required. This resulted, in 1953, in
the creation of the Superintendência do Plano de Valorização Económica
da Amazônia (SPVEA) which was charged with the planning and implementation of agricultural, industrial and infrastructural developments. An
important project initiated at this time was the Belém–Brasília highway,
which opened up large tracts of forest to colonists in Pará and Mato
Grosso. In other respects the achievements of SPVEA were limited, but
its basic function was recognised as valid, and, when the military seized
power in 1964, a successor agency was planned. This was the Superintendência do Desenvolvimento da Amazônia (SUDAM), which was
formed in 1966 and continues to play a role in regional development.
From the start, SUDAM was involved in promoting large-scale commercial enterprises, particularly through the provision of fiscal incentives.
These were partly available for industrial and forestry projects, but most
were used for the development of cattle ranching, notably in Pará and
Mato Grosso.

In 1970, Amazonian development acquired fresh momentum with the
new federal Programa de Integração Nacional (PIN). This sought greatly
to expand the road network in Amazonia, thereby providing easier access
to land for migrant farmers, particularly from north-east Brazil. The prime
axis of this development was the Transamazon highway along which
massive small-scale colonisation was envisaged. A key agency in the
programme was the Instituto Nacional de Colonização e Reforma Agraria
(INCRA) which was responsible for establishing migrant families on the
land. Many problems were encountered along the Transamazon highway
(see Chapter 5), and official enthusiasm for linear penetration and
associated small-scale colonisation soon waned. In 1974, PIN was
superseded by the more selective Programa de Pólos Agropecuários e
Agrominerais da Amazônia (POLAMAZONIA), which provided a contrasting basis for regional land development.

POLAMAZONIA involved the designation of fifteen growth poles,
which were selected for their productive potential and intended as foci for
infrastructural development (Mahar, 1979). Implicit in this programme
was the renewed promotion of large-scale private development, particularly
involving cattle-rearing and mining. Some of the designated growth poles,

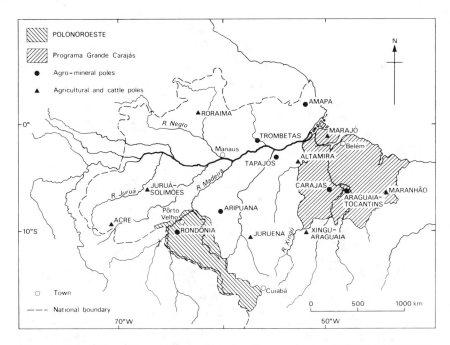

Figure 21 Brazilian Amazonia, showing development poles, POLONOROESTE, and *Programa Grande Carajás* (after Anon., 1976; World Bank, 1981; Kohlhepp, 1987)

like the *pólo agropecuário* Altamira and *pólo agrominerais* Rondônia, were already areas of significant activity, while others were quite undeveloped (Anon., 1976; Valverde, 1979). The POLAMAZONIA strategy has broadly survived and, in places, been elaborated. This is the case in eastern Amazonia where, in 1980, the Programa Grande Carajás was established over a massive 80 million ha of land lying east of the Xingú river (see Figure 21). This area, which contained several pre-existing growth poles, is now a major zone of development activity which encompasses iron mining at Carajás itself, hydro-electric production at Tucuruí, aluminium smelting at Barcarena near Belém, and associated agricultural and transport projects (Goodland, 1985; Kohlhepp, 1987). Likewise, in Rondônia, where major land colonisation started in the mid-1970s after upgrading of the Cuiabá–Pôrto Velho highway, the Programa Integrado de Desenvolvimento do Noroeste do Brasil (POLONOROESTE) was established in 1981 (see Figure 21). POLONOROESTE, covering some 41 million ha, sought to promote orderly land occupation and development by supporting productive activities and providing an economic and social infrastructure (World Bank, 1981; Goodland, 1986). In reality, progress in Rondônia has been compromised by exceptionally rapid inflows of

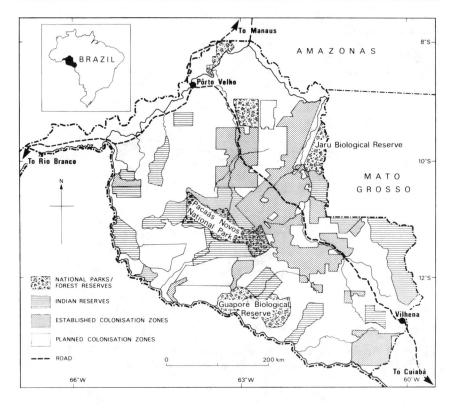

Figure 22 *De facto* compartments in Rondônia, Brazil (after Valverde, 1979; Coy, 1987)

colonists and by sundry technical and organisational problems (Mueller, 1980; Leite & Furley, 1985).

While a broad shift from a linear to a polar pattern of land development arguably facilitates the protection of inter-polar areas, explicit steps are also required to achieve such protection. To some extent, these have been taken by agencies like the Instituto Brasileiro de Desenvolvimento Florestal (IBDF) and the Secretária Especial do Meio Ambiente (SEMA), which, prior to their recent reorganisation, had designated eighteen national parks in Brazilian Amazonia, with a combined area of 9.6 million ha (see Table 25). In addition, three new parks have lately (1989) been created in the region in the wake of released Landsat data that show accelerated rates of recent forest clearance (Margolis, 1988b, 1989a; Neto, 1989a). National parks, however, are still vulnerable to invasion by colonists, and there is an urgent need in Brazil, as elsewhere, for a more integrated approach to land management that will better accommodate the conflicting functions of conservation and development. A strategy for achieving this was outlined by Pandolfo (1974) and Dubé (1980) with their regional zoning models (see Table 22), and is reiterated in the present compartment model (see Table 24). As Nogueira-Neto (1989) indicates, there is as yet no legal basis for 'ecological and economic zoning' in Brazilian Amazonia, although, under pressure of competing land uses, the broad utility of the approach is evident in key project areas like Carajás and Rondônia (see Figure 22).

Prospects for integrated land management

The need for an integrated approach to land management in Amazonia has been elaborated. Some initial steps in this direction are evident, both in terms of creating a suitable range of productive and protective uses for land and of planning a rational, spatial mix of such uses. However, at technical, institutional and political levels, much remains to be done to translate these initial steps into an effective land management strategy for the region. Some important technical and institutional advances have been made in Amazonia. Prior to 1970, limited environmental data were available at the regional level. Aerial photographs existed for a few areas and some local soil and vegetation surveys had been undertaken (Heinsdijk, 1958a, 1958b; FAO, 1966). Latterly, however, new remote sensing techniques based on side-looking airborne radar (SLAR) and satellite multispectral scanners have become available, and SLAR in particular has been used to undertake baseline surveys of natural resources. Venezuela and Brazil were the pioneers in this direction (Aeroservice, 1972; Brasil, 1973, et seq.), and most of Amazonia has now been investigated and mapped at reconnaissance level with the aid of SLAR imagery. Reconnaissance surveys are now being supplemented by more detailed environmental investigations at intermediate and local levels. Additional environmental data may of course initially stimulate land development and hence rates of deforestation, but, in the longer term, such information is prerequisite to integrated land management. As Dubé (1980, p. 100) aptly points out in respect of Brazilian Amazonia, 'uma região bem provida de mapas adequados está em boa via de ser manejada racionalmente'. Clearly, the next step is to establish prompt and accurate systems for routine monitoring of land resources, using satellite multispectral scanners like the NOAA Advanced Very High Resolution Radiometer (AVHRR) and the Landsat and SPOT systems (Eden, 1986b; Nelson et al., 1987; Woodwell et al., 1986, 1987). Significant progress in this direction is now being made in Brazil.

In institutional terms, some progress has also been made towards integrated land management. In general, sectoral government agencies have extended their activities into Amazonian areas, while over the years various dedicated regional agencies have been created. These include

SPVEA (dating from 1953) and SUDAM (1966) in Brazil, CVG (1961) and CODESUR (1969) in Venezuela, and others like DAINCO (1975) in Colombia and INCRAE (1978) in Ecuador. Such institutions have an important role to play in integrated land management, although hitherto their status and relationships within national bureaucracies have often constrained their effectiveness. In Brazilian Amazonia, for example, Dubé (1980) reports that execution of forest policy has involved not only SUDAM and IBDF but also ten other agencies; at times, the 'harmonisation of programmes' has been difficult! Similarly, in Colombia, there are at least seven agencies involved in Amazonian development (Alvarado, 1982), and conflict of roles inevitably occurs. Such institutional arrangements need to be rationalised.

One notable institutional development has been the Treaty for Amazonian Co-operation, or Amazon Pact, which was signed in 1978 by Bolivia, Brazil, Colombia, Ecuador, Guyana, Peru, Surinam and Venezuela. The treaty incorporates principles for collaboration between the signatories in relation to general economic development, conservation and rational use of natural resources, communications, health and other items. Indigenous populations receive scant attention, but there is some emphasis on environmental issues, with preservation of the environment and economic development being specifically designated as objectives of equal weight (Landau, 1980; Medina, 1980b). This is an encouraging premise, although how far the requisite, long-term political co-operation will develop remains to be seen. As yet, practical results have not lived up to expectation (Moniz Bandeira, 1987), but there remains considerable scope for the exchange of scientific, technical and planning information relating to land use systems and to such broader issues as watershed management, flood control and the operation of reserved land. Equally, the Amazon Pact provides a potential vehicle for political collaboration between member states in relation to external issues that affect the region and its general exploitation (Bunyard, 1989).

Technical and institutional developments in Amazonia facilitate integrated land management, but they are no guarantee of its achievement. The latter ultimately depends on the broader political environment. In this respect, there is still major preoccupation in the region with short-term development objectives, and inadequate commitment to the sustainable use and long-term protection of environmental resources. Even so, some progress is being made in the required directions. Three main criteria have emerged in the study against which such progress can be measured, namely the extent to which (a) damaging extractive and pioneer exploitation is being superseded by more sustainable agrosystems, (b) reserved land is being established, and (c) land exploitation is being diversified. A summary assessment of these criteria will serve to conclude the study.

Sustained yield agrosystems

Extraction and pioneer land colonisation remain the dominant modes of land use in Amazonia. They encompass small-scale farming as well as more extensive commercial operations like cattle ranching and extractive logging. Short-term benefits are commonly derived, but, in the longer term, declining productivity is often characteristic and adverse environmental and social effects occur. The inherent instability of such exploitation is particularly evident in agricultural and livestock activities, where low-grade exploitation is widespread and commonly involves a basal equilibrium characterised by low nutrient turnover and minimal yield. Alternatively, declining productivity is followed by land abandonment and the appearance of degraded secondary growth (Eden, 1978). Similarly, the shortcomings of some extractive activities, notably logging and fishing, are increasingly apparent; the scale of such activities has expanded in recent years and is threatening, and in places already causing, severe depletion of resources.

Some attempts have been made to establish more permanent and stable agrosystems as an alternative to the above, and, although recurrent failures have occurred, some progress has been achieved. The Japanese endeavours at Tomé Açu and elsewhere in Brazilian Amazonia have commonly been applauded (Sioli, 1973; Pires, 1978; Gradwohl & Greenberg, 1988) and are examples of persistent and determined efforts to achieve permanent cultivation and settlement. Plantation projects, like those involving rubber in Bragantina and timber at Jari, have also achieved notable progress at technical, if not economic, levels. Elsewhere, compromise systems like agrosilviculture and mixed-forest silviculture are beginning to appear as alternative modes of sustainable exploitation, while options like silvopastoralism and semi-intensive livestock rearing are being explored. How readily sustainable systems of these kinds will be established in Amazonia remains to be seen. Their development faces many ecological and other problems, and it is evident that such systems, if they are to succeed, must be more adapted to local conditions than many of their immediate predecessors on the forested *terra firme*. New exploitation systems in Amazonian wetlands or savannas equally need to be adapted to the specific conditions of their environments.

In respect of extractive activities, which are generally perceived as damaging or 'predatory' in character, there are also some encouraging signs (Sternberg, 1987). In Acre state of Brazil, so-called 'extractive reserves' are currently being promoted as a basis for harvesting diverse forest products in a profitable and sustainable way, while at the same time conserving the forest (Sternberg, 1987; Gradwohl & Greenberg, 1988). Additional data are required on the ecological potential of, and constraints to, such managed extractive systems, which are in effect a form of mixed-forest silviculture. However, as Peters *et al.* (1989) indicate in eastern Peru, there are opportunities for sustained, commercial harvesting of a range of natural non-wood, as well as timber, products from the forest.

Sustained yield systems need to be associated with stable patterns of settlement. Linear road penetration has hitherto stimulated vigorous, and at times overwhelming, migration to new forest land, but has rarely been associated with stable occupance and exploitation. The strategy of growth poles, applied in Brazil as an alternative to linear penetration, is a logical response to this problem and one that recognises the fundamental link between transport development and land exploitation (Nelson, 1973; Fearnside, 1986a; Jordan, 1987). Appropriate transport management, particularly in relation to road building, is thus of critical importance in seeking to establish sustainable exploitation. In addition, sustained yield systems depend on the provision of external services, including agricultural extension, credit support, marketing facilities and the like. Whether government or private agencies are involved, provision of such services needs to parallel innovations at the basic agrosystem level. As yet, sustained yield systems have done little to supersede pioneer exploitation in Amazonia, but there is growing recognition of the need for this change.

Reserved land

Although there are limited scientific data on which to base the designation of national parks in Amazonia, various units have been created, covering an estimated 24.2 million ha, and others are in the process of being established (see Figure 23). Some of the area in question carries savanna or herbaceous wetland, but the vast majority is under forest. Designated national parks currently cover some 4 per cent of the Amazonian forest. While this is a useful beginning, coverage is still well below the minimum suggested for effective biological protection, namely 15–20 per cent of the forest area (see Table 24). Admittedly, there is other protected land in the region, mainly in Indian reserves, but the long-term prospects for such areas are difficult to predict, even where they remain under indigenous control (Lovejoy, 1985b). Indian reserves are currently reported to occupy a massive 52 million ha in Brazilian Amazonia (Anon., 1986) and lesser areas exist in other territories (Corry, 1976; Arvelo-Jiménez, 1980; Bunyard, 1989). In total, they cover some 10–15 per cent of Amazonian forest.

On the ground, many problems exist in regard to both national parks and Indian reserves (Fearnside, 1986b). There are recurrent local difficulties over the demarcation and physical protection of reserved land, while new development plans often encourage or sanction encroachment upon it. In Brazil, an early highway was constructed through the Xingú Indian Park, resulting in substantial loss of indigenous land (Davis, 1977);

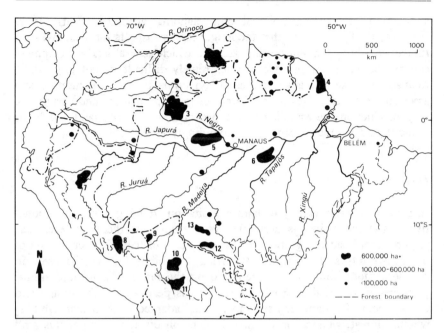

Figure 23 National parks in Amazonia, including 1. Canaima National Park, 2. La Neblina National Park, 3. Pico da Neblina National Park, 4. Cabo Orange National Park, 5. Jaú National Park, 6. Amazonas National Park, 7. Pacaya Samiria Nature Reserve, 8. Manu National Park, 9. Manuripi Heath Nature Reseve, 10. Beni Biosphere Reserve/Chimane Reserve, 11. Isiboro-Sécure National Park, 12. Guaporé Biological Reserve, 13. Pacaás Novos National Park

similar threats currently face Kayapó Indian reserves in other parts of the Xingú basin, as a result of scheduled hydro-electric developments (Anon., 1988). Roads and colonist incursions have likewise affected both national parks and Indian reserves in Rondônia (Fearnside & Ferreira, 1984). National parks in eastern Peru and south-east Venezuela have also been threatened by road-building and other developments (Steyermark, 1977; Anon., 1984). Most alarming of all is the report that 33 per cent (17 million ha) of Indian reserves in Brazilian Amazonia have already been requisitioned by mining companies (Anon., 1986).

In the past, national parks and Indian reserves often gained protection by virtue of their remote or inaccessible location, but such security is diminishing as road and other communications extend. There is thus an urgent need to improve the protection of reserved areas that are already accessible and to establish effective advance protection for those that are still relatively isolated. Also, additional reserved areas need to be designated, particularly national parks, and to be given prompt and effective protection. While the current insecurity of reserved land is very much a function of existing political and planning attitudes (Fearnside & Ferreira, 1984), it is clear that the longer-term prospects for such areas are fundamentally dependent on the extent to which general land development can be stabilised. At present, it is extremely difficult, if not impossible, to maintain reserved land in areas of vigorous pioneer colonisation and associated activities. However, if areas of more permanent and sustainable crop production are established, the pressure on reserved land should be reduced and its maintenance correspondingly eased.

Diversification of exploitation

In general, greater variety of land exploitation, ranging from the productive to the protective, is desirable in Amazonia. At the local level, this requires increased recognition and investigation of habitat diversity and of the constraints and aptitudes of particular habitats for specific uses. In addition, more information is required on the range of plant and animal resources in the region. Such information is pertinent to the design and management of exploitation systems that are adapted to particular habitats, whether forest, wetland or savanna. In general, diversification of this kind would replicate the pattern that evolved spontaneously in pre-Columbian Amazonia. As previously indicated, tribal indigenous groups possess high levels of site-specific and species-specific information that have traditionally allowed them to exploit a range of Amazonian resources, apparently in a sustainable manner. In this respect, tribal groups exemplify a general principle that is relevant to the contemporary colonist and offer a source of useful, specific information on Amazonian habitats and resources.

At the regional level, a full range of ecosystems needs to be appraised for exploitation. In particular, it is important to investigate and, where appropriate, develop the productive potential of more resilient wetland and savanna systems, both within and adjacent to Amazonia, thereby enhancing levels of protection for the fragile forest system. As suggested, a compartment strategy offers a suitable framework for such diversification, facilitating adaptation to the natural variability in the region. At the systemic level, a variety of land use options, ranging from the productive to the protective, are the key components of this strategy.

Conclusion

The patterns of land use mentioned above can be formally accommodated within a compartment model. The model emphasises the value of diverse land exploitation and encourages an appropriate mix and distribution of such exploitation at the regional level. Establishing integrated land management of this kind is not easy. Firstly, the scientific and technical information needed for effective land management, at both agrosystem and regional levels, is frequently in short supply and inadequate to sustain appropriate endeavours on the ground. Secondly, there are constraints at institutional and political levels. As Gilbert (1974) indicates, few groups in Latin America have been accustomed to resolving their problems according to technical criteria, and, in the Amazonian context, this tendency has prejudiced long-term land exploitation and management. The need thus exists for additional ecological and related research in the region and for clear communication of the findings in the public and political arena as an input to official policy-making.

In specific terms, the shortage of scientific and technical data makes formulation of sound land management options difficult and uncertain. This is clearly the case at the agrosystem level, but also applies at the regional level. In the latter context, it is exemplified by the reliance that has been placed on Haffer's (1969) refugia model as a basis for identifying optimal locations for national parks (Wetterburg et al., 1976, 1981). The model provides a rational basis for such identification, but, as recent studies show (Colinvaux, 1987, 1989), the model itself is open to question and may be less reliable than hitherto assumed. Comparable problems exist in regard to predicting the climatic and hydrologic feedbacks likely to affect Amazonia as a result of forest clearance, increasing global fossil fuel consumption, and other variables. This again impinges on conservation planning in so far as it is uncertain whether national parks designated under existing climatic conditions will be sufficiently extensive or physically heterogeneous to retain their biological utility if conditions change (Peters & Darling, 1985; Peters, 1988). Similarly, land development planning currently proceeds on the assumption that existing environmental conditions will persist, whereas it may be that future land use will need to adapt to a drier terra firme and to wetlands that, in places at least, are markedly more flood-prone.

In such circumstances, increased scientific research is urgently required in Amazonia not only to explore current land use options, but also to clarify the longer-term environmental dynamics and thereby provide an improved basis for regional land planning and management. Meanwhile, it seems sensible to adopt a more conservative or 'risk-reducing' approach to the exploitation of forest land (Myers, 1988b). In the present context, this implies the adoption of a 'green' compartment model that retains a high proportion of 'natural land' in the landscape and keeps open more options for the future (see Table 24). At a later stage, if intensive sustainable agrosystems are available for terra firme soils and clear indications exist of the maximum acceptable levels of general forest clearance in relation to likely environmental feedback, a compartment model with an increased area of 'developed land' might be adopted (see Table 24). Mean-while, a 'green' model is more suited to the prevailing uncertainties.

For any kind of compartment strategy to succeed in Amazonia, it will be necessary to regulate extractive and pioneer modes of exploitation. To achieve this will require significant political initiatives. One approach would be to control transport development, particularly by limiting or ending road-building into areas of primary forest (Jordan, 1987). This clearly conflicts with the perceived political requirement to occupy vacant national territories, but would significantly reduce levels of extractive and pioneer land exploitation. Equally, the orientation of available government subsidies to colonists committed to sustain, rather than merely extend, the use of forest land would reduce the attraction, and hence scale, of pioneer exploitation. The application of heavy taxes to extractive activities in the forest, particularly logging, would also regulate the use of forest resources, as well as provide funds for their improved long-term management (Uhl & Vieira, 1989). Such policies, however, presuppose a willingness on the part of national governments to reverse the development-orientated policies that have, in recent decades, generated considerable short-term commercial, and some social, benefits.

While such questions are clearly the responsibility of national govern-ments, the latter have lately come under increasing pressure, domestic and external, to modify their Amazonian development policies. External pressure comes from various directions. International funding agencies like the World Bank and Inter-American Development Bank (IDB), them-selves under pressure from environmentalists, have been increasingly critical and cautious about Amazonian development projects. This is evident in recent World Bank and IDB dealings with Brazil over provision of funds for upgrading the Acre highway, which aims to facilitate linkage with the Pacific basin, via Peru, and offer an easier outlet for Amazonian timber to Japan (Shoumatoff, 1989; Swinbanks & Anderson, 1989). Diffi-culties and delays have also arisen between the World Bank and Brazil over funding for planned hydro-electric projects in the Xingú basin (Byrne, 1989).

There has also been direct pressure on Brazil from environmentalists and politicians in the United States and Europe to moderate Amazonian development policies; similar pressures are also emerging within Brazil itself (Hecht & Cockburn, 1989; Neto, 1989c). An expression of this is the continuing controversy over the accelerated scale of Brazilian forest clearance, as revealed by satellite-based land cover monitoring (Bunyard, 1989; Margolis, 1989a, 1989b). In the face of mounting criticism, the Brazilian government has lately (1989) reiterated its commitment to 'rational development' of Amazonian forest land and brought forward an environmental protection programme, Nossa Natureza, that strengthens existing forestry and mining codes and creates new national parks and forest reserves; in parallel, fiscal incentives for ranching and other projects have been suspended (Margolis, 1988b, 1989a; Neto, 1989b, 1989c).

Whatever their response to specific issues of this kind, Latin American governments fundamentally have the right to formulate their own Amazonian policies, and, in this respect, their continuing concern over territorial sovereignty and vigorous reaction to any suggestion of 'internationalising' Amazonia are quite justified (Hecht & Cockburn, 1989; Margolis, 1989a, 1989b). Nevertheless, just as these countries are an integral part of the global economy, so also are they part of a global ecology, which is self-evidently in need of supportive management. No longer is it realistic for any country, Latin American or otherwise, to adopt a *laissez-faire* attitude to its natural environment. Nowadays, governments have obligations to manage their natural environments, just as they do to direct their national economies, and they must expect to be as accountable for the former as for the latter. That the Amazonian forest is becoming a political, as well as an environmental, issue will inevitably create difficulties for the governments concerned, but may also lead to an extended assumption of responsibility for the region.

Against this background, Amazonian exploitation has to be based on compromise between ecological and other interests. This will inevitably mean some continuing environmental damage, but, under existing conditions, it is scarcely realistic to promote a general 'hands-off' policy for the region. Instead, an integrative strategy needs to be adopted that recognises the requirement for both protective and productive land exploitation, as elaborated in a compartment model. The past experience of the indigenous population shows such a strategy broadly to be feasible and the approach should, in the future, minimise levels of environmental damage and sustain socio-economic benefit.

Implicit in this approach is a critical role for government, although its optimal scale of involvement is clearly open to debate. In this respect, it is true that spontaneous land colonisation in Amazonia has often been more successful than planned colonisation (Nelson, 1973), but this calls for an improvement, rather than abandonment, of government involvement. Ultimately, the matter is a political one, and, in this respect, the outcome is unpredictable. On the one hand, there is growing recognition in the region of the need for more rational land planning and management. On the other hand, there is still a huge gulf between expressed government intentions and the realities on the ground. As Fearnside (1986a) indicates, 'symbolic action' by government is commonplace in Amazonia. Yet, this is better than no action at all, and should encourage the population, if so inclined, to press for fewer symbols and more genuine action. The case for doing so is strong. So-called development is within a decade or two of destroying much of the Amazonian forest. Human energies need to be spent rediscovering how to conserve, as well as clearing, the forest.

Bibliography

Ab'Sáber, A. N., 1982, The paleoclimate and paleoecology of Brazilian Amazonia. In *Biological diversification in the tropics* (ed. G. T. Prance), pp. 41–59, Columbia University Press, New York.

Absy, M. L., 1985, Palynology of Amazonia: the history of the forests as revealed by the palynological record. In *Amazonia* (eds G. T. Prance, T. E. Lovejoy), pp. 72–82, Pergamon Press, Oxford.

Acuña, C. de, 1942, *Descubrimiento del Amazonas*, 2nd edn, Emecé Editores, Buenos Aires.

Adamson, A. H., 1972, *Sugar without slaves. A political economy of British Guiana, 1838–1904*, Yale University Press, New Haven.

Aeroservice, 1972, *Levantamiento radar de la región sur de Venezuela*, 3 vols & maps, CODESUR, Ministerio de Obras Publicas, Caracas.

Aguirre, A., 1963, Estudio silvicultural y económico del sistema taungya en las condiciones de Turrialba, *Turrialba*, **13**: 168–71.

Ahmad, M., 1960, Aluminium toxicity of certain soils on the coast of British Guiana and problems of their agricultural utilisation, *Transactions of 7th International Congress of Soil Science*, Madison, August 1960, **2**: 161–70.

Ahmad, N., 1965, An assessment of the salinity status of the frontland clays of British Guiana, *Compte rendu du congress des recherches agricoles dans les Guyanes*, Paramaribo, November/December 1963 (ed. D. A. Kraaijenga), pp. 125–32.

Alarcón, E., Brochero, M., Buritica, P., Gómez-Jurado, R., Orozco, R., Parra, D., Villamil, L. C., 1980, *Sector agropecuario colombiano: diagnóstico technológico*, Instituto Colombiano Agropecuario, Bogotá.

Allen, J., 1983, In search of the perfect cocoa bean, *New Scientist*, **97**: 293–6.

Allen, R., 1980, *How to save the world*, Kogan Page, London.

Almeida, M. G. de, 1987, A problemática do extrativismo e da pecuária no Estado do Acre. In *Homem e natureza na Amazônia* (eds G. Kohlhepp, A. Schrader), pp. 221–35, Geographisches Institut der Universität Tübingen, Tübingen.

Alvarado, J. N., 1982, Considerations on the Colombian Amazon region. In *Amazonia. Agriculture and land use research* (ed. S. B. Hecht), pp. 41–59, Centro Internacional de Agricultura Tropical, Cali.

Alvim, P. de T., 1977, The balance between conservation and utilization in the humid tropics with special reference to Amazonian Brazil. In *Extinction is forever* (eds G. T. Prance, T. S. Elias), pp. 347–52, New York Botanical Garden, Bronx.

——, 1980, Agricultural production potential of the Amazon regions. In *Land, people and planning in contemporary Amazonia* (ed. F. Barbira-Scazzocchio), pp. 27–36, Centre of Latin American Studies, Cambridge.

——, 1982, An appraisal of perennial crops in the Amazon basin. In *Amazonia.*

Agriculture and land use research (ed. S. B. Hecht), pp. 311–28, Centro Internacional de Agricultura Tropical, Cali.

Anderson, A. B., 1981, White-sand vegetation of Brazilian Amazonia, *Biotropica*, **13**: 199–210.

——, Benson, W. W., 1980, On the number of tree species in Amazonian forests, *Biotropica*, **12**, 235–7.

——, Gely, A., Strudwick, J., Sobel, G. L., Pinto, M. de G. C., 1985, Um sistema agroflorestal na várzea do estuário amazônico (Ilha das Onças, Município de Barcarana, Estado do Pará, *Acta Amazonica*, **15**: 195–224.

——, Overal, W. L., 1988, Pollination ecology of a forest-dominant palm (*Orbignya phalerata* Mart.) in northern Brazil, *Biotropica*, **20**: 192–205.

——, Prance, G. T., Albuquerque, B. W. P. de, 1975, Estudos sobre a vegetação das campinas amazônicas. III. A vegetação lenhosa da campina da Reserva Biológica INPA-SUFRAMA (Manaus-Caracaraí, km 62), *Acta Amazonica*, **5**: 225–461.

Andrade, A., 1986, *Investigación arqueológica de los antrosoles de Araracuara*, Fundación de Investigaciones Arqueológicas Nacionales, Bogotá.

Anlauf, R. R., 1980, Jamaica. Smut and rust diseases add woes to sugar industry, *Foreign Agriculture*, **17** (5): 29–30.

Anon., 1949, *El bajo Orinoco y el alto Caroni (Gran Sabana). Noticias históricas, geográficas, etnográficas y misionales*, Vargas, Caracas.

——, 1966, South American savannas. Comparative studies: llanos and Guyana, *McGill University Savanna Research Series*, **5**: 1–52.

——, 1976, Amazonia, *Brazilian Embassy*, London, **10**: 1–35.

——, 1981, Jari. Uma vitória na Amazônia, *Manchete*, Rio de Janeiro (9 May), 52–75.

——. 1984, Peru's Manu National Park in danger, *Wallaceana*, **36**: 11.

——, 1986, Sarney launches delayed program, *Latin American Monitor*, London. **3**. Mexico and Brazil, **3**: 297–8.

——, 1987, *South America, Central America and the Caribbean* 1988, Europa Publications, London.

——, 1988, Brazil's strongarm tactics fan international opposition to dams, *New Scientist*, **1639**: 21.

Aramburú, C. E., 1984, Expansion of the agrarian and demographic frontier in the Peruvian selva. In *Frontier expansion in Amazonia* (eds M. Schmink, C. H. Wood), pp. 153–79, University of Florida Press, Gainesville.

Arens, K., 1963, As plantas lenhosas dos campos cerrados como flora adaptada as deficiências minerais do solo. In *Simpósio sôbre o cerrado*, São Paulo, December 1962, pp. 285–303, Universidade de São Paulo, São Paulo.

Arvelo-Jiménez, N., 1980, Programs among indigenous populations of Venezuela and their impact: a critique. In *Land, people and planning in contemporary Amazonia* (ed. F. Barbira-Scazzocchio), pp. 210–21, Centre of Latin American Studies, Cambridge.

Ashburn, P. M., 1947, *The ranks of death; a medical history of the conquest*, Coward-McCann, New York.

Askew, G. P., Moffatt, D. J., Montgomery, R. F., Searl, P. L., 1970a, Interrelationships of soils and vegetation in the savanna–forest boundary zone of north-eastern Mato Grosso, *Geographical Journal*, **136**: 370–6.

——, ——, ——, ——, 1970b, Soil landscapes in north-eastern Mato Grosso, *Geographical Journal*, **136**: 211–27.

Aubréville, A., 1961, *Étude écologique des principales formations végétales du Brésil*, Centre Technique Forestier Tropical, Nogent-sur-Marne.

Baal, F. L. J., Mittermeier, R. A., van Roosmalen, M. G. M., 1988, Primates and protected areas in Suriname, *Oryx*, **22**: 7–14.

Bagley, B., 1986, The Colombian connection: the impact of drug traffic on Colombia. In *Coca and cocaine. Effects on people and policy in Latin America* (eds D. Pacini, C. Franquemont), pp. 89–100, Cultural Survival/Latin American Studies Program, Cornell University, Ithaca.

Bajracharya, K. M., 1980, *Forestry development in Suriname. Formulation and implementation of forest policies and programmes*, Food and Agriculture Organization, Rome.

Baker, V. R., 1978, Adjustment of fluvial systems to climate and source terrain in tropical and subtropical environments. In *Fluvial sedimentology* (ed. A. D. Miall), pp. 211–30, Canadian Society of Petroleum Geologists, Calgary.

Balick, M. J., 1985, Useful plants of Amazonia: a resource of global importance. In *Amazonia* (eds G. T. Prance, T. E. Lovejoy), pp. 339–68, Pergamon Press, Oxford.

———, Gershoff, S. N., 1981, Nutritional evaluation of the *Jessenia bataua* palm: source of high quality protein and oil from tropical America, *Economic Botany*, **35**: 261–71.

Barandiaran, D. de, 1962, Actividades vitales de subsistencia de los indios Yekuana o Makiritare, *Antropológica*, **11**: 1–29.

———, 1967, Agricultura y recoleccion entre los indios Sanema-Yanoama o el hacha de piedra y la psicologia paleolitica de los mismos, *Antropológica* **19**: 24–50.

Barrow, C. J., 1985, The development of the várzeas (floodplains) of Brazilian Amazonia. In *Change in the Amazon basin. Vol. 1. Man's impact on forests and rivers* (ed. J. Hemming), pp. 108–28, Manchester University Press, Manchester.

———, 1988, The impact of hydroelectric development on the Amazonian environment: with particular reference to the Tucurui project, *Journal of Biogeography*, **15**: 67–78.

Basso, E. B., 1973, *The Kalapalo Indians of central Brazil*, Holt, Rinehart and Winston, New York.

Baur, G. N., 1964, *The ecological basis of rainforest management*, Forestry Commission, New South Wales, Sydney.

Beard, J. S., 1953, The savanna vegetation of northern tropical America, *Ecological Monographs*, **23**: 149–216.

Becker, B. K., 1974, A Amazônia na estrutura espacial do Brasil, *Revista Brasileira de Geografia*, **36**: 3–36.

Beckerman, S., 1979, The abundance of protein in Amazonia: a reply to Gross, *American Anthropologist*, **81**: 533–60.

———, 1983, Does the swidden ape the jungle?, *Human Ecology*, **11**: 1–12.

Benacchio, S., 1982, Agricultural development in Venezuela's Amazon region. In *Amazonia. Agriculture and land use research* (ed. S. B. Hecht), pp. 115–34, Centro Internacional de Agricultura Tropical, Cali.

Benavides, S. T., Guerrero, R., Calderon, A., Sterling, A., 1975, *Algunos aspectos de suelos, de uso de la tierra y de investigacion agrícola en el sector Puerto Leguízamo–La Tagua, Putumayo*, Centro Inter-Americano de Fotointerpretación, Bogotá.

Benchimol, S., 1985, Population changes in the Brazilian Amazon. In *Change in the Amazon basin. Vol. 2. The frontier after a decade of development* (ed. J. Hemming), pp. 37–50, Manchester University Press, Manchester.

———, 1988, *Amazônia Fiscal. Uma análise da arrecadação tributária e seus efeitos sobre o desenvolvimento regional*, Instituto Superior de Estudos da Amazônia, Manaus.

Bergman, R. W., 1974, Shipibo subsistence in the upper Amazon rainforest, Ph. D. thesis, University of Wisconsin, Madison.

Berrangé, J. P., 1977, *The geology of southern Guyana, South America*, Her Majesty's Stationery Office, London.

Bertrand, J-P., 1988, Soja et dynamique de la region des cerrados: impact des projets nippo-bresiliens de mise en valeur. In *Abstracts of papers, 46th International Congress of Americanists* (ed. J. Lechner), p. 508, 46th International Congress of Americanists, Amsterdam.

Beven, S., Connor, E. F., Beven, K., 1984, Avian biogeography in the Amazon basin and the biological model of diversity, *Journal of Biogeography*, **11**: 383–99.

Biard, J., Wagenaar, G. A. W., 1960, *Crop production in selected areas of the Amazon valley*, Food and Agriculture Organization, Rome.

Bigarella, J. J., Ferreira, A. M. M., 1985, Amazonian geology and the Pleistocene and the Cenozoic environments and paleoclimates. In *Amazonia* (eds G. T. Prance, T. E. Lovejoy), pp. 49–71, Pergamon Press, Oxford.

Bishop, J. P., 1978, Development of a sustained yield tropical agrosystem in the upper Amazon, *Agro-Ecosystems*, **4**: 459–61.

———, 1979a, Development and transfer of technology for small farms in the Ecuadorian Amazonic region. In *Agro-forestry systems in Latin America* (ed. G. de las Salas), pp. 145–50, Centro Agronomico de Investigacion y Enseñanza, Turrialba.

———, 1979b, Family agricultural–swine–forestry production in the Spanish American humid tropics. In *Agro-forestry systems in Latin America* (ed. G. de las Salas), pp. 140–4, Centro Agronomico de Investigacion y Enseñanza, Turrialba.

———, 1979c, Livestock–forestry production in the Spanish American humid tropics. In *Agro-forestry systems in Latin America* (ed. G. de las Salas), pp. 135–9, Centro Agronomico de Investigacion y Enseñanza, Turrialba.

———, 1982, Agroforestry systems for the humid tropics east of the Andes. In *Amazonia. Agriculture and land use research* (ed. S. B. Hecht), pp. 403–16, Centro Internacional de Agricultura Tropical, Cali.

Black, G. A., Dobzhansky, T., Pavon, D., 1950, Some attempts to estimate species diversity and population density of trees in Amazonian forests, *Botanical Gazette*, **111**: 413–25.

Bleackley, D., 1956, *The geology of the superficial deposits and coastal sediments of British Guiana*, Bulletin 30, British Guiana Geological Survey, Georgetown.

Boerboom, J. H. A., 1974, Succession studies in the humid tropical lowlands of Surinam, *Proceedings of 1st International Congress of Ecology*, The Hague, September 1974, pp. 343–5.

———, Maas, P. W. T., 1970, Canker of *Eucalyptus grandis* and *E. saligna* in Surinam caused by *Endothia havanensis*, *Turrialba*, **20**: 94–9.

Bonavia, D., 1981, Flood disaster in China blamed on vanishing forests, *The Times*, London, 8 September.

Bonilla, V. D., 1966, El despertar de la selva. Principales aspectos de la colonización del Caquetá, *Tierra*, Bogotá, **2**: 1–80.

Bonnaire, A., 1970, Instituto Colombiano de la Reforma Agraria (INCORA), experiencias y recomendaciones en el fomento del caucho en la Intendencia Nacional del Caquetá. In *2nd simposio y foro de biología tropical amazonica*, Florencia, January 1969 (ed. J. M. Idrobo), pp. 28–59, Asociación Pro-Biología Tropical, Bogotá.

Bonnefille, R., Riollet, G., 1988, The Kashiru pollen sequence (Burundi) palaeoclimatic implications for the last 40,000 yr BP in tropical Africa, *Quaternary Research*, **30**: 19–35.

Boom, B. M., 1986, A forest inventory in Amazonian Bolivia, *Biotropica*, **18**: 287–94.

Boomert, A., 1976, Pre-Columbian raised fields in coastal Surinam, *Proceedings of 6th International Congress for the Study of Pre-Columbian Cultures of the Lesser Antilles*, Guadeloupe, July 1975, pp. 134–44.

——, 1978, Prehistoric habitation mounds in the Canje river area?, *Journal of Archaeology and Anthropology*, **1**: 44–51.

——, 1980, Hertenrits: an Arauquinoid complex in north west Surinam, *Journal of Archaeology and Anthropology*, **3**: 69–94.

Boster, J., 1983, A comparison of the diversity of Jivaroan gardens with that of the tropical forest, *Human Ecology*, **11**: 47–68.

Bourlière, F., 1973, The comparative ecology of rain forest mammals in Africa and tropical America: some introductory remarks. In *Tropical forest ecosystems in Africa and South America: a comparative review* (eds B. J. Meggers, E. S. Ayensu, W. D. Duckworth), pp. 279–92, Smithsonian Institution, Washington.

Boxman, O., de Graaf, N. R., Hendrison, J., Jonkers, W. B. J., Poels, R. L. H., Schmidt, P., Tjon Lim Sang, R., 1985, Towards sustained timber production from tropical rain forests in Surinam, *Netherlands Journal of Agricultural Science*, **33**: 125–32.

Boza, F. V., Baumgartner, J., 1962, Estudio general, clínico y nutricional en tribus indígenas del Territorio Federal Amazonas de Venezuela, *Archivos Venezolanos de Nutricion*, **12**: 143–225.

Bradley, J., 1980, Remote sensing of suspended sediment in Amazonian rivers using satellite multispectral imagery, Ph.D. thesis, Bedford College, London.

Branford, S., Glock, O., 1985, *The last frontier. Fighting over land in the Amazon*, Zed Books, London.

Brasil, 1973, *Levantamento de recursos naturais. Vol. 1. Parte das folhas SC.23 Rio São Francisco e SC.24 Aracaju*, Departamento Nacional da Produção Mineral, Ministério das Minas e Energia, Rio de Janeiro.

——, 1975, *Levantamento de recursos naturais. Vol. 8. Folha NA.20 Boa Vista e parte das folhas NA.21 Tumucumaque, NB.20 Roraima e NB.21*, Departamento Nacional da Produção Mineral, Ministério das Minas e Energia, Rio de Janeiro.

——, 1976, *Levantamento de recursos naturais, Vol. 11. Folha NA.19 Pico de Neblina*, Departamento Nacional da Produção Mineral, Ministério das Minas e Energia, Rio de Janeiro.

——, 1977, *Levantamento de recursos naturais. Vol. 14. Folha SA.19 Içá*, Departamento Nacional da Produção Mineral, Ministério das Minas e Energia, Rio de Janeiro.

——, 1978, *Levantamento de recursos naturais. Vol. 17. Folha SB.20 Purus*, Departamento Nacional da Produção Mineral, Ministério das Minas e Energia, Rio de Janeiro.

Braun, E. H. G., Ramos, J. R. de A., 1959, Estudo agrogeológico dos campos Puciari-Humaitá, Estado do Amazonas e Território Federal de Rondônia, *Revista Brasileira de Geografia*, **21**: 3–57.

Bray, W., 1986, Finding the earliest Americans, *Nature*, **321**: 726.

Brienza Junior, S., 1982, Freijó em sistemas agroflorestais, *Circular Técnica, EMBRAPA/CPATU*, Belém, pp. 1–15.

Brinkmann, W. L. F., 1985, Studies on hydrobiogeochemistry of a tropical lowland forest system, *GeoJournal*, **11**: 89–101.

Brock, S., 1964, Longhorns of British Guiana, *Geographical Magazine*, **36**: 583–93.

Bromley, R., 1980, The colonization of humid tropical areas in Ecuador. In *Land, people and planning in contemporary Amazonia* (ed. F. Barbira-Scazzocchio), pp. 174–84, Centre of Latin American Studies, Cambridge.

——, 1981, The colonisation of humid tropical areas in Ecuador, *Singapore Journal of Tropical Geography*, 2: 15–26.

Brooks, E., Fuerst, R., Hemming, J., Huxley, F., 1973, *Tribes of the Amazon basin in Brazil 1972*, Charles Knight & Company, London.

Brown Jr, K. S., 1982, Paleoecology and regional patterns of evolution in neotropical forest butterflies. In *Biological diversification in the tropics* (ed. G. T. Prance), pp. 255–308, Columbia University Press, New York.

——, 1985, Biogeography and evolution of neotropical butterflies. In *Biogeography and quaternary history in tropical America* (eds T. C. Whitmore, G. T. Prance), pp. 66–104, Oxford University Press, Oxford.

——, Ab'Sáber, A. N., 1979, Ice-age forest refuges and evolution in the neotropics: correlation of paleoclimatological, geomorphological and pedological data with modern biological endemism, *Paleoclimas*, 5: 1–30.

——, Sheppard, P. M., Turner, J. R. G., 1974, Quaternary refugia in tropical America: evidence from race formation in *Heliconius* butterflies, *Proceedings of the Royal Society of London*, B, 187: 369–79.

Brune, A., Melchior, G. H., 1976, Ecological and genetical factors affecting exploitation and conservation of forests in Brasil and Venezuela. In *Tropical trees: variation, breeding and conservation* (eds J. Burley, B. T. Styles), pp. 203–13, Academic Press, London.

Brush, S., 1979, An anthropological appraisal of Latin American farming systems, *Studies in Third World Societies*, 7: 107–16.

Bryson, R. A., 1972, Climatic modification by air pollution. In *The environmental future* (ed. N. Polunin), pp. 133–73, Macmillan, London.

Buck, E. C., 1919, Proposed railway development of the hinterland of British Guiana, *Timehri*, 6: 99–103.

Budowski, G., 1972, Discussion. In *The environmental future* (ed. N. Polunin), pp. 383–4, Macmillan, London.

——, 1983, Applicability of agro-forestry systems. In *Agro-forestry in the African humid tropics* (ed. L. H. MacDonald), pp. 13–6, United Nations University, Tokyo.

Bulla, L., Lourido, L., 1980, Production, decomposition and diversity in three savannas of the Amazonas territory (Venezuela). In *Tropical ecology and development* (ed. J. I. Furtado), vol. 1, pp. 73–7, International Society of Tropical Ecology, Kuala Lumpur.

Bunker, S. G., 1981, The impact of deforestation on peasant communities in the Medio Amazonas of Brazil, *Studies in Third World Societies*, 13: 45–60.

——, 1985, *Underdeveloping the Amazon: extraction, unequal exchange, and the failure of the modern state*, University of Illinois Press, Urbana.

Bunyard, P., 1989, Brazil and the Amazonian pact, *The Ecologist*, 19: 86–7.

Burnham, C. P., 1975, The forest environment: soils. In *Tropical rain forests of the Far East* (ed. T. C. Whitmore), pp. 103–20, Clarendon Press, Oxford.

Burns, E. B., 1966, Manaus, 1910: portrait of a boom town, *Journal of Inter-American Studies*, 7: 400–21.

Buschbacher, R. J., 1986a, Tropical deforestation and pasture development, *Bio-Science*, 36: 22–8.

——, 1986b, Deforestation for sovereignty over remote frontiers. In *Amazonian rain forests. Ecosystem disturbance and recovery* (ed. C. F. Jordan), pp. 46–57, Springer-Verlag, New York.

Bush, M. B., Piperno, D. R., Colinvaux, P. A., 1989, A 6,000 year history of Amazonian maize cultivation, *Nature*, **340**: 303-5.

Butt, A. J., 1965, The Guianas, *Bulletin of the International Committee on Urgent Anthropological and Ethnological Research*, **7**: 69-90.

——, 1970, Land use and social organisation of tropical forest peoples of the Guianas. In *Human ecology in the tropics* (ed. J. P. Garlick), pp. 33-49, Pergamon Press, Oxford.

Byrne, L., 1989, Historic Amazon meeting, *The Observer*, London, 19 February.

Calvin, M., 1987, Fuel oils from euphorbs and other plants, *Botanical Journal of the Linnean Society*, **94**: 97-110.

Camacho, R. P., 1975, La gente del hacha. Breve historia de la technología según una tribu Amazónica, *Revista Colombiana de Antropología*, **18**: 435-78.

Câmara, I. de G., 1983, Tropical moist forest conservation in Brazil. In *Tropical rain forest: ecology and management* (eds S. L. Sutton, T. C. Whitmore, A. C. Chadwick), pp. 413-21, Blackwell Scientific Publications, Oxford.

Camarão, A. P., de Azevedo, G. P. C., Marcues, J. R. F., Serrão, E. A. S., 1980, Fósforo, leguminosas e nitrogênio no melhoramento de pastagem de capim Jaraguá em Marabá, Pará, *Pesquisa em Andamento, EMBRAPA/CPATU*, Belém, **27**: 1-7.

Camargo, A. P., Alfonsi, R. R., Pinto, H. S., Chiarini, J. V., 1977, Zoneamento da aptidão climática para culturas comerciais em áreas de cerrado. In *4th simpósio sobre o cerrado*, Brasília, June 1976 (ed. M. G. Ferri), pp. 89-105, Livraria Itatiaia, Belo Horizonte.

Camargo, F. C., 1948, Land and settlement on the recent and ancient Quaternary along the railway line of Braganca, State of Pará, Brazil, *Proceedings of the Inter-American Conference on Conservation of Renewable Natural Resources*, Denver, September 1948, **3**: 213-21.

——, 1949, Reclamation of the Amazonian floodlands near Belém, *Proceedings of the United Nations Scientific Conference on Conservation and Utilization of Resources*, Lake Success, August/September 1949, **6**: 598-602.

——, 1958, Report on the Amazon region. In *Humid tropics research. Problems of humid tropical regions*, pp. 11-24, United Nations Educational, Cultural and Scientific Organization, Paris.

Camargo, F. E., 1968, Recursos naturais e humanos da Amazônia, *Revista Brasileira de Política Internacional*, **11**: 84-100.

Camargo, M. N., Falesi, I. C., 1975, Soils of the central plateau and Trans-amazonic highway of Brasil, In *Soil management in tropical America* (eds E. Bornemisza, A. Alvarado), pp. 25-45, Soil Science Department, North Carolina State University, Raleigh.

Carneiro, R. L., 1961, Slash-and-burn cultivation among the Kuikuru and its implications for cultural development in the Amazon basin. In *The evolution of horticultural systems in native South America: causes and consequences. A symposium* (ed. J. Wilbert), pp. 47-68, Editorial Sucre, Caracas.

——, 1968, The transition from hunting to horticulture in the Amazon basin, *Proceedings of 8th International Congress of Anthropological and Ethnological Sciences*, Tokyo, September, **3**: 244-8.

Carvajal, G. de, 1934, *The discovery of the Amazon, according to the account of Friar Gaspar de Carvajal and other documents*, Special Publication 17, American Geographical Society, New York.

Carvalho, J. O. P. de, 1980, Inventário diagnóstico da regeneração natural da negotação em área da Floresta Nacional do Tapajós, *Boletim de Pesquisa, EMBRAPA/CPATU*, Belém, **2**: 1-23.

Casement, R., 1912, *Correspondence relating to the treatment of British Colonial subjects and native Indians employed in the collection of rubber in the Putumayo district, including Sir Roger Casement's report 1912–13*, House of Commons, London.

CETEC-IBS, 1980, The cerrados — an important and economically viable option for food and fibre production, *Brazilian Agriculture and Commodities*, **1**: 18–25.

Chacón, J. C., Gliessman, S. R., 1982, Use of the 'non-weed' concept in traditional tropical agroecosystems of south-eastern Mexico, *Agro-Ecosystems*, **8**: 1–11.

Chagnon, N., 1968a, The culture-ecology of shifting (pioneering) cultivation among the Yanomamö Indians, *Proceedings of 8th International Congress of Anthropological and Ethnological Sciences*, Tokyo, September 1968, **3**: 249–55.

———, 1968b, *Yanomamö. The fierce people*. Holt, Rinehart and Winston, New York.

———, 1983, *Yanomamö. The fierce people*, 3rd edn, Holt, Rinehart and Winston, New York.

———, 1988, Life histories, blood revenge, and warfare in a tribal population, *Science*, **239**: 985–91.

———, Hames, R., 1979, Protein deficiency and tribal warfare in Amazonia: new data, *Science*, **203**: 910–3.

Chaloult, N. B., 1980, Settlement along the Transamazon highway: planning and reality. In *Land, people and planning in contemporary Amazonia* (ed. F. Barbira-Scazzocchio), pp. 139–40, Centre of Latin American Studies, Cambridge.

Chapman, M. D., 1977, Ecological management strategies for Amazonian fisheries, D. Phil. thesis, University of Oxford, Oxford.

Chernela, J. M., 1985, Indigenous fishing in the neotropics: the Tukanoan Uanano of the blackwater Uaupes river basin in Brazil and Colombia, *Interciencia*, **10**: 78–86.

Choubert, B., 1957, *Essai sur la morphologie de la Guyane*, Département de la Guyane Française, Paris.

Church, G. E., 1904, The Acre territory and the caoutchouc region of south-western Amazonia, *Geographical Journal*, **23**: 596–613.

Cobley, L. S., 1967, *An introduction to the botany of tropical crops*, Longmans, London.

Cochrane, T. T., 1984, Amazonia: a computerised overview of its climate, landscape and soil resources, *Interciencia*, **9**: 298–306.

———, Sanchez, P.A., 1982, Land resources, soils and land management in the Amazon region: a state of knowledge report. In *Amazonia. Agriculture and land use research* (ed. S. B. Hecht), pp. 137–209, Centro Internacional de Agricultura Tropical, Cali.

———, Sánchez, L. G., de Azevedo, L. G., Porras, J. A., Garver, C. L., 1985, *Land in tropical America*, 3 vols, Centro Internacional de Agricultura Tropical, Cali.

Cohen, M. N., 1977, *The food crisis in prehistory. Overpopulation and the origins of agriculture*, Yale University Press, New Haven.

Colchester, M., 1984, Rethinking stone age economics: some speculations concerning the pre-Columbian Yanoama economy, *Human Ecology*, **12**: 291–314.

Cole, M. M., 1960, The Brazilian savanna, *Revista Geográfica*, **26**: 5–40.

Colinvaux, P., 1987, Amazon diversity in light of the paleoecological record, *Quaternary Science Reviews*, **6**: 93–114.

———, 1989, Ice-age Amazon re-visited, *Nature*, **340**: 188–9.

———, Liu, K-b., 1987, The late-Quaternary climate of the western Amazon basin. In *Abrupt climatic change. Evidence and implications* (eds W. H. Berger, L. D. Labeyrie), pp. 113–22, D. Reidel, Dordrecht.

Collier, R., 1968, *The river that God forgot. The story of the Amazon rubber boom*, Collins, London.

Combe, J., Budowski, G., 1979, Classification of agro-forestry techniques. In *Agro-Forestry systems in Latin America* (ed. G. de las Salas), pp. 17–47, Centro Agronomico Tropical de Investigacion y Enseñanza, Turrialba.

Connell, J. H., 1978, Diversity in tropical rain forests and coral reefs, *Nature*, **199**: 1302–10.

Cooper, A., 1979, Muri and white sand savannah in Guyana, Surinam and French Guiana. In *Ecosystems of the world. Vol. 9A, Heathlands and related shrublands* (ed. R. L. Specht), pp. 471–81, Elsevier, Amsterdam.

Corry, S., 1976, *Towards Indian self-determination in Colombia*, Survival International, London.

Costa Filho, P. P., da Costa, H. B., de Aguiar, O. R., 1980, Exploração mecanizada da floresta tropical úmida sem babaçu, *Circular Técnica, EMBRAPA/CPATU*, Belém, **9**: 1–38.

Coursey, D. G., Booth, R. H., 1977, Root and tuber crops. In *Food crops of the lowland tropics* (eds C. L. A. Leakey, J. B. Wills), pp. 75–96, Oxford University Press, Oxford.

Coy, M., 1987, Rondônia: frente pioneira e programa POLONOROESTE. O processo de diferenciação sócio-econômica na periferia e os limites do planejamento público. In *Homem e natureza na Amazônia* (eds G. Kohlhepp, A. Schrader), pp. 253–70, Geographisches Institut der Universität Tübingen, Tübingen.

Crist, R. E., Guhl, E., 1957, Pioneer settlement in eastern Colombia. In *Annual report of the Smithsonian Institution 1956*, Publication 4272, pp. 391–414, US Government Printing Office, Washington.

Cunningham, S. M., 1980, Brazil. Recent developments in the centre-west region, *BOLSA Review*, **14** (2): 44–52.

CVG, 1969, *Informe anual*, Corporacion Venezolana de Guayana, Caracas.

Dagon, R. R., 1967, Current agricultural practices among the Waiwai, *McGill University Savanna Research Series*, **8**: 1–23.

DAINCO, 1977, *Orinoquia y Amazonia. Diagnóstico y bases de un plan de desarrollo*, Departamento Administrativo de Intendencias y Comisarías, Bogotá.

DANE, 1986, *XV censo nacional de poblacion y IV de vivienda*, vol. 1, Departamento Administrativo Nacional de Estadística, Bogota.

Dantas, M., Rodrigues, I. A., 1980, Plantas invasoras de pastagens cultivadas na Amazônia, *Boletim de Pesquisa, EMBRAPA/CPATU*, Belém, **1**: 1–23.

Dasmann, R. F., 1973, *Classification and use of protected natural and cultural areas*, Occasional Paper 4, International Union for Conservation of Nature, Morges.

——, Milton, J. P., Freeman, P. H., 1973, *Ecological principles for economic development*, John Wiley & Sons, London.

Davis, S. H., 1977, *Victims of the miracle. Development and the Indians of Brazil*, Cambridge University Press, Cambridge.

Davis, T. A. W., Richards, P. W., 1933, The vegetation of Moraballi creek, British Guiana: an ecological study of a limited area of tropical rain forest, Part 1, *Journal of Ecology*, **21**: 350–84.

——, ——, 1934, The vegetation of Moraballi creek, British Guiana: an ecological study of a limited area of tropical rain forest, Part 2, *Journal of Ecology*, **22**: 106–33.

DeAngelis, D. L., 1980, Energy flow, nutrient cycling, and ecosystem resilience, *Ecology*, **61**: 764–71.

De las Salas, G. (ed.), 1979, *Agro-forestry systems in Latin America*, Centro Agronomico Tropical de Investigacion y Enseñanza, Turrialba.

Denevan, W. M., 1966a, The aboriginal cultural geography of the llanos de Mojos of Bolivia, *Ibero-Americana*, **48**: 1–160.

———, 1966b, A cultural-ecological view of the former aboriginal settlement in the Amazon basin, *Professional Geographer*, **18**: 346–51.

———, 1970, Aboriginal drained-field cultivation in the Americas, *Science*, **169**: 647–54.

———, 1971, Campa subsistence in the Gran Pajonal, eastern Peru, *Geographical Review*, **61**: 496–518.

———, 1973, Development and the imminent demise of the Amazon rain forest, *Professional Geographer*, **25**: 130–5.

———, 1976, The aboriginal population of Amazonia. In *The native population of the Americas in 1492* (ed. W. M. Denevan), pp. 205–34, University of Wisconsin Press, Madison.

———, 1981, Swiddens and cattle versus forest: the imminent demise of the Amazon rain forest reexamined, *Studies in Third World Societies*, **13**: 25–44.

———, 1984, Ecological heterogeneity and horizontal zonation of agriculture in the Amazon floodplain. In *Frontier expansion in Amazonia* (eds M. Schmink, C. H. Wood), pp. 311–36, University of Florida Press, Gainesville.

———, Padoch, C., 1988, Swidden-fallow agroforestry in the Peruvian Amazon, *Advances in Economic Botany*, **5**: 1–7.

———, Treacy, J. M., Alcorn, J. B., Padoch, C., Denslow, J., Paitan, S. F., 1984, Indigenous agroforestry in the Peruvian Amazon: Bora Indian management of swidden fallows, *Interciencia*, **9**: 346–57.

———, Zucchi, A., 1978, Ridged-field excavations in the central Orinoco llanos, Venezuela. In *Advances in Andean archaeology* (ed. D. L. Browman), pp. 235–45, Mouton, The Hague.

Detwiler, R. P., Hall, C. A. S., 1988, Tropical forests and the global carbon cycle, *Science*, **239**: 42–7.

Dew, E., 1978, *The difficult flowering of Surinam*, Nijhoff, The Hague.

De Wit, C. T., 1967, Photosynthesis: its relationship to overpopulation. In *Harvesting the sun* (eds A. San Pietro, F. A. Greer, T. J. Army), pp. 315–20, Academic Press, New York.

Diamond, J. M., 1975, The island dilemma: lessons of modern biogeographic studies for the design of natural reserves, *Biological Conservation*, **7**: 129–46.

———, May, R. M., 1976, Island biogeography and the design of natural reserves. In *Theoretical ecology. Principles and applications* (ed. R. M. May), pp. 163–86, Blackwell Scientific, Oxford.

Dias Filho, M. B., 1983, Limitações e potencial de *Brachiaria humidicola* para o trópico úmido brasileiro, *Documentos*, *EMBRAPA/CPATU*, Belém, **20**: 1–28.

Dickinson, R. E., 1981, Effects of tropical deforestation on climate, *Studies in Third World Societies*, **14**: 411–41.

———, Henderson-Sellers, A., 1988, Modelling tropical deforestation: a study of GCM land-surface parametrizations, *Quarterly Journal of Royal Meteorological Society*, **114**: 439–62.

Dirven, J. G. P., 1965, Some important grassland types in Surinam, *Netherlands Journal of Agricultural Science*, **13**: 102–13.

Döbereiner, J., 1977, Present and future opportunities to improve the nitrogen nutrition of crops through biological fixation. In *Biological nitrogen fixation in farming systems in the tropics* (eds A. Ayanaba, P. J. Dart), pp. 3–12, John Wiley & Sons, Chichester.

Dobson, A., Jolly, A., Rubenstein, D., 1989, The greenhouse effect and biological diversity, *Trends in Ecology and Evolution*, 4: 64–8.

Dobzhansky, T., 1950, Evolution in the tropics, *American Scientist*, 38: 209–21.

Domínguez, C. A., 1975, El río Apaporis: vision antropo-geográfica, *Revista Colombiana de Antropología*, 18: 127–81.

———, 1987, La colonización como ampliación del espacio de dominación. In *Homem e natureza na Amazônia* (eds G. Kohlhepp, A. Schrader), pp. 271–8, Geographisches Institut der Universität Tübingen, Tübingen.

Donselaar, J. van, 1969, Observations on savanna vegetation-types in the Guianas, *Vegetatio Acta Geobotanica*, 17: 271–312.

Dourojeanni, M. J., 1985, Over-exploited and under-used animals in the Amazon region. In *Amazonia* (eds G. T. Prance, T. E. Lovejoy), pp. 419–33, Pergamon Press, Oxford.

Downer, A.V., 1979, *Settlements on the white sands*. Paper presented at 5th Commonwealth Conference on Development and Human Ecology, Georgetown, April 1979.

Dozier, C. L., 1969, *Land development and colonization in Latin America*, Praeger, New York.

Dubé, Y., 1980, *Em busca de uma política florestal para a Amazônia brasileira*, Superintendência do Desenvolvimento da Amazônia, Belém.

Dubois, J. L. C., 1971, *Silvicultural research in the Amazon*, Food and Agriculture Organization, Rome.

———, 1979, *Importância de sistemas de produção agro-florestal para a Amazônia*. Paper presented at 2nd Simpósio Nacional de Ecologia, Belém, November 1979.

Ducke, A., Black, G. A., 1953, Phytogeographical notes on the Brazilian Amazon, *Anais da Academia Brasileira de Ciências*, 25: 1–46.

Dudal, R., 1968, Definition of soil units for the soil map of the world, *FAO World Soil Resources Reports*, 33: 1–72.

———, 1969, Supplement to definitions of soil units for the soil map of the world, *FAO World Soil Resources Reports*, 37: 1–10.

———, 1970, *Key to soil units for the soil maps of the world*, Food and Agriculture Organization, Rome.

Dufour, D. L., 1987, Insects as food: a case study from the northwest Amazon, *American Anthropologist*, 89: 383–97.

Duthie, D. W., 1939, The soils of British Guiana south of the 5th parallel, and of the North-West District, *Agricultural Journal of British Guiana*, 10: 173–93.

Dutra, S., Souza Filho, A. P. da S., Serrao, E. A. S., 1980, Adaptação de leguminosas forrageiras consorciadas com gramineas no cerrado do Amapá, *Pesquisa em Andamento, EMBRAPA/CPATU*, Belém, 14: 1–3.

Eastwood, D. A., Pollard, H. J., 1987, The accelerating growth of coca and colonisation in Bolivia, *Geography*, 72; 165–6.

Eddy, P., Sabogal, H., Walden, S., 1988, *The cocaine wars*, Century, London.

Eden, M. J., 1964, The savanna ecosystem — northern Rupununi, British Guiana, *McGill University Savanna Research Series*, 1: 1–216.

———, 1966, Some problems of Amerindian development in the Rupununi District, *Journal of the Guyana Museum and Zoo*, 42: 36–40.

———, 1971a, Scientific exploration in Venezuelan Amazonas, *Geographical Journal*, 137: 149–56.

———, 1971b, Some aspects of weathering and landforms in Guyana (British

Guiana), *Zeitschrift für Geomorphologie*, N.F. **15**: 181–98.

——, 1974a, Palaeoclimatic influences and the development of savanna in southern Venezuela, *Journal of Biogeography*, **1**: 95–109.

——, 1974b, Ecological aspects of development among Piaroa and Guahibo Indians of the upper Orinoco basin, *Antropológica*, **39**: 25–56.

——, 1974c, Irrigation systems and the development of peasant agriculture in Venezuela, *Tijdschrift voor Economische en Sociale Geografie*, **65**: 48–54.

——, 1978, Ecology and land development: the case of Amazonian rainforest, *Transactions of Institute of British Geographers*, N.S. **3**: 444–63.

——, 1979, Ecological equilibrium and settlement change in the neotropical rainforest, *Actas del 4th Symposium Internacional de Ecología Tropical*, Panama City, March 1977, **3**: 819–33.

——, 1980, A traditional agro-ecosystem in the Amazon region of Colombia. In *Tropical ecology and development* (ed. J. I. Furtado), vol. 1, pp. 509–14, International Society of Tropical Ecology, Kuala Lumpur.

——, 1982, Silvicultural and agroforestry developments in the Amazon basin of Brazil, *Commonwealth Forestry Review*, **61**: 195–202.

——, 1986a, Monitoring indigenous shifting cultivation in forest areas of southwest Guyana using aerial photography and Landsat. In *Remote sensing and tropical land management* (eds M. J. Eden, J. T. Parry), pp. 255–77, John Wiley & Sons, Chichester.

——, 1986b, The management of renewable resources in the tropics: the use of remote sensing. In *Remote sensing and tropical land management* (eds M. J. Eden, J. T. Parry), pp. 3–15, John Wiley & Sons, Chichester.

——, 1987, Traditional shifting cultivation and the tropical forest system, *Trends in Ecology and Evolution*, **2**: 340–3.

——, 1988, Crop diversity in tropical swidden cultivation: comparative data from Colombia and Papua New Guinea, *Agriculture, Ecosystems and Environment*, **20**: 127–36.

——, Andrade, A., 1987, Ecological aspects of swidden cultivation among the Andoke and Witoto Indians of the Colombian Amazon, *Human Ecology*, **15**: 339–59.

——, ——, 1988, Colonos, agriculture and adaptation in the Colombian Amazon, *Journal of Biogeography*, **15**: 79–85.

——, Bray, W., Herrera, L., McEwan, C., 1984, *Terra preta* soils and their archaeological context in the Caquetá basin of southeast Colombia, *American Antiquity*, **49**: 125–40.

——, McGregor, D. F. M., Morelo, J., 1982, Geomorphology of the middle Caquetá basin of eastern Colombia, *Zeitschrift für Geomorphologie*, N.F. **26**: 343–64.

——, Potter, V., 1979, Land colonisation and agricultural development in lowland Venezuela, *Papers in Geography*, Bedford College, London, **1**: 1–29.

Egger, K., 1981, Ecofarming in the tropics — characteristics and potentialities, *Plant Research and Development*, **13**: 96–106.

Egler, W. A., 1960, Contribuções ao conhecimento dos campos da Amazônia. 1. Os campos do Ariramba, *Boletim Museu Paraense Emílio Goeldi; Botânica*, **4**: 1–36.

Eidt, R. C., 1962, Pioneer settlement in eastern Peru, *Annals of the Association of American Geographers*, **52**: 255–78.

Elton, C. A., 1958, *Ecology of invasions by animals and plants*, Methuen, London.

EMBRAPA, 1975, *Mapa esquemático dos solos das regiões norte, meio-norte e centro-oeste do Brasil*, Empresa Brasileira de Pesquisa Agropecuária, Rio de Janeiro.

——, 1978, Recomendações técnicas para o controle da fusariose e outras doenças da pimenta-do-reino, *Comunicado Técnico*, *EMBRAPA/CPATU*, Belém, **1**: 1–8.

Endler, J. A., 1982, Pleistocene forest refuges: fact or fancy? In *Biological diversification in the tropics* (ed. G. T. Prance), pp. 641–57, Columbia University Press, New York.

Erwin, T. L., 1982, Tropical forests: their richness in Coleoptera and other arthropod species, *Coleopterists' Bulletin*, **36**: 74–5.

——, 1988, The tropical forest canopy: the heart of biotic diversity. In *Biodiversity* (ed. E. O. Wilson), pp. 123–9, National Academy Press, Washington.

Evans, C., Meggers, B. J., 1968, *Archaeological investigations on the Rio Napo, eastern Ecuador*, Smithsonian Contributions to Anthropology 6, Washington.

Ewel, J. J., 1986, Designing agricultural ecosystems for the humid tropics, *Annual Review of Ecology & Systematics*, **17**: 245–71.

Falesi, I. C., 1972, Solos da rodovía transamazônica, *Boletim Técnico do IPEAN*, Belém, **55**: 1–196.

——, 1976, Ecossistema de pastagem cultivada na Amazônia brasileira, *Boletim Técnico*, *EMBRAPA/CPATU*, Belém, **1**: 1–193.

Fanshawe, D. B., 1952, *The vegetation of British Guiana*, Institute Paper 29, Forestry Institute, Oxford.

——, 1954, Riparian vegetation in British Guiana, *Journal of Ecology*, **42**: 289–95.

FAO, 1966, *Report on the soil survey project, British Guiana*, 7 vols and maps, Food and Agriculture Organization, Rome.

——, 1976–87, *Production yearbook 1975–1986*, vols 29–40, Food and Agriculture Organization, Rome.

——, 1978a, *Outline of an applied research and experimental development programme for the Latin American Regional Centre for Aquaculture*, Food and Agriculture Organization, Rome.

FAO-UNESCO, 1971, *Soil map of the world. Vol. 4. South America*, United Nations Educational, Scientific and Cultural Organization, Paris.

——, 1974, *Soil map of the world. Vol. 1. Legend*, United Nations Educational, Scientific and Cultural Organization, Paris.

Farley, R., 1953, The rise of the village settlements of British Guiana, *Caribbean Quarterly*, **3**: 101–9.

Farnworth, E. G., Golley, F. B. (eds), 1974, *Fragile ecosystems*, Springer-Verlag, Berlin.

Fearnside, P. M., 1978, Estimation of carrying capacity for human populations in a part of the Transamazon highway colonization area of Brazil, Ph.D. dissertation, University of Michigan, Ann Arbor.

——, 1979, Cattle yield prediction for the Transamazon highway of Brazil, *Interciencia*, **4**: 220–5.

——, 1980a, The effects of cattle pasture on soil fertility in the Brazilian Amazon: consequences for beef production sustainability, *Tropical Ecology*, **21**: 125–37.

——, 1980b, The prediction of soil erosion losses under various land uses in the Transamazon highway colonization area of Brazil. In *Tropical ecology and development* (ed. J. I. Furtado), vol. 2, pp. 1287–95, International Society of Tropical Ecology, Kuala Lumpur.

——, 1982, Deforestation in the Brazilian Amazon: how fast is it occurring?, *Interciencia*, **7**: 82–8.

——, 1983, Development alternatives in the Brazilian Amazon: an ecological evaluation, *Interciencia*, **8**: 65–78.

———, 1985a, Brazil's Amazon forest and the global carbon problem, *Interciencia*, **10**: 179–86.

———, 1985b, Environmental change and deforestation in the Brazilian Amazon. In *Change in the Amazon basin. Vol. 1. Man's impact on forests and rivers* (ed. J. Hemming), pp. 70–89, Manchester University Press, Manchester.

———, 1985c, Agriculture in Amazonia. In *Amazonia* (eds G. T. Prance, T. E. Lovejoy), pp. 393–418, Pergamon Press, Oxford.

———, 1986a, Deforestation and international economic development projects in Brazilian Amazonia. Paper presented at Symposium on Biological Diversity and the Impact of International Economic Development Projects in the Humid Tropics, INTECOL/ESA joint meeting, Syracuse, August 1986.

———, 1986b, Spatial concentration of deforestation in the Brazilian Amazon, *Ambio*, **15**: 74–81.

———, 1987, Jari aos dezoito anos: lições para os planos silviculturais em Carajas. In *Homem e natureza na Amazônia* (eds G. Kohlhepp, A. Schrader), pp. 291–311, Geographisches Institut der Universität Tübingen, Tübingen.

———, Ferreira, G. de L., 1984, Roads in Rondônia: highway construction and the farce of unprotected forest reserves in Brazil's Amazonian forest, *Environmental Conservation*, **11**: 358–60.

———, Rankin, J. M., 1980, Jari and development in the Brazilian Amazon, *Interciencia*, **5**: 146–56.

———, ———, 1982. The new Jari: risks and prospects of a major Amazonian development, *Interciencia*, **7**: 329–39.

Fernández-Baca, S., de Lucía, R., Jara, L. C., 1986, Mexico. Milk and beef production from tropical pastures, *World Animal Review*, **58**: 2–12.

Ferri, M. G., 1960, Contribution to the knowledge of the ecology of the 'Rio Negro caatinga' (Amazon), *Bulletin of the Research Council of Israel*, **8D**: 195–208.

Fifer, V., 1982, The search for a series of small successes: frontiers of settlement in eastern Bolivia, *Journal of Latin American Studies*, **14**: 407–32.

Fittkau, E. J., 1969, The fauna of South America. In *Biogeography and ecology in South America* (eds E. J. Fittkau, J. Illies, H. Klinge, G. H. Schwabe, H. Sioli), vol. 2, pp. 624–58, Dr W. Junk, The Hague.

———, Irmler, U., Junk, W. J., Reiss, F., Schmidt, G. W., 1975, Productivity, biomass, and population dynamics in Amazonian water bodies. In *Tropical ecological systems. Trends in terrestrial and aquatic research* (eds. F. B. Golley, E. Medina), pp. 289–312, Springer-Verlag, Berlin.

———, Klinge, H., 1973, On biomass and trophic structure of the central Amazonian rain forest ecosystem, *Biotropica*, **5**: 2–14.

Fosberg, F. R., 1970, The problem of isolation in the lowland tropical rain-forest, *Tropical Ecology*, **11**: 162–8.

———, 1972, Discussion. In *The environmental future* (ed. N. Polunin), pp. 387–8, Macmillan, London.

Fränzle, O., 1979, The water balance of the tropical rain forest of Amazonia and the effects of human impact, *Applied Sciences and Development*, **13**: 88–117.

Fuchs, H., 1964, El sistema de cultivo de los Deukwhuana (Maquiritare) del alto Rio Ventuari, Territorio Federal Amazonas, Venezuela, *América Indígena*, **24**: 171–95.

Furley, P., 1980, Development planning in Rondonia based on natural renewable resource surveys. In *Land, people and planning in contemporary Amazonia* (ed. F. Barbira-Scazzocchio), pp. 37–45, Centre of Latin American Studies, Cambridge.

————, 1986, Radar surveys for resource evaluation in Brazil: an illustration from Rondonia. In *Remote sensing and tropical land management* (eds M. J. Eden, J. T. Parry), pp. 79–99, John Wiley & Sons, Chichester.

————, Ratter, J. A., 1988, Soil resources and plant communities of the central Brazilian cerrado and their development, *Journal of Biogeography*, **15**: 97–108.

Furtado, J. I. (ed.), 1980, *Tropical ecology and development*, 2 vols, International Society of Tropical Ecology, Kuala Lumpur.

Game, M., 1980, Best shape for nature reserves, *Nature*, **287**: 630–2.

Gansser, A., 1974, The Roraima problem (South America), *Verhandlungen Naturforschende Gesellschaft in Basel*, **84**: 80–100.

Garrido Filha, I., 1980, *O projeto Jari e os capitais estrangeiros na Amazônia*, 2nd edn, Editora Vozes, Petrópolis.

Gasser, J. K. R., 1961, Investigations of rice-growing in British Guiana. 1. Characteristics of some rice soils of the coastland, *Journal of Soil Science*, **12**: 234–41.

Gazzo, J., 1982, Development policies and plans for Peru's Amazon region. In *Agriculture and land use research* (ed. S. B. Hecht), pp. 85–105, Centro Internacional de Agricultura Tropical, Cali.

Gentry, A. H., Lopez-Parodi, J., 1980, Deforestation and increased flooding of the upper Amazon, *Science*, **210**: 1354–6.

Geological Society of America, 1964, *Mapa geológico de América del Sur*, Geological Society of America, Boulder.

Gibbs, R. J., 1967, The geochemistry of the Amazon river system. 1. The factors that control the salinity and the composition and concentration of the suspended solids, *Geological Society of America Bulletin*, **78**: 1203–32.

Gilbert, A., 1974, *Latin American development. A geographical perspective*, Penguin Books, Harmondsworth.

Gliessman, S. R., Garcia, E. R., Amador A., M., 1981, The ecological basis for the application of traditional agricultural technology in the management of tropical agro-ecosystems, *Agro-Ecosystems*, **7**: 173–185.

Goldman, I., 1963, *The Cubeo. Indians of the northwest Amazon*, University of Illinois Press, Urbana.

Goldstein, I. S., 1979, Chemical from wood, *Unasylva*, **31** (125): 2–9.

Gómez Latorre, A., 1978, Las atrocidades de la Casa Arana. In *La nueva dimension de la Amazonia* (ed. G. P. Callejas), pp. 64–78, La Fundación Universidad de Bogotá Jorge Tadeo Lozano, Bogotá.

Gómez-Pompa, A., Vázquez-Yanes, C., 1974, Studies on the secondary succession of tropical lowlands: the life cycle of secondary species, *Proceedings of 1st International Congress of Ecology*, The Hague, September 1974, pp. 336–42.

————, ————, Guevara, S., 1972, The tropical rain forest: a nonrenewable resource, *Science*, **177**: 762–5.

Gonçalves, C. A., Pimentel, D. M., Santos Filho, B. G. dos, 1974, Plantas invasoras de pastagens do Estado do Pará, *Boletim Técnico do IPEAN*, Belém, **62**: 25–37.

Goodland, E. A., 1964, The mound, *Journal of the British Guiana Museum and Zoo*, **39**: 9–17.

Goodland, R. J. A., 1966, South American savannas. Comparative studies, llanos and Guyana, *McGill University Savanna Research Series*, **5**: 1–52.

————, 1980, Environmental ranking of Amazonian development projects in Brazil. In *Land, people and planning in contemporary Amazonia* (ed. F. Barbira-Scazzocchio), pp. 1–26, Centre of Latin American Studies, Cambridge.

————, 1985, Brazil's environmental progress in Amazonian development. In

Change in the Amazon basin, Vol. 1. *Man's impact on forests and rivers* (ed. J. Hemming), pp. 5–35, Manchester University Press, Manchester.

——, 1986, Environmental aspects of Amazonian development projects in Brazil, *Interciencia*, **11**: 16–24.

——, Irwin, H. S., 1975, *Amazon jungle: green hell to red desert?*, Elsevier, Amsterdam.

——, ——, 1977, Amazonian forest and cerrado: development and environmental conservation. In *Extinction is forever* (eds G. T. Prance, T. S. Elias), pp. 214–33, New York Botanical Garden, Bronx.

Gorzula, S., Medina-Cuervo, G., 1986, La fauna silvestre de la cuenca del Rio Caroni y el impacto del hombre, evaluación y perspectivaes, *Interciencia*, **11**: 317–24.

Gottlieb, O. R., Mors, W. B., 1978, Fitoquímica amazônica: uma apreciação em perspectiva, *Interciencia*, **3**: 252–63.

Gottsberger, G., 1978, Seed dispersal by fish in the inundated regions of Humaitá, Amazonia, *Biotropica*, **10**: 170–83.

——, Morawetz, W., 1986, Floristic, structural and phytogeographical analysis of the savannas of Humaitá (Amazonas), *Flora*, **178**: 41–71.

Gould, F., 1988, Genetic engineering, integrated pest management and the evolution of pests, *Trends in Ecology and Evolution*, **3**: 15–18.

Goulding, M., 1980, *The fishes and the forest. Explorations in Amazonian natural history*, University of California Press, Berkeley.

——, 1983, Amazonian fisheries. In *The dilemma of Amazonian development* (ed. E. F. Moran), pp. 189–210, Westview Press, Boulder.

——, Leal Carvalho, M., Ferreira, E. G., 1988, *Rio Negro. Rich life in poor water*, SPB Academic Publishing, The Hague.

Gourou, P., 1949, Observações geográficas na Amazônia, *Revista Brasileira de Geografia*, **11**: 355–408.

Gradwohl, J., Greenberg, R., 1988, *Saving the tropical forests*, Earthscan Publications, London.

Graham-Yooll, A., 1988, Hoyte's recipe for economic recovery, *South*, London, **100**: 41–2.

Greaves, A., 1979, *Gmelina* — large scale planting, Jarilandia, Amazon basin, *Commonwealth Forestry Review*, **58**: 267–9.

Grenand, F., Haxaire, C., 1977, Monographie d'un abattis Wayãpi, *Journal d'Agriculture Traditionelle et de Botanique Appliqué*, **24**: 285–310.

Gross, D. R., 1975, Protein capture and cultural development in the Amazon basin, *American Anthropologist*, **77**: 526–49.

——, Eiten, G., Flowers, N. M., Leoi, F. M., Ritter, M. L., Werner, D. W., 1979, Ecology and acculturation among native peoples of central Brazil, *Science*, **206**: 1043–50.

Guidon, N., Delibrias, G., 1986, Carbon-14 dates point to man in the Americas 32,000 years ago, *Nature*, **321**: 769–71.

Guzman, M. J., 1971, Los Andokes: historia, conciencia etnica, y explotación del caucho, *Universitas Humanistica*, Bogotá, **2**: 53–97.

Haffer, J., 1969, Speciation in Amazonian forest birds, *Science*, **165**: 131–7.

——, 1974, *Avian speciation in tropical South America*, Nuttall Ornithological Club, Harvard University, Cambridge, Mass.

——, 1977, Pleistocene speciation in Amazonian birds, *Amazoniana*, **6**: 161–91.

Hames, R., 1983, Monoculture, polyculture, and polyvariety in tropical forest swidden cultivation, *Human Ecology*, **11**: 13–34.

Hammen, T. van der, 1963, A palynological study on the Quaternary of British Guiana, *Leidse Geologische Mededelingen*, **29**: 125–80.

———, 1972, Changes in vegetation and climate in the Amazon basin and surrounding areas during the Pleistocene, *Geologie en Mijnbouw*, **51**: 641–3.

———, 1974, The Pleistocene changes of vegetation and climate in tropical South America, *Journal of Biogeography*, **1**: 3–26.

Hammond, N., 1980, Prehistoric human utilization of the savanna environments of Middle and South America. In *Human ecology in savanna environments* (ed. D. R. Harris), pp. 73–105, Academic Press, London.

Hansen, J., Fung, I., Lacis, A., Rind, D., Lebedeff, S., Ruedy, R., Russel, G., 1988, Global climate changes as forecast by Goddard Institute for Space Studies three-dimensional model, *Journal of Geophysical Research*, **93D**, 9341–64.

———, Johnson, D., Lacis, A., Lebedeff, S., Lee, P., Rind, D., Russell, G., 1981, Climate impact of increasing atmospheric carbon dioxide, *Science*, **213**: 957–66.

Hanson, E., 1933, Social regression in the Orinoco and Amazon basins. Notes on a journey in 1931 and 1932, *Geographical Review*, **23**: 578–98.

Hare, F. K., 1980, The planetary environment: fragile or sturdy?, *Geographical Journal*, **146**: 379–95.

Harner, M. J., 1972, *The Jívaro. People of the sacred waterfalls*, Doubleday/Natural History Press, Garden City, NY.

Harris, D. R., 1971, The ecology of swidden cultivation in the upper Orinoco rain forest, Venezuela, *Geographical Review*, **61**: 475–95.

———, 1972, The origins of agriculture in the tropics, *American Scientist*, **60**: 180–93.

Harris, M., 1978, *Cannibals and kings. The origins of cultures*, Fontana/Collins, Glasgow.

———, 1984, Animal capture and Yanomamo warfare: retrospect and new evidence, *Journal of Anthropological Research*, **40**: 183–201.

Harrison, P., 1982, The new age of organic farming, *New Scientist*, **94**: 427–9.

Hayter, T., Watson, C., 1985, *Aid. Rhetoric and reality*, Pluto Press, London.

Healy, K., 1986, The boom within the crisis: some recent effects of foreign cocaine markets on Bolivian rural society and economy. In *Coca and cocaine. Effects on people and policy in Latin America* (eds D. Pacini, C. Franquemont), pp. 101–43, Cultural Survival/Latin American Studies Program, Cornell University, Ithaca.

Hecht, S. B., 1981, Deforestation in the Amazon basin: magnitude, dynamics and soil resource effects, *Studies in Third World Societies*, **13**: 61–108.

———, 1982, Agroforestry in the Amazon basin: practice, theory and limits of a promising land use. In *Amazonia. Agriculture and land use research* (ed. S. B. Hecht), pp. 332–71, Centro Internacional de Agricultura Tropical, Cali.

———, 1985, Environment, development and politics: capital accumulation and the livestock sector in eastern Amazonia, *World Development*, **13**: 663–84.

———, Cockburn, A., 1989, Defenders of the Amazon, *New Statesman and Society*, **55**, 16–20.

Hegen, E. E., 1963, The Andean cultural frontier, *Journal of Inter-American Studies*, **5**: 431–6.

———, 1966, *Highways into the upper Amazon basin*, University of Florida Press, Gainesville.

Heinsdijk, D., 1958a, *Report to the government of Brazil on a forest inventory in the Amazon valley. 3. Region between Rio Tapajós and Rio Madeira*, Report 969, Food and Agriculture Organization, Rome.

————, 1958b, *Report to the government of Brazil on a forest inventory in the Amazon valley. 2. Region between Rio Xingú and Rio Tocantins*, Report 949, Food and Agriculture Organization, Rome.

————, Miranda Bastos, A. de, 1963, *Inventários florestais na Amazônia*, Serviço Florestal, Ministério de Agricultura, Rio de Janeiro.

Hemming, J., 1978, *Red gold. The conquest of the Brazilian Indians*, Macmillan, London.

Henderson, P. A., Walker, I., 1986, On the leaf litter community of the Amazonian blackwater stream Tarumazinho, *Journal of Tropical Ecology*, 2: 1–17.

Henderson-Sellers, A., Gornitz, V., 1984, Possible climatic impacts of land cover transformations, with particular emphasis on tropical deforestation, *Climatic Change*, 6: 231–58.

Herbertson, A. J., 1905, The major natural regions: an essay in systematic geography, *Geographical Journal*, 25: 300–12.

————, Jordan, C. F., Klinge, H., Medina, E., 1978a, Amazon ecosystems. Their structure and functioning with particular emphasis on nutrients, *Interciencia*, 3: 223–31.

Herrera, R., Merida, T., Stark, N., Jordan, C. F., 1978b, Direct Phosphorus transfer from leaf litter to roots, *Naturwissenschaften*, 65: 208–9.

Herrera-MacBryde, O., 1988, New Colombian parks, *Threatened Plants Newsletter*, 20: 5–6.

Hershkovitz, P., 1969, The evolution of mammals on southern continents. 6. The recent mammals of the neotropical region: a zoogeographic and ecological review, *Quarterly Review of Biology*, 44: 1–70.

Higbee, E. C., 1951, Of man and the Amazon, *Geographical Review*, 41: 401–20.

Higgs, A. J., Usher, M. B., 1980, Should nature reserves be large or small?, *Nature*, 285: 568–9.

Hills, T. L., 1973, The savanna biome: a case study of human impact on biotic communities. In *Perspectives on environment* (eds I. R. Manners, M. W. Mikesell), pp. 1–33, Association of American Geographers, Washington.

Hiraoka, M., Yamamoto, S., 1980, Agricultural development in the upper Amazon of Ecuador, *Geographical Review*, 70: 423–45.

Hoffmann, H., 1964, Money, ecology, and acculturation among the Shipibo of Peru. In *Explorations in cultural anthropology. Essays in honor of George Peter Murdock* (ed. W. H. Goodenough), pp. 259–76, McGraw-Hill, New York.

Holdridge, L. R., 1951, The alder, 'Alnus acuminata', as a farm timber tree in Costa Rica, *Caribbean Forester*, 12: 47–53.

Holling, C. S., Clark, W. C., 1975, Notes towards a science of ecological management. In *Unifying concepts in ecology* (eds W. H. van Dobben, R. H. Lowe-McConnell), pp. 247–51, Dr W. Junk, The Hague.

Holmberg, A., 1963, The Sirionó. In *Handbook of South American Indians* (ed. J. H. Steward), pp. 455–63, Cooper Square, New York.

Holthuijzen, A. M. A., Boerboom, J. H. A., 1982, The *Cecropia* seedbank in the Surinam lowland rain forest, *Biotropica*, 14: 62–8.

Holz, R. K., Baker, V. R., Sutton Jr, S. M., Penteado-Orellana, M. M., 1978, *South American river morphology and hydrology*, ASTP Summary Science Report, NASA, 412: 545–94.

Homma, A. K. O., Miranda Filho, L., 1979, Análise da estrutura da produção de pimenta-do-reino no estado do Pará — 1977/1978, *Comunicado Técnico, EMBRAPA/CPATU*, Belém, 20: 1–68.

Horn, E. F., 1957, The lumber industry of the lower Amazon valley, *Caribbean Forester*, 18: 56–67.

Hornick, J. R., Zerbe, J. I., Whitmore, J. L., 1984, Jari's successes, *Journal of Forestry*, **82**: 663–7.

Howard-Williams, C., Junk, W. J., 1976, The decomposition of aquatic macrophytes in the floating meadows of a central Amazonian várzea lake. In *Neotropische Ökosysteme. Festschrift zu Ehren von Prof. Dr Harald Sioli* (ed. P. Muller), pp. 115–23, Dr W. Junk, The Hague.

Huber, O., 1982, Significance of savanna vegetation in the Amazon territory of Venezuela. In *Biological diversification in the tropics* (ed. G. T. Prance), pp. 221–44, Columbia University Press, New York.

Hueck, K., 1957, Sôbre a origem dos campos cerrados do Brasil e algumas novas observações no seu limite meridional, *Revista Brasileira de Geografia*, **19**: 67–82.

———, Seibert, P., 1972, *Vegetationskarte von Südamerika*, Gustav Fischer, Stuttgart.

Huffnagel, H. P., 1964, *Rubber production in the Amazon region*, Food and Agriculture Organization, Rome.

Hutchinson, I. D., 1980, *Liberation thinning. A tool in the management of mixed dipterocarp forest in Sarawak*, Forest Department, Kuching.

———, 1987, Improvement thinning in natural tropical forests: aspects and institutionalization. In *Natural management of tropical moist forests* (eds F. Mergen, J. R. Vincent), pp. 113–27, Yale University, New Haven.

Hutton, E. M., 1979, Problems and successes of legume-grass pastures, especially in tropical Latin America. In *Pasture production in acid soils of the tropics* (eds P. A. Sanchez, L. E. Tergas), pp. 81–93, Centro Internacional de Agricultura Tropical, Cali.

IBGE, 1960–87, *Anuário estatístico do Brasil 1959–1986*, vols 20–47, Fundação Instituto Brasileiro de Geografia e Estatística, Rio de Janeiro.

———, 1980a, *Produção agricola municipal 1979. 1. Rondônia–Acre–Amazonas–Roraima–Pará–Amapá*, Fundação Instituto Brasileiro de Geografia e Estatística, Rio de Janeiro.

———, 1980b, *Produção da pecuária municipal 1979. 1. Região norte*, Fundação Instituto Brasileiro de Geografia e Estatística, Rio de Janeiro.

IBRD, 1953, *The economic development of British Guiana*, International Bank for Reconstruction and Development, Johns Hopkins Press, Baltimore.

IDB, 1982, *Economic and social progress in Latin America. 1980–81 report*, Inter-American Development Bank, Washington.

———, 1984, *Economic and social progress in Latin America, 1984 report*, Inter-American Development Bank, Washington.

———, 1987, *Economic and social progress in Latin America, 1987 report*, Inter-American Development Bank, Washington.

INCORA, 1973, *La colonización en Colombia: una evaluación del proceso*, Instituto Colombiano de la Reforma Agraria, Bogotá.

INCRA, 1972, *O programa de integração nacional e a colonização na Amazônia*, Instituto Nacional de Colonização e Reforma Agrária, Ministério de Agricultura, Brasília.

IPEAN, 1974, *Solos da rodavía transamazônica: trecho Itaituba–Rio Branco*, Instituto de Pesquisa Agropecuária do Norte, Belém.

IUCN, 1982, *Directory of neotropical protected areas*, Tycooly International, Dublin.

Jahoda, J. C., O'Hearn, D. L., 1975, The reluctant Amazon basin, *Environment*, **17**: 16–30.

Jankauskis, J., 1978, *Recuperação de florestas tropicais mecanicamente exploradas*, Superintendência do Desenvolvimento da Amazônia, Belém.

Janos, D. P., 1983, Tropical mycorrhizas, nutrient cycles and plant growth. In *Tropical rain forest: ecology and management* (eds S. L. Sutton, T. C. Whitmore, A. C. Chadwick), pp. 327–45, Blackwell Scientific, Oxford.

Janzen, D. H., 1974, Tropical blackwater rivers, animals, and mast fruiting by the Dipterocarpaceae, *Biotropica*, **6**: 69–103.

——, 1975, *Ecology of plants in the tropics*, Edward Arnold, London.

Jonkers, W. B. J., Schmidt, P., 1984, Ecology and timber production in tropical rain forest in Surinam, *Interciencia*, **9**: 290–7.

Jordan, C. F., 1982, The nutrient balance of an Amazonian rain forest, *Ecology*, **63**: 647–54.

——, 1985, *Nutrient cycling in tropical forest ecosystems*, John Wiley & Sons, Chichester.

——, 1987, *Amazonian rain forests. Ecosystem disturbance and recovery*, Springer-Verlag, New York.

——, Russell, C. E., 1983, Jari: productividad de las plantaciones y perdida de nutrientes debido al corte y la quema, *Interciencia*, **8**: 294–7.

——, Uhl, C., 1978, Biomass of a 'tierra firme' forest of the Amazon basin calculated by a refined allometric relationship, *Oecologia Plantorum*, **13**: 387–400.

Journaux, A., 1975, *Recherches géomorphologiques en Amazonie brésilienne*, Bulletin 20, Centre de Géomorphologie, Caen.

Joyce, C., 1985, Tapping the lungs of the earth, *New Scientist*, **1466**: 48–50.

Junk, W. J., 1980, Aquatic macrophytes: ecology and use in Amazonian agriculture. In *Tropical ecology and development* (ed. J. I. Furtado), vol. 2, pp. 763–70, International Society of Tropical Ecology, Kuala Lumpur.

——, 1984, Ecology of the várzea, floodplain of Amazonian white-water rivers. In *The Amazon* (ed. H. Sioli), pp. 215–43, Dr W. Junk, Dordrecht.

——, de Mello, J. A. S. N., 1987, Impactos ecológicos das represas hidrelétricas na bacia amazônica brasileira. In *Homem e natureza na Amazônia* (eds G. Kohlhepp, A. Schrader), pp. 367–85, Geographisches Institut der Universität Tübingen, Tübingen.

Kahn, F., Mejia, K., de Castro, A., 1988, Species richness and density of palms in terra firme forests of Amazonia, *Biotropica*, **20**: 266–9.

Kass, D. C. L., 1976, Simultaneous polyculture of tropical food crops with special reference to the management of sandy soils of the Brazilian Amazon, Ph.D. thesis, Cornell University, Ithaca, NY.

Katzman, M. T., 1977, *Cities and frontiers in Brazil: regional dimensions of economic development*, Harvard University Press, Cambridge, Mass.

Kelsey, T. F., 1972, The beef industry in the Roraima savannas: a potential supply for Brazil's north, Ph.D. dissertation, University of Florida, Gainesville.

Kendall, S., 1985, Economies under the influence of cocaine, *Financial Times*, London, 24 May.

Kershaw, A. P., 1978, Record of last interglacial–glacial cycle from northeastern Queensland, *Nature*, **272**: 159–61.

Key, L., 1974, Village patterns and peasant agriculture — an historical overview. In *Guyana coastal lowlands: geography and environment* (ed. T. L. Hills), pp. 79–110, McGill University, Montreal.

Khobzi, J., Kroonenberg, S., Faivre, P., Weeda, A., 1980, Aspectos geomorfologicos de la Amazonia y Orinoquia colombianas, *Revista CIAF*, **5**: 97–126.

King, K. F. S., 1968a, *Land and people in Guyana*, Commonwealth Forestry Institute, Oxford.

——, 1968b, Agri-silviculture (the taungya system), *Bulletin, Department of Forestry, University of Ibadan*, **1**: 1–109.

King, L. C., 1967, *The morphology of the earth*, Oliver and Boyd, Edinburgh.

Kirby, J., 1976, Agricultural land-use and the settlement of Amazonia, *Pacific Viewpoint*, **17**: 105–32.

——, 1978, Colombian land-use change and the settlement of the oriente, *Pacific Viewpoint*, **19**: 1–25.

Kitamura, P. C., Dias Filho, M. B., Serrão, E. A. S., 1982, Análise econômica de algumas alternativas de manejo de pastagens cultivadas — Paragominas, PA, *Boletim de Pesquisa, EMBRAPA/CPATU*, Belém, **41**: 1–40.

Klammer, G., 1971, Über plio-pleistozäne Terrassen und ihre Sedimente im unteren Amazonasgebiet, *Zeitschrift für Geomorphologie*, N.F. **15**: 62–105.

Kleinpenning, J. M. G., 1975, The integration and colonisation of the Brazilian portion of the Amazon basin, *Nijmeegse Geografische Cahiers*, **4**: 1–177.

——, 1979, *An evaluation of the Brazilian policy for the integration of the Amazon basin (1964–1976)*, Geografisch en Planologisch Instituut, Nijmegen.

——, Volbeda, S., 1985, Recent changes in population size and distribution in the Amazon region of Brazil. In *Change in the Amazon basin. Vol. 2. The frontier after a decade of colonisation* (ed. J. Hemming), pp. 6–36, Manchester University Press, Manchester.

Klinge, H., 1967, Podzol soils: a source of blackwater rivers in Amazonia, *Atas do Simpósio sôbre a Biota Amazônica*, Belém, 1966, **3**: 117–25.

——, 1976, Bilanzierung von Hauptnährstoffen im Ökosystem tropischer Regenwald (Manaus) - Vorläufige Daten, *Biogeographica*, **7**: 59–99.

——, 1977, Fine litter production and nutrient return to the soil in three natural forest stands of eastern Amazonia, *Geo-Eco-Trop*, **1**: 159–67.

——, 1986, Lowland Amazon forests, bioelements and geochemistry. In *Proceedings of 1st Symposium on the Humid Tropics*, Belém, 1984, **1**: 333–46.

——, Herrera, R., 1978, Biomass studies in Amazon caatinga forest in southern Venezuela. 1. Standing crop of composite root mass in selected stands, *Tropical Ecology*, **19**: 93–110.

——, Medina, E., 1979, Rio Negro caatingas and campinas, Amazonas states of Venezuela and Brazil. In *Ecosystems of the world. Vol. 9A. Heathlands and related shrublands* (ed. R. L. Specht), pp. 483–8, Elsevier, Amsterdam.

——, ——, Herrera, R., 1977, Studies on the ecology of Amazon caatinga forest in southern Venezuela, *Acta Científica Venezolana*, **28**: 270–6.

——, Rodrigues, W. A., 1968, Litter production in an area of Amazonia terra firme forest. 1. Litter-fall, organic carbon and total nitrogen contents of litter, *Amazoniana*, **1**: 287–302.

——, ——, Brunig, E., Fittkau, E. J., 1975, Biomass and structure in a central Amazonian rain forest. In *Tropical ecological systems. Trends in terrestrial and aquatic research* (eds F. B. Golley, E. Medina), pp. 115–22, Springer-Verlag, Berlin.

Kloos, P., 1971, *The Maroni river Caribs of Surinam*, Van Gorcum, Assen.

——, 1977, The Akuriyo of Surinam: a case of emergence from isolation, *International Work Group for Indigenous Affairs*, **27**: 1–31.

Knight, P., 1982, How the Amazon defeated an American millionaire, *The Times*, London, 26 January.

Kohlhepp, G., 1987, Problemas de planejamento regional e do desenvolvimento regional na área do Programa Grande Carajás no leste da Amazônia. In *Homem e natureza na Amazônia* (eds G. Kohlhepp, A. Schrader), pp. 313–45, Geographisches Institut der Universität Tübingen, Tübingen.

Kroonenberg, S. B., Melitz, P. J., 1983, Summit levels, bedrock control and the etchplain concept in the basement of Surinam, *Geologie en Mijnbouw*, **62**: 389–99.

Kubitzki, K., 1985, The dispersal of forest plants. In *Amazonia* (eds G. T. Prance, T. E. Lovejoy), pp. 192–206, Pergamon Press, Oxford.

Laeyendecker-Roosenburg, D. M., 1966, A palynological investigation of some archaeologically interesting sections in northwestern Surinam, *Leidse Geologische Mededelingen*, **38**: 31–6.

Lamb, A. F. A., 1968, *Fast growing timber trees of the lowland tropics. 1.* Gmelina arborea, Commonwealth Forestry Institute, Oxford.

Lambert, J. D. H., Arnason, J. T., 1986, Nutrient dynamics in milpa agriculture and the role of weeds in initial stages of secondary succession in Belize, C. A., *Plant and Soil*, **93**: 303–22.

Landau, G. D., 1980, The Treaty for Amazonian Cooperation: a bold new instrument for development, *Georgia Journal of International and Comparative Law*, **10**: 463–89.

Landsberg, H. E., 1961, Solar radiation at the earth's surface, *Solar Energy*, **5**: 95–8.

Langford, M. H., 1953, *Hevea* diseases of the Amazon valley, *Boletim Técnico, Instituto Agronômico do Norte*, **27**: 1–28.

Lathrap, D. W., 1962, Yarinacocha: stratigraphic excavations in the Peruvian montaña, Ph.D. dissertation, Harvard University, Cambridge, Mass.

———, 1968, The 'hunting' economies of the tropical forest zone of South America: an attempt at historical perspective. In *Man the hunter* (eds R. B. Lee, I. Devore), pp. 23–9, Aldine, Chicago.

———, 1970, *The upper Amazon*, Thames & Hudson, London.

Latin America Bureau, 1984, *Guyana. Fraudulent revolution*, Latin America Bureau, London.

Laurent, R. F., 1973, A parallel survey of equatorial amphibians and reptiles in Africa and South America. In *Tropical forest ecosystems in Africa and South America: a comparative review* (eds B. J. Meggers, E. S. Ayensu, W. D. Duckworth), pp. 259–66, Smithsonian Institution, Washington.

Lawton, R. M., 1978, The management and regeneration of some Nigerian high forest ecosystems. In *Tropical forest ecosystems*, Natural Resources Research 14, pp. 580–8, United Nations Educational, Scientific and Cultural Organization, Paris.

Layrisse, M., Wilbert, J., 1966, *Indian societies of Venezuela. Their blood group types*, Fundación La Salle de Ciencias Naturales, Caracas.

Le Cointe, P., 1922, *L'Amazonie Brésilienne*, 2 vols, A. Challamel, Paris.

Leentvaar, P., 1973, Lake Brokopondo. In *Man-made lakes: their problems and environmental effects* (eds W. C. Ackermann, G. F. White, E. B. Worthington, J. L. Ivens), pp. 186–96, American Geophysical Union, Washington.

Leite, L. L., Furley, P. A., 1985, Land development in the Brazilian Amazon with particular reference to Rondônia and the Ouro Prêto colonisation project. In *Change in the Amazon basin. Vol. 2. The frontier after a decade of development* (ed. J. Hemming), pp. 119–39, Manchester University Press, Manchester.

Leopoldo, P. R., Franken, W., Matsui, E., 1985, Hydrological aspects of the tropical rainforest in the central Amazon. In *Change in the Amazon basin. Vol. 1. Man's impact on forests and rivers* (ed. J. Hemming), pp. 90–107, Manchester University Press, Manchester.

Lettau, H., Lettau, K., Molion, L. C. B., 1979, Amazonia's hydrologic cycle and the role of atmospheric recycling in assessing deforestation effects, *Monthly Weather Review*, **107**: 227–38.

Lewin, R., 1984, Parks: how big is big enough?, *Science*, **225**: 611–2.

Lewis, G. P., Owen, P. E., 1989, *Legumes of the Ilha de Maracá*, Royal Botanic Gardens, Kew.

Lima, R. R., 1956, A agricultura nas várzeas do estuario do Amazonas, *Boletim Técnico, Instituto Agronômico do Norte*, **33**: 1–164.

Lizot, J., 1976, The Yanomami in the face of ethnocide, *International Work Group for Indigenous Affairs*, **22**: 1–36.

———, 1977, Population, resources and warfare among the Yanomami, *Man*, N.S. **12**: 497–517.

Loczy, L. de, 1966, Contribuições a paleogeografia e história do desenvolvimento geológico da bacia do Amazonas, *Boletim, Divisão de Geologia e Mineralogia*, Rio de Janeiro, **223**: 1–96.

Lopes, A. S., Cox, F. R., 1977, Cerrado vegetation in Brazil: an edaphic gradient, *Agronomy Journal*, **69**: 828–31.

Lovejoy, T. E., 1985a, Development in a water-dominated ecosystem, or Amazonian ecology in a time of change. In *Change in the Amazon basin. Vol. 1. Man's impact on forests and rivers* (ed. J. Hemming), pp. 66–9, Manchester University Press, Manchester.

———, 1985b, Amazonia, people and today. In *Amazonia* (eds G. T. Prance, T. E. Lovejoy), pp. 328–38, Pergamon Press, Oxford.

———, Bierregaard Jr, R. O., Rankin, J. M., Schubart, H. O. R., 1983, Ecological dynamics of tropical forest fragments. In *Tropical rain forest: ecology and management* (eds S. L. Sutton, T. C. Whitmore, A. C. Chadwick), pp. 377–84, Blackwell Scientific Publications, Oxford.

———, ———, Rylands, A. B., Malcolm, J. R., Quintela, C. E., Harper, L. H., Brown Jr, K. S., Powell, A. H., Powell, G. V. N., Schubart, H. O. R., Hays, M. B., 1986, Edge and other effects of isolation on Amazon forest fragments. In *Conservation biology. The science of scarcity and diversity* (ed. M. E. Soulé), pp. 257–85, Sinauer Associates, Sunderland.

———, de Padua, M. T. J., 1980, *Can science save Amazonia?*, Earthscan, London.

———, Schubart, H. O. R., 1980, The ecology of Amazonian development. In *Land, people and planning in contemporary Amazonia* (ed. F. Barbira-Scazzocchio), pp. 21–6, Centre of Latin American Studies, Cambridge.

Lowe-McConnell, R. H., 1975, *Fish communities in tropical freshwaters; their distribution, ecology and evolution*, Longmans, London.

———, 1977, *Ecology of fishes in tropical waters*, Edward Arnold, London.

———, 1979, On environmental stability and its effects on fish populations in tropical freshwaters, *Actas del 4th Symposium Internacional de Ecologia Tropical*, Panama City, March 1977, **2**: 695–710.

Lowenthal, D., 1960, Population contrasts in the Guianas, *Geographical Review*, **50**: 41–58.

Loxton, R. F., Rutherford, G. K., Spector, J., Jones, T. A., 1958, *Soil and land-use surveys. 2. British Guiana. The Rupununi savannas*, Imperial College of Tropical Agriculture, Trinidad.

MacArthur, R. H., 1955, Fluctuations of animal populations, and a measure of community stability, *Ecology*, **36**: 533–6.

———, Wilson, E. O., 1967, *The theory of island biogeography*, Princeton University Press, Princeton.

McConnell, R. B., 1968, Planation surfaces in Guyana, *Geographical Journal*, **134**: 506–20.

McDonald, L., Fernandes, I. M., 1984, AMCEL, *Journal of Forestry*, **82**: 668–70.
McGregor, D. F. M., 1980, An investigation of soil erosion in the Colombian rainforest zone, *Catena*, **7**: 265–73.
McNeil, M., 1964, Lateritic soils, *Scientific American*, **211** (5): 96–102.
McNeill, W. H., 1979, *Plagues and peoples*, Penguin, Harmondsworth.
McWatt, J. E., 1964, Land development, *Proceedings of a Seminar on Land Development*, Georgetown, December 1963 (ed. D. A. Farnum), pp. 16–30.
Mabberley, D. J., 1983, *Tropical rain forest ecology*, Blackie, Glasgow.
Maguire, B., 1979, Guayana, region of the Roraima sandstone formation. In *Tropical botany*, (eds K. Larsen, L. B. Holm-Nielsen), pp. 223–38, Academic Press, London.
Mahar, D. J., 1979, *Frontier development policy in Brazil: a study of Amazonia*, Praeger, New York.
Mandel, J. R., 1973, *The plantation economy. Population and economic change in Guyana 1838–1916*, Temple University Press, Philadelphia.
Marbut, C. F., Manifold, C. B., 1926, The soils in the Amazon basin in relation to agricultural possibilities, *Geographical Review*, **16**: 414–42.
Mares, M. A., 1986, Conservation in South America: problems, consequences, and solutions, *Science*, **233**: 734–9.
Margolis, M., 1988a, Threat from Amazon burn-off, *The Times*, London, 6 September.
——, 1988b, Brazil moves to save rain forests, *The Times*, London, 13 October.
——, 1989a, Nationalist rhetoric clouds Amazon plan, *The Times*, London, 11 April.
——, 1989b, Brazil labels its critics green 'imperialists', *The Times*, London, 9 March.
Marlier, G., 1973, Limnology of the Congo and Amazon rivers. In *Tropical forest ecosystems in Africa and South America: a comparative review* (eds B. J. Meggers, E. S. Ayensu, W. D. Duckworth), pp. 223–38, Smithsonian Institution, Washington.
Marques, J., Santos, J. M. dos, Villa Nova, N. A., Salati, E., 1977, Precipitable water and water vapour flux between Belém and Manaus, *Acta Amazonica*, **7**: 355–62.
Marques, J. R. F., Teixeira Neto, J. F., Serrão, E. A. S., 1980, Melhoramento e manejo de pastagens na Ilha de Marajó. Resultados e informações práticas, *Miscelânea, EMBRAPA/CPATU*, Belém, **6**: 1–25.
Martine, G., 1980, Recent colonization experiences in Brazil: expectations versus reality. In *Land, people and planning in contemporary Amazonia* (ed. F. Barbira-Scazzocchio), pp. 80–94, Centre of Latin American Studies, Cambridge.
Martínez, H., 1982, *Jenaro Herrera: una experiencia de colonización en la selva baja peruana*. Paper presented at 31st Annual Latin American Conference, Gainesville, February 1982.
Masson, J. L., 1978, *Agrosilviculture in the Pucallpa region of the Peruvian Amazon*, Food and Agriculture Organization, Lima.
——, 1979, *Demostración de manejo y utilización integral de bosques tropicales. Peru — plan de manejo para el Bosque Nacional Alexander von Humboldt*, Food and Agriculture Organization, Rome.
Matallana, R. P. B. de, 1937, La Gran Sabana, *Boletín de la Sociedad Venezolana de Ciencias Naturales*, **4**: 10–82.
May, R. J., 1984, *Kaikai aniani: a guide to bush foods, markets and culinary arts of Papua New Guinea*, Robert Brown & Associates, Bathurst.
May, R. M., 1975, The tropical rainforest, *Nature*, **257**: 737–8.

——, 1979, Fluctuations in abundance of tropical insects, *Nature*, **278**: 505–7.
Medina, M. E., 1980a, Ecology of tropical American savannas: an ecophysiological approach. In *Human ecology in savanna environments* (ed. D. R. Harris), pp. 279–319, Academic Press, London.
——, 1980b, Treaty for Amazonian cooperation: general analysis. In *Land, people and planning in contemporary Amazonia* (ed. F. Barbira-Scazzocchio), pp. 58–71, Centre of Latin American Studies, Cambridge.
Meggers, B. J., 1957, Environment and culture in the Amazon basin: an appraisal of the theory of environmental determinism. In *Studies in human ecology*, Social Science Monographs 3, pp. 71–89, Pan American Union, Washington.
——, 1971, *Amazonia. Man and culture in a counterfeit paradise*, Aldine, Chicago.
——, 1973, Some problems in cultural adaptation in Amazonia, with emphasis on the pre-European period. In *Tropical forest ecosystems in Africa and South America: a comparative review* (eds B. J. Meggers, E. S. Ayensu, W. D. Duckworth), pp. 311–20, Smithsonian Institution, Washington.
——, 1975, Application of the biological model of diversification to cultural distributions in tropical lowland South America, *Biotropica*, **7**: 141–61.
——, 1985, Aboriginal adaptation to Amazonia. In *Amazonia* (eds G. T. Prance, T. E. Lovejoy), pp. 307–27, Pergamon Press, Oxford.
——, Evans, C., 1957, *Archeological investigations at the mouth of the Amazon*, Bulletin 167, Bureau of American Ethnology, Washington.
——, ——, 1973, An interpretation of the cultures of Marajó island. In *Peoples and cultures of native South America* (ed. D. R. Gross), pp. 39–47, Doubleday/The Natural History Press, New York.
Melby, J., 1942, Rubber river: an account of the rise and collapse of the Amazon boom, *Hispanic American Historical Review*, **22**: 452–69.
Migliazza, E. C., 1978, The integration of the indigenous peoples of the Territory of Roraima, Brazil, *International Work Group for Indigenous Affairs*, **32**: 1–29.
Ministerio de Agricultura, 1972, *Algunas consideraciones sobre los problemas del sector agropecuario de la Intendencia de Caquetá*, Ministerio de Agricultura, Bogotá.
——, 1985, *Diagnostico agropecuario del Caquetá*, Ministerio de Agricultura/Gobernacion del Caquetá, Florencia.
Mitchell, W. B., 1969, *Area handbook for Guyana*, The American University, Washington.
Mittermeier, R. A., Milton, K., 1976, Jungle jackpot. Surinam's nature parks can do wonders for a wild-life list, *Animal Kingdom*, **79** (6): 26–31.
Molion, L. C. B., 1976, *A climatonomic study of the energy and moisture fluxes of the Amazonas basin with considerations of deforestation effects*, Instituto de Pesquisas Espaciais, São José dos Campos.
Moniz Bandeira, L. A. de, 1987, Estratégias de planejamento e de desenvolvimento regional a nivél internacional: o Pacto Amazônico. In *Homem e natureza na Amazônia* (eds G. Kohlhepp, A. Schrader), pp. 159–68, Geographisches Institut der Universität Tübingen, Tübingen.
Morales, E., 1988, Coca crop substitution and cosmetic development in Peru. In *Abstracts of Papers, 46th International Congress of Americanists* (ed. J. Lechner), p. 677, 46th International Congress of Americanists, Amsterdam.
Moran, E. F., 1979, Criteria for choosing successful homesteaders in Brazil, *Research in Economic Anthropology*, **2**: 339–59.
——, 1981, *Developing the Amazon*, Indiana University Press, Bloomington.
——, 1982, Ecological, anthropological, and agronomic research in the Amazon basin, *Latin American Research Review*, **17**: 3–41.
——, 1983, Mobility as a negative factor in human adaptability: the case of

South American tropical forest populations. In *Rethinking human adaptation: biological and cultural models* (eds R. Dyson-Hudson, M. A. Little), pp. 117–35, Westview Press, Boulder.

Morey, R. V., 1970, Ecology and culture change among the Colombian Guahibo, Ph.D. thesis, University of Pittsburg, Pittsburg.

———, Marwhitt, J. P., 1978, Ecology, economy, and warfare in lowland South America. In *Advances in Andean archaeology* (ed. D. L. Browman), pp. 247–58, Mouton, The Hague.

Morisawa, M., 1968, *Streams. Their dynamics and morphology*, McGraw-Hill, New York.

Mors, W. B., Rizzini, C. T., 1966, *Useful plants of Brazil*, Holden-Day, San Francisco.

Mott, G. O., Popenoe, H. L., 1977, Grasslands. In *Ecophysiology of tropical crops* (eds P. de T. Alvim, T. T. Kozlowski), pp. 157–86, Academic Press, New York.

Muchovej, J. J., de Albuquerque, F. C., Ribeiro, G. T., 1978, *Gmelina arborea* — a new host of *Ceratocystis fimbriata*, *Plant Disease Reporter*, **62**: 717–9.

Mueller, C. C., 1980, Recent frontier expansion in Brazil: the case of Rondonia. In *Land, people and planning in contemporary Amazonia* (ed. F. Barbira-Scazzocchio), pp. 141–53, Centre of Latin American Studies, Cambridge.

Mueller, C. W., 1975, Pioneer roads and the modernization of Brazilian Amazonia ocidental, Ph.D. dissertation, University of Miami, Coral Gables.

Müller, A. A., 1980, A cultura do dendê, *Miscelânea*, *EMBRAPA/CPATU*, Belém, **5**: 1–22.

Muthoo, M. K., Leader, T., 1978, *Forestry development and research, Brazil. National forest policy planning and development*, Food and Agriculture Organization, Rome.

Myers, H. M., Myers, P. V. N., 1871, *Life and nature under the tropics*, D. Appleton & Company, New York.

Myers, J. G., 1936, Savannah and forest vegetation of the interior Guiana plateau, *Journal of Ecology*, **24**: 162–84.

Myers, N., 1978, The nature of the deforestation problem — trends and policy implications, *Proceedings of the US Strategy Conference on Tropical Deforestation*, Washington, June 1978 (ed. D. R. Shane), pp. 19–22.

———, 1979a, *The sinking ark. A new look at the problem of disappearing species*, Pergamon Press, Oxford.

———, 1979b, Islands of conservation, *New Scientist*, **83**: 600–2.

———, 1980, *Conversion of tropical moist forests*, National Academy of Sciences, Washington.

———, 1984, *The primary source. Tropical forests and our future*, W. W. Norton, New York.

———, 1986, Tropical deforestation and a mega-extinction spasm. In *Conservation biology: the science of scarcity and diversity* (ed. M. E. Soulé), pp. 394–409, Sinauer Associates, Sunderland.

———, 1988a, Tropical forests: much more than stocks of wood, *Journal of Tropical Ecology*, **4**: 209–21.

———, 1988b, Tropical deforestation and climatic change, *Environmental Conservation*, **15**: 293–8.

Naraine, S. S., 1974a, Some aspects of coastal development in Guyana. In *Guyana coastal lowlands: geography and environment* (ed. T. L. Hills), pp. 1–17, McGill University, Montreal.

———, 1974b, The impact of drainage, irrigation and flood control on agriculture in Guyana. In *Guyana coastal lowlands: geography and environment* (ed. T. L. Hills), pp. 35–41, McGill University, Montreal.

Nascimento, C. N. B., Lourenço Júnior, J. B., 1979 *Criação de búfalos na Amazônia*, Empresa Brasileira de Pesquisa Agropecuária, Belém.

——, Moura Carvalho, L. O. D., Lourenço Júnior, J. B., 1979, *Importância do búfalo para a pecuária brasileira*, Empresa Brasileira de Pesquisa Agropecuária, Belém.

Nelson, M., 1973, *The development of tropical lands: policy issues in Latin America*, John Hopkins University Press, Baltimore.

Nelson, R., Horning, N., Stone, T. A., 1987, Determining the rate of forest conversion in Mato Grosso, Brazil, using Landsat MSS and AVHRR data, *International Journal of Remote Sensing*, **8**: 1767–84.

Neto, R. B., 1989a, Disputes about destruction, *Nature*, **338**: 531.

——, 1989b, Destruction area disputed, *Nature*, **339**: 86.

——, 1989c, Outside influences resented, *Nature*, **338**: 286.

Nicholaides III, J. J., Couto, W., Wade, M. K., 1983, *Agronomic-economic research on soils of the tropics. 1980–1981 technical report*, Soil Science Department, North Carolina State University, Raleigh.

——, Bandy, D. E., Sanchez, P. A., Villachica, J. H., Coutu, A. J., Valverde, C. S., 1984, Continuous cropping potential in the upper Amazon basin. In *Frontier expansion in Amazonia* (eds M. Schmink, C. H. Wood), pp. 337–65, University of Florida Press, Gainesville.

Nieuwenhuijs, W. H., 1960, *Development of grazing and fodder resources in the Amazon valley*, Food and Agriculture Organization, Rome.

Nieuwolt, S., 1977, *Tropical climatology*, John Wiley & Sons, London.

Nisbet, E. G., 1988, The business of planet management, *Nature*, **333**: 617.

Nogueira-Neto, P., 1989, We're learning the hard way, *Newsweek*, 30 January.

Nordin, C. F., Meade, R. H., 1982, Deforestation and increased flooding of the upper Amazon, *Science*, **215**: 426–7.

Norgaard, R. B., 1981, Sociosystem and ecosystem coevolution in the Amazon, *Journal of Environmental Economics and Management*, **8**: 238–54.

Noy-Meir, I., 1975, Stability of grazing systems: an application of predator-prey graphs, *Journal of Ecology*, **63**: 459–81.

Nugent, S., 1981, Amazonia: ecosystem and social system, *Man*, N.S. **16**: 62–74.

OCEI, 1987, *Anuario estadistico de Venezuela 1986*, Oficina Central de Estadistica y Informatica, Caracas.

Odum, E. P., 1969, The strategy of ecosystem development, *Science*, **164**: 262–70.

——, 1975, *Ecology*, 2nd edn, Holt Rinehart and Winston, London.

——, Franz, E. H., 1980, Whither the life-support system? In *Growth without ecodisasters?* (ed. N. Polunin), pp. 263–74, Macmillan, London.

——, Odum, H. T., 1972, Natural areas as necessary components of man's total environment, *Transactions of 37th North American Wildlife and Natural Resources Conference*, Mexico City, March 1972, pp. 178–89.

Odum, H. T., 1971, *Environment, power and society*, Wiley-Interscience, New York.

OEA, 1974, *Marajó. Um estudo para o seu desenvolvimento*, Organização dos Estados Americanos, Washington.

——, 1987a, *Minimum conflict: guidelines for planning the use of American humid tropic environments*, Organization of American States, Washington.

——, 1987b, *Programa de desarrollo integral de la Amazonia boliviana: macrodiagnóstico regional y estrategia de desarrollo*, Organización de los Estados Americanos, Washington.

Ojasti, J., 1980, Ecology of capybara raising on inundated savannas of Venezuela. In *Tropical ecology and development* (ed. J. I. Furtado), pp. 287–94, International Society of Tropical Ecology, Kuala Lumpur.

——, Medina, G., 1972, The management of capybara in Venezuela, *Transactions of 37th North American Wildlife and Natural Resources Conference*, Mexico City, March 1972, pp. 268–77.

Olawoye, O. O., 1975, The agri-silvicultural system in Nigeria, *Commonwealth Forestry Review*, **54**: 229–36.

Oltman, R. E., Sternberg, H. O'R., Ames, F. C., Davis Jr, L. C., 1964, *Amazon river investigations. Reconnaissance measurements of July 1963*, Circular 486, US Geological Survey, Washington.

ORSTOM, 1979, *Atlas des Départements d'outre-mer*, Office de la Recherche Scientifique et Technique Outre-Mer, Bondy.

Ortiz, S., 1980, The transformation of Guaviare in Colombia: immigrating peasants and their struggles. In *Land, people and planning in contemporary Amazonia* (ed. F. Barbira-Scazzocchio), pp. 194–205, Centre of Latin American Studies, Cambridge.

——, 1984, Colonization in the Colombian Amazon. In *Frontier expansion in Amazonia* (eds M. Schmink, C. H. Wood), pp. 204–30, University of Florida Press, Gainesville.

Ortolani, A. A., 1980, The importance of agrometeorology to rubber production in Brazil, *Brazilian Agriculture and Commodities*, **1**: 34–6.

O'Shaughnessy, H., 1985, Cocaine: from the Blue Mountains to Soho, *The Observer*, London, 10 November.

Overing, J., Kaplan, M., 1988, Los Wóthuha (Piaroa). In *Los aborigenes de Venezuela. Vol. 3. Etnología contemporánea* (ed. J. Lizot), pp. 307–411, Fundación la Salle/Monte Avila Editores, Caracas.

Pacini, D., Franquemont, C., 1986, *Coca and cocaine. Effects on people and policy in Latin America*, Cultural Survival/Latin American Studies Program, Cornell University, Ithaca.

Padoch, C., Chota Inuma, J., De Jong, W., Unrah, J., 1985, Amazonian agroforestry: a market-orientated system in Peru, *Agroforestry Systems*, **3**: 47–58.

Paiva, M. P., 1977a, *The environmental impact of man-made lakes in the Amazonian region of Brazil*, Eletrobrás, Rio de Janeiro.

——, 1977b, *Algumas considerações sobre a represa de Brokopondo*, Eletrobrás, Rio de Janeiro.

Palca, J., 1987, High finance approach to protecting tropical forests, *Nature*, **328**: 373.

Palmer, J. R., 1977, Forestry in Brazil — Amazonia, *Commonwealth Forestry Review*, **56**: 115–30.

Panday, R. M. N., 1959, *Agriculture in Surinam 1650–1950*, H. J. Paris, Amsterdam.

Pandolfo, C., 1974, *Estudos basicos para o estabelecimento de uma politica de desenvolvimento dos recursos florestais e de uso racional das terras da Amazônia*, 2nd edn, Superintendência do Desenvolvimento da Amazônia, Belém.

——, 1979, *A Amazônia brasileira e suas potencialidades*, Superintendência do Desenvolvimento da Amazônia, Belém.

Panero, R., 1967, *A South American 'great lakes' system*, Hudson Institute, Croton-on-Hudson.

Papadakis, J., 1969, *Soils of the world*, Elsevier, Amsterdam.

Parsons, J. J., 1980, Europeanization of the savanna lands of northern South

America. In *Human ecology in savanna environments* (ed. D. R. Harris), pp. 267–89, Academic Press, London.

——, Denevan, W. M., 1967, Pre-Columbian ridged fields, *Scientific American*, **217** (1): 93–100.

Payne, W. J. A., 1976, Possibilities for the integration of tree crop and livestock production in the wet tropics, *Journal of the Science of Food and Agriculture*, **27**: 888.

Pearman, G. I., Fraser, P. J., 1988, Sources of increased methane, *Nature*, **332**: 489–90.

Peck, R. B., 1982, Forest research activities and the importance of multi-strata production systems in the Amazon basin (humid neo-tropics). In *Amazonia. Agriculture and land use research* (ed. S. B. Hecht), pp. 373–86, Centro Internacional de Agricultura Tropical, Cali.

Pédelaborde, P., 1963, *The monsoon*, Methuen, London.

Penteado, A. R., 1967, *Problemas de colonização e de uso da terra na região bragantina do Estado do Pará*, vol. 2., Universidade Federal do Pará, Belém.

Peters, C. M., Gentry, A. H., Mendelsohn, R. O., 1989, Valuation of an Amazonian rainforest, *Nature*, **339**: 655–6.

Peters II, R. L., 1988, The effect of global climatic change on natural communities. In *Biodiversity* (ed. E. O. Wilson), pp. 450–61, National Academy Press, Washington.

——, Darling, D. J. S., 1985, The greenhouse effect and nature reserves: global warming would diminish biological diversity by causing extinctions among reserve species, *BioScience*, **35**: 707–17.

Petrick, C., 1978, The complementary function of floodlands for agricultural utilization. The várzea of the Brazilian Amazon region, *Applied Sciences and Development*, **12**: 26–46.

Pianka, E. R., 1970, On r- and K-selection, *American Naturalist*, **104**: 592–7.

Pickersgill, B., Heiser Jr, C. B., 1978, Origins and distribution of plants domesticated in the New World tropics. In *Advances in Andean archaeology* (ed. D. L. Browman), pp. 135–65, Mouton, The Hague.

Pimm, S. L., 1984, The complexity and stability of ecosystems, *Nature*, **307**: 321–6.

Pinedo del Aguila, V. M., 1967, *Evaluación economica de los recursos forestales de la Amazonia peruana*, Universidad Nacional Major de San Marcos, Lima.

Pinto, J. M., 1966, *Aspectos econômicos da juta na Amazônia*, Instituto Nacional de Pesquisas da Amazônia, Manaus.

Pires, J. M., 1966, The estuaries of the Amazon and Oiapoque rivers and their floras. In *Scientific problems of the humid tropical zone deltas and their implications*, pp. 211–18, United Nations Educational, Scientific and Cultural Organization, Paris.

——, 1973, Tipos de vegetação da Amazônia. In *O Museu Goeldi no año do sesquicentenário*, *Publicação Avulsa*, *Museu Paraense Emílio Goeldi*, **20**: 179–202.

——, 1978, The forest ecosystems of the Brazilian Amazon: description, functioning and research needs. In *Tropical forest ecosystems*, Natural Resources Research 14, pp. 607–27, United Nations Educational, Scientific and Cultural Organization, Paris.

——, Prance, G. T., 1977, The Amazon forest: a natural heritage to be preserved. In *Extinction is forever*, (eds G. T. Prance, T. S. Elias), pp. 158–94, New York Botanical Garden, Bronx.

——, ——, 1985, The vegetation types of the Brazilian Amazon. In *Amazonia* (eds G. T. Prance, T. E. Lovejoy), pp. 109–45, Pergamon Press, Oxford.

Pitt, J., 1961, *Application of silvicultural methods to some of the forests of the Amazon*, Food and Agriculture Organization, Rome.

——, 1969, *Relatório ao govêrno do Brasil sôbre aplicação de métodos silviculturais a algumas florestas da Amazônia*, Superintendência do Desenvolvimento da Amazônia, Belém.

Polunin, N. (ed.), 1980, *Growth without ecodisasters?*, Macmillan, London.

Portais, M., 1983, Los actores del manejo del espacio en la región amazonica ecuatoriana. In *La región amazonica ecuatoriana*, pp. 5–11, Centro Ecuatoriano de Investigación Geográfica, Quito.

Portig, W. H., 1968, Latin America: dangers to rainfall, *Science*, **159**: 376.

Posey, D. A., 1983, Indigenous knowledge and development: an ideological bridge to the future, *Ciência e Cultura*, **35**: 877–94.

Potter, L., 1979, *Coastal and interior settlements in Guyana: development, problems and prospects*. Paper presented at 5th Commonwealth Conference on Development and Human Ecology, Georgetown, April 1979.

Potter, G. L., Ellsaesser, H. W., MacCracken, M. C., Luther, F. M., 1975, Possible climatic impact of tropical deforestation, *Nature*, **258**: 697–8.

Powell, A. H., Powell, G. V. N., 1987, Population dynamics of male euglossine bees in Amazonian forest fragments, *Biotropica*, **19**: 176–9.

Prance, G. T., 1973, Phytogeographic support for the theory of Pleistocene forest refuges in the Amazon basin, based on evidence from distribution patterns in Caryocaraceae, Chrysobalanaceae, Dichapetalaceae and Lecythidaceae, *Acta Amazonica*, **3**: 5–28.

——, 1977, The phytogeographic subdivisions of Amazonia and their influence on the selection of biological reserves. In *Extinction is forever* (eds G. T. Prance, T. S. Elias), pp. 195–213, New York Botanical Garden, Bronx.

——, 1978, The origin and evolution of the Amazon flora, *Interciencia*, **3**: 207–22.

——, 1979a, Distribution patterns of lowland neotropical species with relation to history, dispersal and ecology, with special reference to Chrysobalanaceae, Caryocaraceae and Lecythidaceae. In *Tropical botany* (eds K. Larsen, L. B. Holm-Nielsen), pp. 59–87, Academic Press, London.

——, 1979b, Notes on the vegetation of Amazonia. 3. The terminology of Amazonian forest types subject to inundation, *Brittonia*, **31**: 26–38.

——, 1982, Forest refuges: evidence from woody angiosperms. In *Biological diversification in the tropics* (ed. G. T. Prance), pp. 137–58, Columbia University Press, New York.

——, 1985, The increased importance of ethnobotany and underexploited plants in a changing Amazon. In *Change in the Amazon basin. Vol. 1. Man's impact on forests and rivers* (ed. J. Hemming), pp. 129–36, Manchester University Press, Manchester.

——, Nelson, B. W., da Silva, M. F., Daly, D. C., 1984, Projeto Flora Amazônica: eight years of binational botanical expeditions, *Acta Amazonica*, **14** (suplemento): 5–29.

——, Rodrigues, W. A., da Silva, M. F., 1976, Inventário florestal de um hectare de mata de terra firme km 30 da Estrada Manaus-Itacoatiara, *Acta Amazonica*, **6**: 9–35.

——, Schubart, H. O. R., 1978, Notes on the vegetation of Amazonia. 1. A preliminary note on the origin of the open white sand campinas of the lower Rio Negro, *Brittonia*, **30**: 60–3.

Preston, T. R., 1975, Intensive beef fattening systems for the tropics, *Proceedings of Seminar on Potential to Increase Beef Production in Tropical America*, Cali, February 1974, pp. 149–82.

PRORADAM, 1979, *La Amazonia colombiana y sus recursos*, 5 vols, Proyecto Radargrametrico del Amazonas, Bogotá.

Purseglove, J. W., 1979, *Tropical crops. Dicotyledons*, Longman, London.

Raintree, J. B., 1986, Agroforestry pathways. Land tenure, shifting cultivation and sustainable agriculture, *Unasylva*, **38** (4): 2–15.

Ramírez, P., 1958, *Estudio preliminar de suelos y otros aspectos de la colonia penal de Araracuara*, Instituto Geográfico 'Agustín Codazzi', Bogotá.

Ramos Perez, D., 1946, *El tratado de límites de 1750 y la expedición de Iturriaga al Orinoco*, Instituto Juan Sebastian Elcano de Geografía, Madrid.

Rankin, J. M., 1985, Forestry in the Brazilian Amazon. In *Amazonia* (eds G. T. Prance, T. E. Lovejoy), pp. 369–92, Pergamon Press, Oxford.

Ratter, J. A., Richards, P. W., Argent, G., Gifford, D. R., 1973, Observations on the vegetation of the northeastern Mato Grosso. 1. The woody vegetation types of the Xavantina-Cachimbo expedition area, *Philosophical Transactions of the Royal Society*, **266 B**: 449–92.

Raven, P. H., 1988, Our diminishing tropical forests. In *Biodiversity* (ed. E. O. Wilson), pp. 119–22, National Academy Press, Washington.

Rayman, P. R., 1979, Experiences in tropical pasture seed production in Brazil. In *Pasture production in acid soils of the tropics* (eds P. A. Sanchez, L. E. Tergas), pp. 377–84, Centro Internacional de Agricultura Tropical, Cali.

Reátegui, R. R., 1979, Development of integrated agricultural, livestock and forestry production systems in tropical Peru. In *Agro-forestry systems in Latin America* (ed. G. de las Salas), pp. 91–100, Centro Agronomico de Investigacion y Enseñanza, Turrialba.

Reichel-Dolmatoff, G., 1976, Cosmology as ecological analysis: a view from the rain forest, *Man*, N.S. **11**: 307–18.

Reinke, R., 1962, *Das Klima amazoniens*, Dissertation, University of Tübingen, Tübingen.

Reis, M. S., 1982, The problem of combining electricity and forest development, *Unasylva*, **34** (137): 28–9.

Reis Altschul, S. von, 1977, Exploring the herbarium, *Scientific American*, **236** (5): 96–104.

Reubens, E. P., Reubens, B. G., 1962, *Labour displacement in a labour-surplus industry: the sugar industry of British Guiana*, University of the West Indies, Jamaica.

Rich, V., 1984, Amazon to yield more secrets?, *Nature*, **311**: 197.

Richards, P. W., 1952, *The tropical rain forest*, Cambridge University Press, Cambridge.

——, 1973, the tropical rain forest, *Scientific American*, **229** (6): 58–67.

——, 1977, Tropical forests and woodlands: an overview, *Agro-Ecosystems*, **3**: 225–38.

Richardson, B. C., 1972, Guyana's 'green revolution': social and ecological problems in an agricultural development programme, *Caribbean Quarterly*, **18**: 14–23.

Richey, J. E., Brock, J. T., Naiman, R. J., Wissmar, R. C., Stallard, R. F., 1980, Organic carbon: oxidation and transport in the Amazon river, *Science*, **207**: 1348–51.

Rivière, P., 1972, *The forgotten frontier. Ranchers of north Brazil*, Holt, Rinehart and Winston, New York.

Roberts, C. R., 1979, Some common causes of failure of tropical legume/grass pastures on commercial farms and suggested remedies. In *Pasture production in acid soils of the tropics* (eds P. A. Sanchez, L. E. Tergas), pp. 399–416, Centro Internacional de Agricultura Tropical, Cali.

Roberts, T. R., 1973, Ecology of fishes in the Amazon and Congo basins. In *Tropical forest ecosystems in Africa and South America: a comparative review* (eds B. J. Meggers, E. S. Ayensu, W. D. Duckworth), pp. 239–54, Smithsonian Institution, Washington.

Robinson, J. G., Redford, K. H., 1986, Body size, diet, and population density of neotropical forest mammals, *American Naturalist*, **128**: 665–80.

Rocha, J., 1982, Brazil buys dream of American billionaire, *The Observer*, London, 24 January.

Rodrigues, W. A., 1961, Aspectos fitossociológicos das catingas do Rio Negro, *Boletim do Museu Paraense Emílio Goeldi; Botânica*, **15**: 1–41.

———, 1967, Inventario florestal piloto ao longo da estrada Manaus-Itacoatiara, Estado do Amazonas: dados preliminares, *Atas do Simpósio sôbre a Biota Amazônica*, Belém, 1966, **7**: 257–67.

Roosevelt, A. C., 1980, *Parmana. Prehistoric maize and manioc subsistence along the Amazon and Orinoco*, Academic Press, New York.

Rosenbaum, H. J., Tyler, W. G., 1971, Policy-making for the Brazilian Amazon, *Journal of Inter-American Studies & World Affairs*, **13**: 416–33.

Ross, E. B., 1978a, The evolution of Amazon peasantry, *Journal of Latin American Studies*, **10**: 193–218.

———, 1978b, Food taboos, diet and hunting strategy: the adaptation to animals in Amazon cultural ecology, *Current Anthropology*, **19**: 1–36.

Rubinstein, E. M. de, 1985, The impact of high yielding rice varieties in Latin America. In *Rice: progress assessment and orientation in the 1980s. Proceedings of 16th Session of the International Rice Commission*, Los Baños, June 1985, pp. 97–109, Food and Agriculture Organization, Rome.

Ruddle, K., Chesterfield, R., 1976, Change perceived as man-made hazard in a rural development environment, *Development and Change*, **7**: 311–30.

Rudel, T. K., 1983, Roads, speculators, and colonization in the Ecuadorian Amazon, *Human Ecology*, **11**: 385–403.

Russell, J. A., 1942, Fordlandia and Belterra, rubber plantations of the Tapajos river, Brazil, *Economic Geography*, **18**: 125–45.

Sagan, C., Toon, O. B., Pollack, J. B., 1979, Anthropogenic albedo changes and the earth's climate, *Science*, **206**: 1363–8.

Sahlins, M., 1977, *The use and abuse of biology. An anthropological critique of sociobiology*, Tavistock Publications, London.

Salati, E., 1985, The climatology and hydrology of Amazonia. In *Amazonia* (eds G. T. Prance, T. E. Lovejoy), pp. 18–48, Pergamon Press, Oxford.

———, Marques, J., Molion, L. C. B., 1978, Origem e distribuição das chuvas na Amazônia, *Interciencia*, **3**: 200–5.

———, Dall'Olio, A., Matsui, E., Gat, J. R., 1979, Recycling of water in the Amazon basin: an isotopic study, *Water Resources Research*, **15**: 1250–8.

———, Vose, P. B., Lovejoy, T. E., 1986, Amazon rainfall, potential effects of deforestation, and plans for future research. In *Tropical rain forests and the world atmosphere* (ed. G. T. Prance), pp. 61–74, Westview Press, Boulder.

Salo, J., Kalliola, R., Häkkinen, I., Mäkinen, Y., Niemela, P., Puhakka, M., Coley, P. D., 1986, River dynamics and the diversity of Amazon lowland forest, *Nature*, **322**: 254–8.

Sanchez, P. A., 1976, *Properties and management of soils in the tropics*, John Wiley & Sons, New York.

————, 1979a, Advances in the management of Oxisols and Ultisols in tropical South America, *Proceedings of International Seminar on Soil Environment and Fertility Management in Intensive Agriculture*, Tokyo, 1977, pp. 535–66.

————, 1979b, Tropical pasture research in acid, infertile soils of Latin America: present status and needs for the future. In *Pasture production in acid soils of the tropics* (eds P. A. Sanchez, L. E. Tergas), pp. 471–6, Centro Internacional de Agricultura Tropical, Cali.

————, Bandy, D. E., Villachica, J. H., Nicholaides, J. J., 1982, Amazon basin soils: management for continuous crop production, *Science*, **216**: 821–7. .

————, Benites, J. R., 1987, Low-input cropping for acid soils of the humid tropics, *Science*, **238**: 1521–7.

————, Isbell, R. F., 1979, A comparison of the soils of tropical Latin America and tropical Australia. In *Pasture production in acid soils of the tropics* (eds P. A. Sanchez, L. E. Tergas), pp. 25–53, Centro Internacional de Agricultura Tropical, Cali.

Sanford, P. A., Wangari, E., 1985, Tropical grasslands: dynamics and utilization, *Nature and Resources*, **21** (3): 12–27.

Santhirasegaram, K., 1975a, Management of legume-grass pastures in a tropical rainforest ecosystem of Peru. In *Soil management in tropical America* (eds E. Bornemisza, A. Alvarado), pp. 434–52, Soil Science Department, North Carolina State University, Raleigh.

————, 1975b, Legume-based improved tropical pastures, *Proceedings of Seminar on Potential to Increase Beef Production in Tropical America*, Cali, February 1974, pp. 49–61.

Sarnthein, M., 1978, Sand deserts during glacial maximum and climatic optimum, *Nature*, **272**: 43–6.

Schmidt, R., 1987, Tropical rain forest management, *Unasylva*, **39** (2): 2–17.

Schmithüsen, F., 1978, *Contratos de utilização florestal com referência especial à Amazônia brasileira*, Ministério da Agricultura, Brasilia.

Schubart, H. O. R., Salati, E., 1982, Natural resources for land use in the Amazon region: the natural systems. In *Amazonia. Agriculture and land use research* (ed. S. B. Hecht), pp. 211–39, Centro Internacional de Agricultura Tropical, Cali.

Schultze-Kraft, R., Giacometti, D. C., 1979, Genetic resources of forest legumes for the acid, infertile savannas of tropical America. In *Pasture production in acid soils of the tropics* (eds P. A. Sanchez, L. E. Tergas), pp. 55–64, Centro Internacional de Agricultura Tropical, Cali.

Schulz, J. P., 1960, *The vegetation of Surinam. Vol. 2. Ecological studies on rain forest in northern Surinam*, Van Eedenfonds, Amsterdam.

Schuurman, F., 1980, Colonization policy and peasant economy in the Amazon basin. In *Land, people and planning in contemporary Amazonia* (ed. F. Barbira-Scazzocchio), pp. 106–13, Centre of Latin American Studies, Cambridge.

Schwarz, W., Rocha, J., 1989, Brazilian police and troops to protect Amazon forest, *The Guardian*, London, 15 February.

Schwarzkopf, L., Rylands, A. B., 1989, Primate species richness in relation to habitat structure in Amazonian rainforest fragments, *Biological Conservation*, **48**: 1–12.

Seiler, W., Conrad, R., 1987, Contribution of tropical ecosystems to the global budgets of trace gases, especially CH_4, H_2, CO, and N_2O. In *The geophysiology of Amazonia: vegetation and climate interactions* (ed. R. E. Dickinson), pp. 133–60, John Wiley & Sons, New York.

Serrão, E. A. S., Simão Neto, M., 1975, The adaptation of tropical forages in the

Amazon region. In *Tropical forages in livestock production systems* (eds E. C. Doll, G. O. Mott), pp. 31–52, American Society of Agronomy, Madison.

———, Toledo, J. M., 1988, Sustaining pasture-based production systems for the humid tropics. Paper presented at MAB Conference on Conversion of Tropical Forests to Pasture in Latin America, Oaxaca, October 1988.

———, Falesi, I. C., Veiga, J. B. da, Neto, J. F. T., 1978, *Produtividade de pastagens cultivadas em solos de baixa fertilidade das áreas de floresta do trópico úmido brasileiro*, Empresa Brasileira de Pesquisa Agropecuária, Belém.

Short, K. C., Steenken, W. F., 1962, A reconnaissance of the Guayana Shield from Guasipati to the Río Aro, Venezuela, *Boletín Informativo, Asociación Venezolana de Geología, Minería y Petroleo*, 5: 189–221.

Shoumatoff, A., 1989, Rain forest martyr, *The Times*, London, 29 April.

Sioli, H., 1966a, General features of the delta of the Amazon. In *Scientific problems of the humid tropical zone deltas and their implications*, pp. 381–90, United Nations Educational, Scientific and Cultural Organization, Paris.

———, 1966b, Soils in the estuary of the Amazon. In *Scientific problems of the humid tropical zone deltas and their implications*, pp. 89–96, United Nations Educational, Scientific and Cultural Organization, Paris.

———, 1967a, Studies in Amazonian waters, *Atas do Simpósio Sôbre a Biota Amazônica*, Belém, 1966, 3: 9–50.

———, 1967b, The Cururú region in Brazilian Amazonia, a transition zone between hylaea and cerrado, *Journal of the Indian Botanical Society*, 46: 452–62.

———, 1968a, Hydrochemistry and geology in the Brazilian Amazon region, *Amazoniana*, 1: 267–77.

———, 1968b, Zur Ökologie des Amazonas-Gebietes. In *Biogeography and ecology in South America* (eds E. J. Fittkau, J. Illies, H. Klinge, G. H. Schwabe, H. Sioli), vol. 1, pp. 137–70, Dr W. Junk, The Hague.

———, 1973, Recent human activities in the Brazilian Amazon region and their ecological effects. In *Tropical forest ecosystems in Africa and South America: a comparative review* (eds B. J. Meggers, E. S. Ayensu, W. D. Duckworth), pp. 321–34, Smithsonian Institution, Washington.

———, 1975a, Amazon tributaries and drainage basins. In *Coupling of land and water systems* (ed. A. D. Hasler), pp. 199–213, Springer-Verlag, Berlin.

———, 1975b, Tropical rivers as expressions of their terrestrial environments. In *Tropical ecological systems. Trends in terrestrial and aquatic research* (eds F. B. Golley, E. Medina), pp. 275–88, Springer-Verlag, New York.

———, 1980, Foreseeable consequences of actual development schemes and alternative ideas. In *Land, people and planning in contemporary Amazonia* (ed. F. Barbira-Scazzocchio), pp. 257–68, Centre of Latin American Studies, Cambridge.

———, 1984, The Amazon and its main affluents: hydrography, morphology of the river courses, and river types. In *The Amazon. Limnology and landscape ecology* (ed. H. Sioli), pp. 127–65, Dr W. Junk, Dordrecht.

———, 1985, The effects of deforestation in Amazonia, *Geographical Journal*, 151: 197–203.

Siskind, J., 1973, *To hunt in the morning*, Oxford University Press, New York.

Skillings, R. F., 1984, Economic development of the Brazilian Amazon: opportunities and constraints, *Geographical Journal*, 150: 48–54.

Smith, A., 1971, *Mato Grosso*, Michael Joseph, London.

Smith, N. J. H., 1974a, Destructive exploitation of the South American river turtle, *Association of Pacific Coast Geographers*, 36: 85–102.

————, 1974b, Agouti and babassu, *Oryx*, **12**: 581–2.

————, 1976, Spotted cats and the Amazon skin trade, *Oryx*, **13**: 362–71.

————, 1978, Agricultural productivity along Brazil's Transamazon highway, *Agro-Ecosystems*, **4**: 415–32.

————, 1979, Aquatic turtles of Amazonia: an endangered resource, *Biological Conservation*, **16**: 165–76.

————, 1980, Anthrosols and human carrying capacity in Amazonia, *Annals of the Association of American Geographers*, **70**: 553–66.

————, 1981a, *Man, fishes, and the Amazon*, Columbia University Press, New York.

————, 1981b, Caimans, capybaras, otters, manatees, and man in Amazonia, *Biological Conservation*, **19**: 177–87.

————, 1982, *Rainforest corridors. The Transamazon colonization scheme*, University of California Press, Berkeley.

————, 1983, Enchanted forest, *Natural History*, **92** (8): 14–20.

Smole, W. J., 1976, *The Yanoama Indians: a cultural geography*, University of Texas Press, Austin.

Soares, L. de C., 1963, *Amazônia*, Conselho Nacional de Geografia, Rio de Janeiro.

Soares, W. V., Lobato, E., Gonzalez, E., Naderman Jr, G. C., 1975, Liming soils of the Brazilian cerrado. In *Soil management in tropical America* (eds E. Bornemisza, A. Alvarado), pp. 283–99, Soil Science Department, North Carolina State University, Raleigh.

Somberg, S. I., Lenhart, J. D., Pericchi D., S. J, 1973, Stand analysis of the Federal Territory of Amazonas of Venezuela, *Turrialba*, **23**: 20–9.

Sombroek, W. G., 1966, *Amazon soils. A reconnaissance of the soils of the Brazilian Amazon region*, Centre for Agricultural Publications and Documentation, Wageningen.

Sommer, A., 1976, Attempt at an assessment of the world's tropical moist forests, *Unasylva*, **28** (112/113): 5–24.

Southwood, T. R. E., 1976, Bionomic strategies and population parameters. In *Theoretical ecology. Principles and applications* (ed. R. M. May), pp. 26–48, Blackwell Scientific Publications, Oxford.

————, May, R. M., Hassell, M. P., Conway, G. R., 1974, Ecological strategies and population parameters, *American Naturalist*, **108**: 791–804.

Souza Filho, A. P. da S., Dutra, S., Serrão, E. A. S., 1980, Níveis de fósforo no rendimento do quicuio da Amazônia (*Brachiaria humidicola*) com leguminosas no cerrado do Amapá, *Pesquisa em Andamento, EMBRAPA/CPATU*, Belém, **16**: 1–2.

Spain, J. M., 1975, Forage potential of allic soils of the humid lowland tropics of Latin America. In *Tropical forages in livestock production systems* (eds E. C. Doll, G. O. Mott), pp. 1–8, American Society of Agronomy, Madison.

————, Navas, G. E., Lascano, C., Franco, L. H., Hayashi, H., 1986, A strategy for the gradual replacement of native savanna on an Oxisol in eastern Colombia. In *Ecology and management of the world's savannas* (eds J. C. Tothill, J. J. Mott), pp. 283–7, Australian Academy of Sciences, Canberra.

Spears, J. S., 1980, Can farming and forestry coexist in the tropics?, *Unasylva*, **32** (128): 2–12.

Sponsel, L. E., 1986, Amazon ecology and adaptation, *Annual Review of Anthropology*, **15**: 67–97.

Spruce, R., 1908, *Notes of a botanist on the Amazon and Andes*, 2 vols, Macmillan, London.

Stark, N., 1971, Nutrient cycling. 1. Nutrient distribution in some Amazonian soils, *Tropical Ecology*, **12**: 24–50.

———, Jordan, C. F., 1978, Nutrient retention by the root mat of an Amazonian rain forest, *Ecology*, **59**: 434–7.

Sternberg, H. O'R., 1973, Development and conservation, *Erdkunde*, **27**: 253–65.

———, 1986, O 'pulmao verde', *Geografia do Brasil*, **11** (22): 1–13.

———, 1987, Reflexões sobre desenvolvimento e o futuro da Amazônia. In *Homem e natureza na Amazônia* (eds G. Kohlhepp, A. Schrader), pp. 463–77, Geographisches Institut der Universität Tübingen, Tübingen.

Steward, J. H., Faron, L. C., 1959, *Native peoples of South America*, McGraw-Hill, New York.

Steyermark, J. A., 1977, Future outlook for threatened and endangered species in Venezuela. In *Extinction is forever* (G. T. Prance, T. S. Elias), pp. 128–35, New York Botanical Garden, Bronx.

Strug, D. L., 1986, The foreign politics of cocaine: comments on a plan to eradicate the coca leaf in Peru. In *Coca and cocaine. Effects on people and policy in Latin America* (eds D. Pacini, C. Franquemont), pp. 73–88, Cultural Survival/Latin American Studies Program, Cornell University, Ithaca.

SUDAM, 1978, *Estudo de viabilidade técnico-econômica da exploração mecanizada em floresta de terra firme região de Curuá-Una*, Superintendência do Desenvolvimento da Amazônia, Belém.

Sutmöller, P., Abreu, A. V. de, Grift, J. van der, Sombroek, W. G., 1966, *Mineral imbalances in cattle in the Amazon valley*, Koninklijk Instituut voor de Tropen, Amsterdam.

Swift, M. J., Sanchez, P. A., 1984, Biological management of tropical soil fertility for sustained productivity, *Nature and Resources*, **20** (4): 2–10.

Swinbanks, D., Anderson, A., 1989, Japan and Brazil team up, *Nature*, **338**: 103.

Tardin, A. T., Lee, D. C. L., Santos, R. J. R., de Assis, O. R., dos Santos Barbosa, M. P., de Lourdes Moreira, M., Pereira, M. T., Silva, D., dos Santos Filho, C. P., 1980, *Subprojeto desmatamento, Convênio IBDF/CNPq-INPE 1979*, Instituto de Pesquisas Espaciais, São José dos Campos.

Terborgh, J. W., 1974, Preservation of natural diversity: the problem of extinction-prone species, *BioScience*, **24**: 715–22.

———, 1986, Keystone plant resources in the tropical forest. In *Conservation biology: the science of scarcity and diversity* (ed. M. E. Soulé), pp. 330–44, Sinauer Associates, Sunderland.

Terra, G. J. A., 1964, The significance of leaf vegetables, especially of cassava in tropical nutrition, *Tropical & Geographical Medicine*, **2**: 97–108.

Thomas-Hope, E., 1987a, Guyana economy. In *South America, Central America and the Caribbean*, pp. 403–5, Europa Publications, London.

———, 1987b, Surinam economy. In *South America, Central America and the Caribbean*, pp. 612–15, Europa Publications, London.

Thompson, K., 1980, Stress environments and economic development, *INTECOL Bulletin*, **7–8**: 53–69.

Thornes, J. B., 1969, Variability in specific conductance and pH in the Casiquiare-upper Orinoco, *Nature*, **221**: 461–2.

Timm, R. M., Albuja V., L., Clauson, B. L., 1986, Ecology, distribution, harvest, and conservation of the Amazonian manatee *Trichechus inunguis* in Ecuador, *Biotropica*, **18**: 150–6.

Tindall, H. D., 1977, Vegetable crops. In *Food crops of the lowland tropics* (eds C. L. A. Leakey, J. B. Wills), pp. 101–25, Oxford University Press, Oxford.

Toledo, J. M., Ara, M., 1977, Manejo de suelos para pasturas en la selva amazonica. Paper presented at Reunión Taller-FAO-SIDA sobre la Ordenacion y Conservación de Suelos en America Latina, Lima, 1977.

———, Morales, V. A., 1979, Establishment and management of improved pastures in the Peruvian Amazon. In *Pasture production in acid soils of the tropics* (eds P. A. Sanchez, L. E. Tergas), pp. 177–94, Centro Internacional de Agricultura Tropical, Cali.

———, Serrão, E. A. S., 1982, Pasture and animal production in Amazonia. In *Amazonia. Agriculture and land use research* (ed. S. B. Hecht), pp. 281–309, Centro Internacional de Agricultura Tropical, Cali.

Tollenaar, D., 1959, Rubber growing in Brazil in view of the difficulties caused by South American Leaf Blight (*Dothidella ulei*), *Netherlands Journal of Agricultural Science*, 7: 173–89.

Tosi, J. A., Voertman, R. F., 1964, Some environmental factors in the economic development of the tropics, *Economic Geography*, 40: 189–205.

Tricart, J. L. F., 1978, Ecologie et développement: l'exemple amazonien, *Annales de Géographie*, 87: 257–93.

———, 1985, Evidence of upper Pleistocene dry climates in northern South America. In *Environmental change and tropical geomorphology* (eds I. Douglas, T. Spencer), pp. 197–217, George Allen and Unwin, London.

Troll, C., 1963, Landscape ecology and land development with special reference to the tropics, *Journal of Tropical Geography*, 17: 1–11.

Turner, H. E., 1938, A short history of the Rupununi savannahs with special reference to the livestock industry, *Agricultural Journal of British Guiana*, 9: 230–6.

Turner, J. R. G., 1971, Studies of Mullerian mimicry and its evolution in Burnet moths and heliconid butterflies. In *Ecological genetics and evolution* (ed. R. Creed), pp. 224–60, Blackwell Scientific Publications, Oxford.

Uhl, C., 1982, Recovery following disturbances of different intensities in the Amazon rain forest of Venezuela, *Interciencia*, 7: 19–24.

———, 1987, Factors controlling succession following slash-and-burn agriculture in Amazonia, *Journal of Ecology*, 75: 377–407.

———, 1988, Restoration of degraded lands in the Amazon basin. In *Biodiversity* (ed. E. O. Wilson), pp. 326–32, National Academy Press, Washington.

———, Vieira, I. C. G., 1989, Ecological impacts of selected logging in the Brazilian Amazon: a case study from the Paragominas region of the State of Pará, *Biotropica*, 21: 98–106.

———, Clark, H., Clark, K., 1982, Successional patterns associated with slash-and-burn agriculture in the upper Rio Negro region of the Amazon basin, *Biotropica*, 14: 249–54.

UNESCO, 1978, *Tropical forest ecosystems*, Natural Resources Research 14, United Nations Educational, Scientific and Cultural Organization, Paris.

———, 1981, *Vegetation map of South America*, Natural Resources Research 17, United Nations Educational, Scientific and Cultural Organization, Paris.

Uquillas, J. E., 1983, Colonización dirigida en el nor-oriente ecuatoriano. In *La región amazónica ecuatoriana*, pp. 71–82, Centro Ecuatoriano de Investigación Geográfica, Quito.

———, 1985, Land grants for indigenous communities in the Ecuadorian Amazon. In *Change in the Amazon basin. Vol. 2. The frontier after a decade of colonisation* (ed. J. Hemming), pp. 200–6, Manchester University Press, Manchester.

USDA, 1975, *Soil taxonomy*, US Department of Agriculture, Washington.

Valverde, O. (ed.), 1979, *A organização do espaço na faixa da Transamazônica*.

Vol. 1. Introdução, sudoeste amazônico, Rondônia e regiões vizinhas, Fundação Instituto Brasileiro de Geografia e Estatística, Rio de Janeiro.

——, 1981, Ecologia e desenvolvimento da Amazônia, Revista Brasileira de Tecnologia, 12 (4): 3–16.

——, Dias, C. V., 1967, A rodovia Belém–Brasília. Estudo de geografia regional, Instituto Brasileiro de Geografia, Rio de Janeiro.

Valverde, S. C., Bandy, D. E., 1982, Production of annual food crops in the Amazon. In Amazonia. Agriculture and land use research (ed. S. B. Hecht), pp. 243–80, Centro Internacional de Agricultura Tropical, Cali.

Vanzolini, P. E., 1973, Paleoclimates, relief, and species multiplication in equatorial forests. In Tropical forest ecosystems in Africa and South America: a comparative review (eds B. J. Meggers, E. S. Ayensu, W. D. Duckworth), pp. 255–8, Smithsonian Institution, Washington.

——, Williams, E. E., 1970, South American anoles: the geographic differentiation and evolution of the Anolis chrysolepis species group (Sauria, Iguanidae), Arquivos de Zoologia, 19: 1–298.

Vega, L., 1979, Profit-making capacities of regular plantations as compared with the agrosilvicultural model: Surinam. In Agro-forestry systems in Latin America (ed. G. de las Salas), pp. 107–21, Centro Agronomico de Investigacion y Enseñanza, Turrialba.

Vicente-Chandler, J., 1968, Agricultural potential of Latin America's hot humid tropics, Journal of Soil and Water Conservation, 23: 51–4.

——, 1975, Intensive management of pastures and forages in Puerto Rico. In Soil management in tropical America (eds E. Bornemisza, A. Alvarado), pp. 409–33, Soil Science Department, North Carolina State University, Raleigh.

Vickers, W. T., 1979, Native Amazonian subsistence in diverse habitats: the Siona-Secoya of Ecuador, Studies in Third World Societies, 7: 6–36.

——, 1983, Tropical forest mimicry in swiddens: a reassessment of Geertz's model with Amazonian data, Human Ecology, 11: 35–45.

Vieira, L. S., Dos Santos, W. H. P., Falesi, I. C., Filho, J. P. S. O., 1967, Levantamento de reconhecimento dos solos da região bragantina, Estado do Pará, Pesquisa Agropecuaria Brasileira, 2: 1–63.

Vining, J. W., 1977, Presettlement planning in Guyana, Geographical Review, 67: 469–80.

Wade, M. K., 1978, Soil management practices for increased crop production for small farms of the Amazon jungle of Peru, Ph.D. thesis, North Carolina State University, Raleigh.

Wadsworth, F. H., 1987, Applicability of Asian and African silviculture systems to naturally regenerated forests of the neotropics. In Natural management of tropical moist forests (eds F. Mergen, J. R. Vincent), pp. 93–111, Yale University, New Haven.

Wagenaar, G. A. W., 1966, Report to the government of Guyana on the development of the settlement schemes at Ebini, Brandwagt-Sari, Kumaka-Kwebanna and Wauna-Jarakita, Food and Agriculture Organization, Rome.

Wagley, C., 1964, Amazon town. A study of man in the tropics, Alfred A. Knopf, New York.

——, 1977, Welcome of tears. The Tapirapé Indians of central Brazil, Oxford University Press, New York.

Walker, B. H., Noy-Meir, I., 1982, Aspects of the stability and resilience of savanna ecosystems. In Ecology of tropical savannas (eds B. J. Huntley, B. H. Walker), pp. 556–90, Springer-Verlag, Berlin.

Wallace, A. R., 1890, *A narrative of travels on the Amazon and Rio Negro*, 3rd edn, Ward Lock & Company, London.

Walsh, J. J., Rowe, G. T., Iverson, R. L., McRoy, C. P., 1981, Biological export of shelf carbon is a sink of the global CO_2 cycle, *Nature*, **291**: 196–201.

Walter, H., 1973, *Vegetation of the earth in relation to climate and the eco-physiological conditions*, translated from German by J. Wieser, English Universities Press, London/Springer-Verlag, New York.

Wambeke, A. van, 1978, Properties and potentials of soils in the Amazon basin, *Interciencia*, **3**: 233–42.

Watters, R. F., 1971, Shifting cultivation in Latin America, *FAO Forestry Development Paper*, **17**: 1–305.

Weber, N. A., 1947, Lower Orinoco river fungus-growing ants (Hymenoptera: Formicidae, Attini), *Boletín de Entomología Venezolana*, **6**: 143–61.

Wellman, F. L., 1972, *Tropical American plant disease*, Scarecrow Press, New Jersey.

Went, F. W., Stark, N., 1968, Mycorrhiza, *BioScience*, **18**: 1035–9.

Werner, D., Flowers, N. M., Ritter, M. L., Gross, D. R., 1979, Subsistence productivity and hunting effort in native South America, *Human Ecology*, **7**: 303–15.

Wesche, R. J., 1967, The settler wedge of the upper Putumayo river, Ph.D. dissertation, University of Florida, Gainesville.

Wetterberg, G. B., Jorge Padua, M. T., Soares de Castro, C., Vasconcellos, J. M. C., 1976, Uma análise de prioridades em conservação da natureza na Amazônia, *Série Técnica, PRODEPEF*, Brasília, **8**: 1–62.

——, Prance, G. T., Lovejoy, T. E., 1981, Conservation progress in Amazonia: a structural review, *Parks*, **2**: 5–10.

Whiffen, T., 1915, *The North-west Amazons, notes of some months spent among cannibal tribes*, Constable & Company, London.

Whitmore, T. C., 1975, *Tropical rain forests of the Far East*, Clarendon Press, Oxford.

——, 1982, On pattern and process in forests. In *The plant community as a working mechanism* (ed. E. I. Newman), pp. 45–59, British Ecological Society, Oxford.

Wickhan, H. A., 1908, *On the plantation, cultivation, and curing of Pará Indian rubber*, Kegan Paul, Trench, Trübner & Company, London.

Wiebecke, C., 1965, *Weltforstatlas*, Verlag Paul Parey, Hamburg.

Wijmstra, T. A., van der Hammen, T., 1966, Palynological data on the history of tropical savannas in northern South America, *Leidse Geologische Mededelingen*, **38**: 71–90.

Wilbert, J., 1972, *Survivors of Eldorado*, Praeger, New York.

Wilhelmy, H., 1952, Die eiszeitliche und nacheiszeitliche Verschiebung der Klima- und Vegetationszonen in Südamerika, *Verhandlungen des Deutschen Geographentages*, **28**: 121–8.

Williams, J. F., 1954, The development of the sugar cane industry in British Guiana. In *Bookers sugar* (ed. A. Woolley), pp. 121–6, Bookers Sugar Estates, London.

Williams, L., 1940, Botanical exploration in the middle and lower Caura, Venezuela, *Tropical Woods*, **62**: 1–20.

Williams, W. A., Loomis, R. S., Alvim, P. de T., 1972, Environments of evergreen rainforests of the lower Rio Negro, Brazil, *Tropical Ecology*, **13**: 65–78.

Wilson, E. O., 1988, The current state of biological diversity. In *Biodiversity* (ed. E. O. Wilson), pp. 3–18, National Academy Press, Washington.

Wolda, H., 1978, Fluctuations in abundance of tropical insects, *American Naturalist*, **112**: 1017–45.

Wood, H. A., 1972, Spontaneous agricultural colonisation in Ecuador, *Annals of the Association of American Geographers*, **62**: 599–617.

Wood, P. J., 1976, The development of tropical plantations and the need for seed and genetic conservation. In *Tropical trees. Variation, breeding and conservation* (eds J. Burley, B. T. Styles), pp. 11–18, Academic Press, London.

Wood, T. W. W., Mora, G., Krijnen, E. M., Romero, J. B., Gillis, M., Castrillo, H., 1977, Valoración preliminar de la estructura forestal y la condición del bosque humedo tropical cerca del campamento Río Grande, Reserva Forestal Imataca, Guayana. Paper presented at Seminario sobre Ecología del Tropico Humedo Americano, Mérida, November, 1977.

Woodwell, G. M., Houghton, R. A., Stone, T. A., 1986, Deforestation in the Brazilian Amazon measured by satellite imagery. In *Tropical rain forests and the world atmosphere* (ed. G. T. Prance), pp. 23–32, Westview Press, Boulder.

——, ——, ——, Nelson, R. F., Kovalick, W., 1987, Deforestation in the tropics: new measurements in the Amazon basin using Landsat and NOAA advanced very high resolution radiometer imagery, *Journal of Geophysical Research*, **92**: 2157–63.

World Bank, 1981, *Brazil. Integrated development of the northwest frontier*, The World Bank, Washington.

Yared, J. A. G., Carpanezzi, A. A., Carvalho Filho, A. P., 1980, Ensaio de espécies florestais no planalto do Tapajós, *Boletim de Pesquisa, EMBRAPA/CPATU*, Belém, **11**: 1–22.

Yde, J., 1957, The agricultural level of the Waiwai Indians, *Timehri*, **36**: 23–35.

——, 1965, *Material culture of the Waiwai*, National Museum, Copenhagen.

Zamora, C., 1975, Soils of the lowlands of Peru. In *Soil management in tropical America* (eds E. Bornemisza, A. Alvarado), pp. 46–60, Soil Science Department, North Carolina State University, Raleigh.

Zimmerman, B. L., Bierregaard, R. O., 1986, Relevance of the equilibrium theory of island biogeography and species-area relations to conservation with a case from Amazonia, *Journal of Biogeography*, **13**: 133–43.

Zonneveld, J. I. S., 1969, Preliminary remarks on summit levels and the evolution of the relief in Surinam (S. America), *Verhandelingen van het Koninklijk Nederlands Geologisch Mijnbouwkundig Genootschap*, **27**: 53–60.

Zucchi, A., 1973, Prehistoric human occupations of the western Venezuelan llanos, *American Antiquity*, **38**: 182–90.

Index

Achuará Indians 76
Acre 7, 9
  extractive reserves 211
  highway 216
Acrisols 31, 35–6
  fertility 35–6
  northern Mato Grosso 114
  Rio Branco-Rupununi savanna 137
Adaptation
  agrosystems 4, 162, 166
  biotic stressors 170
  compartment strategy 214
  cultural 4, 63
  forest species 60
  indigenous land exploitation 63, 77,
    82–3
  land exploitation systems 142, 169
  local conditions 211
  tribal culture 63, 82–5
  wetland cultivation 140
Agroforestry 150
Agrosilviculture 12, 150–2
  advantages 152
  compromise usage 191, 194
  definition 150
  indigenous 75, 85, 150
  potential on *terra firme* 195
  problems 150, 152
  pests and diseases 152
  sustainable exploitation 211
Agrosystems 4
  commercial 87–8
  development 61
  intensive 143–9, 192
  status in Amazonia 171
  sustainable 120, 204, 210–12, 215
  performance on *terra firme* 119–20
Agrovilas 111
Akawaio Indians 78
Albedo 23

Altamira 110
Aluminium toxicity 143
Amazon basin 16
  erosion rates 29
Amazon estuarine zone 27, 53, 140
  rice 166
  soils 33, 37
  water buffalo 166
Amazon Pact (*see* Treaty for
  Amazonian Co-operation)
Amazon river 16, 25
  discharge 28
  erosion rate 29
  fluctuation in level 29
  lower valley 125–9
  sediment load 28
  white water 28–9
Amazonia
  area 16–17
  climate 19–23
  climatic change 22, 175–7
  compartment model 14, 187–8
  compartment strategy 190–3, 195
  definition 2–3, 17
  diversification of exploitation 214
  forest clearance 172–4
  genetic erosion 178–9
  geology 23–4
  geomorphology 23–7
  integrated land management 186–96,
    209–14
  land cover 172–4
  land systems mapping 187
  management model 187–8
  national parks 182–4, 212–14
  population 174–5
  regional planning 193
  reserved land 212–14
  rubber exploitation 88–93
  soil resources 30–7

sustained yield agrosystems 211–12
Amazônia legal 8, 17, 172, 205
Amerindian population
  antiquity 62
  contemporary 63
  density in forest 68
  density in savanna 77
  density in wetland 78–9
  European contact 63
  protein supply 76–7
  regulation 84
Amerindian settlement
forest 68, 76–7, 83
  relocation 69, 76
  savanna 78
  wetland 79
Andoke Indians 72–3, 75, 123, 150
Arenosols 31, 47
  forest regeneration 59
  Guianas 163, 198
  northern Mato Grosso 114
  parent materials 36
AVHRR (Advanced Very High
    Resolution Radiometer) 209

Balbina project 178
Banana 67, 72, 79, 107, 112, 124,
  151
Bauxite 198
Belém
  commercial fishing 167
  early developments 5, 100
  population 99, 103, 205
  rain forest 45
  rainfall regime 21–2
  rubber trading 89
  temperature regime 19–20
Belém-Brasília highway 103, 115, 157,
  206
Belterra clay 26, 32
Belterra plantation 91, 98, 151
Berbice Formation 26, 130
  Arenosols 36
Biocides 170
  natural 180–1
Biomass
  forest animals 49, 64–5
  savanna animals 65
Biotic stressors 37–8, 142, 169–70
  terra firme 119, 146, 149
Birds
  species diversity 39

Black pepper 102–3, 144–5, 147
  fungal disease 112, 146, 148
Boa Vista
  rainfall 20–21
  population 135–6
Bolivia
  forest cover 172–3
  indigenous subsistence 68
  land cover 173
  national parks 200, 213
  population 175
  spontaneous colonisation 203
Bragantina 10, 30, 99, 169
  agriculture 100–4
  failure of planned colonisation 8,
    104, 120
  land holdings 100–1
  out-migration 103
  peasant colonisation 99–104,
    119
  population growth 101, 104
  railway 100
  rubber plantations 91–2, 102–3
Brazil
  agrosilviculture 151
  Amazonian population 175, 205
  cerrado agriculture 162
  colonisation in Bragantina
    99–104
  colonisation at Altamira 110–13
  forest clearance 172–4, 216
  forestry in Pará 93–9
  grass-legume pastures 157–8, 163
  hydro-electricity 178
  Indian reserves 212–13
  indigenous subsistence 69–70, 76
  land cover 173
  Marajó island 166
  mixed-forest silviculture 154–6
  national parks 200, 208, 213
  Nossa Natureza 216
  ranching in Mato Grosso 113–18
  ranching in Rio Branco-Rupununi
    savanna 135–40
  resource use in lower Amazon valley
    125–9
  standing timber volume 46
  zoning 14, 188–9
Brazil nut 6, 145, 149, 156, 179
Brazilian Shield 23
  geology 23–4
  planation surfaces 24–5

Caatinga forest 40, 47–8
  nutrient deficiency 48
  root mass 47
Caboclo 6, 86, 121
Cacao 6, 9, 179
  agrosilviculture 152
  Caquetá basin 109
  eastern Peru 204
  fungal infection 111–12, 120, 146
  genetic resources 181
  Transamazon highway 111–12
  wetlands 121
Caja Agraria 106
Calorie supply
  indigenous subsistence 74–6, 81
  manioc 66, 74
Caquetá basin 105, 123
  peasant colonisation 104–10
  Proyecto Caquetá 105–7
  riparian settlement 122–5
  rubber collecting 89, 123
Carajás
  forestry plantation 98
  Programa Grande Carajás 207
Carbon dioxide 1, 23, 176, 184, 190
Casa Arana 123
Casiquiare 5
Catholic missionaries 5
Cattle
  Amazonian savannas 121, 137–9
  disease problems 108, 138–9
  health and nutrition 159
  improved pastures 139, 159
  lower Amazon valley 55, 129
  Suiá Missú 115
Cattle ranching 13, 88
  Altamira zone 112–13
  Amazonian savannas 140, 163
  northern Mato Grosso 113–18
  overstocking 117
  pests and disease of forage species
    159
  Rio Branco-Rupununi savanna
    135–40
  sustainability 118, 140
Cattle rearing 9–10
  Amazonian savannas 121
  coastal Guyana 135
  experiments in Pará 158
  experiments in Peru 158
  intensive 156–7
  lower Amazon valley 129

  semi-intensive 156–9
  tree plantations 161
  upper Caquetá basin 107–9
Cerradão 40
Cerrado 10, 48, 51
  dry farming 162
  exploitation 162, 165
Cipoal 48
Climatic change
  computer simulation 175–6
  effect of deforestation 175–7
  effect on land use 215
  effect on national parks 215
  forest refugia 41–2
  Quaternary 22, 42, 51
Coca 67, 109, 125, 205
CODESUR (Comisión para el
    Desarrollo del Sur) 199, 210
Coffee
  coastal Guyana 132
  diseases 146
  eastern Peru 146, 204
  upper Caquetá basin 109
Colombia
  colonisation in upper Caquetá basin
    104–10, 203
  conservation of cultivars 181
  forest survey 39
  grass-legume pastures 157
  indigenous subsistence 72, 75, 77
  land cover 173
  national parks 200, 213
  penetration roads 203
  population 175
  resource use in middle Caquetá
    valley 122–5
  standing timber volume 46
Colonisation
  land 8–9, 37, 120, 125
  oriente 203, 205
  Paleo-Indian 62
  peasant 87, 99–113
  pioneer 103, 119, 184–5
  planned 87, 106–7, 197, 203, 217
  Rondônia 207
  southern Venezuela 203
  spontaneous 87, 105, 107, 197, 203,
    217
Compartments
  basis for diversification 214
  compromise 14, 187–8, 191–2, 194
  designation 194–6

landscape planning 187, 215–16
management model 190
model 187–8, 192
productive 14, 187–8, 192–4
protective 14, 187–8, 191–2, 194
regional exploitation 214–15, 217
spatial mix 190
strategy for Amazonia 190–3, 195
urban-industrial 192–3
Conservation 11–12
compartment strategy 195
forest 170, 183–4
hydro-electric projects 178, 193
integration with development 12–14, 182
national parks 182–3
oriente 205
planning 181–5
southern Venezuela 201–2
traditional cultivars 181
Cuiabá-Santarém highway 118, 126, 151
Curare 180
Curuá-Una
silvicultural experiments 96, 154–5
CVG (Corporación Venezolana de Guayana) 199, 210

DAINCO (Departmento Administrativo de Intendencias y Comisarías) 205, 210
Diseases
agrosilviculture 152
biotic stressors 37–8
black pepper 111–12, 146, 148
cacao 111–12, 120, 146
cattle 108, 129, 138–9
coffee 111–12, 146
forage species 159
introduced 63
monocultural cropping 146
rubber 91, 146
South American leaf blight 91–3, 119
sugar cane 134
terra firme 119, 146
Diversification
indigenous exploitation 82–3, 85, 214
modern exploitation 214
northern Mato Grosso 118
resource use 169

Diversity
birds 39
cultivated plants 65
fishes 39
forest refugia 41, 183
forest species 39, 41–2, 45
indigenous fishing equipment 70, 80
indigenous yard gardens 72
insects 39

Ecosystem dynamics 55–61
Ecuador
early maize cultivation 63
indigenous subsistence 65, 74, 76
land cover 173
national parks 200, 213
population 175
silvopastoralism 160–1
spontaneous colonisation 203
Endemism 42, 52
Erosion
accelerated 10
soil 21, 36, 91, 107–8, 111, 143
tree crops 145, 152
Etchplanation 25
Evapotranspiration 12, 23, 176–7
Extinction
forest species 60
megafaunal 60
plants and animals 178–9
Extractive activities 211
mining 87
rubber 86–7, 93, 119
terra firme 119
traditional 6, 86, 206
upper Caquetá basin 105–6
Extractive logging 93, 153, 211
Brazilian production 94
Guianas 198
Pará 93–5, 98
relation to silviculture 156
várzea 128
Extractive reserves 211

FAO (Food and Agriculture Organization)
forest inventories 96
silvicultural experiments 96
Soil map of the World 31
Fauna
aquatic 54–5, 178
fish 54–5

forest 49
  savanna 52
  soil 49
  wetland 54
Faunal resources
  forest 64–5
  savanna 77–8
  várzea 79
  wetland 65, 167–8
Ferralsols 31–6
  Altamira zone 110
  analytical data 35
  Bragantina zone 100
  fertility 33–4
  northern Mato Grosso 114
  Rio Branco-Repununi savanna 137
  upper Caquetá basin 106
Fertiliser
  Amazonian savannas 163
  black pepper 144
  costs 144
  experiments at Yurimaguas 144
  organic 145
  pasture 117, 157–8, 163
  perennial crops 145
  sugar cane 134
  use 9, 34, 143–5, 159
Fiscal incentives 115, 118, 206, 217
Fish
  Amazon estuarine zone 55
  effect of forest clearance 167
  hydro-electric developments 167
  pond culture 168
  species diversity 39
  supplies 54–5, 167–8
Fishing 211
  Caquetá valley 124–5
  commerical 128, 167
  indigenous 69–70, 80
  lower Amazon valley 128
  traditional 167
Fisheries
  management 168
  prospects 168
Fluvisols 32, 36, 130
Fordlandia 91, 98
Forest
  animal biomass 49
  animals 49
  area 3, 41, 172–3
  caatinga 40, 47–8
  canopy 42, 48

cipoal 40, 48
cleared area 41, 172–4
deciduous 40, 48–9
evergreen 40, 42–7
faunal diversity 49
leaf litter 45
lianas 45
litter fall 47
mangrove 53
marsh 52–3
phytogeographic zones 40, 183
phytomass 45, 47
pioneer species 58
Pleistocene refugia 41–2, 59, 179,
    183–4, 215
primary species 58, 179
rooting system 45
secondary 59
seed dispersal 58
semi-deciduous 40, 48–9
species diversity 45, 53
stability 60
standing timber volume 46–7
swamp 52–3
terra firme 42–9
Forest clearance
  area 172–4
  atmospheric carbon dioxide 176–7
  biological effects 178–82
  effect on climate 175–7
  effect on fish 167
  loss of plant resources 179–81
  satellite monitoring 172, 216
Forest regeneration 58–9, 179
  indigenous cultivation 57–8, 75
  primary species 58, 179
Forest reserves 11, 182, 184
  compromise usage 191
  Rondônia 208
  southern Venezuela 154, 202
  Tapajós National Forest 96, 154,
    156
  upper Caquetá basin 110
  watershed protection 194
Forestry
  agrosilviculture 151–2
  Brazilian production 93–4
  Carajás project 98
  Caruá-Una 96
  extractive logging 93–5, 98
  forest inventories 96
  Jari project 96–8, 161, 211

mixed-forest silviculture 153–6
plantation prospects 98
silvicultural experiments 96
silvopastoralism 160–1
Tapajós National Forest 96, 154,
  156
French Guiana 173, 175, 198

Game supply
  forest 64–5, 68–9
  savanna 65
Gathering
  indigenous 64, 68–9
Genetic engineering 170
Genetic resources 10, 42
  cacao 181
  conservation 153, 156, 181–2, 191
  loss 2, 178–80
  plant breeding 181
  rubber 181
Gleysols 32, 35–6, 52, 122, 126
Geology 23–4
Greenhouse effect 177
Growth poles 199, 206–8, 212
Guerrillas 13, 109, 205
Guiana Shield 23–5
Guianas 129, 163, 198–9
  early settlement 5
  timber plantations 146
Guyana
  coastal agriculture 129–35, 165
  coastal soils 130–1
  indigenous subsistence 65, 77–8
  land capability mapping 186
  land cover 173
  national park 200, 213
  plantation surfaces 24–5
  population 135, 175
  ranching in Rupununi savanna
    135–40
  rice cultivation 129, 132, 134–5
  rice production 132
  Rupununi savanna 39, 50–1
  sugar cane production 132
  sugar plantations 130, 132–4

Hunting 49
  Caquetá valley 124
  indigenous 64, 68–9, 78
Hydro-electricity
  Balbina 178
  Brokopondo 167, 178, 198

Caquetá valley 125
dam at Monte Alegre 166
environmental impact 178, 193
fish populations 167
Guri 178, 202
threat to Indian reserves 213
Tucuruí 90, 96, 167, 178, 207
watershed protection 194
World Bank funding 216
Xingú river 178, 213, 216
Hylaea 3, 39, 41

IDB (Inter-American Development
  Bank) 216
INCORA (Instituto Colombiano de la
  Reforma Agraria) 106–7
INCRA (Instituto Nacional de
  Colonização e Reforma Agraria)
  111–12, 206
Indian reserves 182, 184, 212
  compromise compartment 191, 194
  long-term prospects 212
  mining companies 213
  road building 213
  Rondônia 208
  Xingú Indian Park 212–13
Insects
  pests 74–5
  species diversity 39
intensive cropping 143–9
  pests and diseases 146
  productive compartment 188,
    192–4
  prospects 149
  risk 149
  soil problems 143–4
  tree crops 145
Inter-Tropical Convergence Zone 19
Iquitos 16
  flood levels 177–8
  river level 28
Island biogeography theory 182

Jari
  forestry plantation 96–8, 211
  project performance 98
  rice cultivation 127, 165
  silvopastoralism 161
  sustainability 97
  tree infections 146, 149
  wood yields 97
Jute 121, 127

Kayapó Indians 69, 213

Lakes 30
  fish resources 54–5, 80
Land degradation 87, 119
Land management 4, 13–14, 61, 169,
    171
  integrated 186–91, 197–8, 202,
    208–10
  model 190–1
  oriente 13, 205
  compartment model 14, 188
Land reclamation 130–2
Landsat
  forest clearance 172–4, 208
  land cover monitoring 172, 174
  resource monitoring 209
  Pucallpa 204
  river patterns 30
  Río Napo 27
  Santarém 126
  Suiá Missú ranch 116
Landscape ecology 4, 190
Laterite 32, 169
Leaf litter 45, 47, 49
Liana forest 48
Limoncocha 160–1
Llanos 19, 51, 136, 165
  agricultural development 163
  capibara rearing 167
  indigenous subsistence 77
  Venezuelan 163–4, 199
Logging (see extractive logging)

Macusi Indians 77–8
Madeira basin 16
Maize 9, 67, 72, 101–2, 107, 111, 124,
    151
  cultivation on várzea 79, 127
  microfossil evidence 63
  ridged fields 81
  Yurimaguas 144
Makiritare Indians 69, 72
Malva 102, 127
Manaus 5
  climate 19–21
  comercial fishing 128, 167
  forest survey 45
  population 205
  river level 28–9, 125
Manioc 65–6, 101–3, 107, 124, 151
  conservation of cultivars 181

cultivation on várzea 79
indigenous cultivation 72–4
ridged fields 81
Marajó island
  Jesuit estates 7
  pre-Columbian settlement 81
  water buffalo 166
Mato Grosso
  cattle ranching 113–18
  land colonisation 9
  dry forest 48
  forest cover 172
  grass-legume pastures 157
  Suiá Missú ranch 115–16, 118
  timber production 94
  unstable exploitation 120
Medicinal plants 72, 180
Methane 177
Minimum Critical Size of Ecosystems
    Project 183–4
Mixed cropping 85
  indigenous cultivation 72
  reduced pests and diseases
    152
Mojos region 53
  ridged fields 80
  soils 35
Mulching 145
Mycorrhizal fungi 56

Narcotraficantes 13, 109, 205
National parks 3, 11, 182, 200–1
  Amazonia 212–214
  Brazil 200, 208
  effect of climatic change 215
  designation 194
  distribution 182–4
  extent 12, 182–4, 191
  management 61
  oriente 205
  Rondônia 208
  savanna and wetland 195
  size 183
  southern Venezuela 201–2
  Surinam 198, 201
Negro basin 16
  caatinga forest 47–8
Negro river
  black water 30
  erosion rate 29
  gauge height at Manaus 29
  productivity 54

Nitosols 31, 36
  analytical data 35
  Brazilian Amazonia 36, 194
  Rondônia 145
  Transamazon highway 111, 145
Nitrogen fixation 170
  crop legumes 144–5
  forest 56
  pasture legumes 157
  silvopastoralism 160
Nitrous oxide 177
Nordestinos
  Bragantina zone 100
  Altamira zone 110–11
Nossa Natureza 216
Nutrient cycling
  atmospheric inputs 56
  closed 55
  detrital pathway 49
  direct 56
  mycorrhizal fungi 56
  nitrogen 56, 160
  organic residues 145
  savanna 56
  silvopastoralism 160
Nutrient supply
  cattle ranching 107, 117, 138
  Jari 97
  Rio Branco-Rupununi savanna 138
  wetland 57

Oil palm 9, 109, 180, 204
Organic matter
  value in soil 145
Oriente 13, 203–5
  colonisation 9, 197, 204
  population 203
  roads 87
Orinoco river
  reclamation of delta 166
  turbidity 28
Oxisols 32–3

Pará
  black pepper cultivation 144, 146
  Bragantina 99–100
  early Jesuit estates 7
  forestry 93–9
  grass-legume pastures 157–8
  Guamá valley 165
  land colonisation 9, 103, 206
  Nitosols 36

rubber collecting 89, 91
timber production 94
Tucuruí 178
Pasture legumes 109
  grass-legume associations 157–8, 161
  potential 157
  savanna 163
  silvopastoralism 161
Peasant colonisation 87
  Altamira zone 110–13
  Bragantina zone 99–104
  upper Caquetá basin 104–10
Pediplanation
  eastern Brazil 24–5
  Guiana Shield 24–5
Peru
  agrosilviculture 151
  fertilisers at Yurimaguas 144
  fruit trees 179
  grass-legume pastures 157
  indigenous subsistence 76, 79–81
  land cover 173
  mixed-forest silviculture 212
  national parks 213
  penetration roads 203–4, 216
  population 175
  silviculture 154
  soil erosion 10
  spontaneous colonisation 203
  standing timber volume 46
Pests
  agrosilviculture 152
  biotic stressors 37–8, 146
  effects of climate 22
  forage species 119, 159
  indigenous cultivation 74–5
  indigenous knowledge 85
  Jari project 97
  monocultural plantations 88, 146
  savanna and wetland 122
  terra firme 119, 146
Phosphorus 56
  availability 117
  deficiency 138
  fertiliser for pasture 157–8,
    163
  fixation 32, 144
  organic residues 145
Phytochemicals 180–1
Piaroa Indians 69–72, 83
PIN (Programa de Integração Nacional)
    110, 206

Plantations
 Amapá 163
 Belterra 91–2
 coastal Guyana 130, 132–4
 Fordlandia 91–2
 forestry 96–8, 163, 211
 Guianas 7
 Jari 96–8, 161
 problems 87–8
 rubber 8, 91–3, 211
 silvopastoralism 161
 technical progress 211
 terra firme 193
Plinthite 32
POLAMAZONIA (Programa de Pólos
 Agropecuários e Agrominerais da
 Amazônia) 112, 206–7
POLONOROESTE (Programa
 Integrado de Desenvolvimento do
 Noroeste do Brasil) 207
Population (see also Amerindian
 population)
 Amazonia 174–5
 Bragantina 101, 104
 Brazil 205
 Caquetá basin 106, 122
 Guianas 135, 198
 lower Amazon valley 126–7
 oriente 203
Population pressure
 pre-contact period 84
Programa Grande Carajás 207
Projeto Radambrasil
 designation of reserves 187
 forestry surveys 96
 land surveys 12, 96
 soil maps 31
PRORADAM (Proyecto
 Radargrametrico del Amazonas)
 31, 186–7
Protein
 acquisition 63
 animal products 64
 indigenous population 77, 81
 indigenous subsistence 75–6
 maize 67
 manioc 65
 várzea 128
 wetlands 140
Proyecto Caquetá 106

Rabies 138–9

Radar imagery 30, 186–7, 209
Rainfall
 coastal Guyana 130, 134
 distribution 20
 effect of deforestation 176
 effect on grazing 138
 intensity 21–2
 variability 20–2, 134
Refugia 41–2, 59, 179
 conservation 42
 national parks 183–4, 215
Remote sensing 13–14
 monitoring forest clearance 172, 216
 monitoring land resources 209
 reconnaissance land survey 17, 186,
  209
 vegetation mapping 40
Reserved land 3, 12, 184, 187, 190
 invasion 184, 212–14
Resilience
 savanna and wetland 61, 122, 162
 fish population 128, 168
Resources
 deficiencies 37, 142, 169
 genetic 10, 42, 153, 156, 178, 181
 mineral 5
 renewable 5
 variabilities 37, 142, 169
Rice
 Altamira zone 111–12
 Amazon estuarine zone 166
 Bragantina 102–3
 coastal Guyana 129, 132, 134–5, 165
 floating varieties 166
 Jari 127, 165
 pests and diseases 146
 várzea 162
 Yurimaguas 144
Ridged fields 80–1, 83, 140
Rio Branco-Rupununi savanna 39–40,
  50–1, 121, 136
 cattle ranching 135–40
 development potential 139–40, 163
 improved pastures 139
 indigenous subsistence 77–8
Risk
 diversification 169
 flooding 28, 79, 140, 165
 floodplain cultivation 124
 forest land exploitation 215
 intensive cultivation 149
 plantation production 93, 98

Rivers 28–30
  black water 30, 54
  clear water 30, 54
  erosion rates 29
  flooding 177–8
  gauge height at Manaus 29
  productivity 54
  sediment load 28, 178
  white water 28, 54, 168
Roads
  Acre highway 216
  Belém-Brasília highway 101, 115,
    206
  Cuiabá-Santarém highway 118,
    126
  Guyana 198
  limiting road-building 216
  linear penetration 212
  maintenance 113, 120
  oriente 203
  reserved land 213
  Transamazon highway 87, 110, 206
Rondônia
  colonisation 9, 208
  de facto compartments 208
  POLONOROESTE 207
  reserved land 208, 213
  timber production 94
Roraima Formation 24, 26
  Arenosols 36
Rubber 8–9, 88–93, 119
  agrosilviculture 152
  Anandineua 91–2
  Asian plantations 8, 89
  Bahia 93
  Belterra 91
  boom 7
  Caquetá basin 109, 123
  extraction 86–7, 93
  Fordlandia 91
  genetic resources 181
  growth of Belém 100
  Igarape-Açú 91–2
  latex 88, 180
  mixed-forest silviculture 156
  production 89, 93
  seringueiros 89
  South American leaf blight 91–3,
    119, 146
  vulcanisation 88
Rupununi savanna (*see* Rio Branco-
  Rupununi savanna)

San Carlos di Rio Negro
  rainfall 19
Santarém
  fishing 128
  Landsat 126
  rainfall 20
  river level 28, 125
  settlement 126
Savanna 2–3, 40, 49–52
  area 3, 41, 49, 172–3
  burning 50–2, 138
  cattle ranching 135–40, 163
  Colonial settlement 121
  definition 50
  development prospects 163
  modern exploitation 162–3
  fauna 52
  grass-legume pastures 163
  Gran Sabana 77–8, 121
  indigenous resource use 77–8
  islands 41, 50
  Mojos 80
  organic decomposition 52
  Puciari-Humaitá 40, 50, 163
  Rio Branco-Rupununi 40, 50–2,
    77–8, 121, 135–40, 163, 195
  scleromorphism 56
  Sipaliwini 50
  soils 77
  species diversity 50
  resilience 61
  Trombetas-Paru 50
  variability 37–8
Seringueiros 89
Shifting cultivation
  adaptive status 82
  caboclo 6
  field abandonment 74–5
  indigenous 57, 70–5, 78
Shipibo Indians 79, 81
Silviculture
  compromise usage 191, 195
  experiments in Brazil 154–6
  extractive reserves 211–12
  Far East 153
  Jari 96–8
  mixed-forest 12, 96, 153–6, 195,
    211–12
  monocyclic systems 154–6
  polycyclic systems 154
  potential on *terra firme* 156, 195
  sustainable exploitation 211

Silvopastoralism 160–1, 195
Siona-Secoya Indians 65, 74
Sirionó Indians 68
Soils 30–37
    central Amazonia 34
    cerrado 162
    classification 32
    coastal Guyana 131
    compaction 117, 143
    forest 55–6
    mapping 30–31
    savanna 77
Soil fauna 49
Soil fertility 32–7, 56
    biological management 169
    cerrado 162
    pasture 107, 117, 138
    savanna 77
    terra firme 143–4
    wetlands 130, 140
Soil Map of the World 31
Soyabean 9, 144
Speciation 41
SPOT satellite 209
SPVEA (Superintendência do Plano de
    Valorização Económica da
    Amazônia) 8, 206, 210
Stability
    ecosystem 60–1
    exploitation 119, 211
    savanna and wetland 61
    tropical forest 60
SUDAM (Superintendência do
    Desenvolvimento da Amazônia)
    206, 210
    forestry policy 96
    fiscal incentives 115
Sugar cane 7, 67, 101, 109, 112, 121
    coastal Guyana 130, 132–5, 165
Suiá Missú ranch 115–16, 118
Surinam
    agrosilviculture 151
    cacao disease 146
    forest survey 45
    hydro-electricity 178, 198
    land cover 175
    mixed-forest silviculture 153–4
    national parks 198, 201, 213
    planation surfaces 24–5
    population 173
    silvopastoralism 161
    Sipaliwini savanna 50

Sustainable exploitatin 3, 5, 168–70,
    185, 193, 210–12
    agrosilviculture 150
    fisheries 140
    indigenous 84, 169
    institutional support 120
    Jari 97
    oriente 204
    savanna ranching 140
    semi-intensive pasture systems 159
    silvopastoralism 161
    terra firme 120, 194, 215
    transport management 212

Taboos 83–4
    functional nature 83
    indigenous hunting 69, 83
Tapajós basin
    rubber seeds 89
    Tapajós National Forest 96, 154,
        156
Tapajós river 29–30
Temperature regimes 19–20
Terra firme 9–10, 17
    agrosilviculture 150, 152, 194–5
    biotic stressors 37–8
    compromise compartment 194
    effect of climatic change 215
    extractive logging 94–5
    forests 42–9
    indigenous exploitation 67, 79–80
    intensive exploitation 143–9,
        193
    land exploitation 118–19, 142
    productive compartment 194
    regional planning 193
    roads 87
    savannas 49–52
    semi-intensive cattle rearing 156–7,
        159
    silviculture 156, 194–5
    silvopastoralism 160–1
    soils 32–6
    sustainable exploitation 152, 168–9,
        215
Terra preta 79, 127
Terra roxa 36, 111, 194
Tomé Açu 103, 148, 211
Transamazon highway 87, 90, 96
    access to land 206
    Altamira colonisation 110–11
    Nitosols 36

Treaty for Amazonian Co-operation 14, 197, 210
Tucuruí
  hydro-electricity 90, 167, 178, 207
  Programa Grande Carajás 207
  timber extraction 96
Turtles 55, 65, 80, 83, 128
  managed exploitation 167

Uanano Indians 70, 76
Ultisols 32, 35, 144

Várzea 16, 23, 40
  campos de várzea 40, 54, 126, 129
  contemporary cultivation 127, 162
  definition 26
  extractive logging 93–4, 128
  faunal resources 80
  fishing 128, 167
  flood regime 125, 178
  flood variability 28, 80, 127
  forest clearance 167
  indigenous subsistence 78–83
  indigenous settlement 78–9
  productive compartment 194
  Río Napo 27
  soils 33
Vegetation
  change 41–2
  classification 39
  mapping 40
Venezuela
  agriculture in llanos 163–4
  capibara rearing 167
  forest regeneration 58
  forest reserves 202
  Guri barrage 178, 202
  indigenous subsistence 69–70, 72, 75–6, 78
  land cover 173
  national parks 201–2, 213
  population 175
  silviculture 154
  southern 199, 201–3
  standing timber volume 46

Wai Wai Indians 65, 69, 72
Wapisiana Indians 77–8
Warfare
  indigenous 84
Water buffalo 55, 166
Weeds
  biotic stressor 37–8, 142

Bragantina 101–2
  indigenous management 85
  pasture land 108, 113, 117, 158–9
  shifting cultivation 74–5
Wetland 2, 52–55
  Amazon estuarine zone 55
  area 41, 52, 172–3
  Atlantic coastal plain 53
  campos de várzea 53
  coastal Guianas 129
  conservation 192
  effect of climatic change 215
  fauna 54
  faunal resources 65, 167–8
  herbaceous 3, 53
  indigenous resource use 78–81, 85
  indigenous ridged fields 80, 83
  marsh forest 52–3
  modern exploitation 140–1, 162, 165–8, 192–3
  Mojos 27, 53
  natural variability 37
  northern Rupununi 53
  nutrient supply 82
  rise in sea level 177
  seed dispersal 53
  soil fertility 37, 165
  soils 33, 36–7
  species diversity 53
  resilience 61
  sustainable exploitation 168–9
  swamp forest 52–3
  water conditions 56–7
White sands
  origin 26
Wild plants
  indigenous food source 64
Witoto Indians 72–3, 75, 150
World Bank 107, 216

Xavante Indians 114
Xingú river 29–30
  hydro-electric dams 178, 213, 216

Yanomamo Indians 69, 72, 75–7, 84
Yurimaguas 144–5

Zoning
  Brazilian Amazonia 188–9, 209
  ecological and economic 14, 189, 209
  models 14, 209